POLITICAL CHANGE IN
MOROCCO

Princeton Oriental Studies

Social Sciences, 3

POLITICAL
CHANGE
IN
MOROCCO

BY DOUGLAS E. ASHFORD

PRINCETON, NEW JERSEY

PRINCETON UNIVERSITY PRESS

1961

To Peggy

ACKNOWLEDGMENTS

THE author and his family are deeply indebted to the Ford Foundation, whose generosity enabled them to live in North Africa for fifteen months while the research for this study was being completed. The author is also grateful to the Woodrow Wilson School of Public and International Affairs, which engaged him as a Visiting Lecturer while the book was being put into first-draft form, and to the Department of Oriental Studies, which provided funds for secretarial assistance.

The most profound gratitude is reserved for the many Moroccans who tolerated the author's prying questions and academic impatience in 1957 and 1958. Over a hundred government officials and party leaders were interviewed at length, many of them several times. They cannot all be acknowledged individually, but credit has been given as discretion permits in the footnotes of the book. Two Moroccan leaders were especially generous with their time, hospitality, and confidence—Mohammed Lyazidi, of the Istiqlal's Executive Committee, and Mehdi Ben Barka, now leader of the National Union. Both Marvine Howe and Margaret Pope were also most kind in introducing the author to their friends and to much of Morocco's charm. The author takes full responsibility for any misrepresentation of the views or facts given to him during his visit to Morocco.

The Information and Press Service of the French Embassy in Rabat was particularly kind in letting the author rummage through all its publications and translations since the date of Morocco's independence. The United States Embassy gave the author copies of its press translations. These Arabic press translations were supplemented with translations from the Moroccan French-language press and by the author. Where one of these services was used, the footnotes so indicate. Without this help the author could not have completed the field work, but any errors from multiple translations are his own responsibility. He would also like to acknowledge the invaluable assistance of several French officials working in Morocco, whose names are not divulged.

The book conforms to the French system of transliterating Arabic. Although this creates several anomalies for the English-speaking student of classical Arabic, it is consistent with the bulk of scholarly research on North Africa and conforms to current practice in Morocco. Moroccans sometimes transliterate the same proper name in different ways. Conforming to personal usage, which is employed in all reports from North Africa, also facilitates the following of events subsequent to this study.

The author is most grateful to Professor Dankwart A. Rustow, who encouraged his initial interest in underdeveloped countries and gave support to this project in every way possible. Professor Rustow later took time from his research in Turkey, in 1958-1959, to comment on this manuscript in detail. The manuscript received a second and most helpful polishing from Professor Manfred Halpern, who gladly took on the extra task while he was carrying a full teaching load. A third reading was performed by Professor Lewis Thomas at the close of a busy academic year. David Hart was also kind enough to read the manuscript and make suggestions on sections dealing with the tribes. The book undoubtedly reflects the scholarship and imagination of these men. Mrs. Barbara Thorson and Mrs. Sondra Hardis deserve mention for having pleasantly endured the author's secretarial demands. A note of thanks also belongs to John and Joan Lawson, who first alerted the author to the fascinating complexities of Moroccan politics.

The last and most important acknowledgment is to the author's wife, Peggy. She cheerfully supported his decision to leave a secure government post several years ago and with equal good humor helped plan the North African trip. With little help she moved home and family to a strange and occasionally hazardous environment, and added a second child to the family under something less than pleasant circumstances. Without her encouragement this task would scarcely have been possible and certainly would not have been so memorable.

Douglas E. Ashford

Princeton, August 1959

CONTENTS

Acknowledgments   vii

I. Introduction   3

The Setting of the Study   3
The Setting in Morocco   9

II. Background to Moroccan Nationalism   25

Doctrines and Dilemmas of the Early Years   25
Emergence of a Political Party   34
Islah and Intrigue in the North   45

III. Organizing the Istiqlal and Achieving Independence   57

Growth and Suppression of the Istiqlal   57
Independence by Default or Design?   74

IV. Government and Administration   93

Toward a "Homogeneous" Government   93
From Balafrej to Ibrahim   105
Lawmaking and Legal Reform   111
New Wine in Old Barrels?   116
Separation of Whose Powers?   124

V. Citizens and Privileges   132

Who Is a Moroccan?   132
Purge: Who, When, and How Many?   134
Civil Liberties for What?   145

VI. Violence and Coercion   157

Violence and Independence   157
Urban Terrorism and the Police   163
An Army with No Country to Defend   167
Two Armies in Dispute   177

VII. Rural Administration and the Tribes 185

The Reorganized *Bled* 185
Politics Comes to the Countryside 194
Problems in Distant Provinces 203
The Tribal Revolts of Late 1958 211

VIII. Independence and the Istiqlal 219

Transition and Conflict of Leadership 219
Reconstruction of the Party Cadre 232
How National Is the Istiqlal? 243
The Shattering of Nationalist Solidarity 260

IX. The Moroccan Labor Movement 270

Growth of the Labor Movement 270
Labor's Strength and National Politics 279
Labor Solidarity Bows to Politics 291

X. Opposition Political Parties 302

Nationalists Without a Party 302
Tribesmen Form a Party 319
Intellectuals Without a Party 326
Formation of the Democratic Istiqlal 334

XI. Development of Representative Government 344

The Experimental Assembly 344
Rural Communes and Popular Participation 355
Elections in Search of a Role 363

XII. Formation of Interest Groups 373

Industrialists and Merchants Unite 373
The Moroccan Farm Bureau 381
The Silent Half and the Students 387
Interests Without an Organization 398

XIII. Conclusion 405

Bibliographical Notes 419

Index 423

TABLES

1. Percentage Division of Active Population by Occupation (Ex-French Zone Only)   15
2. Source of National Income by Percentages   17
3. Members of the First Five Councils of Government   98
4. Number of Civil Servants per Ministry (October 1958)   120
5. Number of Posts for Rural Officials (Filled, Vacant, and Total Posts in December 1957, with Ranks)   190
6. Dates of Appointment of Rural Officials (from December 1955 to December 1957 by Quarters)   191
7. Continuity of Istiqlal Leadership from 1929 to 1958   223
8. Istiqlal Cadre Training Program in 1956 and 1957   237
9. Istiqlal Sections and Subsections by Inspectorate (with Ratios of Popular Strength and Organizational Strength per Subsection)   247
10. Estimated Linguistic Differentiation of the Istiqlal and Comparison to Rural Administrative Organization   258
11. Membership of the U.M.T. by Federations and Local Unions in 1958   280
12. Plan for Rural Communes of Fès and Tafilalet Provinces (Average Membership, *Caids*, and Tribes per Commune)   359
13. Estimated Participation in Istiqlal Youth Activities in 1956 and 1957   391
14. Estimated Participation of Men, Women, and Teachers in the Literacy Campaigns of 1956 and 1957   400

MAPS

Major Physical Features   23
Administrative Map—1955-1960   187

POLITICAL CHANGE IN
MOROCCO

CHAPTER I

INTRODUCTION

The Setting of the Study

THE Moroccan people have known three political regimes in the twentieth century. At the turn of the century the country was ruled by the traditional central government, the Makhzen, which had existed in various forms for nearly a millennium. From 1912 to early 1956 final authority rested with the Protectorate powers, France and Spain. The last twenty years of this period were marked with increasingly bitter and effective nationalist agitation, which culminated in the independent Morocco of today. The subject of this inquiry will be the politics of independent Morocco from 1955 to 1959, the most recent period of rapid political development. Partly by adaptation of old habits and partly by innovation a new political structure has been created. The magnitude of the change in these four years probably compares with that of the previous millennium in its direct effect on the lives of all Moroccans. Although there are many controversies over Morocco's accomplishments since independence, she has successfully created a nation. This act bears further examination, for it will be repeated in many countries in the southern half of the world in the coming decade.

In this book Morocco becomes a case study for the student of comparative politics and particularly for the student of the non-Western world. The practical lessons to be learned from the Moroccan experience are rivaled by the insights provided for theoretical formulations. The analytical benefits of the study can best be distinguished by emphasizing our need to understand how the creation of a nation affects the lives of all its members or citizens. To think of the nation or the introduction of national politics as the property of only the advanced segment of the population can be grossly misleading, but to think of politics in more comprehensive terms requires suitable concepts and theory. Although the formulation of new frameworks of inquiry is in itself a major endeavor, this book tries to suggest what seem to be the more promising ways for improving our ability to analyze new nations.

The rapid political and social changes that are characteristic of the emerging countries of the world have compelled scholars to reexamine their tools of analysis. Frequently it has seemed advisable simply to abandon concepts that seemed to work well in Western contexts, and in many instances old theories have been refurbished with new qualifications. Undoubtedly many new nations today have been required to make decisions and provide for a developing political system much more rapidly than was required of the countries of Western Europe at a comparable stage in their development. The new Moroccan nation, for example, has become the focus for patterns of behavior relating all Moroccans in an endeavor that is certainly different from that pursued under the Protectorate regime. The concrete characteristics of the new nation obviously include certain activities that were denied the Protectorate administrations in the North, South, and Tangier. How one can best analyze these activities in relation to national political problems is the ultimate purpose of this inquiry, although a satisfactory framework must eventually stand the test of comparative use.

Since this book emphasizes political behavior in independent Morocco, there is neither the amount nor kind of description of the Protectorate period that an historical study might have. This is not intended to neglect either the injustices or the contributions of French and Spanish rule, but to underscore those aspects of Morocco's recent development that seem most pertinent to the scope of the inquiry. The Protectorate powers,[1] important as they were in preparing Morocco for independence, certainly favored granting something less than independence. They introduced many new kinds of behavior, but it would be risky to assume that such behavior had the same significance both before and after independence. For any study of politics in the foreseeable future, the state or nation will continue to be a means of demarcating behavior patterns, although this convenient focus still contains many ambiguities.

Sufficient historical information is included in this book to enable the reader to orient himself and to describe those characteristics of

---

[1] As yet there is not a good history of the Protectorate period, although there are several books of memoirs of ex-Resident Generals of Morocco. Stephane Bernard is doing a detailed analysis of the colonial diplomacy leading to independence under the auspices of the Carnegie Endowment for International Peace. The most recent basic handbook is Nevill Barbour's *A Survey of North West Africa (The Maghrib)*, London, Royal Institute of International Affairs, 1959. A fairly objective summary of the French side is "Morocco 54," *Encyclopédie d'Outre-mer*, Special Issue, Paris, n.d. Summaries by nonparticipants are Jean d'Esme (pseud.), *Le Maroc que Nous Avons Fait*, Paris, Librairie Hachette, 1955, and Albert Ayache, *Le Maroc: Bilan d'une Colonisation*, Paris, Editions Sociales, 1956 (hereafter simply noted as *Le Maroc*). There is no similar work by a Moroccan.

Morocco that appear to have changed little with independence. For example, the growth of the nationalist movement, led by the Istiqlal or Independence party in the French zone and the Islah or Reform party in the Spanish zone, is clearly of particular importance in Morocco's development. CHAPTER II deals briefly with the orgins of Moroccan nationalism and with the history of the Islah. CHAPTER III traces the postwar growth of the Istiqlal and the negotiations of the summer of 1955, immediately prior to independence. The reader will find most of CHAPTER IV a closely packed summary of changes in the formal structure of the government since independence.

However, this study does not proceed solely as an historical inquiry into the adjustment of a modern nationalist movement to independence. The nationalists are among the most active participants in contemporary Moroccan politics, but from the point of independence *everyone* is, to some extent, a nationalist, good or poor, historic or recent, fervent or indifferent. The author's desire to place emphasis on political relationships among *all* members of the new nation has, therefore, led him to include in this book consideration of how the less active citizens exercise influence. As the government of every overpopulated country well knows, merely for citizens to *be present* is for them to participate in politics in a way and to place certain demands on the political system of a new nation. Devoting more attention in this book to participation in such comprehensive terms may help us to avoid the pitfalls that Rupert Emerson sketched several years ago when he wrote: "Much of what is glibly and habitually said about nationalism rests on a very slim foundation of positive knowledge and, more important, of precise, meaningful concepts. Much of what passes for solid scientific analysis is actually done with mirrors or with a sleight of hand which may deceive the unwary but should not be allowed to deceive the manipulator himself."[2]

Another student of modern nationalism, Karl Deutsch, has cautioned against handing all our problems to the psychologist, who may be as baffled as the political scientist in handling the intricate and unfamiliar problems of new countries.[3] Many of the difficulties to which these men refer stem from the tendency to slight the analytical structure of inquiry and, thereby, to be unclear as to which

[2] "Paradoxes of Asian Nationalism," *Far Eastern Quarterly*, vol. 13, no. 2, February 1945, p. 131.
[3] *Nationalism and Social Communication*, Cambridge, Technology Press, 1953, p. 12. His precise words were, "The political scientist has passed the baby to the psychologist, but the psychologist does not seem eager to take it."

concrete problems can be meaningfully discussed in any selected framework of inquiry. While this study does not hope to resolve all the issues involved in systematic inquiry, it is hoped that this book will contribute to better theory and concept formation.

The shortcomings to which Rupert Emerson refers have been recognized in the past decade. Several studies have appeared that apply extremely rigorous forms of analysis to discrete problems of new countries,[4] although the study of political behavior is still weak in more general theory. In response to the need for more comprehensive and more systematic theory, several studies have been made to which the author of this book is indebted.[5] The improvement of the suggested approaches and the development of new approaches to general theory doubtless will continue to be one of the major aspects of the study of new nations.

With the intent of being useful for this purpose, this book attempts to discuss the actions of individuals and of groups in reference to the entire nation or the political relationships existing among all Moroccan citizens at any given moment. The immediate benefit of such a viewpoint is to detract attention from the more dramatic figures in Moroccan politics and to focus attention on particular relationships as they are related to politics on the national level. In Morocco, as in many other underdeveloped nations, there are large numbers of citizens whose political roles are easily overlooked. The broad range of social differentiation may very easily divert the observer's eyes toward the most familiar and encourage the implicit assumption that the more readily observable is sufficient. Thinking in terms of participation at the national level some heuristic advantage, at least, and may suggest new forms of systematic analysis that are applicable to large groups of persons.

Throughout this inquiry the author has avoided the word "power" as it refers to the relationship of several actors. The logical pitfalls of the use of this word have been well demonstrated by Herbert A.

[4] For examples of successful studies dealing with well-defined problems see Morroe Berger, *Bureaucracy and Society in Modern Egypt: A Study of the Higher Civil Service*, Princeton, Princeton University Press, 1957, and Lucian Pye, *Guerrilla Communism in Malaya*, Princeton, Princeton University Press, 1956.

[5] See Dankwart Rustow, *Politics and Westernization in the Near East*, Princeton, Center of International Studies, 1956; Rustow, "New Horizons for Comparative Politics," *World Politics*, vol. 9, no. 4, July 1957, pp. 530-549; Leonard Binder, "Prolegomena to the Comparative Study of Middle Eastern Governments," *American Political Science Review*, vol. 51, no. 3, September 1957, pp. 651-669.

Simon.[6] Although a problem of the complexity of the Moroccan experience cannot be handled with the refinement that has been brought to the study of influence, much can be learned from this study that is useful in working toward systematic theory suited for more general concrete problems. Thus, this book is primarily concerned with how actors interrelate at particular moments and in reference to stated concrete problems of the new nation. Although it is easy to replace one abused term with another, in this book the phrase "political system" refers to the entire pattern of relationships in the various situations described. A consistent effort has been made to avoid teleological and ontological use of the phrase, although it must be admitted that this compromise falls far short of the exact usage that the term implies.

For descriptive purposes four general relationships in the political system have been singled out. These relationships refer to particular ways in which Moroccans are related in the political system, and they are extremely useful as one attempts to refer discrete situations and actions to national politics.[7] For the needs of this book it is sufficient to refer to political relationships as being predominantly charismatic, coercive, institutional, or traditional.

In Morocco charismatic relationships are found between the King and, to a lesser extent, the Leader of the Istiqlal, Allal Al-Fassi, and the populace. Such a relationship enables one of the actors in a situation to establish moral imperatives for some part of the behavior of another actor or other actors.[8] Commanding personalities have

[6] "Notes on the Observation and Measurement of Power," *Journal of Politics*, vol. 15, no. 4, November 1953, pp. 500-516. The article contains some basic definitions for the study of influence, which have been highly refined and applied. See, for example, James A. March, Jr., "An Introduction to the Theory and Measurement of Influence," *American Political Science Review*, vol. 49, no. 2, June 1953, pp. 431-451.

[7] For further progress in the use of these concepts or of study in terms of the political system, more precise observational terms would be needed, which it is to be hoped would permit application of the theory using more precise methodological techniques and eventually the proof or disproof of this theory. In other words, so long as one continues to speak of the political system or characteristics of political relationships as is being done here, the best that can be hoped for is that one will not assert conclusions that contain the more obvious contradictions of the use of the word "power." Only when more precise meaning is given to such relationships can they be studied systematically. The discovery of useful and valid means for accomplishing this is the heart of systematic inquiry and will not be considered at length in this book.

[8] The usage here refers to charisma as a characteristic affecting interrelationships and not as a psychological characteristic. The distinction has been clearly made by Talcott Parsons, "Personality and Social Structure," Alfred H. Stanton, ed., *Personality and Political Crisis*, Glencoe, Free Press, 1951, pp. 61-80.

played such dramatic roles in the developing nations that we tend to forget how important they have been in the politics of more advanced nations. As a subject of systematic inquiry, charismatic relationships are elusive and confusing, but their importance in national politics cannot be disputed.

Coercive relationships are those in which one actor can compel another actor to perform certain actions. The use of the term in political studies generally refers to activities of the forces of order, but in the case of Morocco and many other new countries coercive relationships may be found in other concrete forms. It should also be noted that ostensibly coercive groups like armies may be so fully integrated into the network of institutional relationships in a country that the group never or seldom uses coercive influence. What is often thought of as the isolation of the military and the police in more advanced political systems is more properly analyzed as the successful and near total institutionalization of their influence. Such an accomplishment has, in fact, characterized the democratic nations and has also been a major problem in new countries. This term occurs in this book in the discussions of the transition of the urban terrorist organization, the Moroccan Army of Liberation, and the tribal structure of Morocco. Coercion should be distinguished from violence, a state of affairs in which the populace no longer is able to restrain the destruction of its members.

Institutional relationships mean formalization of relations between actors, usually by a written or well-understood set of rules. While there are many groups in Moroccan society that may be institutionalized in this sense, it will be seen that there are wide differences in the ability of various Moroccans to relate their institutions to national politics. Institutional relationships involve a wide range of formalization. Their study is further complicated by the frequent occurrence of well organized groups that do not exercise influence along institutional lines. This distinction is clearer in the study of new nations than in the study of older nations, where there tend to be an abundance of organizations.

Traditional relationships characterize those Moroccans who still live in almost separate societies from the persons included in modern Morocco. The obvious reference is to the tribes, although there are undoubtedly many other Moroccans partially integrated into the life of the nation who are still strongly influenced by traditional ties. In an extreme sense traditional relationships may virtually exclude groups from national politics, although there are ways in which fairly intact societal subgroups in the nation may be related to national politics.

The Setting in Morocco

Generalization requires that some rough delimitation be made of the range of action open to Moroccans. Many alternatives have clearly been closed to them due to their own material shortcomings. The ways in which the game of politics could be played were certainly limited and conditioned in various ways by the capabilities of the participants. Policy decisions and political activity among informed Moroccans can generally be studied with the assumption that these citizens were aware of the major physical realities of their country. For this more active segment of the population and their more isolated compatriots there have been certain immovable factors in the Moroccan environment which all must acknowledge. The purpose of this chapter is to give a brief summary of the characteristics of the Moroccan setting that will be most important in the reader's understanding of the new nation's transition. Although there are still many gaps in the information on basic conditions in Morocco, the colonial powers left the country with remarkably well-developed statistical services, which provide a fairly complete sketch of the nation's human resources and physical conditions.

Perhaps the most striking characteristic of the Moroccan population, of particular importance to political analysis, is the very small number of citizens prepared to participate in political life as we know it in the advanced nations. There are a number of indicators of such preparation, of which literacy, occupational categories, and urbanization are among the most frequently cited.[9] Literacy estimates for Morocco usually agree that no more than a tenth of the population can read and write Arabic, although the enthusiastically received literacy drives since independence may have slightly increased this amount. Urbanization studies indicate that Morocco, like several other states of the Arab world, is a country of overcrowded, highly Europeanized cites surrounded by primitive villages. The contemporary world has no doubt penetrated in some form to nearly all areas of concentrated population, but par-

[9] These and other similar indicators have been combined systematically to study societies in transition in Daniel Lerner's *The Passing of Traditional Society*, Glencoe, Free Press, 1958.

ticular social and political problems are very likely created by the pattern of urbanization. Including cities of over 10,000 persons, nearly four fifths of the urbanized group are in the five largest cities: Casablanca, Marrakech, Rabat, Fès, and Meknes.[10] The bulk of the urbanized population is in large cities where they not only encounter the conventional abuses of new city dwellers but also must survive the gradual decline in business activity since independence. Although nearly two million Moroccans live in cities with a population of over 10,000, many of them are still in the initial phases of the transition from tribal life and many more come only to bolster the income of their families in the countryside. The total effect of this rotating subproletariat in the shanty towns surrounding the cities has never been thoroughly studied, but many Moroccans receive their first political indoctrination during seasonal visits to the cities, as they struggle to increase their families' subsistence income.[11]

The immediate problems of government as well as of general political participation can be related to the rapid growth of Moroccan cities. Over the last forty-five years approximately one million persons have emigrated from the more seriously depressed or overpopulated areas of the country.[12] The mass of newly urbanized Moroccans are illiterate and seldom possess skills permitting their assimilation into industrial occupations even if enough jobs could be found. Nearly a fourth of the Moroccans live in an urban setting if towns over 20,000 are counted, or slightly over a third are urbanized if one counts towns over 2,000.[13] These persons are readily accessible for political agitation and have easily exploited grievances. The concentration of about one and a half million persons in the five largest cities further aggravates the social problems of rapid urban growth and facilitates political activity.[14] Although no reliable estimates have been published, at least half a million of

[10] R. Forichon and P. Mas, "Les Problèmes de la Repartition du Peuplement au Maroc," *Bulletin Economique et Social du Maroc*, vol. 21, no. 76, March 1956, p. 485.

[11] The most complete study, but without any information on political behavior, is Robert Montagne's (ed.) *Naissance du Proletariat Marocain*, Paris, Peyronnet, 1950.

[12] *Ibid.*, pp. 13-14.

[13] Albert Ayache, *op.cit.*, p. 12. If one used the latter criterion, France would be fifty-five per cent urbanized.

[14] The best recent study of Moroccan urbanization is by R. Forichon and P. Mas, *op.cit.*, pp. 471-505. Dealing with towns over 10,000, these authors place thirty-five per cent of the urbanized population in Casablanca and seventy-eight per cent in the five cities over 100,000.

the urban dwellers live in substandard housing, of which a large proportion are slums. The rise of nationalism in Morocco with the growth of these large cities over the past twenty years is certainly not entirely coincidental. The new Moroccan government is devoting large sums to the removal of slums, as well as to the improvement of rural living conditions in hopes of stemming the flow from the countryside, but it seems likely that the exodus will continue for some time.

There has been ample evidence of the difficulty that a large segment of the Moroccan population has had in relating its political concerns to those of the new nation. The most distant people are probably those living a tribal existence, where the nation probably has taken on only a symbolic meaning and where the political aspect of their own social structure fulfills most of their needs. There is no way of making a reliable estimate of the size of this segment, although the center of strength of the preindependence Al-Glaoui empire in the High Atlas Mountains is a partial indicator. The revolts of Addi ou Bihi and the tribesmen of the Rif and Taza regions are further evidence. The government revealed that nearly a million tribesmen were involved in the Rif-Taza uprisings and passive resistance. Two million is probably a conservative estimate of the number of Moroccans who still rely more heavily on the subordinate political system of their tribe than on the national political system. Although the effort was probably mismanaged, the discouraging results of the first attempts at closer integration of these tribesmen suggest the difficulty the new country faces. That there has not been more serious trouble is most likely due to the influence of the King, whose political role merits closer attention.

In a study of the national political contacts of the tribesmen, it should not be forgotten that their experience with politics on this level has been based on the Protectorate and the Moroccan Liberation Army. The Protectorate was established by coercion and continued to use coercion to isolate and protect tribal institutions that could easily be manipulated. The Liberation Army certainly had a profound impact on the tribal areas, for it was organized with the precise purpose of achieving independence and recovering Mohammed Ben Youssef's throne. But even in this case introduction to politics on the national level was through an army or organized coercion. That military organization was compatible with the tribal system proved to be true even after the bulk of the Liberation Army had been assimilated into the Royal Army. The tribesmen understood the use of violence and, when circumstances brought them into conflict with the new nation, they used it. Whether or not their actions were justifiable is a question involving value judgments, and not of direct concern to this inquiry. But the fact remains that these tribesmen were able to exercise influence on national politics. For an analysis of the national political system it is important that we see how this was done and how the way in which this was done related to the new nation. (This will be discussed further in CHAPTER XIII.)

In contrast to the tribal participants in the national political system are the well-organized groups of the cities. These groups are gradually being extended to the countryside in some cases and include not only the political parties, but also the pressure groups, the unions, and the nascent representative body, the National Consultative Assembly. It is probably safe to claim that all members of these specialized bodies are aware of the purpose and problems of the new nation. A liberal estimate of the number of citizens who fall within this politically advanced portion of the population is about one million. As the experience of these groups indicates, these persons are probably as well prepared to participate in a national political system as are members of any representative cross section of the population of an advanced, industrialized nation. The politically active segment of the population has begun to differentiate its goals and to seek specific avenues of influence to the government and the administration in a way that is roughly comparable to the politics of advanced nations.

Although Morocco faces many difficult economic and social problems, she is probably much better off than many of her Arab neighbors. In the late 1940's and early 1950's Morocco enjoyed a sizable boom in economic activity, which left her with a highly developed economic infrastructure. This includes a network of over 6,000 miles of paved roads and over 20,000 miles of improved secondary roads. There are 1,200 miles of railroad, of which nearly a third is electrified. Morocco has seven improved ports and many smaller ones. The largest Moroccan port, Casablanca, ranks eleventh among European ports in annual tonnage handled and under the Protectorate was the third most important French port. Well-equipped airports have been built at Tangier, Rabat, Casablanca, Oujda, and Agadir. Morocco has eight dams producing enough electricity to meet present industrial needs, and kilowatt output has multiplied nearly five times since 1945. Much of the basic structure for Morocco's future economic development has been implanted.[15] The largest part of this development was achieved under French planning and financing during the Protectorate. (Much less was done in the ex-Spanish zone, where highway development and exploitation of resources lag considerably behind the progress made in the south.) In many respects this infrastructure was designed to meet French expectations and needs and is, therefore, not entirely harmonious with Moroccan plans today. Nevertheless, it must be acknowledged that the large investment carried many indirect benefits to the Moroccan people and left Morocco with a basic economic structure capable of handling large increases in industrial activity.

Morocco is still recovering from a decline in business activity that began before independence. The return of prosperity to France, the withdrawal of French capital from Indo-China, the rise in world prices of raw materials due to the Korean War, and stock-piling all contributed to a rate of growth that would have been most difficult to sustain. Economic activity began tapering off in 1952 even before the first violent clashes of the Protectorate forces and the nationalists in Casablanca. Independence and particularly the Meknes riots in late 1956 stimulated a flight of capital from the new nation, but the effects of this must be qualified with the trend that had already begun several years before. The concentration of much of the industrial growth in Casablanca, which contains near-ly half of the industrial and commercial firms of the country,[16] probably meant that the improvement was not uniformly apparent to the Moroccan people. Even in the major cities hundreds of thousands lived and continue to live in shanty towns or *bidonvilles*, where sanitation, nourishment, and housing are often worse than among isolated tribes in the mountains. Presence of these shanty towns is due not only to the artificially large economic boom in Morocco but also to growing population pressure.

Throughout the underdeveloped areas of the world change has been accompanied with lowered death rates, increasing birth rates, and lower birth mortality. Though Morocco is not an exception, her position is somewhat more hopeful since she can possibly feed

[15] For the above data and more detail see *Maroc: Travaux Publics*, Rabat, Ministry of Public Works, 1957, *passim*.
[16] *Le Maroc au Travail*, Rabat, Ministry of Labor, 1958, p. 20.

herself and has been able to export some grain and other foodstuffs. Since the Treaty of Fès in 1912 the average annual increase in the Moroccan population has been about 150,000.[17] Her population has increased from about three million for both zones shortly after the turn of the century to about ten million today. Like most new countries Morocco has a young population. The last reliable census was in 1952, when it was calculated that a third of the population was less than 10 years of age and a half under 20 in the ex-French zone. The pressure of population growth becomes more meaningful when translated into the obligations it puts on the new nation: 160,000 more persons to feed each year; 30,000 additional children to educate; and 50,000 more persons seeking employment.[18] There are, of course, very few Moroccans who will be content simply to see their country hold its own, even though this alone would be a considerable accomplishment. Some reflection is needed to comprehend the problems created by a population that has nearly quadrupled from 1900 to the present. There are few signs that the present rate of increase will change. Demographic projections suggest that by 1975 the Moroccan population will be about fifteen million persons or about a third larger than it is today.[19]

It is probably fair to assume that those people in the advanced occupational categories are those most accustomed to politics, as politics is understood in the advanced nations. The last census for the ex-French zone estimated the Muslim active population at slightly less than three million, of which over two million occupied positions in agriculture and forestry. About a tenth of the active population or 300,000 persons held jobs in industry and handcrafts. The remainder, approximately 500,000, were employed in transport, commerce, administration and other service occupations. These occupational groups have generally been more active than other groups politically, as the history of the nationalist party demonstrates and as circumstances of proximity, leisure, and income would suggest. Though all professional categories undoubtedly include many illiterates, it is probably fair to estimate that about one

[17] *Facts and Figures About North Africa*, Paris, Office of Technical Publications of the French Prime Minister, 1952, p. 8.

[18] A good short summary of Morocco's demographic situation will be found in Pierre Bertrand's "L'aspect démographique des problèmes marocains," *O. R. Maroc*, pp. 17-26.

[19] *Ibid.*, p. 23, projects a population of fifteen million for 1975. A population of fifteen and a half million for the southern area is projected for in *The Future Growth of World Population*, New York, United Nations, 1958, p. 72.

tenth of the Moroccan population is in fairly close contact with Moroccan politics. Since the million Moroccans in the northern zone are generally more isolated, no more than 100,000 persons in the north are likely to fall into similar categories. Thus, of the present Moroccan population of about ten million, there are only about a million who enjoy the opportunities for political action on the national level that urbanization and specialized professions generally encourage. Although these figures are open to a variety of interpretations, in any context they provide some understanding of the broad dimensions of Moroccan political life.

The statistics of the active population of Morocco present a dramatic brief picture of the social and economic problems of the new country. The following table divides the active population of the ex-French zone into three categories by percentages:[20]

TABLE 1

Percentage Division of Active Population by Occupation
(Ex-French Zone Only)

Occupation	1926	1931	1936	1952	1952 Real Numbers[a]
Agriculture	86.2	76.6	77.1	70.0	2064
Industry and artisan	3.3	10.9	10.7	11.2	330
Administrative and commercial	10.5	10.5	12.2	18.8	558
Percentage of total population	27.2	22.5	27.0	38.6	
Real active population[a]	1307	1171	1646	2953	
Real total population[a]	4797	5192	6042	7641	

[a] Actual figures given to nearest thousand.

The table provides an insight into several aspects of the growth of Moroccan society over the past thirty years. Although industrial expansion has proceeded rapidly since the last war, the percentage of the active population that could be absorbed into industrial and artisan occupations has not changed. The general population increase has tended to wipe out each industrial advance.

[20] Taken from the article of R. Forichon and P. Mas, *op.cit.*, p. 482. The basic figures came from the censuses of 1952 and of 1936 (the latter during the French Protectorate). For the 1952 figures, which are the most recent, broken down into twenty-six occupational groups, see *Annuaire Statistique de la Zone Française du Maroc*, Rabat, Central Service for Statistics, 1953, p. 29.

Probably about two thirds of the total figure of 330,000 persons in industrial and artisan pursuits are in the latter category. Handicraft industries have been severely disrupted since cheaper and more attractive European products began to be imported. Undoubtedly these industries are suffering from severe underemployment. The relative increase in employment has been in less productive administrative and commercial occupations, many of which are devoted to the operation and management of the sizable economic infrastructure already mentioned. In this sector, as with the industrial portion of the second sector, Moroccans are heavily dependent on foreign technical and supervisory personnel. The bulk of the Moroccan active population still remains in agricultural occupations. The percentage is even higher when one includes the total number of people dependent on agriculture, which is usually placed at about eighty per cent of the population. As the exodus to the cities has taken place, the tendency has been to leave elders and children in the rural villages.[21] Although a man-power survey of Morocco has not yet been made, Moroccan officials conservatively estimate that 200,000 persons, or a fifth of those in non-agricultural occupations, have no special training or skills.[22]

The agricultural sector of the Moroccan economy is indisputably the most important, although officials have had difficulty in instituting reforms that have had effect beyond the commercialized segment of the rural economy.[23] National-income figures are controversial, but the most frequently cited percentages of sources of national income follow:[24]

[21] The tendency is also to leave women behind. Pierre Bertrand estimates that sixty-five per cent of the male working population and eighty-four per cent of the women depend on agricultural pursuits, *op.cit.*, p. 22. Those wishing to make more use of the French census material on Morocco will find the criteria and procedures the same as those defined for the census of France.

[22] *L'Evolution Economique du Maroc*, Rabat, Ministry of National Economy, 1957, p. 81.

[23] An analysis of the economy of an underdeveloped country in terms of the money economy alone is most unreal for obvious reasons. A large proportion of the farmers have only a subsistence income. There are many economists who have recognized this, but the most forceful presentation of the Moroccan case and an extremely ingenious analysis is the United Nations study, "Morocco," *Structure and Growth of Selected African Economies*, New York, United Nations, 1958, pp. 80-147. The author is particularly indebted to Emanuel Keukjian of the United Nations Bureau of Economic Affairs, who wrote the study just cited.

[24] The table and following estimates appear in Jean and Simonne Lacouture's *Le Maroc à l'Epreuve*, Paris, Editions du Seuil, 1958, p. 268. See also Paul Ripoche, *Problèmes Economiques au Maroc*, Rabat, n.d., p. 6.

TABLE 2

Source of National Income by Percentages

Source of National Income	Per Cent
Agriculture	42
Mines	7
Industry, commerce, and artisans	40
Public services and government monopolies	7
External revenue	4
	100

On the basis of these figures, it has been estimated that the four fifths of the Moroccan population relying on agriculture receive about one third of the national income. The disparities in distribution of income are not entirely accounted for by the larger and more wealthy farms of Europeans. About ninety per cent of the cultivated land is held by Moroccans, even though settlers from abroad have taken some of the best land. The best estimates are extremely speculative, but suggest that ten per cent of the rural Moroccan population owns over half the land, that small independent farmers—including about thirty per cent of the rural population—own slightly less than half the land, and that about sixty per cent of the rural population is landless. These persons are agricultural laborers in the more advanced rural areas and sharecroppers, or *khames* farmers, who receive a fifth of the produce of the land under Muslim landownership practice.[25]

The Moroccan government has repeatedly recognized that rural modernization and improved farming methods are essential to development of the nation. The commercialized segment of agricultural production demonstrates the advancement of the European settler over the Moroccan farmer. In both absolute and relative terms the modern farms of Europeans are superior. Their rate of increase in income is higher and their income per hectare in 1955 was three times that enjoyed by the Moroccan farmer.[26] Changes in landownership are by no means a reliable solution, especially because

[25] *Structure and Growth . . . , op.cit.*, p. 85. For discussion of the segment of the rural economy under foreign landownership, see *ibid.*, p. 87. Political activity of Moroccan farmers will be discussed in CHAPTER XII.

[26] See *L'Evolution Economique du Maroc, op.cit.*, pp. 36-37.

the bulk of agricultural exports come from European farms and their disruption would adversely affect Morocco's trade balance with France. To the end of 1958 the government's policy was to concentrate on improving the methods of the Moroccan farmers through large-scale agricultural-aid programs like the "Operation Plow." Perhaps more significant for long-run calculations is the decline in wheat output per capita over the past twenty years, although total production has been increasing in both absolute and relative terms for all types of farms.[27] Although Morocco's agricultural economy holds promise of further improvement, the result of the past twenty years' improvements is another example of how hard a new nation must work in order to stand still. The population pressures are severe and the consequent problems are further complicated from year to year by droughts, which can reduce the subsistence farmers to starvation and destroy their reserves of seed for the coming year.

The United Nations study of the Moroccan economy provides the best insight into the disparity between the income of the farmer and that of those in other occupations, as well as between the European and the Moroccan. The inquiry makes allowance for subsistence income, but the European's per capita income for all occupations still comes out about eight times that of a Moroccan. The new country, of course, derives certain benefits from the presence of the Europeans, and the government can probably justify this inequality of income for the present. When one considers only Moroccans, one finds that the farmers' per capita income was one half that of persons in other employment in 1952. With allowance for subsistence farming, the per capita income of the farmer was 29,500 francs; in other occupations, per capita income was 61,600 francs; and the total per capita income was 41,700 francs a year, or about $120.[28]

The Moroccan government is well aware of these disparities, which complicate many of the proposed programs for both rural and urban improvement. In some occupations the long-run trend has been even more striking. For example, income in the civil service has increased three times as fast as total national income. Government officials recognize with some concern that in the period 1951-1955 the rate of increase in the allocation of national product was

---

[27] *Ibid.*, p. 21.

[28] *Structure and Growth . . . , op.cit.*, p. 119. Monetary figures will usually be given in francs in this book in order to discourage comparison with the high-priced American economy.

greater for services and commerce than for agriculture and industry.[29] This is no doubt partly the result of the expansion of the economy during the period, but it also suggests that the economy was being geared increasingly to the interests of a modernized minority and in the area of generally less productive endeavors. Very likely many new countries display this trend during their early economic development, but economic necessity may not be apparent to those seeking jobs or observing unequal distribution of wealth. The initial industrial development of an underdeveloped country leads unavoidably to the political mobilization of a segment of its population which the new government must often recognize as the most influential group in the new nation.

Like many new nations, Morocco is restricted in her plans to reorient her economy by the structure of her foreign-trade balance. Mining contributes less than a tenth of Morocco's national income, but represents a third of the value of her exports. Agricultural products constitute almost half of her exports and have increased in importance over the past six years, while the proportion of industrial and handicraft exports decreased.[30] But even this apparent advantage for the economy is partially dependent on price-fixing agreements and duty-free import quotas with France, which French farmers in Morocco have enjoyed under the Protectorate and have preserved to the common benefit of Moroccan farmers. In some respects the government has more control over its mineral wealth than over its agriculture. The export market of Morocco's most important mineral, phosphate ore, has become increasingly spread over recent years. Although many of the associated enterprises are privately operated, the exploitation of the mines is reserved to a semipublic corporation, the Cherifian Phosphate Office. About a fifth of the world's phosphate comes from Morocco, whose phosphate output is about half the value of all her mineral exports. This industry employs about 12,000 Moroccans. An additional 30,000 are employed in mining lead, manganese, zinc, iron, and coal. As is often the case, as production

[29] Charles Benier, "Essai Statistique sur l'Economie Agricole Marocain," *Bulletin Economique et Social du Maroc*, vol. 20, no. 74, October 1957, p. 184. 1956 figures can be found in *L'Evolution Economique du Maroc, op.cit.*, p. 284. See also the Table of Values of Principle Exports and Imports, *ibid.*, p. 256.

[30] In the case of artisans, it is not unusual for an artisan to employ his entire family or several families in the small home industry. These employment figures are taken from *Structure and Growth . . . , op.cit.*, p. 97, and are based on the period 1952-1954.

and investment in valuable resources has steadily increased, total employment has decreased with improvement of production and transportation methods.

Moroccan industry produces largely consumer products for local consumption, many of which are imported in partially finished form. Modern industries probably do not employ more than about 125,000 workers, of whom many are employed only seasonally. The last survey indicated that about 160,000 persons were engaged in handicraft or artisan industries, but higher estimates are frequently given by local Moroccans.[31] This makes a total of approximately 300,000 Moroccans employed by the industrial and handicraft industries. The artisans are scattered throughout the country, although the inland cities by-passed by modern industry, such as Fès and Marrakech, have probably felt the decline of the home industries most severely. The artisan and industrial structure of the economy have characteristics similar to those of the subsistence agricultural and commercialized agricultural economies. The United Nations study found that with a smaller labor force the modern industrial establishments made a contribution to the national economy four times as great as the traditional industrial segment.[32] The alleviation of the depression of traditional industries is probably the second most important economic problem of Morocco, of which the most important is improving agricultural production. The human adjustments that remain to be accomplished in Morocco are likely to be as costly to effect and as slow to bring monetary returns as the initial phase of industrialization through which the country has passed.

Among the manufacturing enterprises of Morocco, those handling food, beverages, and tobacco account for forty per cent of the value added in manufacturing.[33] The artisan industries are most important in the textile and leather-goods industries, which account for twenty-five per cent of value added in manufacturing. Some individual enterprises, most of them under European ownership, have prospered with the first phase of expansion, but have experienced some difficulties since the decline in business activity. A thriving fishing in-

---

[31] *Ibid.*, p. 97.

[32] *Ibid.*, p. 98. See also the chart of manufactures, pp. 101-104. The same chart can also be found in *L'Evolution Economique du Maroc, op.cit.*, p. 164, but without the value-added calculations.

[33] France, which purchases only twelve per cent of the Moroccan phosphate, receives seventy per cent of the other minerals, *L'Evolution Economique du Maroc, op.cit.*, p. 17.

dustry was started that once accounted for a tenth of Moroccan exports, but it has had increasing difficulty competing in foreign markets with lower-priced products in recent years. A large sugar-refining plant, which relies heavily on imports of raw sugar, has succeeded, but has considerable excess capacity. A cement industry began with the postwar building boom, and today Morocco is nearly self-sufficient in cement production. Some small plants have been started to purify lead and zinc and to refine chemical products of phosphate and manganese, but the bulk of these ores is exported in crude form or as it is extracted.[34] All this industry, of course, is part of the monetary economy of Morocco and, except for purchases of tea, sugar, and a few consumer goods, is almost isolated from the bulk of subsistence farmers and tribesmen. The United Nations study calculated that, with subsistence income deducted, the per capita money income of the Moroccan farmer was from 6,500 to 8,000 francs per year and from 60,000 to 65,000 francs for the urbanized Moroccan.[35] These averages have probably increased over the past four years, but it should also be remembered that they represent a range of income which in more isolated areas may drop to half the rural average.

Since many geographical references will be made in this study, some introduction to Moroccan geography will be helpful.[36] Morocco includes slightly over 170,000 square miles, or about the same area as Washington and Oregon. The population is concentrated in the Atlantic coastal zone, which extends about one hundred miles inland from the southern port of Safi to the Rif mountains.[37] The coastal

---

[34] *Ibid.*, p. 108.

[35] Many of the factors producing problems for the Moroccan economy have been slighted here in order to concentrate on the relationship of the Moroccan himself to the present economy. For example, the large volume of raw-material exports makes the economy especially vulnerable to world prices, as was the case in Morocco during the stockpiling of the Korean War and the subsequent slump. The generally inelastic price structure of such commodities also places the underdeveloped nation at a disadvantage. Likewise, the exporter of raw materials often has high transportation costs due to heavy tonnage hauled in one direction. This is particularly so in Morocco, whose minerals must be hauled from the interior. Foreign-trade statistics and trade-balance trends have been excluded as less pertinent to this study, but ample statistics exist and will be found in nearly all the documents cited in this section.

[36] There are several good geographical studies of Morocco. The most complete is probably Jean Despois, *L'Afrique du Nord*, Paris, Presse Universitaire de France, 1949. Another is F. Joly, A. Ayache, and J. Fardel, *Géographie du Maroc*, Paris, Delagrave, 1949.

[37] If one uses a delimitation such that this zone was one tenth of the Morocco's total area, one sees that one third of the population lives here. R. Forichon and P. Mas, *op.cit.*, p. 473.

zone is the location of most commercialized farming, which is distributed over the three plains of Doukkala in the south, Chaouia inland from Casablanca, and Gharb between Rabat and the Rif. The plains are sheltered from the Sahara by a double ridge of mountains, the High Atlas and the Anti-Atlas, which run northeasterly to cut the country approximately into halves. The High Atlas Mountains merge with the Middle Atlas range, situated below Fès and running in the same direction. The Rif Mountains run east and west along the northern Mediterranean coast and spread out to connect with the Middle Atlas range around Taza. Though much drier than the Atlantic plains, the area around Oujda is partially arable with irrigation. South of a line running roughly from Oujda to Agadir is an area receiving only brief showers in the rainy season and depending for water on springs and melting snow from the mountains. Rains are much heavier to the north of the mountains, where dams have been concentrated to conserve water, irrigate, and generate electricity. Although subsistence agriculture is largely at the mercy of the annual rains, Morocco is much more fortunate than most Arab countries in having sufficient water for irrigation schemes—some of which have been started—and for the generation of large amounts of electricity.

The approaches to the mountains from the north support a large pastoral economy of the tribes. Stretches of forest are also found on the northern slopes of the mountains, which help support the tribal communities. In general, the tribesmen along the coast are of Arab background or fully Arabized Berbers. Berber tribal communities are largely confined to the mountains of the High Atlas, Anti-Atlas, and the eastern portion of the Rif. Some of the more isolated Berber tribes are still fairly intact, but Arabization has spread rapidly during the past generation. Many of the tribes of the Moroccan Sahara are of Arab origin.

As the geography of Morocco suggests, the extreme southerly and northeasterly tips of the country are relatively isolated from the more heavily populated Atlantic plains, where most economic activity is concentrated. Oujda and Agadir are sizable cities, but are more remote from the capital, Rabat, than the other major cities, which are at most only several hours' drive from the capital. Present communication patterns are also somewhat distorted because of the former division of the country into two zones under the Proctectorate. Since the Spanish did less to develop their area, it is now seriously isolated from the communication system built in the ex-French zone, as well

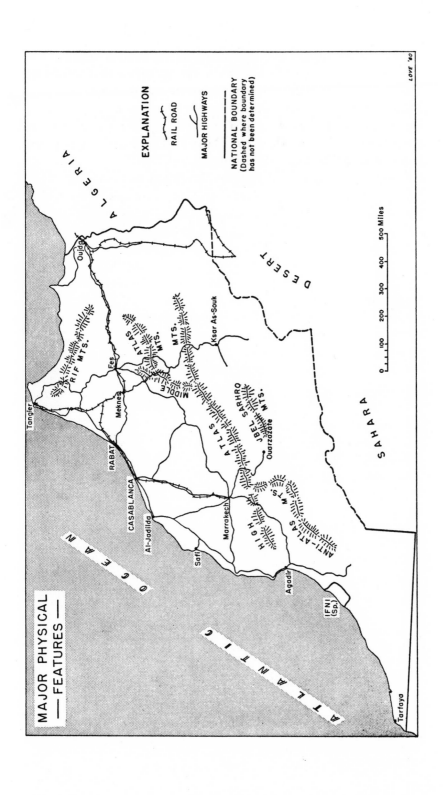

MAJOR PHYSICAL
— FEATURES —

EXPLANATION

RAIL ROAD

MAJOR HIGHWAYS

NATIONAL BOUNDARY
(Dashed where boundary
has not been determined)

ALGERIA

ATLANTIC

OCEAN

SAHARA

DESERT

0   100   200   300   400   500 Miles

Tangier
Oujda
Fes
Meknes
RABAT
CASABLANCA
Al-Jadilda
Safi
Marrakech
Agadir
IFNI (Sp.)
Tarfaya
Ouarzazate
Ksar As-Souk

RIF MTS.
ATLAS MTS.
MIDDLE ATLAS MTS.
HIGH ATLAS MTS.
ANTI-ATLAS MTS.
JBEL SARHRO MTS.

LOVE '60

as being more difficult to reach because of the rugged mountains of the Rif. To the south of Morocco lie the Spanish colonies, Tarfaya (ex-Spanish Meridional Morocco), which has been given to Morocco, and Seguia Al-Hamra and Rio de Oro, which are claimed by some Moroccans. Below them and extending over a vast territory three times the size of Morocco is Mauritania, a French colony that is also claimed by some Moroccans.

CHAPTER II

BACKGROUND TO MOROCCAN NATIONALISM

Doctrines and Dilemmas of the Early Years

FROM the nationalist movement have come the leaders of the new nation of Morocco. Only fourteen years after the Treaty of Fès established French and Spanish supervision of Morocco (1912), this movement began with two small groups of young men. From the beginning of their activity they hoped to make Morocco again independent,[1] but the goal was not publicly announced until 1944. Their eventual conflict with the Protectorate regime was inherent in their goal. Given the conditions existing in Morocco during the youth of these men, the slow progress made before World War II is not surprising. Most of the leaders had not yet finished their education. Mohammed Ben Youssef, now usually referred to as King Mohammed V, was eighteen when he was selected by the French in 1927 for his apparent docility. Ahmed Balafrej and Allal Al-Fassi were eighteen when they separately became the spokesmen for two small groups of nationalists meeting in Rabat and Fès in 1926. Though the goals of each group were somewhat differently inspired, the formation of a new Moroccan state was inherent in the ambitions of both. More difficult to explain is the striking absence of the elders of these young men in the movement, an absence which continued even after they had begun their early organization. With rare exceptions the nationalist movement was the organization of men who had grown up under French and Spanish colonial rule and not of the men who had witnessed the pacification and occupation of Morocco.

The pacification was a long and arduous military operation which was not completed until 1934, when the core of the nationalist movement was already well formed. The occupation followed the general lines of the historic division of Morocco between the *bled al-makhzen* and *bled as-siba*, meaning the areas under the control of the central or Cherifian administration of the King and the areas ruled by local *caids*. The *caids* were nominally under the control of

[1] See Hadj M'Hammed Bennouna's speech given in the late 1920's and quoted in Mehdi Bennouna's *Our Morocco: The True Story of a Just Cause*, Morocco, 1951, p. 34.

the King and the tribes they supervised were supposed to pay tribute to the King, but throughout the present dynasty, the Alaouite, this was a constantly shifting relationship. The areas belonging to the Cherifian government up to the time of the French occupation included roughly the plains of eastern Morocco around Oujda, the areas surrounding Fès and Taza, and most of the plains along the Atlantic coast from Tangier to the High Atlas below Safi.[2] Tribal hostilities were frequently exploited by the French and, even before the Treaty of Fès, many of the more powerful *caids* were in collusion with the French.[3] Expeditions were first sent into Morocco in 1907 after several attacks on French citizens. One occupied Oujda and its surrounding area in eastern Morocco and the other parts of the rich Chaouia plain surrounding Casablanca. Other early military operations of the occupation established French control in the southern cities of Agadir and Marrakech, where they used a strategy of counterbalancing tribal alliances, known as the policy of the "great *caids*." By 1913 the areas that constituted the *bled al-makhzen* had all been occupied and operations were begun to open up communications with eastern Morocco by taking the mountainous regions around Taza. Communications between the cities of the Gharb and Chaouia plains were also precarious because of the activities of nearby tribes. These tribes were the victims of the next campaign in the Khenifra area, which took eight years to complete.[4]

[2] Henri Terrasse, *Histoire du Maroc*, Casablanca, Editions Atlantides, 1950, tome II, pp. 356-358. Bordering most of this region were tribes or tribal fractions that were generally friendly to the dynasty and protected its holdings from more distant tribes. For example, three tribes, the Zemmour, the Zaer, and the Ziane, occupy most of the hilly Middle Atlas region that extends toward the coast in the area below a line formed by Fès, Meknes, and Rabat. They have a long history of intermittent cooperation with the dynasty and originally were given their relatively choice lands to protect those coastal areas and cities against attack and population pressure of other, more belligerent Berber tribes. For their role under the present dynasty see *ibid.*, "Le Maroc Isolé et Anarchique: La Dynastie Alaouite," CHAPTER VII, *passim*.

[3] The most complete study of the tribal structure outside the Maghzen is Robert Montagne's *Les Berbères et le Makhzen dans le Sud du Maroc*, Paris, Alcan, 1930, with another more anthropological study by the same author, *Villages et Kasbahs Berbères*, Paris, Alcan, 1930.

[4] A short history of the tribal campaigns will be found in Jean d'Esme, *op.cit.*, pp. 180-203. An interesting sidelight to this interlude in the pacification of Morocco is the revolt allegedly inspired by German agents at Khenifra in the Ziane tribe. One also took place near Tafilalet. See *ibid.*, pp. 204-207 and 210. See also the estimates of Allal Al-Fassi, which may be exaggerated but give an impression of the large scale of the "colonial" war and the fierce resistance of the Berbers, *The Independence Movements in Arab North Africa*, Washington, American Council of Learned Societies, 1954, p. 92.

During World War I, Marshall Lyautey, military commander and first Resident General, decided to try to hold his gains by relying heavily on the support of the tribes in the south. After the war, fighting resumed with the tribes in the Taza and Middle Atlas areas, while new campaigns were started in the south. The Rif War also began shortly after World War I. Fighting ranged throughout the area north of Fès, Ouazzan, and Taza. The region south of the High Atlas, including the present provinces of Agadir and Tafilalet, was not pacified until the early 1930's. In 1933 after an heroic struggle, the Berber forces in the southern sector of Tafilalet were defeated. This broke the last center of strong opposition. The next year the Sous valley of Agadir and the fringes of the Sahara Desert beyond the Anti-Atlas Mountains were occupied. At huge costs in human lives and material Morocco was finally pacified at the moment when new centers of opposition were forming in the cities.

The significance of the pacification for the present study is twofold. Through coercion the historic problem of the relationship of the *bled as-siba* and *bled al-makhzen* was solved, at least temporarily. Whether or not the nationalists approved of the means by which Morocco was first capable of founding a single, uniform administrative structure, the hegemony established by the French was an essential prerequisite for the development of Morocco as a modern nation. Though possibly this administrative unity might have been attainable by other means, the history of Berber resistance to firm central control or even supervision suggests that coercion would have had to be used in any case. Regardless of the lost secrets of historic possibility, France united Morocco, established the French claim to superior military capability, and took upon herself the responsibility for continuing central rule without the constant use of coercion. The French unification of Morocco made the aspirations of the young nationalists more realistic and gave them a defined sphere of organization. The French administration provided the nationalists with a possible source of discontent and a specific target for criticism, both of which could be used to build their movement.

The uprising in the northern zone of Morocco under Abdelkrim is a distinct phase of the pacification of Morocco and was certainly an important source of inspiration for the young nationalists.[5] The

[5] Charles-André Julien considers it the "decisive event" in the rise of the nationalist movement in his *L'Afrique du Nord en Marche*, Paris, Julliard, 1952, p. 145. Allal Al-Fassi, *op.cit.*, selects this phase of the pacification for detailed description, pp. 94-105.

Spanish occupation had not gotten started on any large scale before World War I, and in 1920 a major campaign was launched. Led by Abdelkrim, the tribes of the then almost-impenetrable Rif Mountains extended their resistance to include large parts of the ex-Spanish zone and later the northern fringe of the ex-French zone. Large stores of arms and ammunition were captured in 1923, and the Spanish, suffering great loss of men and great humiliation, were driven back into the port areas of Mellila and Alhucemas. In the first attempts at negotiation the Rif forces insisted on complete independence.[6] A new campaign began at the end of 1923 as Abdelkrim's revolt extended into the plains east of Tangier and the low mountains south of Tangier. General Primo de Rivera tried again to open negotiations with Abdelkrim, who was distracted by the discontent among Rifian tribes. Abdelkrim had also begun to organize the Rif Republic, which was complete with president, legislature, and plans for a constitution.[7]

France was brought into the conflict over disputes in the area between the Rif Mountains and Fès, where the border remained unclear. Skirmishes which began in 1924 eventually brought about a massive French campaign under General Pétain, with 200,000 French troops. In the face of Abdelkrim's continued refusal to accept any compromise of his plans for a republic, French concern multiplied. In May 1925, France and Spain planned a joint campaign, should he further decline offers to give a measure of local autonomy along the lines of the "great *caids*" like Al-Glaoui. Abdelkrim refused and just one year later the Rif hero was taken prisoner and exiled to Reunion Island, where he remained until he escaped to Egypt in 1947.[8] The importance of this episode to the growth of the nationalist movement is not easily evaluated. The magnitude of the effort by the French and the Spanish to make good their colonial claim suggests that in the absence of overwhelming

---

[6] The failure of this campaign weakened the Spanish monarchy and contributed to the situation that led to the dictatorship of General Primo de Rivera in September 1923. The war had cost forty-three million pounds. Rom Landau, *Moroccan Drama: 1900-1955*, San Francisco, American Academy of Asian Studies, 1956, p. 167. The size of Spanish losses are suggested in the figures of captured weapons, including 200 cannons and 20,000 rifles, according to Al-Fassi, *op.cit.*, pp. 96-98.

[7] *Ibid.*, pp. 103-105.

[8] Robert Montagne devotes one chapter to Abdelkrim in his book, *Révolution au Maroc*, Paris, Editions France-Empire, 1953, pp. 151-178. He discusses his role in accentuating tribal rivalries in order to weaken Abdelkrim, *ibid.*, pp. 163-164, though Al-Fassi maintains that the Rif War served to overcome such tensions, *op.cit.*, p. 102. This tactic was used throughout the Protectorate to increase French control among the tribes.

military force Morocco would have been most difficult to reduce to colonial status. On the basis of this discontent and resentment, a nationalist movement could find ample support, though obviously it would not easily be modeled into a form suitable for a modern state. The colonial powers realized this, and their efforts to prevent tribal tensions from being utilized led them to try to institutionalize the separation of the tribes from the more advanced areas of Morocco. This, of course, gave the nationalists a great stimulus.

Aside from indirect aid, the importance of the Abdelkrim uprising to the nationalist cause is not clear. The nationalists were certainly heartened by witnessing the struggle the Rif tribes could sustain. For a variety of reasons the nationalist movement itself was largely confined to the sections of Morocco where Arabic culture was predominant. The declaration of a republic with little official recognition of the role of Islam and the monarchial tradition of Morocco would certainly cause misgivings among the nationalists.[9] As a symbol Abdelkrim has been, of course, of great value to the nationalists throughout their struggle for independence, and his uncompromising position is the one that they themselves accepted shortly after his defeat. Being a devout Muslim he abolished customary tribal law wherever possible and strongly supported the Salafiya reform movement of Islam during the time of his short-lived republic. During the last days of Abdelkrim's struggle an emissary, Si Abdelkader Tazi, the brother of the pasha of Fès, was sent to the Rif as a representative of the nationalist group then gradually forming in Fès,[10] but no other direct relationship existed until after World War II.

The intellectual and religious inspiration for the early period of the nationalist movement is even more difficult to evaluate in reference to the problem of this study than the pacification of Morocco by the colonial powers. Aspects dealing with the motivation of such nascent movements are, of course, important, but do not fall within the framework of this book. For background purposes they will be described briefly. Like other Arab nations of this epoch, Morocco saw the influx of a variety of reformist opinion. The early group assembled in Rabat heard Hadj M'Hammed Bennouna recite from memory the speeches of Saad Zaghloul, memorized while he studied

[9] Al-Fassi, *op.cit.*, p. 103, defends Abdelkrim against charges of disloyalty to the Alaouite dynasty. Though the issue is not central to this study, it is important to remember that on several occasions since he has taken refuge in Egypt Abdelkrim has severely criticized the Istiqlal party and has always stoutly defended the King.

[10] Interview with Si Abdelaziz Ben Driss, Istiqlal Inspector for Agadir Province, Agadir, March 13, 1958.

in Cairo.[11] The reforms suggested by Jamal Din Al-Afghani and Mohammed Abdu were propagated among the young nationalists in Fès by Si Mohammed Ben Al-Arabi Al-Alaoui. Much attention was given to the efforts of the Destour group in Tunisia under Abdelaziz Taalibi and to the exploits of Mustapha Kemal in Turkey, although the absence of religious inspiration in his reforms troubled many of the young nationalists. Through Mohammed Lyazidi the doctrines of Sheikh Bouchaib Doukkali were carried to the small nationalist group at Rabat.[12] The Fès group of nationalists was particularly influenced by Ben Al-Arbi, and the young Mohammed Ghazi was arrested for his agitation for religious reforms before the nationalist group took on a distinct political significance. With some minor exceptions the common element of nearly all these early intellectual preoccupations of the nationalists was religious reform, specifically along the lines of Mohammed Abdu's philosophy and Salafiya doctrines. The political implications of this philosophy are not precisely clear, but the protest soon brought the young reformers into politics in search of the authority to enforce their values and the power to counteract colonialist encouragement of heretical sects and brotherhoods.[13]

The complexities of this intellectual ferment tended to grow less important as the nationalist movement advanced and need not be explored in detail to follow the growth of modern Morocco.[14] In a sense, the early reformers themselves were the first members of the new state to be "nationalized." Cause for their change in focus was provided by the French, whose policy was purposefully designed to differentiate the Berber population from the Arab and more strongly Islamized sectors. The Berber *dahir*, or law, of 1930 placed the bulk

[11] Mehdi Bennouna, *op.cit.*, p. 34. It is perhaps significant that his discourse on Egypt was interrupted by Ahmed Balafrej, who said: "Let us come to our subject. Aren't you going to deliver a speech?" *Ibid.*, p. 34.

[12] Robert Rezette, *Les Partis Politiques Marocains*, Paris, Armand Colin, 1955, p. 63, and Al-Fassi, *op.cit.*, p. 111.

[13] Parallel to Doukkali's efforts in Morocco is the work of Sheikh Abd Al-Hamid Ben Badis in Algeria and Sheikh Abdelaziz Taaibi in Tunisia. See Julien, *op.cit.*, pp. 111-118. An excellent study of the problem of bringing this body of belief, along with other reform movements in the Arab world, into one political organization is the doctoral thesis of Mahdi Saadi Al-Mandjara, *The League of Arab States: 1945-1955*, presented in November, 1957, to the University of London, London School of Economics and Political Science. Further elaboration of these trends as they came to bear on concrete problems can be found in Hazem Zaki Nuseibeh's *The Ideas of Arab Nationalism*, Ithaca, Cornell University Press, 1956, *passim*.

[14] In Al-Fassi's discussion of the Salafiya movement, *op.cit.*, pp. 111-116, he admits the difficulty of incorporating contemporary political concepts into its theory and defends it against charges of a negative kind of battle against superstition.

of the tribes under French criminal law, recognized the judicial competence of the tribal *jemaâ,* or customary courts, and provided for a higher customary court of appeal. All of these acts tended to reduce the application of the Shariah law of orthodox, Sunni Islam. The implications of this policy are replete with paradoxes. If the French had been prepared to permit the steady spread of Islam in its orthodox form, as had been continuing for centuries, the volatile issue of religion would conceivably have been removed from the sphere of political issues and would no longer have been a source of meaningful political differentiation.

The Berber *dahir* was particularly important in the early expansion of the nationalists, who highly valued their Arab culture and orthodox Islam. Furthermore, this new challenge to Islam provided the starting point for the appeal of Pan-Arabism, whose political meaning is more clearly defined and, therefore, generally more suitable for political agitation than Pan-Islamic doctrine. Above all, for purposes of this book, the segregation of a near majority of the potential members of a new Moroccan state under a separate legal system, regardless of its religious implications, focused the attention of the young nationalists on the importance of the nation itself. The *dahir* applied roughly from all the territory south of Fès and Meknes to the Sahara and from Rabat to the Algerian border.[15] The *dahir* also meant that all the participants in the early nationalist movement could appear as "champions of Islam" and thereby reduce the chances of internal conflict between members having a near fanatical attitude toward Islam and others having less religious motivation, which became a source of tension in the nationalist movements of Algeria and Tunisia.

The *dahir* gave new importance to Chekib Arslan, the Pan-Arab leader and one-time student of Mohammed Abdu. In 1930 he opened an office in Geneva, which became the European headquarters for nationalists from the Levant and North Africa. Several members of the northern group of nationalists came under his influence, and Arslan was invited to speak in Tetouan in 1930, from where he established relations with Allal Al-Fassi and Mohammed Hassan

[15] Among the largest tribal confederations to be included were the Beni Ourain, Beni Mguild, Zemmour, Ziane, Ait Segrouchen, and Ait Yafelmane. *Al-Maghreb,* 1è année, no. 11, May-June 1933, p. 32, carries a map of the included territory. This early nationalist publication has at least one article on the Berber *dahir* in almost every issue. A summary of the Pan-Islamic and Pan-Arab movements will be found in G. E. von Grunebaum's essay, "Problems of Muslim Nationalism," *Islam and the West,* Richard N. Frye, ed., The Hague, Mouton, 1958, pp. 9-29.

Ouazzani. From 1930 to 1933 Ouazzani was his secretary in Geneva, but Arslan's influence in the south was limited by the strict control of the French. He became spokesman and European organizational focus for the young nationalists, to whom he opened his journal and many of whom, like Ahmed Balafrej in 1932, took refuge at his Geneva office. The effort in the south, however, remained oriented toward Paris, while the nationalist group in the north tended more toward Pan-Arab and Levantine opinions. When the government of Spain came under General Franco, Arslan continued to work with the northern group. The committee at Rabat and Fès, at that time working closely with the Socialists of the Popular Front in France, could not risk being associated with the new dictatorship. After 1938 Arslan's prestige diminished as a result of his support of the Axis powers, although his ideas probably continued to have appeal in the north, where some *modus vivendi* had to be continued with Franco.[16]

These early contacts with Chekib Arslan are of interest not only because of the revelation of the nebulous form the ideas of the nationalists took before independence. They also reveal the element of selectivity of doctrine, perhaps not calculated, that involved the nationalists of the north and south in somewhat different courses of action. The predominance of the Pan-Islamic thought in the ex-French zone and Pan-Arabic thought in the ex-Spanish zone suggests that these early doctrines had a usefulness that rested more in their suitability for handling existing political problems than for the solutions to future problems that they might embody. The somewhat disappointing experience of the northern nationalists with this doctrine also anticipates the discouraging reception that the Moroccan nationalists were to receive in the post-World War II era by the new organization for Pan-Arabic action, the Arab League. At that time the harsh political realities of Palestine were to have more significance than the goals of either Pan-Arabic or Pan-Islamic thought,[17]

[16] This curious divergence between the intellectual orientation of the northern and southern nationalists is in part a result of the French policy of not permitting known nationalists from the northern zone to study in France. So they turned to Madrid, Jerusalem, and Egypt where Pan-Arab doctrines were freely propagated. If France had been prepared to take some risk in countering Franco's influence in Morocco, it might have been a skillful strategy to admit these young nationalists to French institutions and give them as strong a French background as one finds in the case of many nationalists in the southern zone. At this time, of course, France was not envisaging sustaining her influence in a unified country.

[17] It is interesting to note that Pan-Islamic leaders were committed to independence for Morocco *and* return of Mauritania in the 1917 Congress, Al-Fassi, *op.cit.*, p. 108.

just as did the immediate political problems of a movement working with two different colonial administrations in the prewar era.

In connection with the reform of Islam in Morocco, brief comment should be made on the activities of the *confréries*, or religious brotherhoods. Their political role, on the whole, has not been so great since independence as before independence. Their importance is more of historical interest, for it was the early attentions of the French colonial administration to the brotherhoods as possible powers in tribal interplay in the pacification of Morocco—and later in the governing of Morocco—that stimulated the nationalists of Qarawiyn to press for reforms.[18] Like Sunni Islamic doctrine in other Arab states, the Malekite school of Sunni Islam of Morocco was firmly opposed to the growth of these sects, generally called Sufi sects in the other areas of the Muslim world. The brotherhood is led by a sheikh, who may be of Cherifian descent, that is, from the Prophet Mohammed, or may be a *marabout*, or saint, to whom are attributed mystic powers. The initial cell of a brotherhood is called a *zaouia*, which has various categories of members, some of whom can bestow a divine benediction, or *baraka*, with various degrees of potency. The *zaouia* may be loosely knit or scattered throughout the country. In 1953 they were estimated to have slightly over a quarter of a million members, or 3.8 per cent of the Muslim population.[19] Among the most active in the politics of the Protectorate were the Derkaoua and the Kettani brotherhoods, the sheikh of the latter becoming a colleague of Al-Glaoui during General Juin's Residency and having a history of cooperation with the Protectorate going back at least to 1927.[20] Their reputation for betrayal of the nationalist cause, combined with the tremendous prestige of Mohammed V after his exile, who also possesses a powerful blessing, has barred them from overt political activity.

---

[18] Mehdi Bennouna, *op.cit.*, p. 38. The early Salafiya reformers, including some of Al-Fassi's ancestors, started the campaign against the brotherhoods before World War I. Al-Fassi, *op.cit.*, p. 87.

[19] Rezette, *op.cit.*, p. 117. The most complete historical account of the brotherhoods is in George Drague's *Esquisse d'Histoire Religieuse du Maroc*, Paris, J. Peyronnet, n.d. A shorter summary will be found in Rezette, *op.cit.*, pp. 19-27, although their manipulation by the French tends to give them more importance in his book than they have had subsequently. It should be noted that the common impression of *marabouts*, or brotherhood leaders, as tattered ascetics is incorrect. Abdul Hai Kettani was a brilliant scholar of Islam and Arabic. His magnificent library has now been seized by the government and is being collated and redistributed.

[20] Abdul Hai Kettani was instrumental in the arrest of Mohammed Ghazi in 1927. Mehdi Bennouna, *op.cit.*, p. 29. Unlike Glaoui, Kettani did not receive the King's pardon in 1955.

Emergence of a Political Party

From the small group of students at Rabat, led by Ahmed Balafrej, and the group at Qarawiyn University, led by Allal Al-Fassi, emerged the first political party of the French zone. Formed during the final steps of the pacification, its struggle in 1937 to become a rudimentary, poorly organized party was stifled with the approach of World War II. During this entire period the group of young nationalists never operated with complete freedom or with any legal protection. Although they were permitted for short intervals of a month or two to operate quite openly, most work was done clandestinely in anticipation of the next wave of suppression. Only in the brief period from December 1936 to March 1937 did they enjoy a measure of legality, when General Noguès granted a general amnesty and many new papers were started. This amnesty was partly due to the establishment of the Popular Front government in France in June 1936. Its desire to solidify the loyalty of the Moroccans were reinforced by the initiation of the revolution under Franco in Spain the next month. Before this time the nationalists had had the blessing of some Socialists. They had subsidized and written in the early French review of the nationalists, *Al-Maghreb*, in 1932 and 1933.[21] For nearly all the first half of the period from 1926 to 1939 French Morocco was still in a state of open warfare and complete military occupation except for the secure areas along the coast. Under these conditions it is not surprising that little was done.

In April 1927 the Fès group, called the Students Union, and the Rabat group, called the Supporters of Truth, began collaborating and clandestinely took oaths in a new organization, the Moroccan League. The next month, after having been denounced by the head of the Kettani brotherhood, the first nationalist, Mohammed Ghazi, was arrested. Mohammed Ghazi had started the first free school of the nationalists in Fès in 1926. This school was an institution that was to take on its full political implications only after World War II. After these early meetings the young nationalists again returned to their studies, mostly at Qarawiyn or in Paris. Until the Berber *dahir* the most important goal of the group left in Morocco was their opposition to the increasing activity of the brotherhoods. Al-Fassi became famous for his lectures on this subject at Qarawiyn Univer-

[21] This small review was published in Paris and edited by Robert-Jean Longuet. Among its Spanish contributors was Ortega y Gasset. It was smuggled into the Protectorate. Discussed by Al-Fassi, *op.cit.*, p. 127, and Rezette, *op.cit.*, pp. 69-70.

sity. Indeed, the first primitive organization of the nationalists in Morocco consisted of groups of Islamic scholars and students who exchanged information throughout the regions of the country where orthodox Islam was strongest and who convened in the privileged sanctuary provided by the mosques.[22]

In view of the small percentage of the Moroccans who belonged to brotherhoods, this original goal of the nationalists was actually more an intellectual protest than a theme that could be developed into an imperative for political action. As has been noted, this need was admirably filled by the Berber *dahir* of May 1930. It brought the cause of the nationalists to the attention of the Socialists in France, who from this time on sympathized with the young nationalists. Shortly after the issue of the *dahir*, Chekib Arslan made his visit to Tetouan and made contact with the nationalists of the French zone.[23] Arslan made the *dahir* a central theme of his Pan-Arabism, and his protégé, Mohammed Hassan Ouazzani, started a French-language newspaper, *L'Action du Peuple*, in Fès in 1933. While some nationalists with more French background, like Mohammed Lyazidi and Omar Abdeljalil, wrote for its columns, the nationalist *ulema* of Qarawiyn in the same city contributed nothing and little appeared pertaining to their Islamic-inspired protests.[24] Through Arslan's efforts the campaign reached all parts of the Arab world, and committees to defend Islam in Morocco were started in Egypt, India, and Indonesia. The young nationalists were convinced that the *dahir* was the initiation of a program to divide Morocco into smaller colonies and to begin the proselytism of the Berbers by Christian missionaries.

In 1929 the Moroccan League had formed a loosely bound Committee of National Action, which included members from both the old Spanish and French zones. The committee took on new significance after the enactment of the 1930 *dahir* and was broken into separate parts for the north and south to facilitate its

[22] Rezette, *op.cit.*, pp. 7-11, gives some examples of the better-known meetings in mosques. These meetings were, of course, important throughout the period before the war and, in addition, in the absence of permission for the nationalists to meet publicly, were used to reach the public and to overcome the obstacle of illiteracy to political agitation.

[23] Rezette, *op.cit.*, pp. 68-71. Though not directly pertinent to this inquiry, it is indicative of the plight of the young nationalists between the appeal of France and the Arab world that Chekib Arslan declined an invitation to a Socialist-sponsored rally on behalf of the Moroccans in 1933.

[24] "*Ulema*" is the plural form of the word "*alim*," or "religious scholar in Islam." For a more detailed view on this early publication, see Rezette, *op.cit.*, p. 76.

activities in the French Protectorate. Allal Al-Fassi continued his lectures at Qarawiyn and late in 1933 made visits to Tetouan, Madrid, and Paris. On his return in May 1934 he was received by the King— the first contact between the nationalists and Mohammed V. Shortly afterward the nationalist newspapers, now four in number and coming from Tetouan and Paris as well as Fès, were banned. Allal Al-Fassi and his colleagues were forbidden to continue their public lectures.

During this same early period the organization of students and youth began. When Balafrej returned to Paris after the first meeting of 1926, he helped start the Association of North African Muslim Students. Congresses were held in Tunis in 1931 and in Algiers in 1932. The 1933 Congress, scheduled for Rabat, was forbidden there and was held in Paris. At the same time graduates of the Muslim colleges of Fès, Rabat, Marrakech, and Casablanca began to form alumni associations, though their initial reluctance to engage in direct political agitation drew the criticism of the *L'Action du Peuple*.[25] An unsuccessful attempt was made by the alumni associations, in November 1933, to condemn the banning of the meeting of the Association of North African Muslim Students. Another source of potentially more aggressive support for the nationalists, the Movement of Moroccan Scouts, also started in 1933. Though under French auspices, its Moroccan directors were known for their nationalist leanings, and by the end of World War II the scouts had become an important nationalist adjunct. Efforts of the nationalist press to establish as a national holiday November 18, the day on which Mohammed Ben Youssef became King, also succeeded from the fall of 1933.

Up to 1933 the French authorities had not forcefully intervened in nationalist activities, which were still largely confined to small groups in Rabat, its neighboring city of Salé, and Fès. Allal Al-Fassi and his colleagues had been removed from their positions as *ulema* at Qarawiyn and a few of their students had been briefly detained by the police. Early in 1934 the King made a visit to Fès, where the spectacular ovation he received produced serious concern among the French authorities. They canceled his trip to the mosque on the Friday of that week and abruptly hustled Mohammed V back to Rabat. The riots resulting from the arbitrarily foreshortened visit alerted the nationalists to the problem they would have in pursuing their ac-

[25] *Ibid.*, p. 77.

tivity among a population whose enthusiasm was so easily turned into violence.[26] This incident was violently attacked by the nationalist press, which was forbidden soon afterward in Morocco. The nationalist leaders appear then to have entered a period of reflection and consultation, from which emerged the Plan of Reforms of 1934, described in the following paragraph. It must be remembered that at this time they possessed almost no organization outside of the small groups in the major cities, loosely held together in the Committee of Action. From this incident of the riots following the King's forced return to Rabat came the more conciliatory opinion embodied in the Plan of Reforms and also the decline in the importance of Arslan and Mohammed Hassan Ouazzani, the most outspoken critics of France.

After the Fès riots a small committee of ten persons had been formed in Fès to work on a new plan of action.[27] Six were clearly of predominantly Arabic background and of the four who had some French background only Mohammed Hassan Ouazzani represented what might be termed an extreme modernist viewpoint. In December 1934 the Plan of Reforms, which this committee had prepared, was presented to the King, Premier Laval, and the Resident General. The document[28] justified Julien's evaluation that "[the] program constitutes a catalog of claims more than an elaborated plan of reforms."[29] The first part of the Plan reiterated the original conditions under which the Protectorate had been established and outlined how this agreement had been violated. This was followed by five sections on proposed changes in the realm of political and administrative procedures, judicial and penal institutions, general social and health measures, economic and financial practices, and, last, special needs, including the abolition of the Berber *dahir* and the use of Arabic as the official language. The goal of independence was not discussed, nor was any suggestion made that the Moroccans be given a voice in foreign affairs or national defense. The section on economic reforms was probably the most naïve, starting off with the unex-

[26] Interview with Mohammed Lyazidi, executive committee, Istiqlal party, Rabat, January 10, 1958.

[27] Julien, *op.cit.*, p. 151, lists them as Omar Abdeljalil, Abdelaziz Ben Driss, Ahmed Cherkaoui, Mohammed Diouri, Allal Al-Fassi, Mohammed Ghazi, Boucker Kadiri, Mohammed Lyazidi, Mohammed Mekki Naciri, and Mohammed Hassan Ouazzani.

[28] Comité d'Action Marocaine, *Plan de Reformes Marocaines*, Paris, 1934.

[29] Julien, *op.cit.*, p. 154. His general discussion of the document will be found in *ibid.*, pp. 151-154. See also Allal Al-Fassi, *op.cit.*, pp. 136-142, and Rezette, *op.cit.*, pp. 87-90.

plained injunction to "raise the standard of living of Moroccans by the creation of work and the development of economic activity." The section on justice was outlined the most systematically and completely, which was to be expected since many members of the committee had a thorough knowledge of Islamic law and Moroccan history. The political and administrative section was a mixture of sound suggestions and obviously ambitious schemes, particularly in the area of representative institutions, as the authors of the document learned after three years of independence. The Plan of Reforms is valuable for this study not so much for what it specifically contained, as for its tacit testimony as to how little the nationalists changed their thinking over the next twenty years regarding the actual problems of running a nation.

To expect the young nationalists to be familiar with the intricacies of government while at the same time carrying on their campaign for independence would be unreasonable, but it is important in understanding events after independence. Their organized membership was restricted to Rabat, Casablanca, Fès, Salé, and Kenitra (Port Lyautey).[30] A few members were just beginning nationalist activity in Safi, Meknes, and Marrakech. Finances were provided largely by contributions of a few wealthy members. Very little attention had been given to developing a disciplined following even in the cities, though it was possible to create a potentially violent demonstration. The nationalists' strength for the entire area of Morocco was reliably estimated to include twelve leaders, 150 militants, and from 200 to 300 sympathizers.[31]

The Plan of Reforms marked the entry of the nationalists into official politics. Though it is probably an exaggeration to say that the Plan "had far-reaching repercussions in French and Moroccan circles,"[32] it alerted the French to the growing threat to their control and showed the nationalists how difficult it would be to negotiate for reforms. The Plan was rejected in its entirety and the nationalists again were dispersed, many of them going to Paris to try to bring

[30] Most of the organizational information in this paragraph is from Rezette, *op.cit.*, p. 255 and pp. 263-267. The cited figures were taken from "an official document," according to Rezette. Since he is known to have received some assistance from French authorities in Rabat and Paris in writing his book, these figures are probably the work of the French administration. Even if minimized considerably, they indicate how small a group were active participants at this time.

[31] The two leaders in addition to the ten authors of the Plan of Reforms are probably Ahmed Balafrej and Mohammed Zeghari.

[32] Allal Al-Fassi, *op.cit.*, p. 141.

their case to the attention of officials there. Their efforts were renewed with vigor late in 1935, when the French residents demanded representative institutions. This was regarded by the nationalists as the first step in the incorporation of Morocco in the French Empire and also, of course, as the denial of equal privileges to Moroccans in their own affairs. Allal Al-Fassi and his colleagues met with the Resident General to discuss the matter on the eve of the formation of the Popular Front. This was the first meeting of the nationalists with a Resident General and soon broke down into a round of mutual incriminations, but the establishment of the Blum government postponed the controversial issue. The same Resident General also forbade the convening of the annual congress of the Association of North African Muslim Students in Morocco in the fall of 1936. By this time the nationalists had established their first local sections, four being formed in Casablanca, five at Fès, and one each at Kenitra, Rabat, and Salé.[33]

With the Socialists in power in Paris new opportunities were opened for the nationalists in Morocco. In July 1936 a nationalist delegation was sent to Paris and was received by Paul Viénot, the Under Secretary of State for Foreign Affairs and one of their sympathizers. Though they did not receive any specific concessions, the unpopular Resident General Peyrouton was recalled, only to be replaced by General Noguès, who was suspect because of his role in the suppression of the demonstrations following the Berber *dahir*. Nevertheless, the nationalists were hopeful and a series of meetings was held in the cities where they had members. A list of "urgent demands" was formed, for the most part a summary version of the Plan of Reforms of 1934. The same delegation was sent again to Paris in October to present these demands to Viénot, but the delegation was not received because of the curt tone of its petition. Toward the end of October a general meeting took place and plans were made for a series of public rallies in other major cities.[34]

In this first congress plans were made for a series of public rallies to begin to build up a popular base for the Committee of Action and its followers. Early in November 1936 public meetings were held in

[33] Rezette, *op.cit.*, p. 270.

[34] Julien, *op.cit.*, p. 160. The members of the delegation were Omar Abdeljalil and Mohammed Hassan Ouazzani. See also Al-Fassi, *op.cit.*, pp. 156-157. Rezette contends, *op.cit.*, p. 98, that this general meeting took place before Mohammed Hassan Ouazzani could return from Paris on the insistence of Allal Al-Fassi and that this was one of the immediate causes of the personal friction leading to the later split of the committee.

Fès and Salé, with several hundred participants and no disorder. Another meeting was planned for Casablanca in mid-November, which was to have been devoted to the problems of press censorship and the ban on Arabic-language newspapers. To maximize the impact of their grievance the nationalists had invited French sympathizers and the press, who were to be entertained at a reception the following day. Alarmed, possibly by the throngs waiting for the rally or by the poor publicity for Protectorate policy that might be released in France, the French authorities decided at the last moment to forbid the meeting and the crowds turned into the streets carrying the nationalists on their shoulders.

Luckily the situation did not break out into violence, but Allal Al-Fassi, Mohammed Lyazidi, and Mohammed Hassan Ouazzani were arrested soon after. This was the first of what was to be a long series of attempts by the French to "decapitate" the movement and, like the others, it reflected the misjudgment of the colonial authorities as to the potential strength of the movement. Over the next days violent demonstrations occurred in Fès, Salé, Casablanca, Oujda, and Taza. Abdeljalil was sent off to Paris to plead the nationalist case before Viénot, who apparently was very worried over the possible outbreak of widespread violence in Morocco under the newly formed and fully occupied Popular Front government. At the same time Abdeljalil opened the first permanent office of the nationalists in Paris, and started a new French-language journal there.

After a month the nationalist leaders who had been arrested were freed and consultations were begun between the Resident General and Abdeljalil, now back from Paris. The committee met with the Resident and received permission to publish an Arabic weekly and several other newspapers, although all press activity remained under the discretionary powers of the Resident General. Trade unions were also authorized for the first time toward the end of 1936, but were reserved to Europeans. In practice it was not possible to prevent Moroccans from participating when a French union would accept them and many began joining the Moroccan branch of the C.G.T. (*Confédération Générale du Travail*). The Casablanca incident also helped to strengthen the ties between the Socialists of France and the nationalists, although the association carried certain dilemmas for both parties. Perhaps most important for the movement, the demonstrations gave the organization recognition and popularity among a larger circle of followers and new sections were established in Meknes, Sefrou, Ouazzan, and Kasba-Tadla.[35] For the first time the nationalists began to extend their influence to the heretofore isolated and generally impenetrable Berber countryside, commonly called the *bled*. More evidence of this advance appeared the next year.

In this interval of relatively free activity the nationalists decided to undertake a reorganization of their followers. Faced with problems of allocating authority and formally recognizing status within the loosely formed group of leaders, conflict was produced that led to the split of the committee. Al-Fassi and Ouazzani were designated to compose a new set of party regulations and procedures. In January 1937 twenty-one leaders met to elect new central committees. During the nominations for the Executive Committee Ouazzani criticized the nomination of Al-Fassi for chairman, arguing that his totally Islamic background would be a handicap in negotiations with the French and that his inability to speak French would make understanding more difficult. Confronted with the prospect of extending their organization in Morocco the leaders decided that Al-Fassi was too valuable to relegate to a secondary position. He was elected chairman and Ouazzani was given the secondary post of secretary general.

For Ouazzani, graduate of the École Libre des Sciences Politiques in Paris and up till now a leader in the nationalists' contacts both in Paris and in Geneva, this minor defeat was too humiliating and he resigned. Both Arslan and the Tunisian nationalist leader, Sheikh Taalibi, intervened in attempts to reconcile the two figures, but without success. In view of the problems facing the committee at that time, the selection of Al-Fassi is not so surprising as the facility with which personal frictions could erupt. Ouazzani's failure to realize that his position as secretary general could easily become more important than the post as chairman is also indicative of the organizational inexperience of the leaders. Ahmed Balafrej was made secretary general and an office was opened in Fès, where new members were registered in numbers that apparently caused considerable concern to the Resident General.[36]

In March 1937 the Resident issued a decree dissolving the committee and closing its office in Fès. The Resident and Viénot hoped that the nationalists could be persuaded to become a kind of Moroccan Fabian Society and to avoid mass political action. Abdeljalil and Balafrej were dispatched to Paris, while the leaders remaining in

[35] Julien, *op.cit.*, p. 166.
[36] Rezette, *op.cit.*, p. 277, comments on the recruiting methods.

Morocco met in Rabat and reconstituted the committee under the name "National Party for the Realization of the Plan of Reforms." The suppression served to increase the group's appeal and their clandestine organization grew rapidly. By the end of 1937 twenty sections had been created, in addition to the cities in which sections had existed since 1935.[37] The extension into the towns of the *bled* was considerable, though many of them were mining communities that possibly are not properly included here as an actual foothold among the tribesmen. Several of these towns, particularly along the coast, were regions inhabited by Arabic-speaking Berbers or those of solely Arab origin and thus do not indicate a penetration of the French-dominated countryside. This marks, nevertheless, the first time that the nationalists were able to extend their activity to the *bled*, even though that activity was confined to the regions near the large cities.

The progress of the nationalists in the *bled* was facilitated as more French colonists arrived and as the large French landowners contrived plans to enrich their holdings. Support was given to tribesmen resisting such plans near Kasba-Tadla, Marrakech, and Sefrou. The climax came when many people were killed in riots near Meknes after plans had been announced to divert the course of the local river for the benefit of French "colons." At the same time the nationalists were alarmed when the French Catholic Church announced an official pilgrimage to the Berber town of Khemisset. Soon afterward a proposed general meeting of the Koranic schoolteachers in the region of the Zemmour and Ziane tribes was banned.[38] Early in October the local delegates and Executive Committee of the newly formed party assembled in Rabat and prepared a list of grievances for the Resident General.[39] An outspoken attack was unleashed in all the nationalists' papers and demonstrations culminating in violence occurred in Casablanca, Oujda, Khemisset, and Marrakech. In the face of a rapidly deteriorating situation, the Resident General decided to arrest Allal Al-Fassi, Mohammed Lyazidi, Omar Abdeljalil, and several other leaders. For the first time troops were sent to occupy the Fès *medina*, and Qarawiyn University, where many na-

[37] *Ibid.*, p. 271. The new sections of most importance were Oujda, Sidi-Kacem (Petitjean), Es-Saouira (Mogador), Oued-Zem, Berkane, Souk-Al-Arba du Gharb, Al-Jadiid (Mazagan), Moulay Bouchaib, Boujad, Taza, Ouazzan, Safi, and Settat.
[38] Interview with Mohammed Lyazidi, executive committee, Istiqlal party, Rabat, January 10, 1958, and Julien, *op.cit.*, pp. 170-171.
[39] The petition will be found in Al-Fassi, *op.cit.*, pp. 188-190.

tionalists had taken refuge, was surrounded. Rather than risk defamation of their ancient holy place, the nationalists surrendered. Soon afterward Mohammed Hassan Ouazzani was also arrested, after he had refused an opportunity to abandon the nationalist cause.

Though Al-Fassi and Ouazzani were sent into exile until 1946, the nationalists were allowed to continue under less favorable conditions. The party was again assembled under Mohammed Lyazidi, who was released in 1938. Abdeljalil and Balafrej were free to continue their efforts from Switzerland, Spain and France. At least one nationalist publication continued to appear, and several more moderate nationalists were given permission to start papers. The Resident General decreed minor administrative changes toward the end of 1937 that brought the blessing of Arslan. The nationalist party continued to operate an office at Fès that enjoyed immunity because it was on the premises of a friendly British banker, and also one at Rabat, which became its permanent headquarters from this time.[40] The organizational progress of the party during 1936 and 1937 was great. Since the party still was most active in the three large urban centers of Fès, Rabat, and Casablanca, each of these regions selected a committee of directors of about twenty persons and, from this, a smaller regional executive committee. The central organization also had its Executive Committee, a national council made up from this committee plus delegates from the various sections, and a series of directors for specific tasks. The Executive Committee continued its work under camouflage as the "Board of Editors" of one of the authorized nationalist papers.

In early 1937 a system for collection of dues and a loyalty oath had been introduced as the membership drive started. During the period of open activity up to October 1937, the party most likely did not issue more than 10,000 cards to adherents.[41] The signifi-

[40] Rezette, *op.cit.*, pp. 272 and 274. The British enjoyed immunity under the terms of the original capitulatory agreement for Morocco. Communications also relied heavily on the system of British post offices that were established under this agreement. See Mehdi Bennouna, *op.cit.*, p. 42.

[41] See Rezette, *op.cit.*, pp. 272-279, for organizational information. The *anciens* of the party almost unanimously refuse to venture estimates of their prewar strength, but much prefer to talk in terms of "confidence of the people," which, indeed, may be more meaningful. The firm military control by the French made the possible uses of a highly developed organization very limited. Inasmuch as there was definite limitation of the ways in which the nationalists could exercise influence, a mass demonstration was often the most suitable method. Two party inspectors, who have been working in their regions since this epoch, offered estimates of prewar strength that were actually a bit below Rezette's.

cance of this membership is limited by the short interval of time available to promote the party. After the end of 1937 the number diminished considerably, though the grievances and demonstrations had produced a small body of members who were to form the first cadre for the reorganized party after the war.

More interesting for the future of the party was the introduction of recruitment techniques in the *bled*, perhaps not purposefully, not unlike the procedures used by the brotherhoods. Al-Fassi was frequently referred to as "sheikh," leading members as "Allaliynes," and the dues as "*ziara*," all terms used by the brotherhoods.[42] Until his exile Al-Fassi was undoubtedly the leading figure of the party. Lyazidi, who took over the direction of the party in Morocco upon Al-Fassi's exile, is certainly entitled to the appellation *"éminence grise"* of the party.[43] In the top ranks with these two were found the same men who had been associated with the movement for the previous ten years: Balafrej, Mohammed Ghazi, Abdeljalil, Ahmed Mekouar, who comprised the Executive Committee during most of this period. Ahmed Cherkaoui, Boubker Qadiri, Abdelaziz Ben Driss, Mohammed Diouri (not related to the later Minister of Public Works), from the old Committee of Action, and Hachemi Al-Filali, Hassan Bouayad, and Bouchta Jamai, militants from the first days and students of Al-Fassi, comprised the Superior Council, an enlarged version of the Executive Committee. The actual function of this council, outside of providing a position for the *anciens* of the party, was not clear. The group of leaders does not seem as notable for their French background as Rezette suggests.[44] The large majority of the leaders, eight of the thirteen, not only had strong Islamic roots, but were educated at Qarawiyn University and could not even speak French.

The interlude of open activity had taught the nationalists and also the French colonial administration two important lessons. The first was how rapidly the party organization could be expanded if given minimum freedom of action. The second and closely related lesson was how easily this following—both the adherents and the sympathizers—would break away from the control of the party. The consequent violence could be disastrous, either from sheer self-destruc-

---

[42] Rezette, *op.cit.*, pp. 282-283. He also notes that, whereas the militants were called "friends" in 1934, by 1936 the usual term was "brother" or "*khouan*." While such changes should not be exaggerated for their significance among the sophisticated members, in the *bled* their meaning is clear. See also Julien, *op.cit.*, p. 155.

[43] Rezette, *op.cit.*, p. 287.   [44] *Ibid.*, p. 287.

tion or from the subsequent repressive measures by superior French forces. As Rezette has admirably summarized, "The party is a 'sorcerer's apprentice,' than can order the masses to act, but that releases at the same time forces of which it is no more the master."[45] The first lesson led the nationalists to realize how much could be achieved if their following could be organized freely. The second brought home the necessity of doing so effectively, which would mean more education and more organizational restraints. This experience was reflected in their activity after the war, particularly in the intensive organization of free schools. Although Al-Fassi criticized both French personalities and policies freely, it is also evident that the nationalists welcomed the support of the French Socialists, accepted nearly every offer of a Resident General to discuss mutual problems, and repeatedly sent delegates to Paris to consult government officials. With the upper hand so firmly with the French, the surprising aspect of this period, as well as the postwar period, is not the basically conciliatory attitude of the nationalists, but the unimaginativeness and occasional pure blundering that characterized French policy.

In the period after 1937 until World War II, French policy in Morocco was tempered by the friendly reception and concessions being given to the nationalists in the Spanish zone. Some feeble attempts were even made to introduce a few persons of known nationalist connections into advisory organs of the Resident General. Under the tactful guidance of Mohammed Lyazidi the party managed to begin to rebuild its organization. A few other activities were carried on by Islamic reform groups favorable to the party. When the war broke out in August 1939, a delegation of four nationalists called on the Resident General to assure him of the cooperation of Moroccan youth in the event of a conflict in North Africa.

Islah and Intrigue in the North

The historical development of the northern nationalist movement differs from events in the south for a number of reasons. The many gyrations of Spanish colonial policy alone suggest the need for a strategy more flexible than that of the southern nationalists. Spain's policy was heavily influenced by French policy, especially by the animosity between the two powers following the rise of Franco. In addition to these external conditions, there are many factors within the Moroc-

[45] *Ibid.*, p. 288.

can setting itself that are important background. Except for the vicinity of the two cities of the north, Tangier and Tetouan, the area is nearly all occupied by fiercely independent tribes. Tangier was isolated by its special international status and used by all nationalist groups.[46] In Tetouan the aristocratic leading families tended to frown on agitation among the tribes and no doubt welcomed the subduing of Abdelkrim in 1926, who threatened to engulf their city in his "republic." The domination of political life in the north by a few wealthy families, plus the strong personalities of the few leaders from the French zone who took refuge under the generally more tolerant Spanish administration produced much more personal bickering than in the south.

These internecine quarrels were encouraged by the Spanish, both under the republic and under the dictatorship. Posts in the administration were given to nationalists with great skill and surprising success in order to maximize interpersonal strain among the nationalists. When one considers the bargaining power the nationalists of the Spanish zone possessed through the large numbers of Moroccan troops sent to fight for Franco,[47] one realizes that they might have accomplished much more if they had been as willing to manipulate the tribes and brotherhoods of the Rif Mountains as the Spanish were. The northern nationalists were—partly because of the above factors and also because of the relatively stronger appeal of the Axis-aligned aspects of Pan-Arabism—much more deeply involved with the rise of fascism in Europe than those of the French Protectorate. The strategy appears to have been one of each nationalist group's exploiting to the maximum the plight of the European power involved—a strategy which is by no means new in the history of colonial rule.

The early Rabat meeting of young nationalists in 1926 included two representatives from Tetouan, who established a similar group in Tetouan under the leadership of Hadj Abdeselam Bennouna, a former Minister of Finance in the Spanish zone. In 1927 another

[46] There were, of course, many nationalists from the French zone in Tangier also—a fact which may have restrained efforts to enlist members in either single group. During the war Balafrej spent some time there and, along with the elder *ancien* from the south, Abdallah Gennoun, discouraged Torres' attempts to organize in Tangier while it was occupied by Spain during the war. See Rezette, *op.cit.,* pp. 132-133.

[47] Mehdi Bennouna, *op.cit.,* p. 49, places the figure at 135,000. The Spanish were aware of the possible infiltration of these Moroccan units by nationalists. Enlistment preference was given to tribesmen.

small committee was formed in Tangier under Abdallah Gennoun, an *alim* from Fès. When the Committee of National Action was initially formed, two years later, Abdeselam Bennouna and Mohammed Daoud were included from the northern zone. So long as the nationalists were only a group of students meeting informally, joint direction was possible. Once they began to engage in political activity, this arrangement broke down. After the Berber *dahir* demonstrations most of the members in the south found themselves in prison or else dispersed. Consequently, it was decided to have a separate National Committee for the north, which was given the special task of developing relations with Egypt and other Arab nations. While relations with the Middle East were not so completely monopolized by the nationalists of the Spanish zone as this would indicate, their educational connections with Palestine and Egypt, together with the preoccupation of the French-zone nationalists with France, made this a feasible arrangement.

From this early date Tetouan became a center for nationalist activity, particularly for those activities forbidden in the south after the more serious clashes there with the French administration. Chekib Arslan came to Tetouan in 1930 to make his first local contact with both the northern and southern nationalists. Because of the international tension between France and Spain during much of this period, repressions seem to alternate between the north and south, which enabled the group in Tetouan to carry on press and propaganda activities in support of the south in the early 1930's. Though demonstrations were held in support of the south at the time of the Berber *dahir*, the attention of the Spanish-zone nationalists was quickly drawn back to their own situation in 1931, when the brief republican regime was installed in Spain. Abdeselam Bennouna left for Madrid with a petition of "demands," which were also presented locally that fall at municipal elections in Tetouan. But enthusiasm died down and the willingness of the Spanish republic to make concessions was soon restrained as a result of their friendly diplomatic relations with France, who was still fighting in the southern zone.

Liaison between the northern and southern nationalist groups was maintained through frequent meetings outside of Morocco. They met often through their contacts with Chekib Arslan and at international nationalist meetings. The Arabic publications permitted in the north were circulated in large numbers in the south, where none were permitted until 1937. In this period the National Committee in the Spanish zone added a new member, Abdel Khalek Torres, who was to become a major figure in the politics of the north. Al-Fassi cemented relations with the north in mid-1933 and again on his return voyage in early 1934. On the trip he also visited the newly founded Arab center at Madrid, where several southern nationalists worked.[48] In addition to their exchanges in Madrid, the nationalists established a Committee for the Defense of Morocco in Cairo and jointly participated in the Muslim World Conference in Jerusalem in 1932. Apparently open activity was subdued in the north as well as the south during the gestation of the Plan of Reforms, on which the Tetouan group was consulted when Abdeljalil and Ouazzani carried a copy to Paris. Members from the two committees met again early in 1935 in memory of Hadj Abdeselam Bennouna, one of the original elders of the movement. At this time plans were made for future activities in the face of the stalemate being imposed by the two colonial powers. For the Tetouan group, however, new opportunities were soon to be offered with the outbreak of the civil war in Spain.

General Franco, who had received much of his early military training in the pacification of the Spanish zone, made promises of concessions to the northern group in return for the preservation of calm and for help in recruiting troops from among the tribesmen. The fascist revolution alarmed French Socialists, both in North Africa and France, who tried to arrange some kind of *rapprochement* between the northern nationalists and the Spanish republicans, while simultaneously pressing for liberalization of the controls on the southern group. The nationalists held out for complete independence of the northern zone, which, of course, neither the authorities of France nor Spain could accept.[49] Franco was aware of the nationalists' threat to his success in the civil war and authorized several new nationalist papers in the north.

[48] Rezette, *op.cit.*, pp. 129-131. The directors were Mohammed Al-Fassi, one of Balafrej's associates in the founding of the Association of North African Muslim Students and later Minister of National Education, and Mekki Naciri, the roving, Cairo-educated *ancien* from Rabat.

[49] The nationalists played fully on all the confusion of this prelude to World War II. After the republican government at Barcelona rejected their offer, they opened negotiations with the anti-France groups of Catalonia, who did accept these conditions. See Al-Fassi, *op.cit.*, pp. 149-153. Though the Protectorate officials probably did not do all they could to promote the success of these negotiations, the extreme demands being made by the nationalists does not justify the conclusions of Al-Fassi.

In view of the concessions being considered by the Popular Front government of France, it was clearly impossible for the nationalists to continue as an overtly coordinated group. After brief consultation the northern and southern nationalists formed separate parties. Each was to be free to pursue its own goals with the provision that they retain the basic goals of independence, territorial unity, and loyalty to the Alaouite dynasty and Mohammed V.

No sooner had the Tetouan group begun to benefit from their association with Franco than personal rivalries split the National Committee of the north. Mekki Naciri, a refugee from the French zone, formed the Maghrib Unity party and Torres founded the Islah or National Reform party, both of which continued to exist until Moroccan independence.[50] Torres had become leader of the Tetouan group after the death of Abdeselam Bennouna and was assisted by Thami Al-Ouazzani, who was a disciple of Abdeselam. Like the split in Fès, this conflict testifies to the fragility of the nationalist group when confronted with new problems and relieved of the unifying pressure of an adamant colonial administration. In this case the quarrel was even more pointless than the one between Al-Fassi and Ouazzani, for both Naciri and Torres were in agreement on basic policy. The split, of course, made the Spanish task much easier.

The subsequent history of the administration of the new High Commissioner from Spain, Colonel Beigbeder, is largely a series of maneuvers to play one group against the other. The nationalists' confidence in Franco soon proved to be misplaced, for his concessions were highly circumscribed by the supervision of Spanish officials. Nevertheless, the northern nationalists were willing to compromise. Torres became Minister of Habous and Mohammed Daoud was made Inspector of Education. Spain received the support of the Khalifa of Tetouan, the King's representative in the north. The lasting concessions were nearly all cultural, such as permission for the teaching of Arabic in primary schools, Islamic cultural centers in Granada and Cordova, the construction of "Morocco House" in Cairo, and the creation of the Khalifian Institute at Tetouan. The experiment soon failed. Both Torres and Mohammed Daoud resigned from their positions within a few months, and at an Islah

[50] Torres had recently been in contact with the Spanish parties of the left and was, therefore, initially imprisoned by the Franco forces. On assurance of his readiness to rally to Franco, he was released. Rezette says the immediate issue of the quarrel was the selection by Torres of Taib Bennouna in preference to Naciri for director of a free school in Tetouan, *op.cit.*, pp. 153-154.

gathering early in 1937 Mohammed Bennouna reiterated the Islah's continued adherence to the goal of "complete and absolute independence."[51] These expressions of dissatisfaction signaled the rise of Naciri as the Spanish favorite for the moment, though the two factions joined in protest of the arrest of their brothers to the south in the fall of 1937. Activities of the Islah were largely confined to Tetouan, where Torres became "colonel" of a phalangist-sponsored scout movement that was dissolved in 1942 when its usefulness to Spain was in doubt.[52]

With help from Beigbeder, the Unity party of Naciri embarked on an organizational drive early in 1937. From its offices near the Protectorate border, the party was particularly effective in fomenting discontent in the French zone, but in 1938 the High Commissioner gave his support in this area to the pasha of Larache, Moulay Khaled Raisouni, whose loyalty to Franco was uncompromised with nationalist ambitions. Naciri retired to the directorship of the Khalifian Institute in Tetouan, later to voyage to Egypt to recruit Arabic teachers, while the short-lived Unity party disappeared as rapidly as it had grown.[53] Both groups were permitted to make some overtures in the Rif, but this was much too volatile a region for the High Commissioner to allow any intensive activity. As World War II drew near and the Spanish were reinforcing their control in that area, both parties drew together and participated in a rally in memory of Abdelkrim's son, who had been killed in the Rif War. In anticipation of the conflict, control had been tightened on all the northern nationalists and Beigbeder was replaced with General Asensio in 1938. The Islah tried to take advantage of the situation by submitting a new set of demands in 1938, which were firmly denied. During the late thirties the activities of Germany and Italy also increased and an openly pro-Axis group was established in Tetouan under Brahim Al-Ouazzani, a refugee from the 1937 arrests in the French zone.[54]

[51] *Ibid.*, p. 118.

[52] *Ibid.*, p. 264, and Al-Fassi, *op.cit.*, p. 154. According to Rezette, Torres was tempted in 1937 to concede the permanent separation of the two zones of Morocco and became disillusioned with Mohammed V's leadership.

[53] For organizational details on the northern parties at this time see *ibid.*, pp. 119-125. The four offices of the Unity party were at Tetouan, Larache, Chaouen, and Ksar Al-Kbir. Ksar Al-Kbir and Larache are near the old border between the zones.

[54] A summary of German activity will be found in Julien, *op.cit.*, pp. 158-160. See also Al-Fassi, *op.cit.*, pp. 198-201, and Rezette, *op.cit.*, pp. 126-131.

As events since World War II have demonstrated, political creeds rapidly diminish in value when survival is at stake. The Islah joined in the celebrations of German victory in 1940 at Tetouan and Torres visited Berlin with a delegation of his party. His enthusiasm for the Nazi regime produced misgivings in Spain, who did not wish to see her control displaced even by German designs. Early in 1941 a new High Commissioner arrived and the nationalist press was suppressed. Naciri's group was also restrained. The anti-French propaganda of the northern nationalists was likely to pose new demands for the Spanish authorities as well, and, thereby, stimulate popular discontent. With the landing of the Allies in November 1942, the setting was drastically changed again. The decline of the Axis and the accompanying change in attitude by the Spanish induced the northern nationalists to form a "national pact" a month later calling for full independence of both zones under the Alaouite dynasty. At this time both groups were working with Balafrej in Tangier, while Naciri established contacts with the British and Torres with the Americans.

With the liberation of North Africa the Islah party found itself in an extremely embarrassing position and engaged in little political activity for some time. Naciri, being much less compromised, was involved with British efforts to find support for the Arab League in 1945, whose appeal to Moroccans increased as the French suppressed the independence movements in Syria. These ties were reinforced in 1945 by the return to Tetouan of Mehdi and Taib Bennouna, who were the sons of Abdeselam and had been studying in Palestine and Cairo since 1938. The new prestige and importance of the Arab world after the war also opened opportunities for Spain, now eager to reestablish both her world position and her popularity in North Africa. Just as her policy toward the nationalists before the war had been more generous in cultural affairs, she could still make cultural concessions more easily than the French. The Islah gradually came back into favor (though, as Spain found ten years later, the entire strategy was to the ultimate advantage of only the nationalists themselves). Spain was, no doubt, further attracted to this new tactic, potentially very troublesome to France, by the outspoken and uncompromising French opposition to Franco after the war.

Franco's tactics changed little after World War II, although the nationalists benefited from his desire to build Spain's international prestige. In 1946 the Spanish authorities permitted a delegation from the north to visit Cairo to participate in the Cultural Committee of the Arab League. Not until the next year was the delegation joined by Allal Al-Fassi and the role of the southern-zone nationalists increased, though the Tetouan group continued to be the most active in relations with the Arab world. Also, in 1946 the Spanish authorized the revival of the Islah party under Torres and Taib Bennouna. Precautions were taken to remove those aspects of the party most characteristic of its phalangist sponsorship, like the paramilitary Green Shirt youth group. From this time Naciri's opposition activity was largely confined to Tangier, where he made his permanent headquarters. Annoyed over his exclusion from the mission to the Arab League in Cairo, where he had for many years represented Moroccan nationalism, he did not yield to the change of Spanish policy as did Torres. He was more in agreement with Istiqlal policy than with that of the Islah, which, being recently revived and based largely in Tetouan, was more vulnerable to Spanish repression.

The goal of the nationalists made any *rapprochement* with the Spanish temporary. Without official permission, Taib Bennouna and Torres assembled a mass meeting in Tetouan at the end of Ramadan in 1946, and violence was averted largely by the restraint of the Spaniards. In this same period new intrigues were undertaken in the Rif, involving the Spanish, the Unity party, and the National Reform party. After five hundred tribesmen of the western Rif descended on Tetouan to petition their grievances, the Spanish decided to make new concessions in the hope of reducing nationalist agitation and also, no doubt, to embarrass France. In September 1946 Taib Bennouna represented the Islah in Rabat at a policy meeting with the Istiqlal leaders. The northern group promised to abandon its policy of accepting gradually increasing concessions in favor of a demand for independence alone.

Confronted with a unified national movement in both zones, the Spanish policy was threatened. The Khalifa was informed of Spanish plans to establish new ministries for Finance, Agriculture, and Education, designed probably both to bolster this institution against the rising prestige of Mohammed V and also to lure the more ambitious northern nationalists away from their policy of coordinated opposition. The northern nationalists, however, seemed to have anticipated the encouragement the policy of complete Moroccan unity would receive with the projected trip of the King to Tangier in early 1947. They held fast and made new attacks on the Spanish policy, while refusing to accept these administrative concessions. In the enthusiasm of the approaching visit of the King, the Unity party of Naciri and the Islah party were able to unite temporarily and prepared an agreed list of claims to be presented at Tangier. The rebuffed Spaniards countered by banning the nationalist papers and imposing a heavy fine on the Islah.

From 1947 on, the Istiqlal and the Islah cooperated fully. A cell of Istiqlal adherents was established at Tetouan to facilitate liaison, and officials of the two parties pooled their efforts to induce Abdelkrim to take refuge in Egypt.[55] Fearing agitation among the Rif tribes under the direction of their hero, Abdelkrim, newly freed in Cairo, Spain decided to forbid Torres to re-enter the northern zone after his visit to Egypt.[56] While Torres waited in Tangier, demonstrations were held in Tetouan that degenerated into violence, and the party was confined to clandestine activity until a change in Spanish policy early in 1952. The Unity party, now consisting of only Naciri and his personal circle in Tangier, was also barred from further activity in the Spanish zone. In the pattern of earlier coalitions, the parties were able to resolve their differences in the face of adversity and a National Moroccan Front was formed in 1951. It also included the conflicting parties of the French zone, the Istiqlal, and the Democratic party. The Arab League, whose interest in North Africa returned with the threat to the Moroccan throne and the cooling of hostilities over Israel, encouraged the agreement and sent a representative to the meeting. The Front appears to have been formed largely to impress world opinion and to increase the effectiveness of the Moroccan case at it was being raised in the United Nations. The parties retained full internal freedom of action and there are no signs that any mergers were even considered.

As the popularity of the European powers declined in the Arab world, Spain found renewed opportunities to establish herself as an influence in both North Africa and the Middle East. Bolstered with American military aid, she sought to increase her diplomatic recognition by reviving her role as friend of the Islamic states. As a prelude to the mission of her Foreign Minister to the Middle East in the

[55] See Al-Fassi, *op.cit.*, pp. 303-310, and Rezette, *op.cit.*, pp. 184-185.

[56] Two charges were brought against him to justify invalidating his entry papers. He was alleged to have embezzled a million pesetas from a utility firm in Tetouan where he was an officer and a plot was revealed between the National Reform party and the Derkaoui brotherhood, particularly strong in the north, to start an insurrection with the aid of Spanish republican sympathizers. See Rezette, *op.cit.*, pp. 186-187.

spring of 1952, the new Spanish High Commissioner in the north, General Garcia Valino, began to relax the restrictions on nationalist activity. The appeal of this tactic for Spain was increased by her hope of resurrecting old nationalist in-fighting. The Spanish move was also strengthened by the unpopularity of the French administration to the south under Juin and Guillaume. Late in 1951 Valino returned the offices and equipment of the Islah in Tetouan and Torres made a triumphal return after three years' exile. He was accompanied by Taib Bennouna, coming from Cairo, and Mehdi Bennouna, who had been representing the party in New York. The reconstruction of the party organization began almost immediately in Larache and Ksar Al-Kbir, but the nationalists were barred from activity in tribal areas. Naciri's Unity party also made a weak comeback, but after the failure of a scheme to enlist the Rifian tribes he left for the United States to attend the approaching United Nations debate.

The *rapprochement* between the Spanish and the nationalists was furthered by the increasing suppression of the Istiqlal, which culminated in total prohibition after violent demonstrations in December 1952. Confronted with the severe policy of the French, the nationalists turned again to the Arab League and to Spain. After a voyage to Madrid, Torres received permission for public celebration of the anniversary of the Arab League. New contacts were established clandestinely with the southern nationalists. Instructors were sent to replace those arrested from the staffs of Istiqlal free schools. When Mohammed Hassan Ouazzani took refuge in the north, the Spanish saw another opportunity to stimulate personal friction, but their plans were cut short by the forced exile of the King in August 1953. In a speech of the High Commissioner, later endorsed by Franco, Spain denied any knowledge of the plot and considered the unilateral deposition of the King as grounds for a break in Spanish-French cooperation in the administration of Morocco.

Spain refused to recognize the puppet King, Ben Arafa, and throughout the suppression of the Istiqlal, northern religious services continued to be held in the name of Mohammed V. His exile stimulated the organization of an active resistance to the French, which used Tetouan, Tangier, and the Spanish coastal ports in the north as supply, training, and communication centers. Two months after the King's deposition, in the midst of public demonstrations of loyalty to the King in Tetouan, Cairo announced that Torres would be the "chief of the liberation movement of all the Maghrib." The next month the assistant secretary of the Arab League was welcomed by the High Commissioner, the Khalifa, and the Islah.[57] Fearful lest Spanish opportunism might result in proclaiming the Khalifa regent of a government in exile, France took some diplomatic and military precautions. Such a move, however, would have come very close to Spain's relinquishing her own position, and the agitation was confined to the proclamation of nonrecognition by the High Commissioner.

As the Spanish rejected the French repression, the north became the base for the mounting resistance organization in the cities and the *bled* to the south, and also the location for a Liberation Army. Both these efforts brought many nationalists from the south into the cities and countryside of the ex-Spanish zone. For the first time the nationalists were permitted to move freely among the Rifian tribes, who were recruited and trained for the Liberation Army.[58] The Spanish may have considered creating an independent nation from the northern zone, though the scheme would undoubtedly have been rejected by the nationalists as a betrayal of their comrades in the ex-French zone and their agreement on independence only for a unified Morocco. General Valino, nevertheless, pursued a policy of cooperation. Late in 1954 Islah leaders were appointed as Ministers of Social Affairs, a new ministry created under Torres—Justice—and also a joint Department of Education and Welfare. The nationalists' major endeavor, however, remained concentrated in the growing resistance effort, which was to reach its full strength in the midst of the French-Moroccan negotiations for independence. The French concession of early 1956 found the Spaniards unprepared, and celebrations of the Franco-Moroccan Agreement in Tetouan were suppressed in March 1956 with some bloodshed. With the inner contradictions of Spanish policy exposed and probably confused by the sudden capitulation of the French government, Franco had no choice but to follow suit the next month.

Preoccupied with the international contacts of the nationalist movement in New York and Cairo and restricted from activities

---

[57] Rezette, *op.cit.*, pp. 236-237, but the new friendship of the nationalists and the Spanish authorities was not without limits. The same month Taib Bennouna and Mohammed Khatib were imprisoned over an alleged intrigue with the Residence in Rabat. One of the victims claims that it was because of articles extremely critical of Spanish economic policy in the north that were found in his luggage on arrival. Interview with Taib Bennouna, Governor of Tetouan, Tetouan, February 25, 1958.

[58] Interview with Taib Bennouna, Governor of Tetouan, Tetouan, February 8, 1958.

among the tribes by the High Commissioners, the Islah made little organizational progress in the period from World War II to independence. Though prepared to take advantage of Spanish tactics, the small elite of the party was from its origin too closely bound to the leaders of the Istiqlal to consider seriously the permanent division of Morocco. The occasional opportunism of men like Torres was more the manifestation of the strong personalities and personal feuds that are found in both the Islah and the Istiqlal than evidence of any basic difference.

The geographic base of the Islah was confined largely to the northwestern corner of Morocco, excluding Tangier, where the Istiqlal also had its followers. No doubt partly by Spanish design, the offices that existed during the periods of tolerance were mostly along the French-zone border, where they could cause maximum embarrassment to the Resident General. With the exception of the free schools and cultural activities permitted by the High Commissioner, few parallel organizations were set up or dominated by the Islah, in sharp contrast with the Istiqlal. No large recruiting efforts were made like those of the Istiqlal after the war. Whatever opportunities were presented by the organization of the Liberation Army were not directly under the auspices of the Islah. While it is now maintained that the party had a following of 100,000, it is doubtful if more than a tenth of this number was ever organized in a formal way and it is admitted that this number did not increase after the relaxation of controls in 1952.[59] During its whole history the core of Islah remained under the direction of "influential notables, rich proprietors, large merchants, industrial leaders or directors of large corporations, who constitute the financial aristocracy of the Spanish zone."[60] In cooperation with the old families of Tetouan and sometimes alone, Torres remained the leading figure and the "Allal Al-Fassi of the north." The circumstances of geography, tradition, and Spanish strategy that barred the Islah from developing a popular base simultaneously prevented the rise of new leaders.

[59] *Ibid.*, and with Mohammed Tanana, Istiqlal Inspector, Tetouan and Region, Tetouan, February 9, 1958.
[60] Rezette, *op.cit.*, p. 365.

CHAPTER III

ORGANIZING THE ISTIQLAL AND ACHIEVING
INDEPENDENCE

Growth and Suppression of the Istiqlal

MEANWHILE in the French zone the Allied landings in North Africa in November 1942 were the signal for the revival of nationalist activity. Mohammed V remained in Rabat during the landings, against the wishes of the Resident General, who would have preferred to remove the King farther from danger and possible American interference. The King had already given some evidence of increased intransigence by refusing to permit the enforcement of Vichy-inspired, anti-Jewish regulations and a program of obligatory military service without concessions to the Moroccan cause. During 1943 several demonstrations occurred in support of rapid return to civil rule, which very likely were encouraged by the presence of American forces.[1] Hopes were further raised by the historic meeting of the King with Roosevelt, Churchill, and Hopkins in mid-1943. This initial optimism was, however, dispersed with the appointment of a new Resident General, Gabriel Paux, who was well known for his suppression of the independence movements in Syria and Lebanon. Led by Ahmed Balafrej and Mohammed Lyazidi, the nationalists began making postwar plans. To the *anciens* was added an important new element of younger men, who had participated in the movement as students in the late 1930's. Though the new group still represented mainly the nationalist-oriented urban intelligentsia, the social background of the young leaders was often less distinguished than that of the party elders.

In December 1943 the Istiqlal was formed in a meeting of the old nationalists, merchants, teachers, high civil servants, and college graduates from alumni associations of Fès, Rabat, Salé, Marrakech, Azrou, Oujda, Safi, and Meknes. The decision was made to ask for full independence in a petition to the King, the Resident General, and the governments of the Allied Powers. The authors of the petition, or Independence Manifesto, were not only the *anciens*, but

[1] Julien, in *L'Afrique du Nord en Marche*, Paris, Julliard, 1952, pp. 339-343, discusses the encouragement the nationalists received from the liberation by American troops.

also included the newer arrivals. In their bold demand of full independence the nationalists, like many others of that epoch, were to some extent carried away by the solidarities created by the war. The plans for the United Nations and the deceiving promises of the Atlantic Charter strongly influenced this group of intellectuals. They had also been in touch with the King, who had read the Manifesto before it was released, and whom the nationalists considered completely sympathetic with their plan.[2]

While they did not expect immediate results, the nationalists thought that it was an opportune time to state their reforms clearly in view of the approaching Conference of Brazzaville, where French colonial problems were to be discussed, and also to give direction to the growing interest of Moroccan youth in the postwar development of Morocco. The Istiqlal was also aware that the French might try to disassociate the postwar purposes of the King and the party, to the latter's detriment, and they wished to establish their common goals publicly. Though the alliance of the King and the Istiqlal had not yet achieved the intimacy that was to develop, they were in daily contact with the monarch. Through their palace contacts the nationalists were kept informed of the reactions and policies of the Resident General. The alarm created in French circles by the Manifesto led the nationalists to issue a modifying statement. They assured the authorities that they did not wish to "curtail the war effort" or "to bring about the realization of our ideal through violence."[3] Massigli, representing the French National Committee for Liberation, was sent from Algiers to Rabat. After conferring with the Resident General and the King, he announced that the French government in exile was prepared to make speedy reforms in Morocco.

As evidence of the development of nationalism in Morocco, the Manifesto was more interesting as testimony to the acceptance of new elements and to the important role attributed to the King than as a proclamation of the goal of independence. Independence had always been implicit in the goal of the nationalist leaders. The resistance of the French administration to the Plan of Reforms had only reinforced this belief. More important was the modifying letter to the King, which assured him that he would be "the source of legislative and executive powers" and that the conduct of the admin-

[2] Interview with Mohammed Lyazidi, Executive Committee, Istiqlal Party, Rabat, January 10, 1958.

[3] *Istiqlal Party Documents: 1944-1946*, English Edition, Paris, 1946, p. 9.

istration must be completely under his control.[4] The association with the King was still sufficiently new to require this kind of assurance, and his potential value as a symbol of nationalism apparently was anticipated. Among the fifty-eight signatures on the Manifesto could be found evidence of new leadership emerging from the group of young students who had taken important secondary posts in the party. In addition to the familiar *anciens* and the many presidents of alumni associations were Mehdi Ben Barka, Driss M'Hammedi, and Abderrahmin Bouabid, all of whom were to be associated with the progressive faction of the Istiqlal fifteen years later. The intellectualist trend of the movement appeared to be preserved, for the group included eighteen teachers, ten *ulema*, eight lawyers or judges, and six high civil servants. There was no representation of artisans or workers, though eight merchants of wealthy Moroccan families joined the group.[5] From 1944 until independence very few new names were to be added to the top ranks of the movement. Nearly all the Istiqlal Ministers, many of the Ambassadors, and high party officials of independent Morocco were signatories of the Manifesto.

As had happened so often before, the Resident General reacted to the Manifesto with provocative measures. During the consultations with the French authorities over the Manifesto the public appeal of the new party became apparent. Crowds gathered outside the palace and spontaneous meetings were held in the more distant cities of Safi, Marrakech, and Oujda. Violence was avoided until the Resident General decided to arrest Balafrej, Lyazidi, and sixteen other nationalist leaders, on charges of collaboration with the Germans.[6] When the news of the arrests leaked out the next day, violent demonstrations of several thousand persons took place at the palace, the Residency, and in Salé. Several deaths resulted among the Moroccans, and the French forces sent to restore order. In Fès the first day's demonstration was calm, but, with subsequent arrests, broke into a full battle in the Muslim sections of the *medina*. Order was not restored until after a week without food, water, and electricity.

[4] *Ibid.*, pp. 6-8.

[5] The occupational differentiation of the signatories is given in a chart by Rezette, *Les Partis Politiques Marocaines*, Paris, Armand Colin, 1955, p. 301, and their positions are also listed after their signatures on the Manifesto, *Istiqlal Party Documents . . . , op.cit.*, pp. 3-5.

[6] Though the nationalist leaders were in contact with their colleagues in the north at irregular intervals and, like all exiled groups, knew Germans in Tangier during the war, these charges were beyond doubt fabricated. See Rezette, *op.cit.*, p. 145, and Julien, *op.cit.*, p. 345.

As one anticipates later events, it is interesting to note that Al-Glaoui helped preserve order in Marrakech and that no demonstration took place in Casablanca, where a general strike was soon suppressed by French troops.

The reprisals of the Resident General were indications of the new strength of the movement. In the palace the Minister of Justice and early nationalist teacher, Mohammed Ben Al-Arabi Al-Alaoui, and the Minister of Education were removed. The Rabat free school supported by Balafrej was closed, as was also Qarawiyn University in Fès and a school for Berbers started by the French at Azrou. Though momentarily suppressed, the nationalists emerged from this conflict with the strongholds of Rabat, Fès, and Salé thoroughly aligned with their cause. The Istiqlal cell at Azrou was also reinforced; this was the nationalists' first effort to neutralize the French tactic of segregated schools for Berbers. The nationalists also learned that their future success would require the ability to control crowds of sympathizers. Mass discontent deteriorated quickly into violence and destroyed any chance of minor reform or even of continued party organization.

The Istiqlal began to reform its ranks some months later, though Bouabid and ten others were held until 1946. A National Council and Executive Committee were again assembled, but there is no evidence of any new organizational effort under the Residency of General Paux. Probably because of their experience with the riots of early 1944, the nationalists decided at this time to initiate a policy of dividing members into "active" and "supporting" categories, with only the former being permitted to participate in party elections. A special commission was also started for the "orientation and indoctrination of party supporters"[7] though there are no indications of its success. For the time being the party restricted itself to verbal protests and petitions, which reveal a new tactic that was to persist until independence.

With the petition for representation at the United Nations in March 1945, the Istiqlal began to seek international recognition of Moroccan problems. Another note was submitted during the meeting of the signatories of the Algeciras Treaty, who met later that year to consider the re-establishment of the Tangier Statute. The reforms suggested by the Resident General soon after the riots were rejected

[7] Al-Fassi, *The Independence Movements in Arab North Africa*, Washington, American Council of Learned Societies, 1954, p. 92.

by the Istiqlal, who would not accept reforms without recognition of Morocco as in independent country.[8] The formation of the Fourth Republic in France posed another threat to the legal status of Morocco, when consideration was given to representing the French in Morocco through colonial constituencies. The nationalists were alarmed over the possible "departmentalization" of Morocco, as had been done in Algeria. With the support of the King their protest was successful. After the elections for the French Constituent Assembly in October 1945, the Resident General admitted that, due to the importance of the event, an extraordinary privilege was being given to French citizens in Morocco.

Confined to a clandestine existence, the Istiqlal could do little to organize popular support. The leaders realized that no organization would be possible without trained cadres who could indoctrinate and control a mass membership. Most of the Istiqlal's little prewar cadre of organizers remained intact, and a small party journal was secretly published. With its membership of only about 3,000 the Istiqlal did not need an elaborate organization in 1944.[9] A Directing Committee supervised a number of local committees established where groups of militants were centered from before the war. The central committee of twelve members was assisted in turn by six commissions, also having twelve members each. The commissions were for executive, financial, information, administrative, propaganda, and liaison activities. Under the conditions imposed by the repression of the movement this central organization, if it ever had been fully achieved, would probably have been unwieldy, and it was reduced sharply with the reorganization of the party in October 1945. The purpose of the party at this time was to train cadres, and the preoccupation of such a large number of militants with central policy and planning very likely proved to be a handicap. From 1945 the central committees of the Istiqlal ceased to meet alternately in Fès and Rabat. Permanent party headquarters were established in Rabat, where the party press had operated since 1937.

The central organization of 1945 was smaller and simpler. The Directing Committee was replaced by a Superior Council of twenty-

---

[8] The Istiqlal seems to have realized the possible bad impression of this intransigent stand and their refusal was accompanied by a long exposé of each of the major items involved. See Al-Fassi, *op.cit.*, pp. 235-237, and Julien, *op.cit.*, pp. 348-350.

[9] The organizational information for this period can be found at more length in Rezette, *op.cit.*, pp. 294-309, and has been partially confirmed by interviews. The organization of 1945 reveals the influence of Mehdi Ben Barka, who became Balafrej's administrative assistant after the war and supervised the reorganization of the party.

five members. A smaller Executive Committee of five members conducted party affairs between meetings of the labor council. Where adherents were sufficiently numerous, a regional committee was formed or, particularly in the less accessible parts of the *bled*, a single regional director was selected. Beneath these regional centers were the sections and then the groups of cells subordinate to their designated section. The cells had from ten to fifteen members each at first, but they were approximately doubled as the party grew up to 1952. They were organized on both a neighborhood and a factory basis, with a secretary, a treasurer, and an instructor. The latter was required to be literate, led in discussions, gave lessons in reading and writing, and apparently was the key figure in the party cadre at the base level. His importance is suggested by the ex officio designation of the cell instructors as the "section committee," from whom a section president was elected. The section president was given large powers and appears to have been a key figure in the horizontal liaison of the party. He planned propaganda and selected the times for its release; decided on the level of dues for the members and ruled on the use of the dues in local projects; supervised the division of members among the cells and sections; and was responsible not to the regional committee, but to the Superior Council.[10] Since contact among the cells was discouraged, especially during periods of clandestineness, the section committee and its president were in privileged positions in the communication system of the party.

The regional committee was elected by an assembly of all the instructors of the region, but was not in the chain of command from the Superior Council. While it helped coordinate the work of the sections, it seems to have served more as an honorific position and was held responsible more to the subordinate sections for assigned tasks and responsibilities than to the Superior Council. The prestige of older adherents and the special qualification of literacy for all offices above the cell meant that the selections were in many instances predetermined and that the electoral procedure was only a formality. It is important to note that this was an organization initially formed during the period of suppression in 1945 and, therefore, designed to operate secretly. The cells were not in contact with one another, and the sections were almost self-regulating units under the directives of

[10] The important role of trained militants is also most suggestive of Ben Barka's work. He continued to concentrate on their training after independence and led the split of the party partly to give them a more important role in the new Democratic Istiqlal.

the Superior Council and the Executive Committee. In subsequent efforts to abolish the Istiqlal, it was quite possible to arrest the most easily detected group under the central organization, a regional committee, leaving most of the sections and cells intact.

After 1947 the system of two classes of adherents was discontinued. The "active" members were trained to form the first large cadre of the Istiqlal, which was then prepared to begin large-scale recruitment and indoctrination. Elder party militants met secretly with newer leaders in the large cities and informal courses were prepared in Rabat for small numbers of the more trusted new militants. Though the Istiqlal by necessity adapted itself for clandestine activity, it was not designed for terrorism. As the function of the instructor suggests, the leaders were impressed with the need to educate the base of the movement and to develop the controlling cadre. Their subsequent strategy of seeking international recognition of their goal and of accepting limited participation in the Protectorate's administration made organized violence a hazardous tactic. The Istiqlal undertook to enlist in important administrative positions members whose adherence was kept secret and whose selection was made with great care for fear of infiltration. Recruitment was often on a lateral basis, in that key persons were freely brought into the Istiqlal in high positions if their importance warranted immediate prestige. For example, Ahmed Lyazidi, wealthy brother of Mohammed Lyazidi and ex-officer of the French Army, and Mohammed Laghzaoui, a heavy contributor to the Istiqlal after the war, both appeared in the Superior Council in 1945. Care was also taken at this time to cultivate contacts in France, and early in 1946 a distinguished group of French professional figures submitted a petition to the French government on behalf of the Istiqlal.

During the crisis of 1944-1945 the Istiqlal remained largely in the hands of Lyazidi. He sent a new appeal to France on the second anniversary of the 1944 Manifesto and also presented a petition to the new Resident General, Labonne, in March 1946.[11] The latter document reiterated the party's intention to work within the "framework of legality" and acknowledged the French economic contribution to the development of Morocco. The grievances listed concerning judicial, administrative, and social reform were much the same as those in earlier documents, though special stress was laid on the role of the King, public liberties, and the basically constructive role

[11] Both these documents appear in *Istiqlal Party Documents . . . , op.cit.*, pp. 30-43.

envisaged by the Istiqlal since its foundation. A special appeal was made for the return of Al-Fassi and Ouazzani, who had been in exile since 1937, and Balafrej, in exile since 1944. The new Resident General indicated his desire to form some kind of *rapprochement* with the nationalists by releasing these prisoners and by giving permission for the publication of nationalist papers. The papers, however, were heavily censored and frequently appeared with half of the front page blank.

During Labonne's Residency the Istiqlal expanded rapidly in many directions. Moroccan students in Paris, London, Cairo, Damascus, and Tangier were organized to operate information bureaus. Delegations were sent to Paris to attempt to present the Moroccan cause directly to the French government and to seek publicity. Through the Berber College at Azrou new efforts were made to extend the appeal of the party to tribal areas of the Middle Atlas Mountains. In spite of its illegality in the French zone, the scout movement under Driss M'Hammedi made new clandestine efforts and a new youth organization was founded in Casablanca. Sports clubs, stemming from the first successful effort of Laghzaoui in Fès in 1944, became popular centers for nationalism. Many new free schools were founded by the Istiqlal in 1946 to provide a Muslim education, but also to serve as important centers for the training of cadre and for the recruitment of new adherents. Thus, the development of the party beyond small cells of local adherents can almost be followed with the spread of the free schools into the countryside from the major cities.[12]

Shortly after his arrival Resident General Labonne described to the French consultative bodies his plan for sweeping economic reform, which was promptly rejected by both the Istiqlal and the conservative French groups.[13] The Superior Council of the party met

[12] Before the war free schools existed in Rabat, Tetouan, Fès, Mazagan, and Oujda. In the period 1946-1947 free schools were started in Taza, Midelt, Khemisset, Boujad, Kasba Tadla, Safi, Beni Mellal, Es-Saouira (Mogador), and Marrakech. From interviews with regional inspectors of the Istiqlal.

[13] The Labonne reforms are discussed by Julien, *op.cit.*, pp. 353-360, with some sympathy and from the nationalist viewpoint by Al-Fassi, *op.cit.*, pp. 251-263. The first college of the Council of Government comprised of "colons" and the second college, including French merchants and industrialists, both opposed the proposed program. The third college of representatives of professions did support the plan, whose defeat meant the decline of Labonne and his liberal-inspired proposals. The "colons" were particularly suspicious of plans for rural modernization centers and rudimentary rural consultative groups to include Moroccans. The financial interests, strongly backed by banks in Paris, were hostile toward his decision to limit private capital to thirty per cent of the investment in coal, lead, and oil exploitation. See also *Le Monde*, July 25, 1946, p. 2.

two days after the reforms were outlined and sent a delegation to the King to state its opposition. Several party leaders were offered executive positions in the proposed new public corporations, but all declined, and the party formed a boycott of the investment program by Moroccan financiers. The nationalists sent several delegations to Paris to publicize Moroccan opposition to the plan and thereby, perhaps unwittingly, played into the hands of the French financial interests whose virtual control of the Moroccan economy was threatened. While there were no doubt some obvious omissions in the area of political liberties, the nationalists chose to forego any negotiation for subsidiary concessions.

By refusing to accept any change under the aegis of the Protectorate the Istiqlal contributed to the success of those wishing to destroy the movement, lost the opportunities for party organization and educational advancement entailed in such a program, and insured the direct control of the Moroccan economy by foreign investors. Had the Istiqlal leaders more realistically evaluated their economic problems, whether in independent or colonial status, and had they been able to divine that Labonne's administration was to be replaced by the "proconsulate" of General Juin, they might have taken a more conciliatory position. The party felt, of course, that it would be difficult to explain any intermediary position to its largely uninformed and illiterate following, especially during a period when it was engaged in the formation of a disciplined, militant cadre.

The immediate cause of the change in the colonial regime was the King's famous Tangier speech in the spring of 1947. It was preceded by a few days by the brutal retaliation of French forces over a minor quarrel in one of the Casablanca *medinas*.[14] The visit was the occasion of large nationalist demonstrations, with representatives from both zones participating. Though the King undoubtedly shocked both French and Spanish officials by referring to the "legitimate rights of the Moroccan people," the most provocative phrase is generally considered to be "that Morocco, being a country attached by solid bonds to the Arab countries of the East, desires to strengthen those bonds ever more resolutely, especially with the Arab League."[15]

[14] See Al-Fassi, *op.cit.*, pp. 263-266, where his observation that all Moroccan troops of the French forces had been disarmed before the event suggests that it may have been a premeditated attempt to prevent the Tangier trip of the King and to discredit the unfortunate Labonne. The importance attached to the Tangier visit by the Istiqlal is suggested by the seventeen pages devoted to it by Al-Fassi, *ibid.*, pp. 266-283.

[15] Landau, *Mohammed V*, Rabat, Ministry of Foreign Affairs, 1957, p. 46.

No reference was made to France or the future of the Protectorate. From the conference Al-Fassi proceeded to Cairo with Torres, while in the French zone the Istiqlal began its first, intensive membership drive with the aid of the cadre formed over the past year and a half.

Juin's arrival convinced the nationalists that the French tactic would now be to separate the King from the Istiqlal, so as to leave the party without the symbol whose powers had been demonstrated at the Tangier rally. During the first two years of Juin's Residency the nationalists, though certainly apprehensive and closely watched, did not find their activity seriously curtailed. Their papers continued to appear, though more heavily censored than before. Perhaps aware of the effort to disassociate the party from the King, the Istiqlal decided in 1948 to participate in the elections for Moroccan representatives to the Council of Government. To the end of 1950 eleven members of the party participated in this consultative group, where little more was done than discuss the budget. The party looked upon the elections as a chance to demonstrate their good intentions as their international campaign increased. The campaigns and sessions were also a source of publicity in Morocco. To boycott the elections would have been to repudiate an offer directed toward giving a measure, however qualified, of democratic influence to Moroccan political life,[16] and to lose an opportunity to prove their popular support. Tension between General Juin and Mohammed V began, however, from the first days of the new Residency, when, without French permission, the King appointed a committee to examine the budget of 1947-1948 and personally presided over its sessions. Many *dahirs* submitted to the Palace for the reforms planned initially by Juin were left unsigned.

Whatever plans may have been made in France for drawing Morocco into the French Union were shattered by palace spokesmen shortly after the arrival of the new Resident General. The Istiqlal Superior Council believed that these proposed reforms were part of the new French strategy of integration. A few preliminary changes in the Makhzen's organization were made on orders from the Resi-

[16] See the correction issued by the Palace when these charges appeared in the French press, Al-Fassi, *op.cit.*, pp. 329-331. Suffrage was limited to only a few thousand Moroccans, mostly those in commercial and minor industrial activities. Nearly all the elected Moroccans were from wealthy families, for example, Ahmed Lyazidi, Omar Sebti, Mohammed Laghzaoui, Abbès Benjelloun, and Mohammed Laraki. It should not be forgotten that the electoral procedure also put nationalists in important posts in the local chambers of commerce, which provided both business opportunities and another subordinate area of activity for nationalist expansion.

dency. The Istiqlal leaders met to denounce any future implementation of what might be interpreted as a mixed government. Similar statements were issued by the King after the French press and some French officials publicly talked of the new formation of a mixed government. Though the open break between the King and Juin did not occur until the first attempt to dethrone Mohammed V in 1951, their animosity toward each other was well known from the time that the King walked out during a conference with the General late in 1947. The Speech from the Throne in the fall of 1947 contained new reference to "the legitimate rights" of Moroccans and the aspirations of the Moroccan people to become "an Arab, Muslim nation which occupies a worthy place in the community of free nations."[17] From this time Juin began to select administrative officials unilaterally, and soon afterward the Residency was involved in a completely fabricated scheme to defame the King.[18]

After a meeting in 1948 of the French Resident General and the Spanish High Commissioner, policy hardened toward the nationalists in both zones. The nationalists, while opening their ranks within the country to mass enrollment, turned to peaceful means outside the country to gain recognition. The visit of Torres and Al-Fassi to Cairo in the spring of 1947, coincided, probably not by chance, with Abdelkrim's journey to France through the Suez Canal. He was persuaded to become a political refugee in Egypt, from where the nationalists renewed their efforts to get support from the Arab League. Unsuccessful attempts were made in 1947 and again in 1949 to raise the Moroccan problem in the United Nations, but the nationalists persevered in their policy of seeking international recognition. In preparation for their international campaign, the Istiqlal took steps in 1949 to eliminate Communist influence.[19] The international strategy of the movement was obstructed by the preoccupation of the Arab countries with the war in Palestine and by the new tensions between the Soviet-controlled world and the West that held priority in the United Nations.

Preparation of the international campaign entered a new phase with the visit of Mohammed V to Paris in late 1950 on the invitation of President Auriol. While there is some evidence that this offer to

[17] Al-Fassi, op.cit., p. 333.
[18] Ibid., pp. 335-336. This is the first example in Morocco of the now well-demonstrated capacity for French colonial administrations to make policy for France by fait accompli. After an investigation a French colonel, chief of the political department of the Residency, was sent back to Paris.
[19] Julien, op.cit., p. 372.

negotiate was not unanimously supported by the nationalists,[20] the monarch decided to accept after having been given permission to appoint a private council of advisors and assurance that discussions would be held involving the status of Morocco. The reply to his first note to the French cabinet made no mention of reconsideration of Moroccan sovereignty and a second note was sent by the King, to which reply was never received.[21] This challenge to the policy of the Resident General, coupled with the massive demonstrations welcoming the King on his return, including a large number of Berbers from the Middle Atlas, sufficed to alarm General Juin into a direct attempt to demolish the nationalist movement. The ominous clue to the new trend of Protectorate policy was the welcoming of Al-Glaoui with all honors of a monarch, as he returned from his own consultations held in France after the King's departure. From the end of 1950 until the exile of the King in 1953, the rapport between the nationalists and the French deteriorated from distrust to open violence.

The failure of the King's Paris mission convinced other nationalists that the policy of negotiated progress was hopeless and that firmer measures would have to be tried. Early in December 1950 the Istiqlal group in the Council of Government began attacking the budget presented by the Resident General. The clash during these meetings reached a climax with Laghzaoui's report, and Juin ordered him to leave. Laghzaoui was followed by all the nationalists, who shortly afterward were received by the King in tacit defiance of Juin's action. Several weeks later the pro-French tribal leader, Al-Glaoui, provoked Mohammed V into banishing him from the royal palace, while the French embarked on a new campaign to rally the tribes under Glaoui against the King.[22] The crisis mounted the next month when

[20] Landau, *Moroccan Drama: 1900-1955*, San Francisco, American Academy of Asian Studies, 1956, p. 267.

[21] For accounts of this exchange see Julien, *op.cit.*, pp. 372-373, and Landau, *op.cit.*, pp. 268-269. In his Speech from the Throne in 1951 the King publicly stated what is generally considered to have been his goal in these negotiations when he referred to "our desire to see the Franco-Moroccan relations defined by a convention which guarantees for Morocco her full sovereignty." Bennouna, *Our Morocco: The True Story of a Just Cause*, Morocco, 1951, pp. 92-93.

[22] The strategy of playing tribes against the Makhzen was used by European powers even before the Protectorate was imposed. The history of the relations between the Glaoui tribe and the Alaouite dynasty extends back to 1894, when Thami, Al-Glaoui's older brother, participated in pro-French activities in the Marrakech area. A brief account of the tribal manipulation in 1951 will be found in Bennouna, *op.cit.*, pp. 96-97, and Landau, *op.cit.*, p. 274.

the Resident General delivered his first threat of exile to the King. Juin demanded that the King dismiss all the nationalist members from his secretariat and publicly disavow the Istiqlal. When Juin returned from a visit to the United States to discuss the construction of American air bases, he again posed his demands and added that sixty-eight unsigned *dahirs* must also be issued immediately. When both the palace officials and the *ulema* supported the King, Juin threatened to have the tribes unleashed against the cities.[23] The King appealed to France, where there was some opposition to the arbitrary behavior of Juin. Distracted by internal bickering and by the extension of the Indo-China war to Korea, Paris decided to let the Resident have full power over the King.[24] There was no alternative but open insurrection, for which the nationalists were not yet prepared. The King yielded,[25] after consulting the nationalists. From this time the trend toward terrorism grew in the lower ranks of the Istiqlal, where it was felt that nothing more could be done by negotiation. Without central direction rudimentary preparations were made for an active resistance and even some of the Istiqlal leaders began to consider organizing a terrorist branch of the party.

The crisis did much to prepare the nationalists for future trouble. New sympathy was created for Morocco throughout the Arab world and the Arab League revived its interest in North Africa. Upon their return to the mountains, the misled Berber tribes displayed some discontent before the French rural officials. Some asked for the return of the nationalist *caids* who had been summarily removed. Although members of the Istiqlal Executive Committee were arrested, the Istiqlal remained quiet. The party feared that any demonstration would be used as an excuse to exile the King, who was at that time an invaluable symbol and an important source of information.

[23] See *Le Monde*, February 14, 1951, p. 1, and Claude Bourdet, "La crise Marocaine," *Espirit*, February, 1951, pp. 276-284. It should be understood that these actions and also the petitions obtained from Berber tribesmen supporting the French were obtained through a variety of subterfuges and false promises; they did not mean that the tribesmen were aware of the political significance of their opposition or even, in many instances, were aware that they were opposing the King.

[24] Though this crisis was not directly pertinent to the Moroccan problem, the French government found itself trying to resolve it, as so often happens in French colonial problems, after the problem was out of the control of Paris. Fès and Rabat were already surrounded by tribesmen and the palace under siege when the decision was made in Paris.

[25] An airplane was waiting near the palace to fly him into exile and his personal guard had been disarmed. He told his cabinet he was signing under pressure and, refusing to use the royal seal, noted on the *dahirs* only "It is known to us." Bennouna, *op.cit.*, p. 101.

Istiqlal leaders tried to explain to the party militants that the maintenance of order was all that kept Juin from a full-scale repression of the Istiqlal, which would, in turn, isolate the King from organized popular support. Even so, nationalist Berbers in the region of Tadla staged an open revolt after refusing to sign a petition of Al-Glaoui against the King.

With the new threat to the monarch, the nationalists placed greater emphasis on support from the Arab League and the United Nations. In the presence of a delegate from the League, the Istiqlal, the Islah, the Democratic party, and the Unity party signed a pact in April 1951, forming a National Front.[26] The parties retained complete internal autonomy, but agreed to advocate only complete independence for Morocco. To some of the Istiqlal leaders the Front was only a hindrance, but, nevertheless, was important in presenting a united movement when they were seeking aid from Arab nations or submitting complaints before the General Assembly of the United Nations. To prepare internally, the Istiqlal began to organize multiple sections for the same group of cells, so that arrests of local leaders would not fully decapitate the movement. The party newspapers continued to appear, but local manifestations were discouraged.

Juin's replacement by General Guillaume in the spring of 1951 made little change in Protectorate policy. The National Front decided to boycott the elections of late 1951. The nationalists were given no opportunity to campaign, to form electoral lists, or to recall their leaders who were in prison or scattered throughout the world. The election was also to be held on a working day. The symbolic victory of the nationalists was considerable, since in all the major cities only about a tenth of the eligible voters took part, even though the Moroccan electorate had been enlarged to 220,000 persons selected by the French. On election day the nationalists relaxed their policy against demonstrations and permitted a strike in Casablanca, where several persons were injured. The elections were partially intended to discredit a nationalist petition that was about to be considered in the United Nations, where Guillaume had recently declared that "perfect order" existed in Morocco.

[26] Rezette, *op.cit.*, pp. 190-193, and Julien, *op.cit.*, p. 381. The signatories for each of the parties were, respectively, Al-Fassi, Torres, Ahmed Ben Souda, and Naciri. The Arab League delegate was Saleh Abou Riakik.

The new Resident General had further aroused the nationalists by sponsoring a congress of religious brotherhoods and forwarding a petition that denounced the King from 270 *caids* under French control.[27] Meanwhile the Istiqlal had continued to enroll new members. By 1951 it had about 100,000 adherents who had taken the oath of the party and regularly paid dues. Of course, the number of sympathizers was much greater, but their unorganized and violent actions were discouraged. In 1951 the party leaders appear to have realized that by lowering membership standards they risked losing control of their adherents. Though no cells were dissolved, the instructors no longer met with the cells that were regarded as unreliable.[28] Though no figures are available, the proportion of workers being recruited in the party probably increased in this period also, since they had been allowed to join the C.G.T. under the Juin regime.

The nationalist offensive on the international front mounted under the efforts of leaders throughout the world, particularly from the New York Information Office. During 1952 Allal Al-Fassi went on a world tour and visited Scandinavian and South American countries from whom the nationalists hoped to get support in the United Nations. Confronted with serious problems at home, the French government began to consider some kind of compromise, and early in 1952 Foreign Minister Schuman made reference to a possible "cosovereignty" arrangement. In the spring the Resident General forwarded to Paris a memorandum from the King,[29] proposing negotiation of the Protectorate statute, personal freedom for the King to select his own government, and revision of French-Moroccan relations as suggested in the King's memoranda of late 1950. The reply of the Quai d'Orsay suggested only some minor reforms. The King expressed his regret soon afterward and in the fall of 1952 renewed his demand for a constitutional monarchy. During the summer the nationalists had a minor victory in a decision of the Hague Court that reiterated the trusteeship character of French rule and the legal preservation of

[27] For more details on their tribal tactics see Claude Bourdet, "El Glaoui ou le féodalecapitalisme (le complôt Juin-Glaoui)," *Les Temps Modernes*, 9e année, no. 92 (July 1953), pp. 135-137. Many *caids* loyal to the King refused to sign, among them Bekkai, and also the pashas of the large cities, Casablanca, Fès, and Rabat.

[28] For more organizational detail at this period see Rezette, *op.cit.*, pp. 303 and 308. There is no evidence to suggest that it was these cells that were to take the initiative in later terrorist activity, as Rezette suggests, though it is quite possible that the abandoned members were of more extreme views. The released cells may also have been infiltrated by the Communist party.

[29] The memo remains secret, but its contents leaked out in both French and Istiqlal newspapers in Morocco. See Julien, *op.cit.*, pp. 387-388.

Morocco as an independent nation. Though the United Nations action in late 1952 was not all the nationalists had hoped for, they received international recognition of their problem on a much larger scale than ever before.

As the number of impatient militants and constrained sympathizers became larger, it was increasingly difficult to prevent popular demonstrations, especially in Casablanca where Moroccans had been joining unions and where the bond of workingmen's solidarity had been added to the desire for independence. With the permission of the Istiqlal the workers decided to hold a sympathy strike in protest over the assassination of the Tunisian trade-union leader, Farhat Hached. The exact circumstances of the deterioration of the strike into violence are not known. There are some indications that the French administration of Casablanca, dominated by a man long known for his bitter opposition to the nationalists, helped to provoke the bloodshed. In other union strongholds where the authorities showed more restraint and benefited from their long experience in handling Moroccan crowds, the strike was held without incident.[30]

The incident may have been provoked by the French officials who feared that the Moroccans would peacefully take over the Central Committee of the C.G.T. and thereby give themselves a quasi-legal institution for organization and agitation. The Moroccan C.G.T. office was a branch of the French trade union, but Maghjoub Ben Seddik and Taib Bouazza were on the Central Committee. They were convinced that they could win the next election for the Central Committee.[31] The strike, however, precluded such an election, for the Istiqlal and the Communist party were immediately outlawed. Using a plan that must have been prepared long in advance, the police proceeded to arrest all the officers and most of the leading militants of the Istiqlal—about four hundred men.[32] Scores of workers and leaders still carry the scars of the well-organized and brutal suppression. Since the United Nations was meeting at the time, many

[30] Julien, op.cit., p. 391, and P.-M. Déssignes, "Les journées sanglantés de Casablanca," France Observateur, December 11, 1952, p. 9. For accounts of the brutal suppression see Claude Bourdet, "La deuxième crime de M. Boniface," France Observateur, December 18, 1952, pp. 5-6.

[31] Interview with Said Sedikki, Press Officer, U.M.T., Casablanca, February 13, 1958. The Moroccan union leaders were clearly caught in a dilemma between demonstrating on behalf of their Tunisian hero and displaying their strength or staking everything on the chance of winning the union elections. Because of the Protectorate's skill in delaying and abusing such procedures, it is unlikely that the C.G.T. would have been allowed to come under Moroccan control.

[32] See Rezette, op.cit., pp. 216-219.

of the Istiqlal officers and leading members of other parties were in New York and thus escaped arrest. For the next three years this small circle, along with little groups of members visiting or studying in Tangier, Paris, Madrid, and Cairo, constituted the Istiqlal party.

With the Istiqlal and its trade-union support dispersed, the conservative French officials and businessmen of Morocco increased their influence and became more daring. There had been many signs of the deterioration of the administration during the first attempt to exile the King in 1951. In early 1953 the control of Paris over the colonial administration disintegrated completely. With French help, Al-Glaoui now entered into a new campaign to discredit the King. He tried to attack the King's religious position and organized another petition of pashas and *caids* opposing Ben Youssef. With the cooperation of the French administration, a congress of religious brotherhoods was held in the spring and Al-Glaoui, seeking support from tribal leaders, went on a tour of the Berber areas.[33] Under official French auspices he then left on a trip to England to attend the Coronation. He stopped at Paris on his return to hear the controversial, initial address of General Juin to the French Academy.

When Al-Glaoui returned, he again met with the Resident General and then embarked on a new tour of the Berber regions, where he openly denounced Mohammed V. The plot was tacitly revealed when the Resident General went on vacation in the midst of this turmoil. Control of the French zone was left in the hands of the small clique that had fought the nationalists since 1944. The King was well aware of the threat to his throne and sent a message to the President of the French Republic. Although orders had come from Paris to stop the coup, at the last moment the aging Ben Arafa was proclaimed king at a rally of Al-Glaoui forces in Marrakech. The last days before the King's deposition are filled with frantic exchanges between Paris and Rabat, with the descent of the tribes on Rabat and Casablanca because of promises of sugar and orders for vaccination, and with the final exile of Mohammed V.[34]

The absence of all respected authority from this time opened the way for a full-scale resistance effort. For the time being it was spo-

[33] See A. R. Vignon, "Le film d'un complôt," *France-Observateur*, August 27, 1953, pp. 7-8. There are several reports that after the December strikes General Guillaume, who had been opposed to the King's deposition, changed his mind.

[34] The details of this intrigue are not yet fully known and of secondary interest to this study. For further information see Vignon, *op.cit.*; Roger Stephane, "C'est Juin qu'il nous fait," *France-Observateur*, September 3, 1953, p. 5; and Jean-Marie Domenach, "Leçons d'une coup de force," *Espirit*, no. 206, September 1953, pp. 351-356.

radic and poorly organized, but the readiness of some of the nationalists was displayed a few days after the King's departure when the Casablanca-Algiers express train was derailed. Nearly every known Istiqlal militant was arrested and the party, now almost without central control, could make only weak appeals for moderation in the face of mounting terrorism. The country remained under a state of virtual military siege and police rule, though the nationalist leaders continued their propaganda campaign from abroad. For the future Moroccan political system the most important effect of the exile was the martyrdom of the King, who became a national symbol and hero far beyond the stature of any other Moroccan. His sacrifice was the basic theme of every nationalist activity from this date and was also a tribute to his temperance. If he had made an appeal to the countryside in August 1953, there is little doubt but that he could have created a bitter, but probably futile uprising. Until the return of Mohammed Ben Youssef the populace refused to attend the mosques, where prayers were said in the name of Ben Arafa. The myth of Mohammed V spread into the most remote corners of the country.[35] The suppression of the Istiqlal organization, the rise of the resistance movement, and the overpowering prestige of the King were to be basic factors in the reconstruction of the Moroccan nation after independence.

Independence by Default or Design?

The two years between the exile of Mohammed V and his return to Europe set the stage for the development of the new political system of Morocco. Diplomatic intrigue and the manipulation of forces in the French government form a complex web that cannot be untangled with presently available documents. However, such information as can be found is pertinent to future Franco-Moroccan relations. The Moroccans' diplomatic experience before independence helps to explain the disillusionment of those Moroccans who had hoped for a rapid and friendly reconciliation with France. To some extent the experience broke down confidence in France, especially among Moroccans who looked to her for inspiration and guidance.

The reign of the puppet King, Ben Arafa, was marked by an in-

[35] See the account given by Lacouture, *op.cit.*, pp. 108-112, of the tribesmen's commentary on the King's mystical powers and appearances, and Landau, *op.cit.*, pp. 323-335.

creasing intensity of violence as the forces of the resistance became more effective and the French, in turn, more desperate in defending their position. In the history of the nationalist movement the period is important because two new organizations were established as entities separate from the Istiqlal—the resistance and the trade-union movement. The resistance along with its rural manifestation, the Army of Liberation, became the instrument of organized terror. By the fall of 1955 the Army was sufficiently developed to launch attacks against French occupation troops. The unions, which had already emerged as effective organizations in the general strikes of 1952, were also revived in the spring of 1955, more than six months before the return of the King. The extent to which membership of the unions and the Istiqlal overlapped in the cities before independence cannot be measured accurately. With independence there is no doubt but that the trade unions became a well-organized movement with considerable political influence and a well-defined set of goals apart from the major nationalist party.

The period is also important in that it includes the decapitation of the Istiqlal, whose organization almost completely disintegrated during the two years of virtual police rule. The discontinuity of the Istiqlal was a major factor in the development of the new political system, which was, therefore, based not on a sole group, but on the interplay of three organizations and the King. Though the previous decades of nationalist activity, dominated by the Istiqlal, were no doubt basic to the development of popular activity to achieve independence, one of the paradoxes of this development was that the movement reached its goal in the company of two other organizations, each with its own basis of solidarity and its own conception of the future of the new nation. The resistance effort was obviously the result of the new military occupation and arbitrary suppression of Morocco, which reached its height after the exile of the King. The union movement, of course, derived solidarity and prestige from its brutal suppression in 1952 and later skillfully managed to establish itself as a leader in the struggle for independence before the King's return.

After the strike of December 1952, the Istiqlal organization had been demolished with an efficiency that testified to its vulnerability in any situation of violence. There are few indications that the upper hierarchy of the party either had correctly anticipated or properly prepared for the suppression, which had been a constant possibility since General Juin had been appointed Resident General in 1947. The estimates of arrests run as high as 30,000.[36] Though accurate figures are probably impossible to obtain, the leaders of the party are unanimous in their admission that from this time until the return of the King their party was completely suppressed. Of the Executive Committee only Al-Fassi and Balafrej had escaped, since they had been abroad. For several months complete confusion had prevailed among the militants of the base of the party who remained free and who were without orders, preparation, or communications. Central direction had been slowly rebuilt around a Provisional Executive Committee in Casablanca.[37] Late in 1952 most leaders had thought that it would take ten years to regain their old position, which might very possibly have been the case had not the King been exiled eight months later.

The Provisional Executive Committee had had representatives in the major cities, but its meetings had been difficult to arrange under the strict surveillance.[38] The main function of the group had been to maintain liaison among the King, the leaders in prison, and the leaders who had escaped. Some feeble efforts had been made to regroup small cells of from five to ten persons under completely clandestine conditions. This skeletal organization had worked mostly to collect funds for the growing resistance organization, international propaganda, and the support of families of the imprisoned and dead. Under siege conditions it had also tried to sustain the morale of the party sympathizers and the population in general, though no effort could be made except by verbal contacts in the *medinas* and occasional early-morning meetings of cells. Contacts with resistance members had been forbidden in Morocco. All communications had taken place through a chain of stations to Tangier and Tetouan, where representatives of both groups worked until independence.

The few party members who held together from December 1952 to the exile of the King had been concentrated in the cities, with roughly a third of them in Casablanca. Written records do not exist, but estimates based on remembrance of dues collections suggest that

[36] See Bouabid's speech at the Istiqlal Congress of 1955, *Al-Istiqlal*, August 17, 1956, p. 10. He gave this figure as the total number sentenced or detained administratively without any legal process from 1950 to 1955.

[37] The members of the Committee were Abdelkebir Al-Fassi, Ben Bachir Ben Abbès, Mohammed Douiri, Ahmed Boucetta, Mesaoud Chiguer, and Abdelkrim Ghallab.

[38] Interview with Ben Bachir Ben Abbès, Governor of Marrakech City, Marrakech, March 15, 1958.

at the most 50,000 persons had been contacted up to August 1953. The Istiqlal's clandestine organization had not worked well by the leaders' own admission. The police had needed to arrest only one man in the communication chain in order subsequently to arrest all the members of the chain. Those either above or below him in the chain had had no way of knowing what was happening. Few of the leaders or members had been trained or prepared for clandestine work. The committee in Casablanca had been discovered soon after the King's departure, though it had made some efforts to provide legal counsel for the arrested nationalists.

The Provisional Executive Committee had been in daily contact with Mohammed V. Until his exile he had continued to disapprove of terrorist acts, even though there was increasing pressure from the militants of the party and the small resistance movement that had existed at that time. From the time of the King's exile, Mohammed Douiri and M'Hammed Boucetta were the only top-echelon leaders in Morocco until the release of the Istiqlal leaders from prison late in 1954. Douiri had organized groups of teachers, engineers, pharmacists, doctors, and civil servants into professional associations, where a limited number of people could still meet and continue some propaganda efforts. In Casablanca Boucetta had made a similar effort, where he had concentrated on making contact with liberal French opinion in that city, which disapproved of the reactionary junta of military and industrial officials that ruled the Protectorate under the Ben Arafa regime. He had arranged the "Letter of the Seventy-Five," a protest to the French government signed by many prominent Frenchmen in Morocco.

Scattered remnants of the Istiqlal organization had been absorbed into the resistance movement. The activities of the terrorist organization had imposed a self-selecting process for leaders and a necessarily close-knit organization. The leaders were those most capable of performing the most violent acts. There was also a variety of sympathizers and members unsuited for more heroic deeds who performed tasks of arms manufacture, smuggling, fund-collecting, and communications. The time needed before terrorism became a threat to French activity in Morocco suggests that the resistance was poorly prepared and relatively small in August 1953. The Istiqlal had been confronted with the demands of those unwilling to wait for a negotiated settlement for several years.[39] With the encouragement of the King, the party had been successful in controlling pressure from below for direct action. The French clique who virtually ruled Morocco from 1953 on had destroyed the one device at their disposal for preventing the bloodshed and destruction that followed.

The deterioration of the French administration during this period is significant for several reasons. It helps to explain, first, the mistrust that was manifested during the early months of independent Franco-Moroccan relations. In view of the virtual disintegration of metropolitan control over the Residency, even so far as its ability to protect liberal-minded Frenchmen in Morocco, this deterioration is important in evaluating France's role in independent Morocco. The delicacy of questions involving Franco-Moroccan relations is also better understood if due allowance is made for the experience of the mass of the Moroccan populace under French police rule. Secondly, it is of historic and political interest to note the skillful and often successful campaign waged in Paris by the entire North African lobby. Events in other parts of the French colonial empire have since verified how easily her colonial administration can ignore and even reverse decisions made in Paris. Moroccans were well aware of the near-dictatorial authority of the ruling clique after the exile of their monarch—a fact which gave the return of Mohammed V heroic meaning. It was also the last-ditch stand of conservatives in Rabat and their colleagues in Paris that gave the resistance movement time to unleash the Moroccan Army of Liberation in the north. If this intrigue had not occurred, the role of the King might have been appreciably diminished and France might have more easily delayed providing Morocco with arms for her own forces of order in 1956.

Within two months of the King's exile there were reports of increasing reliance on police rule and of suspension of the most elementary individual protections in the case of Moroccan offenders.[40] The terrorist acts were still isolated, but the resistance was able to stage isolated blows, such as the bombing of the market at the Carrières Centrales in Casablanca. The larger *medinas* of Casablanca

[39] Leaders of the resistance movement have publicly admitted since independence that the "Istiqlal party was a political formation faithful to pacific methods in all circumstances" and that the members of the resistance "distrusted their own comrades of the Istiqlal party whose leaders refused to see the cells of their party transformed into terrorist cells," *Al-Istiqlal*, June 22. 1958, p. 24. Both the resistance and the Army of Liberation will be discussed in detail in CHAPTER VI.

[40] See "Les 'Ratissages' au Maroc," *France Observateur*, October 1, 1953, p. 14, and Roger Paret, "Comme Hitler: otages au Maroc," *ibid.*, December 24, 1953, pp. 14-15.

were soon under the undisputed control of resistance cells. A campaign against informers, enforcement of the boycott of French products, and obtaining the full cooperation of recalcitrant Moroccans were the first tasks of the resistance movement. Several attempts were also made on the life of the puppet King. Though France was distracted from events in Morocco by the war in the Far East and the problems of European integration, a delegation of liberal French Deputies visited Morocco early in 1954 to investigate the situation. It was promptly followed by a delegation from the right of the Assembly, which was ostentatiously given full military honors and all official courtesies.[41]

By early 1954 Morocco resembled a large collection of prison camps as the French Army cut off travel and communication between tribes and as the police sealed off the major quarters of the cities. French forces had undergone a sizable reinforcement, though special precautions were taken to prevent members of the resistance from infiltration into the French forces of order.[42] The bankruptcy of French rule was further exposed when liberal-minded French of Morocco, led by Lemaigre-Dubreuil, began to seek a compromise solution with some Moroccan businessmen who were acceptable to the nationalists. The compromise of Mendes-France in Tunisia also alarmed conservative Frenchmen. The French administration was reaching a point where it could no longer control the counter-terrorist activities of the Présence Française, and the first evidence appeared that important members of the administration were actually assisting in counter-terrorist operations.[43] The Mendes-France government established the new Ministry of Moroccan and Tunisian Affairs at Paris and sent a diplomat, Lacoste, to replace General Guillaume as

[41] See the comparison of these two missions by Roger Paret, "Le fiasco Marocain," *France-Observateur*, February 11, 1954, pp. 10-11. Shortly after this the American visitor, Admiral Fechteler, was steered by the authorities into the hands of Al-Glaoui to discredit U.S. interest in the Moroccan problem, much as David Bruce was treated in 1951. See "L'amiral Fechteler mise sur Al-Glaoui," *ibid.*, March 25, 1954, p. 17.

[42] The reorganization of the administration under the Director of Security is described by Roger Paret, "Maroc: les enchères de la terreur," *France Observateur*, April 22, 1954, p. 15. For the activities of individuals from the Vichy regime in this effort see his article, "Relance 'liberale' au Maroc?" *ibid.*, p. 17, May 20, 1954. The French pressure groups, with identification of their relation to industrial, Vichyite, and Juin interests in France, are described with names in C. B. (Claude Bourdet?), "Le fonctionnement du 'lobby' Marocain," *ibid.*, September 2, 1954, pp. 14-15.

[43] Ten counter-terrorists were arrested, *London Times*, June 23, 1954, p. 9, and soon after the deputy police chief of Casablanca was also arrested, *ibid.*, June 24, 1954, p. 10.

Resident General, but denied any intention of returning Mohammed V to the throne.

Like Guillaume, Lacoste was the victim of his staff. His proposals were completely unacceptable to the resistance movement and to the remnants of the Istiqlal abroad. In his contacts with the various nationalist groups he proposed a "third man" policy, which would put a new member of the royal family on the throne who would be acceptable to both the Moroccans and the French. One possible candidate was the Khalifa of Tetouan, who had been recognized by the Spanish as legal guardian of the dynasty when they refused to acknowledge the French coup of August 1953. In the nationalists' view, such a compromise was unacceptable because it would abolish the center of resistance operations tolerated by the Spanish in the north; condone the exile and possibly prevent return of the King; disarm international public opinion and eliminate the usefulness of Spain as a diplomatic lever against France. Though Mendes-France's regime fell before his suggestions of either a substitute king or Throne Council were seriously considered, he did succeed in freeing the higher-ranking leaders of the Istiqlal and the trade unions.

The release of the nationalist leaders, who had been held on legal technicalities and without trial for nearly two years, was tacit admission that a settlement of the Moroccan problem required a bargaining agent who would be recognized by the Moroccan people. The nationalists found themselves in a difficult position, for the junta under Lacoste continued to rule Morocco under siege conditions and no further concessions were made to indicate a change in French policy. Many of the released Istiqlal leaders went to Paris, while those remaining behind could do nothing to rebuild their organization. The initiative continued to rest in the hands of the resistance movement and the growing French counter-terrorist effort and left the *ancien* nationalists as idle spectators.

The French counter-terrorist effort testified to the growing effectiveness of the Moroccan resistance movement. If a more friendly government had existed in Paris under Mendes-France, his views were not reflected in Morocco. The administration was increasingly involved in aiding and abetting French counter-terrorism from mid-1954. Between August 1954 and January 1955, leading Moroccan and French moderates aired their conciliatory views in the columns of *Maroc Presse*. The editor was Lemaigre-Dubreuil, a wealthy Casablanca industrialist, a hero of World War II and a member of a distinguished French family. The offices of his newspaper were attacked several times and eventually the newspaper was banned. Many of the Moroccans with whom he had established contact were assassinated, including members of several of the wealthiest families of Casablanca. Since the Casablanca police were no longer regarded as trustworthy by the Resident General himself, he sent police from Rabat to investigate these crimes.[44]

After attempted lynchings by mobs of their countrymen, many French liberals fled from Morocco. The climax of the French counter-terrorist effort was the assassination, in June 1955, of Lemaigre-Dubreuil. His death was followed by the removal of several police officials and the appointment of a new Resident General, Gilbert Grandval, the day following the assassination.[45] According to some nationalists, the shock of his violent death did more to advance the Moroccan cause than all their efforts since 1952. Soon afterward Paris papers were full of reports of the complicity of the police and "colons." Grandval expelled the head of the Présence Française and tried to bring the police under control. In the tradition of the Berber *dahir* of 1930, conservative French of Morocco had again done the thing best calculated to discredit their position. Though violence continued, discussions began to agree on a new Moroccan regime that could receive the approval of the exiled King.

A major overhaul of French policy in Morocco was in process from mid-1955, but the results were seen only after nine months of tortuous diplomacy and intrigue. The history of the months leading up to the Franco-Moroccan Agreements of March 1956 suggests some of the distrust and deception on which future relations were to be built. Perhaps even more important for the future political system of Morocco, the background to the Agreements and the subsequent negotiation for the conventions on matters of common concern show how interlocked Morocco and France had become over the past thirty years' development. As conditions varied in France, Morocco, and the

[44] "Le contre-terrorisme Francais au Maroc," *France Observateur*, February 10, 1955, pp. 11-12.
[45] See "Ce que M. E. Faure n'a pas dit sur le contre-terrorisme marocain," *ibid.*, June 27, 1955, pp. 16-18, and *Le Monde*, July 19, 1955, p. 5. The importance of the incident is suggested by the report that one police official was called to Paris to report personally to Faure. At the time there were reported to be two French terrorist groups, Organisation de la Defense Anti-Terroriste (ODAT) and Avant-Garde des Ideologies Républicaines (AGIR). Their relations to the overt, right-wing club, the Présence Française, is not known, but there was very likely considerable overlap. Reportedly the President of the Republic had been discreetly sounded out on the possible assassination of Lemaigre-Dubreuil and had strongly disapproved.

world these problems could be a continued source of strength or vulnerability to each of the negotiating powers.

French procrastination is of particular interest, for it was in the interlude between the opening of talks with the King and his triumphal return that the Moroccan Liberation Army came into full activity. Had the French been more decisive, they might have prevented the formation of this military organization, which was to have a continuing role in Moroccan politics. They might also have prevented the massacre of French farmers and officials that occurred as the Liberation Army and the populace in general began to express their impatience in violence. The sequence of late 1955 and early 1956 suggests that the guerrilla army, aided by the tolerance of the Spanish authorities in the north, and possibly in coordination with a similar thrust from Tunisia, could have produced a general conflagration in North Africa. French fears of such aid to the Algerians no doubt helped to hasten the granting of Moroccan independence. In so far as this act deprived the Algerian revolutionaries of support and opposed Moroccan and Algerian immediate interests, France clearly gained from giving independence.

From the arrival of Grandval in July 1955, there was no doubt that some new French policy would be forthcoming. He lost no time in conferring with the puppet King and there were many reports that his consultations were leading up to a new solution to the Moroccan problem. More political prisoners were released and he was enthusiastically received by Moroccan crowds at public appearances. Morocco remained in a state of siege, of course, and the counter-terrorist activities continued, though restrained by the expulsion of leading French counter-terrorists. Grandval himself was publicly disgraced and abused by French mobs on several occasions.[46] With the end of Ramadan, terrorism by both Moroccan and French became more serious and a Committee of Coordination was formed to help to establish a minimum of order so negotiations could be started.[47]

Active in these early contacts was Bekkai, a voluntary exile since

[46] See accounts in Le Monde, July 19, 1955, p. 5, and Landau, op.cit., pp. 370-371, for the anti-Semitic attack on him. During the funeral of General Duval, Grandval's person and uniform were insulted in the crudest fashion.
[47] See Le Monde, July 1, 1955, p. 1. The Committee included Grandval, Boyer de Latour, later to become Resident General, and Soustelle, who at this time was among those hoping for a rapprochement in North Africa. During a funeral for an Algerian terrorist victim at Phillipeville, Algeria, a wreath sent by Soustelle was torn up by the local mayor.

the expulsion of the King, later to become the first President of the Council of Government. He visited Morocco during these consultations and later confirmed his known loyalty to the King by stating that only Mohammed V could resolve the Moroccan problem. The most reliable rumor at the time appeared to be that a Throne Council would be formed after Bekkai had arranged a compromise with the nationalists. Grandval returned to Paris for talks with Faure early in August where it became apparent that there were strong forces within the Faure government, led by Pinay, that opposed any compromise permitting the return of Mohammed V.

The government in Paris was working under considerable pressure during this period, for the preparations of the Army of Liberation must have been known to the authorities and the anniversary of the exiled King's accession to the throne was less than two weeks away. The most conciliatory proposal that the Faure government could agree on was a weak appeal to Ben Arafa to form a coalition group to govern Morocco—a proposal which was immediately rejected by the Istiqlal. With the intervention of the President of the Republic preparations were slowly made for a conference with representatives of the nationalists at Aix-les-Bains. While Faure apparently was seeking to obtain the voluntary withdrawal of Ben Arafa, time ran out and the rural uprising of Throne Day, August 1955, took place as feared. For the first time a serious breach was made in the French Army's occupation of the countryside. The estimates of the dead from clashes of French troops and Berber tribesmen, plus the massacre of French colonialists around Oued Zem and Khenifra, ran as high as 800.[48]

The outburst of violence provided grounds on which the conservatives could further disrupt the Faure government on the eve of the Aix-les-Bains talks, which brought French officials and nationalist leaders together for the first time since 1953. Grandval's removal was the final price for a compromise. The results of the Aix-les-Bains Conference are still secret, though it is generally assumed that the nationalists' minimal conditions were the removal of Ben Arafa and the appointment of a Throne Council approved by Mohammed V, with the way being left open for him to return to his throne. The Istiqlal reserved any judgment on the Throne Coun-

---

[48] Accounts of the tribal uprisings can be found in the *New York Times*, August 21, 1955, p. 1, and August 22, 1955, p. 1. See also *Le Monde*, August 21-22, 1955, p. 1; August 23, 1955, p. 1; and August 24, 1955, pp. 1-2.

cil plan until it was further clarified by the French government.[49] Ben Arafa refused to accept any compromise and was supported by Faure's own Minister of Defense, General Koenig, who was allegedly the representative of the conservative military bloc led by General Juin. The sacrifice of Grandval to the desires of the right-wing in France and Morocco was only the first manifestation of their influence during these negotiations. They were yet to delay the return of the King for two months and, by so doing, were to be instrumental in multiplying the disorder and bloodshed in Morocco.

The exiled monarch approved the principle of a Throne Council[50] after a visit to Madagascar by General Catroux and Henri Yrisson, one-time cabinet director of Pinay and generally regarded as delegate of the right-wing elements on this mission. The planning for the Throne Council entailed two decisions, which revealed the entrenchment of the French conservatives and also discord within the Istiqlal leadership. One was the composition of the Council. The second was under what terms, if any, Mohammed V would be permitted to return to Morocco. While the Catroux mission was in Madagascar, Al-Fassi flew from his Cairo headquarters to Rome to meet with the party leaders. During the conference Al-Fassi is reported to have rejected any scheme that might keep the King from returning to the throne and returned to Cairo, leaving the other members of the Istiqlal Executive Committee to their own devices. On his arrival in Cairo Al-Fassi immediately issued a sharply worded statement that he had refused to participate in the sessions of the Executive Committee because "some persons" had already accepted the idea of a Throne Council.[51]

The next day he corrected his statement by adding that the Throne Council was acceptable if it remained possible for the King to return eventually to Morocco. The differences of opinion within the Istiqlal were never openly discussed, particularly after the arrival of the King in France a few weeks later. As the Istiqlal showed signs of tension, the French conservatives marshalled their strength. Pinay and General Koenig, without resigning from his post under Faure, renewed their attack on the negotiations, while last-minute efforts were made by "colons" in Morocco to bolster the discredited Ben Arafa admin-

---

[49] See the party statements that appear in *Le Monde*, August 25, 1955, p. 3, and August 29, 1955, p. 1. The party was represented by Lyazidi, Abdeljalil, and Bouabid.
[50] *Le Monde*, September 11-12, 1955, p. 1.
[51] *Ibid.*, September 8, 1955, pp. 1 and 4.

istration. They appear to have been successful in postponing the implementation of a reported ultimatum to Ben Arafa delivered by General Catroux, which was then fortified with a letter from the President of the Republic asking Ben Arafa to abdicate.[52]

Meanwhile the new Resident General, Boyer de Latour, had been exploring the situation in Morocco. His indecisiveness no doubt reflects both conditions in Paris and de Latour's sympathy for the conservatives.[53] He was called back to Paris as the opposition started a new dispute over the composition of the Throne Council. One of the Resident's first visits in Paris was with General Juin, while simultaneously Pierre Montel, chairman of the Assembly's National Defense Committee, arrived in Rabat with full military honors to rally opposition to Moroccan independence. Paris stood firm to this challenge, however, and de Latour returned to Morocco in a few days with orders to try to persuade the French opposition elements to permit the departure of Ben Arafa. On the weekend that Ben Arafa finally left Rabat, fighting broke out in the Oujda area and soon spread to all the Rif Mountain area bordering on the French zone.

As the National Assembly began debate on the final plan for the Throne Council, Al-Fassi announced from Cairo that the Moroccan Liberation Army had begun combat to free the King and all North Africa.[54] The outbreak of open warfare drove Faure to more drastic action. He dismissed his director of cabinet and his Minister of Defense, General Koenig, both of whom were openly scheming to obstruct the policy of their government. He was supported by the Assembly, except for the Gaullist group and the right wing. Simultaneously, rioting "colons" distributed handbills in Morocco calling for further resistance. In Rabat a delegation of French conservatives received assurance from de Latour that the Throne Council would not be installed, but would be replaced by a delegate selected by Ben Arafa.[55] His statement that the return of Mohammed V was excluded from all negotiations may well have been instrumental in

[52] These two documents are described in *ibid.*, September 11-12, 1955, p. 2, and September 16, 1955, p. 1.

[53] Boyer de Latour was a career diplomat and former chief of the French mission to the U.N.O. His selection was probably based on the need to gain the confidence of rightist elements in France and Morocco and to deal with specifically diplomatic problems of the negotiations of the summer. The success of France in keeping the Algerian question out of the U.N. bolstered his reputation with the conservatives.

[54] *Le Monde*, October 6, 1955, p. 1.

[55] *La Chronique Marocaine*, Embassy of France, Press and Information Service, October 15, 1955, p. 5, for October 2, 1955. This is an extremely well-done chronicle and will be cited hereafter as *C.M.*

unleashing the Liberation Army offensive. The reception of the discredited Présence Française by the Protectorate's Director of the Interior also revealed the last desperate maneuvering of the opposition to Moroccan independence.

Amid this confusion the Throne Council was announced in mid-October: Bekkai, the moderate nationalist and friend of the King; Si Tahar Ouassou, an obscure chieftain reportedly selected by de Latour; Hadj Omar Sbihi, pasha of Salé with restrained nationalist sympathies; and Si Mohammed Al-Mokri, the adaptable Grand Vizier of Morocco for the preceding forty years.[56] Since the Council never fully assumed its role it is difficult to evaluate, but at least two of the members could have been dominated by the French administration—Al-Mokri and Ouassou. Bekkai was the only tested supporter of the King and there was no strong militant of the Istiqlal. If there were leaders of the Istiqlal who were inclined to accept a compromise on the return of the King, the Throne Council was certainly not selected to preserve their conciliatory attitude.

The period from the installation of the Throne Council to the King's return to Morocco remains one of the most obscure interludes in the sequence of events up to Moroccan independence. The Council had received the approval of the exiled King, and Si Fatimi Ben Slimane was selected to begin consultations for its formation. Though recognized by the minority Democratic party, the Council was soon attacked by the Istiqlal. The Istiqlal line was probably hardened by the hostilities of the Liberation Army, which was under an oath of personal loyalty to Mohammed V. The statements of the party spokesman in Morocco, Lyazidi, and the Leader in Cairo, Al-Fassi, reveal continued discrepancies and confusion. In France the Minister of Moroccan and Tunisian Affairs declared to the Assembly that the government could not enter into negotiations with the Istiqlal unless Al-Fassi were disowned. However, the Faure government was already committed to the nationalists in the exchanges of the past three months and its survival under the new attack from rightist groups in Paris and Rabat depended heavily on continued

[56] *New York Times*, October 16, 1957, p. 1. This list generally followed the outline published nearly six weeks earlier in *Le Monde*, September 1955, p. 1, including a delegate of the makhzen (Al-Mokri), a traditionalist (Ouassou), an independent (Bekkai), and a nationalist (Sbihi), though the latter's qualification is doubtful. Al-Mokri later appeared first on the list of those to be purged. Ouassou became the governor of one of the smaller provinces, Safi, and was later removed under the Balafrej government.

progress with its announced policy. While Lyazidi voiced the party's solidarity with Al-Fassi, he also made the surprising, and perhaps defensive, revelation that Al-Fassi had not been in contact with the party since the meeting in Rome.[57]

There is some evidence to support the view that the Istiqlal leaders in Morocco and Paris resented the veiled interference of Egypt in its affairs and did not want to become embroiled in the Algerian war when the fruits of its own thirty-year struggle were so near. In mid-October Lyazidi made the ambiguous statement that the return of the King had never been "excluded" from the negotiations and that it was the "Moroccan people who should finally decide this point, when they can do so according to democratic procedures."[58] Since there would be no doubt of the results of a referendum on the return of the King, such a statement from Lyazidi would pacify aroused opinion in Cairo, while the qualification also entailed several months' delay and the restoration of order before such a vote could be held; this would be reassuring to Paris. The exact nature of the tensions within the party leadership at this time have never been publicly discussed. The Istiqlal finally rejected the Throne Council after a week's delay.

The party objected to the addition of a fourth member to the Throne Council, which, they maintained, disrupted the agreed balance of power in the group, and objected to the presence of Al-Mokri, whom they considered a tool of Ben Arafa.[59] The Istiqlal further objected to the delay in the return of the King, anticipated for mid-October, and the failure of the French to annul the Treaty of Fès. The most revealing section was the comment regarding Al-Fassi: "We are in agreement with him on purposes. But our methods are different. However, we do not want a rupture as occurred in Tunisia. We seek by all means to persuade him to avoid a rupture over the agreements concluded with French government." No comment was made concerning the King's recognition of the Throne Council, though this had figured prominently in an Istiqlal communiqué from Paris before the trouble with Al-Fassi.

The enlargement of the Throne Council to four members was indisputable grounds for objection, but it is difficult to see how France could have withdrawn from her other promises dealing with

---

[57] See *Le Monde*, October 10, 1955, p. 4, and October 11, 1955, p. 3.

[58] *C.M.*, October 13, 1955, p. 29.

[59] The party's rejection appears in *Le Monde*, October 20, 1955, p. 2, and *New York Times*, October 22, 1955, p. 1.

the abdication of Ben Arafa and the freeing of Mohammed Ben Youssef. Before this time the Istiqlal itself had not publicly taken a firm policy on the King's return to Morocco. The rejection also seems to underestimate the importance of the massive popular support that the King and the party would have under a Council even it it were not composed with a clear nationalist majority. The action of Al-Fassi and the Army of Liberation probably necessitated the King's return to Morocco, but it is doubtful if the Istiqlal had a coordinated and agreed policy on the question. Previous party statements were always phrased in terms of the Throne Council and expressed only minor objections to it.

November 1955 contained a jumble of events following the Faure government's decision to free Morocco and to permit the King to return. Mohammed V arrived in France the last day of October. The uprising of the Army of Liberation, together with the chaos of the countryside once it was known that the King had been freed, paved the way for his triumphal return, which occurred slightly over two weeks later. In the absence of any organization capable of restoring even minimal order and in view of the overwhelming popularity of Mohammed V after his two years' exile, his presence in Morocco became essential to the French policy of reconciliation. Relationships within the Istiqlal and, most likely as a consequence, between the Istiqlal and the King were confused in this period. Though action was already under way for the King's return to Rabat and the Throne Council had been extended at the King's request, the Istiqlal publicly reaffirmed its loyalty to him and commented on the conditions for the formation of a new government.

The St. Cloud Declaration of the King outlined the interim governmental structure and the goal of future negotiations. While the two references to "interdependence" in this document were later to become the center of some controversy, it also specifically mentioned "sovereignty" and that Morocco would "achieve the status of an independent state." It recognized the King's intention to organize a government for negotiation and to proceed with institutional reforms, establishing a constitutional monarchy. The Declaration was reported to have fallen short of Istiqlal desires. Several days later Al-Fassi, who was still in Cairo, announced that the King's statement must have been made under pressure from the French. The next day a delegation of the Istiqlal leaders in Paris visited the King to reaffirm their devotion and a meeting of the Executive Committee was called for the following week in Madrid. How this second dispute among the nationalist leaders was resolved is not known, though the party Executive Committee issued a statement from an emergency meeting in Madrid retracting its extreme position concerning the new government.[60]

These events suggest that the party was still in disagreement on the goals of the interim government or on the priority to give them. When the Istiqlal group arrived at Tangier from Madrid, unaccompanied by Al-Fassi, they felt it necessary to reassert the "perfect unity" of the party's leaders. They also expressed their complete support for the King's recent speech, but added that they hoped the Treaty of Fès would be annulled. Whether this curious concentration on the historic document of 1912, which was superseded by the St. Cloud Declaration, represented mistrust of French intentions or the reiteration of the old claims of the party is not clear. The former seems unlikely because of the existing commitments of the French government, the *fait accompli* of the King's return to Rabat, and the Liberation Army. If it were the latter, it suggests the strong influence of the elder members of the Executive Committee. It also reveals the party's increasing difficulty in distinguishing itself from other organizations that had participated in the struggle for independence.

France prepared for the return of the monarch by appointing a new Resident General, André Dubois, former prefect of police in Paris. His profession indicates an accurate anticipation by French authorities of the major problems the new country would face and also a judicious break with the tradition of appointing Resident Generals associated with the military occupation or the administration of the Protectorate. Amid a tumultuous acclaim the King was welcomed back to Morocco on the fourteenth of November; rejoicing nearly reduced the country to anarchy. Ben Slimane, distrusted by the nationalist leaders, was dropped as the prospective chief of interim government and consultations were begun to form the first government under independent status. Though the Istiqlal had stated earlier that it would only accept Bekkai as President of the government on the King's request, he was appointed during these consultations. Temporary arrangements were made to give limited

[60] An account of the second difference with Al-Fassi will be found in *Le Monde*, November 6-7, 1955, p. 1; November 9, 1955, p. 4; November 10, 1955, p. 4; November 16, 1955, p. 4; November 19, 1955, p. 2.

powers to the new Moroccan ministers and Dubois conducted a series of meetings with the King to plan the immediate changes that would be made in the Protectorate administration.

The King also received delegations of the parties, following which the Istiqlal announced that it would prefer to form the new government alone, but that under the special circumstances it would accept a position of "debatable representativeness." A different source of discontent within the Istiqlal was voiced from Tetouan, where Al-Fassi had stopped on his way to Cairo from the Madrid session of the Executive Committee. He strongly asserted the basic Muslim orientation and Arab character of Morocco, while it was reported that he had refused to return to the French zone so long as any French remained.[61] The Istiqlal Extraordinary Congress was held in the midst of Bekkai's negotiations for the formation of the new government and without the Leader, Al-Fassi.

The negotiations for the final independence agreement were delayed by the fall of the Faure government, elections, and the formation of the Mollet government in early February 1956. During the crisis in France the King continued to affirm the goal of complete independence, and a ministerial negotiating commission was formed to represent Morocco. Before the official negotiations opened in Paris, a temporary accord was signed by Bekkai and Dubois. On leaving Rabat for Paris, Dubois confirmed the fears of the Moroccan nationalists who had demanded the annulment of the Treaty of Fès by stating that all those matters contained in the Treaty—foreign affairs, defense, and finance—would remain in the control of the Residency until specific agreements had been made.[62] As negotiations began under the supervision of the King and Pineau, the new Minister of Foreign Affairs, there were new signs of protest from French conservative elements in Morocco. The Présence Française repeated its demands for representation in Paris by a special delegation during the negotiations and foretold a mass exodus if complete equality were established.[63] General Lejeune, commander of French forces in Morocco, also chose this delicate moment to announce that every

[61] *Ibid.*, November 30, 1955, p. 5.

[62] *C.M.*, February 11, 1956, p. 1.

[63] They then sent their own delegation unofficially to Paris and were also received in Rabat by Dubois. This protest brought complaint from liberal French groups in Morocco and the head of the Présence Française delegation, returning to Morocco before the final agreement was reached, deplored the lack of unity among the French of Morocco.

measure must be taken to insure the maintenance of French forces in Morocco.

On March 2, 1956, the Franco-Moroccan Agreement was signed by Bekkai and Pineau. It explicitly recognized Morocco's right to have an army, to conduct her own diplomacy, and to maintain her territorial integrity. Conventions were anticipated in fields of common interest—defense, foreign relations, economy, and culture—which would be determined on a basis of equality and would guarantee the rights of the French in Morocco. Most important from the nationalists' view was the recognition that the Treaty of Fès was "no longer consistent with the requirements of modern life and can no longer govern Franco-Moroccan relations." The annexed protocol gave the representative of France the right to submit "observations" on acts of the Moroccan government; provided that the status of French forces would remain unchanged during the "transitional period"; admitted Morocco to the Committee of the Franc Area; continued the existing guarantees for French civil servants in Morocco; and endowed the French Ambassador with the title of High Commissioner and permanent diplomatic seniority. With this document the new nation officially entered into existence.

The contingent diplomatic conventions have been concluded according to their urgency and difficulty. Thus, the diplomatic accord was completed with relatively little delay. Commissions have been organized for each major outstanding problem between Morocco and France, but their progress has been slow.[64] Their work was delayed by the break in diplomatic relations with France after the arrest of the Algerian leaders. The Moroccan Foreign Office was also occupied in the early months of independence with similar negotiations with Spain, with the supervisory powers of Tangier, and with its admission to the United Nations. During the first crisis of the Council of Government it was announced that the conventions on technical assistance, cultural, and judicial affairs were ready, but no final action was taken until months later.

Not until early 1957 was the second convention signed to provide technical and administrative assistance. By the fall of 1957 all the other conventions were ready for signature, according to the French

[64] See *C.M.*, March 24, 1956, p. 2 and Annex II. The commissions were for technical and administrative cooperation; cultural affairs; judicial affairs; resolution of problems of French civil servants; military affairs; diplomatic affairs; economic, financial, and monetary affairs.

Chargé d'Affaires, except the intricate problem of restitution and compensation for property.[65] The judicial convention was initialed in June 1957, and the cultural convention was signed in October 1957. The most difficult agreements are those on military and property relations. Negotiations on the Convention of Establishment, or property transfer and compensation, were suspended by the Moroccan government in the fall of 1957, while the resolution on the role of French troops was regularly postponed up to the end of 1958.

[65] *C.M.*, September 5-8, 1957, pp. 1-2. The disposition of property was extremely complex since much of the land had been taken by French farmers at great advantage to them, if not simply seized or occupied forcefully. A good inventory of how much land had been taken and under what conditions it had been occupied did not exist. On the Moroccan side, there was considerable hesitancy over signing a convention that would be unfavorably received at home, but at the same time it was necessary to sustain the productivity, income, and employment that these farms represented.

CHAPTER IV

GOVERNMENT AND ADMINISTRATION

Toward a "Homogeneous" Government

THE formal structure of the Moroccan government and administration changed little during the first three years of independence.[1] Some leaders of the Istiqlal often claimed that the failure to remove the external appearances of the Protectorate regime was due to the presence of a few opposition party ministers in the Council of Government. The party advocated a "homogeneous" government which would miraculously resolve all governmental problems—an argument that is not substantiated by the actions of the Istiqlal ministers or by the program of the Balafrej government after May 1958. In some respects it was more difficult to agree on proposals concerning the relatively well-defined, procedural problems of the central government and administration than on more complex programs having profound implications for the future of the society. The political system appears to have been better suited to deal with distant problems and vague issues than with immediate and fairly familiar problems of the central government. Understanding why little was done with the more specific problems of government may help to explain why progress was slow in advancing the more intricate and costly programs for general social and economic reform.

In the early months of independence Morocco continued to use almost the identical central organization as the old French Protectorate. A few names were changed and some offices were shuffled about among ministries but fundamentally the governmental structure was unchanged. The colonial supervision ceased and the entire organization was put under the King, to whom the ministers were directly and individually responsible. Under the Franco-Moroccan Agreement of March 2, 1956, the King retained all sovereign powers.[2] Before independence the central government and administration had included the Makhzen or historical governing body under the

[1] "Government" will refer to the Council of Government and all subordinate officials and civil servants; "administration" refers only to civil servants of the governmental unit being discussed.

[2] Available in English from the Service de Presse et d'Information, Ambassade de France, "Moroccan Affairs—No. 12," March 1956; in French in *Maroc*, no. 1, Rabat, Ministry of Foreign Affairs, n.d.

King and the offices of the Residency General. Under the terms of the Treaty of Fès the Makhzen was to be preserved, but could be "reformed."[3] For the colonial powers the Makhzen represented Moroccan sovereignty and through this device the King kept nominal control of the entire Cherifian Empire, including special delegates of the Makhzen in Tangier and at Tetouan in the ex-Spanish zone. All the new social and economic services that were sponsored by the French were, however, organized under the Resident General. Since this organization also controlled the police, army, and communications the Makhzen had little influence on the administration of Morocco.

There were two conditions to the Residency's authority, both of which were crucial to the development of the nationalist movement. First, since sovereignty legally continued to rest with the Makhzen, all laws or *dahirs* had to be submitted through the Makhzen for the King's signature. By withholding his endorsement, which was done for the first time in 1944, the King could prevent legislation from going into effect, though the Residency began to develop means of circumventing this veto. Secondly, the clause of the Treaty of Fès recognizing the preservation of Moroccan sovereignty prevented the Protectorate from reorganizing the Moroccan government under any colonial scheme similar to that of Algeria or under some form of the French Union. Though the denunciation of the Treaty of Fès was the key condition for the nationalists in Franco-Moroccan Agreement of 1956, it should be noted that the conditions it also imposed on France, Spain, and the Tangier governing body provided the obstacle to the abolition of Morocco's legal existence. The occupying powers were, nevertheless, able to carry on the bulk of the governing process outside the Makhzen, which by 1955 was completely incapable of governing without the agencies organized during the Protectorate.

Though the Makhzen as the central administrative agency of the Moroccan government was outmoded by the changes introduced during the Protectorate, it has been continued in a new form as the office of the King, the Royal Cabinet, and the Secretary General of the government. The Secretary General and his staff have been the King's personal administrative agency and the most important agency

[3] An English text of the Treaty will be found in Landau, *op.cit.*, Appendix VI, pp. 392-393. A complete study of the juristic basis for the preservation of Cherifian unity will be found in Jacques Bonjean, *L'Unité de L'Empire Cherifian*, Rabat, Institute des Haute-Etudes Marocaines, 1955.

for the coordination and planning of policy. To some extent it has functioned as the country's highest governmental and administrative agency. The Royal Cabinet manages the King's personal and ceremonial affairs. The Council of Government, or cabinet of ministerial officers, supervises the agencies previously operated by the French. Organizing the offices of the Royal Cabinet and the Secretary General were among the first acts of the new government. With the staff provided in this legislation the administrative structure surrounding the King remained unchanged until the crisis leading to the second Council of Government in October 1956.

With the formation of the second government, which was more fully under the control of the Istiqlal, the King decided to provide himself with a private Crown Council. Through the Crown Council affairs that might be difficult to handle in ministries of the Council of Government could be segregated, and some obstacles in forming the new Council were removed. The Minister of the Interior, Caid Lahcen Lyoussi, had long been a friend of the King, but his activities since independence made him unacceptable to the Istiqlal. He took one of the three positions of the Crown Council, reportedly to give some representation to tribesmen. The second Crown Councillor, Si Mokhtar Soussi, was an active member of the Istiqlal and Minister of Habous in the first Council of Government. Bringing the supervision of Habous under the control of the Palace was in harmony with the King's desire to preserve this institution without radical change and also provided some Istiqlal representation in the Crown Council.[4] The third Crown Councillor, Si Ben Al-Arabi Al-Alaoui, was a distinguished elder of the nationalist movement and a friend of the King, though not in an important position in the Istiqlal. Of all three men he was probably the most respected mediator for problems involving the Palace.

The office of the President of the Council of Government was not important in the first two governments. Although it was given all legislative powers "now in force" when established,[5] the circumstances of the emergence of the new political system, as well as the legal technicalities of the Franco-Moroccan Agreement of March

---

[4] Si Mokhtar Soussi was also a good friend of Allal Al-Fassi and gave indirect recognition to Al-Fassi's Sahara campaign. Soussi was one of the original sponsors of Al-Fassi's journal, *Sahara Al-Maghrib.*

[5] *Bulletin Officiel*, no. 225, January 13, 1956, "Dahir du 6 janvier 1956, (24 joumada I 1375), relatif aux pouvoirs du President du Conseil," p. 3. This bulletin will be cited hereafter by the abbreviation *O.B.*

95

1956, meant that the King remained the dominant figure. In addition, M'Barek Ben Bekkai, who was President of the Council of Government until May 1958, looked upon his duties as coordinating a "government of negotiation." He was not a member of the Istiqlal and thereby lacked the organized popular support the party could claim. Like Caid Lahcen Lyoussi, he was a rural official who had resigned over the Protectorate's abuse of the Palace. He was a confidant of the King and showed complete deference to the King's position. Bekkai's position after the change of government in October 1956 was even more delicate. The Istiqlal ministers later admitted that they had agreed to participate in the second government only on the specific request of the King. After President Bekkai's statement of defense during the crisis leading to the second cabinet, the Istiqlal decided that it would henceforth participate in the cabinet only if the King were presiding.[6] The President participated in all the commissions and committees that were organized during his period of office, but the conditions under which he originally took office precluded using his office to build personal support.

A comparison of the first Councils of Government appears in Table 3. The King designated Bekkai as President of the Council of Government and received delegations from each party. The Istiqlal representatives were dissatisfied with the number of ministries given to them and made it clear that they accepted responsibility only because of the unusual conditions existing in the country. The Istiqlal was troubled by the failure to abrogate fully the Treaty of Fès and the reference to "interdependence" derived from the St. Cloud Declaration of November 1955. During the Extraordinary Congress Abderrahim Bouabid revealed that the Istiqlal had requested half the seats in the Council and had been given just under half, a minimum below which they refused to go. He added, "It is far from expressing the importance that we actually have in the country, and numerous are our cadres and militants who have accepted it only with resignation."[7]

On December 7, 1955, the first Council of Government of independent Morocco[8] swore loyalty to the King. The Istiqlal had ten of

<hr />

[6] *Al-Alam*, from series of articles between August 19 and September 4, 1957, U.S. Embassy Press Translations, "Where Are We?"

[7] See "Motion de la Commission Politique de Congrès Extraordinaire du Parti de l'Istiqlal, réuni à Rabat du 2 au 4 décembre 1955," *Al-Istiqlal*, August 17, 1956, pp. 5 and 9.

[8] See *O.B.* no. 2252, December 23, 1955, "Dahir 7 décembre 1955 (22 rebia II 1375), relatif à la constitution du gouvernement," pp. 1870-1871.

the twenty-one cabinet posts, but directed only two major ministries, Agriculture and Justice. Two of the three Ministers of State were Istiqlal members, which suggests the importance they attached to the negotiations. Allal Al-Fassi, the Leader of the party, and Balafrej, the Secretary General, decided not to take posts, though they were certainly entitled to them. Before the first change of government the Istiqlal enlarged its representation considerably. Balafrej joined the Council late in April as Minister of Foreign Affairs and Driss M'Hammedi was "Acting" Minister of the Interior from the time of the Franco-Moroccan Agreement. After that time the Istiqlal had all the important posts in the Council except the Ministry of Defense, created just before independence, which was given to a leader of the Liberal Independent party, Reda Guedira. Though the Democratic party was given more seats than its strength probably would merit, they were all among five smaller ministries. The Democratic party, nevertheless, had two important posts for building its popularity and strength, Youth and Sports and Labor and Social Questions. Among the ministries filled by "independents" was found a post to represent the Jewish minority. The three most important independents, all in important positions, were the confidants of the King, Bekkai, Zaghari, and Lyoussi. The subordinate administrative structure of the first Council of Government corresponded almost exactly to the Directorates and Services under the Protectorate.

Only two months after the Franco-Moroccan Agreement the Istiqlal began to criticize the accomplishments and policy of the first Council, even though they occupied important positions in it.[9] In August 1956 the party's National Council agreed that the first government "had been imposed by artificial circumstances created during the Aix-les-Bains conversations."[10] During the meeting of the National Council the party newspaper admitted that there were serious differences between the Istiqlal ministers and the rest of the Bekkai government, though it also admitted shortly after the meeting that the mission for which the first Council had been assembled was not yet actually accomplished.[11] The General Resolution called

[9] *Al-Alam*, July 10, 1956, French Embassy Press Translations (to be abbreviated hereafter as Fr. Trans.), editorial stressing growing problem of unemployment and worsening economic crisis. It acknowledges the necessary concern of the government with the immediate problems of independence, but stresses the many economic reforms that are needed urgently.

[10] *Al-Istiqlal*, August 24, 1956, "Resolution Générale," p. 7.

[11] *Al-Alam*, August 26, 1956, Interview with Allal Al-Fassi, p. 1, Fr. Trans.

TABLE 3
Members of the First Five Councils of Government

Ministry	First (December 7, 1955, to October 27, 1956)	Second (October 28, 1956, to May 11, 1958)	Third (May 12, 1958, to December 23, 1958)	Fourth (December 24, 1958, to May 23, 1960)	Fifth (May 24, 1960—)
President	M'Barek Ben Bekkai— Independent	M'Barek Ben Bekkai— Independent	Ahmed Balafrej— Istiqlal	Abdallah Ibrahim[a]— Istiqlal	Mohammed Ben Youssef— the King
Vice President	Mohammed Zeghari— Independent	vacant	Abderrahmin Bouabid— Istiqlal	Abderrahmin Bouabid[a]— Istiqlal	Moulay Hassan— the Prince
Foreign Affairs	Ahmed Balafrej[a]— Istiqlal	Ahmed Balafrej— Istiqlal	see President	see President	Driss M'Hammedi— Istiqlal
Justice	Abdelkrim Benjelloun— Istiqlal	Abdelkrim Benjelloun— Istiqlal	Abdelkrim Benjelloun— Istiqlal	M'Hammed Bahnini— Independent	Abdelkhader Torrès[a]— Istiqlal
Interior	Lahcen Lyoussi[b]— Independent	Driss M'Hammedi— Istiqlal	Messaoud Chiguer[a]— Istiqlal	Driss M'Hammedi— Istiqlal	M'Barek Ben Bekkai— Independent
Defense	Ahmed Reda Guedira[c]— Liberal Independent	Mohammed Zeghari— Independent	Ahmed Lyazidi— Istiqlal	Mohammed Aouad— Istiqlal	see Vice President
Agriculture	Ahmed Ben Mansour Nejjai— Istiqlal	Omar Abdeljalil— Istiqlal	see Vice President	Thami Ammar[a]— Istiqlal	Hassan Zemmouri— Independent
Finance	Abdelkader Benjelloun— Democrat				
Commerce and Industry	Ahmed Lyazidi— Istiqlal	Abderrahmin Bouabid[a]— Istiqlal	see Vice President	see Vice President	Mohammed Douiri— Istiqlal
Industrial Production and Mines	Thami Ouazzani— Democrat				
Public Works	Mohammed Douiri— Istiqlal	Mohammed Douiri— Istiqlal	Mohammed Douiri— Istiqlal	Abderrahmin Ben Abdellai— Independent	Abderrahmane Ben Abdellali— Istiqlal
Urban Affairs and Housing	Mohammed Ben Bouchaib— Democrat				

nistry	First (December 7, 1955, to October 27, 1956)	Second (October 28, 1956, to May 11, 1958)	Third (May 12, 1958, to December 23, 1958)	Fourth (December 24, 1958, to May 23, 1960)	Fifth (May 24, 1960—)
ucation	Mohammed Al-Fassi— Istiqlal	Mohammed Al-Fassi— Istiqlal	Omar Abdeljalil— Istiqlal	Abdelkrim Benjelloun— Istiqlal	Abdelkrim Benjelloun— Istiqlal
uth l Sports	Ahmed Ben Souda— Democrat				
blic Health l Sanitation	Dr. Abdelmalek Faraj— Independent	Dr. Abdelmalek Faraj— Independent	Dr. Abdelmalek Faraj[a]— Independent	Dr. Youssef Ben Abbès— Independent	**Dr.** **Youssef** **Ben Abbès—** **Independent**
bor and cial estions	Abdelhai Boutaleb— Democrat	Abdallah Ibrahim— Istiqlal	Al-Bachir Ben Al-Abbes— Independent	Maoti Bouabid— Independent	Dr. Abdelkrim Khatib— Popular Movement
st, Tele- ne, and legraph	Leon Benzaquen[d]— Independent	Leon Benzaquen— Independent	Mohammed Aouad[a]— Istiqlal	Captain Mohammed Medboh— Independent	Mohammed Cherkaoui— Istiqlal
ormation l Touring	Abdallah Ibrahim— Istiqlal[e]	Reda Ahmed Guedira— Liberal **Independent**	[b]		Moulay Ahmed Al-Alaoui[b]— Independent
bous	Mokhtar Soussi— Istiqlal	[b]			
vil Service	none	Rachid Mouline[e]— Liberal Independent	[b]		M'Hammed Boucetta[c]— Istiqlal
nisters of te	Driss M'Hammedi[f]— Istiqlal Abderrahmin Bouabid— Istiqlal Reda Ahmed Guedira— Liberal Independent				

TABLE NOTES FOLLOW

First Council:

ᵃ Balafrej was not appointed until April 26, 1956, when the ministry was created.

ᵇ Replaced by Driss M'Hammedi as Acting Minister on May 4, 1956.

ᶜ Not appointed until ministry was created on April 26, 1956.

ᵈ Not appointed until December 26, 1955.

ᵉ At rank of Secretary of State in this Council.

ᶠ The Ministers of State ceased to function with the signing of the Franco-Moroccan Agreement of March 2, 1956.

Second Council:

ᵃ The Ministry of National Economy was formed from the three previous ministries with a Secretary of State for each.

ᵇ Although continuing to function as a ministry, it has not been included in the list of governmental appointments since the first Council. For all practical purposes it operates as an autonomous ministry under the Palace.

ᶜ Created with this Council and merged with the President's Office thereafter.

Third Council:

ᵃ Denotes ministers objected to by the progressive wing of the Istiqlal.

ᵇ Both ministries merged under the President of the Council from this government.

Fourth Council:

ᵃ Ministers associated with the Istiqlal splinter party founded in late 1959.

Fifth Council:

ᵃ Torrés was not appointed until late in 1960. M'Hammed Bahnini, Secretary General of the government in this Council, served as interim Minister of Justice.

ᵇ Information was again given ministerial status. Al-Alaoui had been the Press Officer of the Palace since independence.

ᶜ Civil Service was again given ministerial status, but with the additional responsibility of "Moroccanization."

---

for the resignation of the Istiqlal ministers and the formation of a "homogeneous" government, but, after a meeting with the King, the Executive Committee denied that such would be done. The Istiqlal attack was followed by a sharp reply from Bekkai, who pointed out that the protesting ministers had over half the posts in the Council and concluded, "There is no crisis of the government, but a crisis of trust."[12] With this exchange the disagreement within the Council was fully revealed, but the King declined to change the

[12] *C.M.*, August 31, 1956, p. 1, and Annex IX; see the Istiqlal reply in *Al-Alam*, September 2, 1956, p. 1, Fr. Trans., charging that he had broken the "rules of government" and that he had no right to make such a statement without permission of the other ministers, though the Istiqlal had felt free to attack him.

Council. The immediate cause of the fall of the first government was not the Istiqlal, which was apparently sufficiently satisfied with the present Council to preclude a full-scale government crisis. Not until two months later, with the abduction of the F.L.N. leaders by the Algerian French administration and the subsequent uprising against French residents in the Moroccan province of Meknes, did Bekkai feel compelled to submit his resignation.

Since the change of government resulted from a crisis in relations with France, the Istiqlal was not free to take full advantage of the situation. Still in the midst of negotiations for the integration of Tangier and for cultural, administrative, technical, and economic aid, the Moroccans needed to preserve a government most likely to reconstruct French confidence. The second Council of Government[13] represented the first major rearrangement of the administrative structure inherited from the French. The Secretaries of State for Finance and Commerce and Industry were placed under the common direction of a new Ministry of National Economy. The Ministry of Urban Affairs and Housing was merged with the Ministry of Public Works, and the Secretary of State for Youth and Sports was subordinated to the Ministry of National Education. The changes in personnel are no doubt more significant as an indicator of the evolution of the political system over the first eleven months of independence. The Democratic party chose not to participate at all, since the posts offered them were not considered proportionate to their strength.

The Liberal Independents received two seats on the new Council, though not important posts. Reda Guedira was removed from his direction of the Ministry of National Defense, to be replaced by an independent and confidant of the King, Mohammed Zeghari. Guedira became Minister of Information and Tourism, a post that was a secretary of state, while another Liberal Independent, Rachid Mouline, became Minister of State for the Civil Service.[14] With the exception of the Minister of Defense and the President of the Coun-

[13] See *O.B.*, no. 2301, November 30, 1956, pp. 1365-1366, "Dahir no. 1-56-269 du 23 rebia I 1376 (28 octobre 1956), portant constitution du nouveau ministère," and Appendix II.

[14] See *O.B.*, no. 2307, January 11, 1957, "Dahir no. 1-57-001 du 3 joumada II 1376 (5 janvier 1957), relatif aux attributions du ministre d'Etat chargé de la fonction publique," p. 42. The office was to supervise regulation of the civil service, control its formation, supervise the Moroccan School of Administration, and, in general, coordinate all activities of the civil service. It is not clear whether the tardiness of defining the powers of the ministry were because of opposition from other ministers or because of administrative problems in its organization.

101

cil, all major posts were in the hands of Istiqlal members. Among the Istiqlal ministers, the most important changes were the appointments of Omar Abdeljalil as Minister of Agriculture and Abderrahmin Bouabid as Minister of the National Economy. Aside from the formalization of Driss M'Hammedi's position as Minister of the Interior, which he had held since early May, the other Istiqlal members of the Council remained in the same posts. With the exception of Bekkai and Guedira, the second Council of Government was virtually the "homogeneous" government that the Istiqlal had demanded the preceding summer.[15]

In 1957 the new country was occupied with reconstructing its relations with France, combatting the effects of a serious drought, and starting the conversion of the administrative structure left from the Protectorate. Though the Istiqlal put severe pressure on the Democratic party, no open party disputes began until the attacks by the Istiqlal on the Liberal Independents. As has frequently been the case in other nations, the first criticism came from the Istiqlal Youth, who held their second congress at Tangier in September 1957. In their final motions they protested the "incapacity" of the Ministry of Information and Tourism, particularly for its negligence in publicizing the campaign to regain Morocco's historic boundaries.[16] Soon afterward Guedira was personally criticized in an editorial of Mehdi Ben Barka, and criticism continued in the party newspaper.

Early in 1958 the Istiqlal's criticisms turned again to the Democratic party, whose presence at the Cairo Afro-Asian Conference had given the opposition party a new appeal. This was followed by a series of demonstrations in the *bidonvilles* of Casablanca and a series of exchanges between the Istiqlal and the Democratic parties regarding the propriety of making political issues of foreign policy problems. Whether the subsequent action was more justified because of the potential threat to public order or to Istiqlal influence is not clear, but the Minister of the Interior forbade all public meetings. With special powers given him during the Sakiet-Sidi-Youssef at-

[15] In its editorial comment following the installation of the new Council, *Al-Alam* admitted that this was a "homogeneous" government under the King, October 28, 1956, p. 1, Fr. Trans.
[16] *Al-Istiqlal*, no. 734, October 5, 1957, p. 14. Since youth activities have not yet been considered in this book, it should be cautioned that they are not quite the same as similar groups in the United States. In Morocco "youth" generally include many up to twenty-five or even thirty years of age and, including a large proportion of the most articulate members of the country, has much more political interest than its American counterpart.

tack in Tunisia, he also banned all publications of the Democratic party.

Perhaps the most important element contributing to the second change in the Council was the development of a new political group, the Popular Movement. Its first public manifestation was a press conference in October 1957, in which Mahjoub Ahardane, then governor of Rabat City, was the spokesman. The governor was immediately removed for his "indiscipline" and for starting a political movement illegally, though the regulations concerning political bodies had not been changed since the Protectorate. Severely attacked by the Istiqlal as remnants of "colonialism," the group was officially inactive until the spring of 1958, when Bekkai decided to endorse a petition to the King on civil liberties presented to him by representatives of this group and other opposition parties. The Istiqlal ministers resigned the same day and charged that Bekkai had engaged in "secret activity" and had betrayed his promise to preserve "independence of opinion" in his office.

The immediate cause of the crisis was alleged to be the excessive powers of the Minister of the Interior in a new *dahir* regulating the activities of political groups. The King began consultations to form a new government immediately, but the tense period in Algerian affairs at that time, the difficulties in assigning posts to new members, and the definition of the conditions under which the Istiqlal would take full control of the Council delayed the final selection for nearly a month. The King received delegations of every opinion, including the Popular Movement, the resistance, the Liberation Army, and the Moroccan Federation of Labor. Before the announcement of the new President of the Council was made, the King issued a Royal Charter outlining the conditions under which the new government would take office and the major problems concerning the country at that moment. In last-minute difficulties over the selection of ministers, the new Council[17] was not announced until three days after Balafrej had been designated President. Though the Istiqlal had once again demanded that a "homogeneous" government be formed, the new Council included two independents and one Istiqlal minister who did not qualify as a strong party man. The Istiqlal paper gave full support to the new ministers, but admitted that three of them were not chosen by Balafrej. A signed editorial of Mehdi

[17] See *O.B.*, no. 2378, May 23, 1958, "Dahir no. 1-58-152 du 22 chaoual 1377 (12 mai 1958) portant constitution du nouveau ministère," p. 806.

Ben Barka not only admitted that the government was not "entirely homogeneous," but specified that the Ministers of the Interior, Public Health and Post, Telegraph and Telephone were not approved by the party.[18]

The two members of the Council generally regarded as independents were Faraj, of the Ministry of Public Health, and Mohammed Aouad, of Post, Telegraph and Telephone, although the latter belonged to the Istiqlal party. In line with the recommendations made during the crisis by the Istiqlal,[19] the ministries accorded to the Civil Service and Information and Tourism were reduced to secretaries of state under the President of the Council. The new structure meant that both organizations built up under the Liberal Independents would be integrated under Istiqlal ministers. This left a Council of twelve ministries that were divided among ten men, since Balafrej continued as Foreign Minister, as well as President of the Council, and Bouabid directed both the Ministries of National Economy and of Agriculture, as well as occupying the office of Vice President of the Council. Both the Minister of Post, Telegraph, and Telephone, Mohammed Aouad, and the Minister of the Interior, Messaoud Chiguer, had close connections with the Palace. The former had been Chief of the King's cabinet and the latter had been Director of the Royal Cabinet since independence.[20] The appointment of what was regarded by the party as a weak Istiqlal member in the Ministry of the Interior was a considerable concession by the party. The ministry was still engaged in drafting legislation for civil liberties, elections, and supervision of the regional administration of the country. A more difficult change to interpret was the departure of Abdallah Ibrahim as Minister of Labor and Social Questions. Ibrahim was the strongest spokesman of the trade unions in the previous Council. The absence of any prominent leader of the labor movement was a serious weakness in the new Council; it also revealed the increasing differences of the Istiqlal leaders.

[18] Translation from *Al-Alam* in *Al-Istiqlal*, May 18, 1958, p. 5.

[19] *Al-Istiqlal*, April 20, 1958, p. 7. They actually occur in a resolution passed by the National Consultative Assembly, which was in session during part of the crisis. Though there are some representatives of other parties in the Assembly, it includes a majority of Istiqlal adherents, according to the party press, *Al-Alam*, April 27, 1958, p. 1, U.S. Trans.

[20] See particularly the comment of *France Observateur*, no. 418, May 15, 1958, p. 8, and *Le Monde*, May 13, 1958, p. 3, for more background on the new ministers.

From Balafrej to Ibrahim

The formation of the Balafrej government was accompanied with two precedents—the proclamation of a Royal Charter by the King and a statement of program by the new President. Substantively they are of interest as an inventory of the progress of the country and as an indication of the priority placed on the goals of the country. The Royal Charter was noticeably different from the statement of Balafrej. The immediate concern of the King was reflected in the Charter's concentration on anticipated institutional reforms dealing only with politics: delegation of authority to the ministers, a law on civil and political rights, elections, and an indirectly elected representative body.[21] In line with these reforms the King also acknowledged that the rural communes were a prerequisite of elections and that the communes could not be based on the deteriorating tribal structure. In the former two years of formal independence none of these issues had been settled. By the time the Balafrej government fell in December 1958, only the charter of civil liberties had been promulgated and this had been under study by the Secretary of the Government for at least a year.

Balafrej did not give this exclusive emphasis to political problems. This was, no doubt, in part the reflection of the differences among the leaders of the Istiqlal. Balafrej may have been trying to gain popular support, which would indirectly accumulate to his benefit via the members of the party. His inclusive program sounded more like a party platform than a projected course of action for a single government. There were subsections on each major activity of the government that coincided almost exactly with the work of each ministry. In slightly more detail the statement also included all the points made by the Charter. The most striking difference was the carefully prescribed economic program, which probably was outlined by Bouabid. The specific economic reforms were a law to encourage investment, tariff reform to protect local industry, and a renewed effort to complete the economic plan. Of these reforms, only the investment law was completed over the next seven months of the government, although some attempt was made to design an

[21] Both the King and Balafrej discussed briefly the aims of the new government in speeches at the formal appointment of the third Council of Government, though they seem to have been of ceremonial significance. The series of palace and government communiqués surrounding the appointment is indicative of the difficult circumstances under which Balafrej took office. See *O.B.*, no. 2379, pp. 835-836, for these two speeches.

economic plan. The Balafrej government did manage a thorough overhauling of the educational system, which had suffered seriously from too rapid expansion. This was completed in the fall of 1958. Of the legal reforms envisaged in new penal, civil, and nationality codes, only the latter was prepared by the end of 1958.

As Lacouture commented six weeks after the formation of the Balafrej Council of Government, a situation that had been viewed originally as the achievement of the Istiqlal's ideal of homogeneous government rapidly became "a crisis of unprecedented virulence and gravity."[22] By July 1958 there was a serious strike in Rabat, where the police intervened in a sympathy strike of all workers, including government workers. Labor disorders rose sharply throughout the country, while the labor leaders abandoned their seats on Istiqlal executive committees and refused to contribute to the party newspapers. Ben Barka published in *Al-Istiqlal* a speech of Ibrahim which sharply denounced the "intellectual aristocracy, whose members live among themselves, totally separate from the people, distant from its realities."[23] Over the summer the newspaper disappeared during an internecine party struggle, in which two friends of Balafrej, Douiri and Boucetta, literally seized the paper's plant in Casablanca. If the existing institutions were unsuitable for an expression of the popular will, they were, nonetheless, sufficient to bring about an expression of the divisions in the party. The experience of the Balafrej government is a warning against discounting the importance of institutions in a new country, no matter how ineffective they might be in relation to the entire political system.

The new government became the focus of party tensions before it was in office and by December 1958 had given way to the leadership of Ibrahim, its most outspoken critic. For a moment in September it looked as if the Balafrej group had won out. Ibrahim was detained by the police in Casablanca, who had been directed to investigate his finances. Ben Barka made plans for an extended voyage to Yugoslavia and the Chinese Republic, after having been removed as editor of *Al-Istiqlal* and reportedly severely censured. A *rapprochement* was established by agreeing within the party to suspend the controversy until the Istiqlal Congress, planned for January 1959.[24] The party leaders and their supporters were alarmed by the growing un-

[22] *Le Monde*, July 2, 1958, p. 3.
[23] *Al-Istiqlal*, June 22, 1958, p. 9.
[24] Interview with Mehdi Ben Barka, President, National Consultative Assembly, Rabat, November 4, 1958.

rest in the countryside. They were especially concerned over the diffusion of their dispute into the ranks of the Liberation Army around Bou Arfa. At least one small battle took place between factions loyal to the old-guard leader, Al-Fassi, and to Fqih Mohammed Al-Basri, the leading resistance delegate on the party's Political Committee and also a friend of Ibrahim.

The catalyst in this momentary reconciliation was Bouabid, who had been abroad during much of the summer. Immediately on his return, two days after Ibrahim had been detained, he visited the King, along with the leaders of the dissident faction of the Istiqlal. The use of the police to discredit a leader of the Istiqlal Left undoubtedly infuriated the critics of the Balafrej government, of whom Bouabid was the only one remaining in the Council of Government. He was also perturbed over the rural discontent and slowness of the implementation of the economic reforms.[25] Balafrej offered to resign at that time, but was dissuaded by Bouabid, who favored making changes in the existing cabinet.[26] The posts in question were probably the Ministers of the Interior, of Labor and Social Questions, and of Post, Telephone, and Telegraph, which had been questioned by the radical group when Balafrej formed his Council of Government.

The development of the conflict over the fall of 1958 is an interesting commentary on the difficulties of designating authority in a new country. When Balafrej returned from Paris talks in mid-October he let slip the comment that "internal tensions of the government are no longer a secret from anyone."[27] Although he later denied having made the statement, each day brought a new flood of rumors about the reconstruction of the Council of Government. Bouabid later revealed that he had submitted his resignation for the first time in October, perhaps because some of the promises made in the September compromise had not been fulfilled. In November the localized rural rebellions spread to the Rif and the Middle Atlas Mountains. With governmental authority rejected by the countryside and by the urban Istiqlal progressives, the country was dangerously near collapse. Though it was not announced for two weeks,

[25] See the comment in *Le Monde*, November 27, 1958, p. 1, after the crisis became public. Also Bouabid's letter of resignation, *La Vigie*, November 23, 1958, p. 1.
[26] According to a letter by Balafrej written in reply to Bouabid's letter of resignation, *La Vigie Marocaine* (hereafter referred to as *La Vigie*), November 25, 1958, p. 1. Balafrej drove his point home by suggesting that Bouabid had betrayed the responsibility assumed thereby, although no changes were made in the cabinet between this time and Bouabid's resignation on November 10, 1958.
[27] *Le Monde*, October 18, 1958, p. 3.

Bouabid had submitted his resignation to the King on the tenth of November.

The seriousness of the crisis was underlined in late November when Bouabid decided to make his resignation public—an unprecedented step that forced the issue. Balafrej also sought popular support by releasing to the press his letter of reply to Bouabid. Balafrej was especially firm in his rejection of a change in the Minister of the Interior; he wrote that the "intransigence" of the group favoring the return of M'Hammedi was "incomprehensible."[28] During the following weeks the unsuccessful attempts at compromise reportedly included appointing the moderate Ahmed Lyazidi to the Ministry of the Interior, Ben Barka to the Ministry of National Education, and returning Ibrahim to the Ministry of Labor and Social Questions. A complete dissolution of the Council of Government was, however, postponed. With the revolts in the countryside becoming more serious and many signs of violence spreading to the cities, the Council was under heavy pressure to keep the machinery of government going.

To resolve the crisis the King turned first to Allal Al-Fassi, the only major political figure of the country who was still publicly uncommitted. The Leader no doubt hoped to avoid an irreparable split of the Istiqlal. The gravity of the conflict was indicated when Al-Fassi's "mission of conciliation" failed. The changes he proposed were to make Ibrahim the Minister of the Interior, Ben Barka the Minister of National Education, and M'Hammedi the Minister of Justice.[29] This arrangement failed because Bouabid insisted that M'Hammedi, who was very familiar with the tribes and spoke the Berber dialect, should be given the Interior post. More surprising was the refusal of Balafrej to continue at the head of such a Council of Government, even with the plan of Al-Fassi. With this check, the King, who had tried to remain the mediating figure, could no longer abstain from taking a leading role.

The Istiqlal was certainly the losing player. Not only had it been unable to take advantage of the opportunity given by the King to mend the split, but it had publicly revealed its inability to help the nation in a moment of national emergency. Harassed by a new

[28] *La Vigie*, November 25, 1958, p. 1. Because of his own long association with the Ministry of Foreign Affairs, he also took strong exception to Bouabid's comment that the ministry should have been separated from the Presidency of the Council.

[29] *Le Monde*, November 29, 1958, p. 6.

rash of bitter attacks from the trade unions and more clashes between the Royal Army and the tribes, the King decided to designate the next Council of Government without reference to political parties. Balafrej resigned early in December, and for nearly three weeks during this troubled period Morocco went without a government. The provisional program for the new government leaked out through the Istiqlal press before the Council was finally selected. It was announced that the new Council would concentrate on reform of the security forces, unemployment, preparation for elections, and improvement of the rural administration.[30]

When Ibrahim was called upon by the King, the limited purpose of the new Council was further outlined. The King decided that the members would participate "personally" (*à titre personnel*), that the main purpose of the Council would be to prepare for elections, and that, therefore, the term of this Council would be of limited duration. On December 24 the fourth Council of Government was formally appointed under Ibrahim's Presidency and without any associates of Balafrej.[31]

The opinions of Ibrahim were last stated in a speech to Istiqlal students before he took office, though it is doubtful if the conditions laid down by the King for the new government would permit their fulfillment: "The riches of the country are inequitably divided among the inhabitants. A hundredth of the population, including the Europeans, possess twenty per cent of the Moroccan land. European capital directs our economy in a manner that does not profit the Moroccan nation. We wish to revise our social and economic orientation, taking account of the interests of the masses. Our program should be realistic and progressist."[32] Perhaps a more sober appraisal of the future of the Ibrahim government was given by the agenda of the first official meeting of the Council of Government. The problems to be discussed were how to end the fighting in the Rif, how to adjust the Moroccan franc to the recent devaluation in France, and the first concrete steps toward holding elections.

The fourth Council of Government made no important changes

[30] *Al-Alam*, translated in *Le Monde*, December 13, 1958, p. 2.

[31] For biographical notes on Ibrahim see *Le Monde*, December 18, 1958, p. 5, and *La Vigie*, December 17, 1958, p. 2. See also *O.B.*, December 26, 1958, no. 2409, "Dahir no. 1-58-409 du 12 joumada II 1378 (24 décembre 1958) portant constitution du nouveau ministère," p. 2096.

[32] *Le Monde*, December 26, 1958, p. 3. Some allowance should be made here for the fact that he was speaking before a youth group, which is generally more radical than an adult group.

in the government's administrative structure. The Ministry of Agriculture returned to its pre-Balafrej status outside the Ministry of National Economy, but was headed by a man aligned with Bouabid, Thami Ammar. A special secretary of state, who was probably to be concerned with the mechanics of the elections, was established under Hassan Zemmouri.[33] The striking innovation was, of course, the change of personalities. Of the eleven ministers, seven had never participated in the Council of Government and at least four had had very little experience in government. The King had followed his intention of selecting men according to their technical competence. He had also lost several very competent men of Balafrej's entourage who had refused to participate.

The extent to which the King had been drawn into the bargaining was also much clearer than in former Councils. M'Hammed-Bahnini, the new Minister of Justice, was a long-time confidant of the King. The King's friend, Mohammed Aouad, became the Minister of Defense, a post closely supervised by the Palace since independence, which was one of the main controversies during the Balafrej government. Captain Medboh was a Royal Army officer who was also trusted by the King and no doubt included as a concession to the tribesmen. Maoti Bouabid, Abderrahmin Ben Abdellai, and Dr. Youssef Ben Abbès were newcomers and supposedly specialists in their fields: labor and social affairs, public works, and public health, respectively. The "team" of Ibrahim was clearly Bouabid, Ammar, and M'Hammedi, who had been the key man in the controversy. Among them they supervised the economic sector of governmental activity and the rural administration. The emphasis on elections was also made clear by putting the two men who had had the largest part in the electoral planning, Bahnini and Zemmouri, in key posts for the supervision of elections.

The experience of the Balafrej Council and the formation of the Ibrahim Council were of particular importance, for they encompassed a period when the new political system probably came close to disintegration. Probably not by coincidence it was also the period when traditional, coercive, institutional, and charismatic influence all came into play on related problems or aspects of the same problem

[33] Zemmouri had been the assistant to Ahmed Bahnini, formerly Director of Political Affairs in the Ministry of the Interior and Minister of Justice in the new government. Zemmouri had been in charge of all local commissions working on the formation of electoral districts.

at the national level. The societal substructure of the new nation no longer resolved or diverted demands from a large number of participants, who expressed themselves at the national level in the various ways that their background permitted. For a moment the national government felt the burden of resolving interests and expectations of many Moroccans—a problem that seldom impinges directly on the governments of advanced nations. A new nation cannot specialize in the highly formal way common to political systems of advanced nations until its citizens understand such specialization. Such specialization itself means that the more delicate, concrete governmental structures of advanced nations are insulated in ways quite difficult to reproduce in new nations.

Another particularly interesting aspect of the crisis was the demonstration of the part that formal institutions may play in rapidly developing political systems. The Council of Government was inherited from the Protectorate, whose main problem had been harmonizing the pattern of influence in Morocco with that of France. When the same institution was transposed to the new nation, its significance changed completely. By coercion, guidance, and close supervision the French and Spanish had made such specialized institutions operate smoothly. The entire organizational foundation for this control was swept away by independence and was only gradually being rebuilt, while the educated members of Moroccan society carried on their political struggle in the outmoded Council of Government. The formal structure of the government did not change noticeably, although very likely it was unsuitable and often meaningless to large numbers of players in the new political system.

Lawmaking and Legal Reform

The usefulness of the Council of Government as a supervisor of the administration has been increasingly limited since independence. The interministerial commission has been a device to circumvent the Council and to permit direct representation of elements particularly concerned with various specific problems. The administrative structure was not equipped for many functions that, under the Protectorate, were neglected or simply left to administrative services of France or Spain. Many problems, such as the selection and training of professional and technical cadres, had been simply left to the political systems of France or Spain, which were no longer directly concerned with the future need for skilled man power in Morocco.[34] The special commissions did not become numerous until after the first change in government, though a group designated by the King early in 1956 to make plans for the Royal Army was certainly an indication of the administrative improvisation needed for carrying on the affairs of the new state. Among the commissions that were started to deal with temporary problems was the Committee of Aid for the North, a group of government ministers and representatives of private organizations assembled to give help to the newly integrated citizens of the ex-Spanish zone before the appropriate governmental agencies existed on a scale sufficient to handle the problem.

The first major interministerial committee was for economic affairs.[35] Directions for this committee suggest some of the difficulties of the government at that time. It was to supervise the execution of decisions taken in the Council and to assure "permanent coordination" between those departments concerned with them. Except for the President of the Council, all the ministries represented on the committee were directed by Istiqlal members. In view of the Istiqlal criticisms of the economic affairs under the direction of the Democratic party in the first Council, the formation of this commission indicates that the economic reorientation of the new nation, even under ministers of the same party, was not easy to accomplish.

The institution of interministerial commissions, often with representatives from outside the government, was expanded under the second Council. In the absence of a legislative body, it appeared to be a convenient and workable method for permitting more highly organized groups not only to present their views, but to take a part in making basic decisions regarding the future of Morocco. The administrative function of such commissions for the government no doubt remained, but added to this was the provision of direct representation of other organizations and indirect representation of groups. Perhaps even more important, such participation in policy-making took place without publicity and final reports did not record individual contributions. In this way members of nongovernmental groups

---

[34] Whether or not France or Spain ever gave full attention to this general problem of the economic and social development of Morocco is another question, and one that is quite impossible to study with available data. The important point is that whatever was done by them along these lines is no longer being done except as specifically requested and authorized through diplomatic channels.

[35] *O.B.*, no. 2307, January 11, 1957, "Dahir no. 2-56-1382 du 21 joumada I 1376 (24 décembre 1956) portant création d'un comité économique interministériel," pp. 36-37.

have virtually acted in ministerial positions, although not in the government, and have also enjoyed bureaucratic anonymity.

The most important of such bodies was the Superior Council of the Plan,[36] which was established in mid-1957 to prepare an economic program for 1960 to 1964. The Council included all the ministers of the interministerial commission for economic affairs, plus three members from the National Consultative Assembly, three workers' representatives, and six from various segments of the economy itself. The latter nine members were appointed on recommendation of the Minister of National Economy. With the predominance of the Istiqlal in the Council of Government and in the National Assembly, the party had a predominant voice in economic planning. Given the important role of economic affairs in the transition from colonial status and the concentration of economic supervision in the Moroccan Ministry of National Economy, this Council began to approximate the importance of the Council of Government itself.

The new Council of the Plan was somewhat slow in getting started, particularly in view of the constant stress by the Istiqlal on economic planning and reorientation of the productive system. Handicapped by a poor agricultural year, formation of a national budget, integration of the economy of the Spanish zone, and adjustments with the deteriorating French franc, coordinated effort began slowly. The Plan Council met only once in 1957 and the working commission was not in operation until 1958.[37] The first working meetings of the Plan Council took place after the formation of the third Council of Government, when it was convened to consider the interim plan for 1958-1959. The published discussions of this meeting indicate that the Plan remained largely the individual efforts of various ministries to ameliorate various, long-standing problems in their respective fields of activity.

A second interministerial commission for social affairs[38] was started to coordinate all activities of the concerned ministries, except those affairs already under the supervision of the commission on

[36] *O.B.*, no. 2333, July 12, 1957, "Dahir no. 1-57-183 (22 juin 1957) prescrivant l'établissement d'un plan de developpement économique et social et instutuant un conseil supérieur du plan," p. 861.

[37] *O.B.*, no. 2353, November 29, 1957, "Dahir no. 2-57-1604 du 27 rebia II 1377 (21 novembre 1957) portant nomination des membres de la commission centrale d'études et de financement," p. 1509. Of the eighteen members of the study group, ten are French.

[38] *O.B.*, no. 2344, September 27, 1957, "Dahir no. 2-57-1130 du 16 safar 1377 (12 septembre 1957) portant création d'un comité social interministériel," p. 1268.

economic affairs. The social affairs commission held its first meeting in December 1957 and decided to form a subordinate group, the Commission for Professional Training. Gradually, and sometimes rapidly, losing the professional and technical cadre of French nationality, considerable effort was needed just to replace losses as well as to provide for new social services and economic growth. No doubt stimulated by their own desire to be independent of French assistance, some progress had been made through efforts of individual ministries. In the third Council of Government an undersecretary of state was designated for the "formation of cadres and technical education."

In early 1958 another special group was designated to begin the complete revision of Morocco's legislation.[39] Since the commission included the entire Council of Government, the first step was to divide the revision among subgroups, which apparently were to review all legislation inherited from the Protectorate applicable to each ministry. The commission did not meet until six months later under the third Council of Government. Responsible to the King and including only those ministers directly concerned were three other important commissions dealing with the codification of Muslim law, national defense, and the investigation of those persons accused of offenses against the King and nationalists before independence. The King's reservation regarding the codification of Muslim law stemmed both from his position as *imam*, or spiritual leader, of the faithful of Morocco and his historic interest in the problem.

The legal reforms were an essential prelude to reorganization of the government. The historic complaint of the nationalists was that the French had unjustifiably restricted the application of Muslim law. Under the French administration the delegation of judicial powers to local administrators and the concentration of authority under the central administration had been used to suppress the nationalist movement and also to preserve tribal customary law instead of orthodox Muslim law. Two of the first acts of the new nation were to relieve all local administrative officials of their judicial powers and to proclaim the "principle of separation of powers." The goal of the new legal system was to revive the application of Muslim law in modified form.

[39] *O.B.*, February 14, 1958, no. 2364, "Dahir no. 1-57-300 du 7 rejeb 1377 (28 janvier 1958) relatif à la création à la présidence du conseil d'une commission d'étude chargée de la revision totale de la législation en vigueur dans le royaume du Maroc," p. 287.

Over the first two years of independence most of the basic judicial reforms were begun. In the fall of 1956 the first two hundred judge-delegates (*juges-deleguées*) were appointed and the famous Berber *dahir* was officially rescinded.[40] By 1958 six hundred judge-delegates, roughly equivalent to justices of the peace, had been appointed and eighty-five courts of the lowest level organized.[41] These courts were limited to giving sentences of two years' imprisonment in criminal proceedings and 90,000 francs' fine in civil proceedings. Special efforts were made to appoint the first new judges in regions where colonial separatist activity among the tribes had been most intensive, like Tafilalet, or where Rabat had been weakly represented, as in the ex-Spanish zone. Available evidence does not permit evaluation of local tribal resistance to the abolition of the customary courts. Although the tribal revolts of late 1958 took place in areas of strong tribal loyalties, there have been no signs of tension in other parts of Morocco where tribes remain similarly intact.

The new nation needed help from France in even this distinctively Muslim endeavor. The organization of the higher courts was delayed until the judicial convention could be signed with France. In late 1958 one hundred and seventy French judges were on loan to the Moroccan government. Even more restrictive than the delay in negotiations for French aid, which stemmed from the Algerian incident of late 1956, was the lack of Moroccan personnel to fill the lower posts in the new judicial system. Commenting on the problem of implementing the "separation of powers" in early 1957, the Istiqlal's *Internal Bulletin* said: "There do not exist enough trained persons to fill these different posts in order to implement separation of authority. Capable judges, *caids*, and pashas are few so that the project has moved slowly, but the Ministry of Justice is doing its best to establish courts over all Morocco to facilitate the separation of administrative authority from judicial authority by the end of next March."[42]

Although Morocco was probably better prepared to institute legal reforms than any other major change in the political system, the ease with which this apparently was accomplished merits further

[40] See account of press conference of Minister of Justice, *Al-Istiqlal*, October 5, 1956, p. 3.

[41] Much of the following information on the court system at the end of 1958 is from an interview with Ali Benjelloun, Chief of Cabinet, Ministry of Justice, October 29, 1958.

[42] (New Series), no. 3, March 1957, p. 4.

examination. The main delay was due to administrative obstacles, which were partially a function of French relations. That Morocco should need foreign help on such an ostensibly purely Muslim problem is in itself well worth underlining, but notice should also be made of the success Morocco has had in rewriting her legal codes. The reformulation of Muslim law to suit modern needs has been a serious stumbling block in many Muslim countries and has often required severe coercion to be accepted. The first three books of reformed Muslim law, dealing with marriage, divorce, and filiation, were unobtrusively put into effect in the spring of 1958. With strong support of the King, it was simply stated that the new law would help to strengthen Moroccan families and facilitate the work of the new judges.[43] The over-all effect of the first reforms was to protect women from unjust divorce, forced marriages, and desertion.

Although the arbitrary Muslim divorce procedure was not totally outlawed, the old system was officially discouraged and several restraints were placed on the husband. With these reforms only inheritance procedures and rights remained as a basic area of judicial reform that was still under the generally outmoded form of the Shraa. While the influence of the King, both among the more advanced nationalists and among the citizens still attached to other customary legal procedures, undoubtedly did much to enable the harmonious transition to reformed Muslim law, it should also be noted that it was probably not a significant source of differentiation in the period being considered in this book. Some of the most isolated Berber tribesmen may have been reluctant to give up tribal practices, but even the marginally integrated citizen could hardly avoid being impressed with the overwhelming unanimity of all colorations of nationalists on judicial reform.

New Wine in Old Barrels?

The problem of training technicians and administrators will reappear in many ways in the study of the Moroccan transition. Its general dimensions can be sketched most accurately for the civil service, though this is only one part of the training problem. For the political system as a whole many kinds of changes have been limited by the lack of technical skills. Those who are prepared are, of course,

[43] For example see *Al-Istiqlal*, April 27, 1958, and the speech of the Minister of Justice, *La Vigie*, December 1, 1957, p. 4.

limited in what they can do by the literacy level, general knowledge of organization procedures, and familiarity with the role of government among the population. Over the first two years of independence almost nothing was done on the national level to attack this problem. Individual ministries did allot funds for advanced training of Moroccans as they saw fit, but no summary of national needs was made nor were the scattered efforts of the ministries coordinated. Since then at least three ministries have their own programs in operation, but there are still few signs that these programs are carefully planned and scaled to anticipated needs or agreed priorities.

The industrial and agricultural sectors appear to have come under the aegis of the Commission for Professional Training. Ibrahim was in the post of Minister of Labor and Social Questions only long enough to establish the commission and to estimate future needs. His plans called for the training of 80,000 skilled industrial workers per year, 50,000 skilled agricultural workers, 1,000 technicians, 1,000 engineers, and 1,400 teachers.[44] These goals were no doubt extremely ambitious for the new country and were probably influenced by Ibrahim's known desire to eliminate foreign assistance as fast as possible. A touch of realism is added by noting that, of the approximately 2,500 engineers working in Morocco, twenty are Moroccan.[45] Actual progress probably has been greatest in a second effort under the Ministry of Public Works, which has operated schools for railroad and port workers since early 1957. The ministry also had a program under way to provide training in language and basic skills for the Casablanca port workers. The third program was under Mohammed Tahiri, who was made Undersecretary for Technical Education and the Training of Cadres in the Ministry of Education under the Balafrej government. His work appeared to be concentrated on professional training within the existing structure of the educational system and its proposed expansion.[46] The main contribution to the end of 1958 was the supervision of about 250 scholarships given for advanced study in key technical and professional fields.

[44] *La Vigie*, January 21, 1958, p. 2. It is interesting to note that Ibrahim made his report via the Consultative National Assembly, which was under the Presidency of Ben Barka. These two later became leaders of the split from the Istiqlal party.

[45] Charles F. Gallagher, Jr., "The Moroccanization of Morocco," American Universities Field Staff Report, CFG-2-58, p. 4.

[46] See his report at the opening of the school year, *La Vigie*, September 13, 1958, p. 1.

The problem of technical training is highly complex and much of the basic data for planning as well as evaluation of progress has not been collected. More information is available on the transition of the civil service, which involves both the problem of technical training and highly controversial political issues. Like the problem of training nongovernmental technicians, change in the administrative structure provides some insight into the functioning of the political system as a whole. It has received more attention than any similar problem because the government has been limited in what it could do to alleviate more general social problems by the quality and number of civil servants. "Moroccanization" has also become a volatile political issue. Many Moroccan leaders regard foreigners in the administration with even more apprehension than they feel about their prevalence in the industrial and commercial life of the new country.

Presentation of data on the civil service is complicated by French practices that have been incorporated in the Moroccan administration, which was structurally almost identical to that of France. No complete attempt will be made to describe the grades of civil servants, of which there were seven main classifications in late 1958, with many possible levels of seniority and skill in each classification. There are also two general classifications of civil servants that were kept to the end of 1958. There were "titled" and "nontitled" civil servants, corresponding roughly to American practice of tenured and nontenured civil servants. The other broad differentiation was between the "mixed cadre" and the "reserve cadre," a distinction made to segregate Moroccans from French civil servants working in the Protectorate. The "reserve" was totally Moroccan, while a few Moroccans of higher level were admitted to the "mixed" group. This distinction was considered as extremely discriminatory by Moroccans, especially because the "mixed" group received larger family allowances and other extra benefits. The difficulty of changing the civil service to suit new national needs is suggested by the delay in changing this provision until the end of 1958.[47]

There were no official figures on the total number of civil servants in the new country in late 1958 and estimates vary considerably. At the end of 1955 there were approximately 80,000 government work-

[47] See the announcement in *Al-Istiqlal*, October 18, 1958, p. 13, which is accompanied with charts giving the differences in allowances between the two groups according to number of children.

ers, including all levels of government and all nationalities. A census of civil servants in the central administration shows that just over 51,000 of them were working in national offices.[48] A less accurate estimate of the situation at the end of 1958 puts the total number of civil servants at about the same number, 80,000, though some high Moroccan officials estimate there may be as many as 110,000. That there has been little, if any, change in the total number is confirmed indirectly by the decrease to about 48,000 in the number of civil servants in the central government at the end of 1958. Although these figures do not include the Royal Army or the security forces under the Ministry of the Interior, it is remarkable that the new nation has been able to establish the new offices required by independence without a large increase in the administrative force. The charge is frequently made that the administration is overcentralized and top-heavy, but this is difficult to evaluate without more precise data on the functions and number of civil servants at the municipal and regional levels.[49]

Comparisons of the Protectorate and the new Moroccan administration are hazardous, because many new services have been added and functions have been redistributed. In general, it is probably fair to conclude from Table 4 that the independent country has managed to take on its new administrative duties while slightly reducing the number of civil servants. The largest increases appear to have been the Ministries of Justice and National Defense. A comparison of the additional personnel of the forces of order is difficult. The Royal Army is about 30,000, the police about 10,000, and there are probably at least an additional 10,000 men paid through the auxiliary forces of the Ministries of the Interior and National Defense. This is much less than the 80,000 troops used by the French during the fighting from 1954 to 1955.

To have from one half to three fifths of the civil servants of any country of foreign nationality would be a serious national problem. In a nation leaving colonial supervision, it also becomes a delicate and controversial issue. In 1955 three fifths of the civil servants in

[48] "Agents des Services Publiques du Protectorate," Recensement de 17 décembre 1955, Service des Statistiques, Ministère de l'Economie Nationale.
[49] It is unfortunate for scholars and experts not officially connected with the government that officials are so loathe to part with more accurate information. The benefits that would indirectly accrue to the advantage of the Moroccan government by study of such data are impossible to realize and the government gives the impression of being much less capable than it probably is.

TABLE 4
Number of Civil Servants per Ministry (October 1958)[a]

Ministry	Civil Servants	Ministry	Civil Servants	Ministry	Civil Servants
Royal Establishment[b]		National Defense[d]	4648	National Education	8345
Palace	148	Interior[e]	2608	Youth and Sports[g]	655
Royal Khalifas	123				
Protocol	54	Police	8906	Labor and Social	
National Assembly	27			Questions	234
Royal Guard	11	National Economy			
Habous	58	National Economy	137	Public Health[h]	3064
		Finance	2234		
Total	421	Customs	1582	Post, Telephone, and	
		General Treasury	331	Telegraph	4269
Secretary General		Commerce and			
of the Government	233	Industry	500	Annexed Budgets,	
				Official	
Foreign Affairs	124	Total	4784	Printing Office	74
				Port of Casablanca	71
Civil Service[c]	83			Port of Safi	11
		Public Works[f]	2128	Port of Kenitra	34
Information and				Port of Agadir	20
Tourists	53	Agriculture & Forests		Secondary Ports	48
		Agriculture	1711		
Justice and Prisons		Forests	1205	Total	287
Justice	3353				
Prisons	712	Total	2916	Grand Total	47,794
Total	4065				

[a] From the pay-roll totals of the Undersecretary of State for Finance, Ministry of National Economy.

[b] The Royal Guard does not include the troops of the palace guard. Habous is carried separately, but has been included with the palace here since its work is closely supervised by the King.

[c] Including 14 civil servants in a government pool.

[d] Including 8 civil servants working with the *gendarmerie*, a group of security forces outside the army and under this ministry. They are not included.

[e] Including 656 civil servants working with the Auxiliary Forces, a group of security forces under this ministry. They are not included.

[f] Including 73 civil servants carried separately for equipment maintenance.

[g] This ministry has changed status several times. In the last two governments included in this study it was under the Ministry of National Education as a "Service."

[h] Including 99 civil servants on "prolonged leave," probably for special training.

the central governmental offices were French.[50] These men were essential to the operation of the government in the early months of

[50] From a report now with Statistical Service, Ministry of National Economy, entitled "Agents des Services Publiques du Protectorate" and dated December 17, 1955. The Protectorate categories "Muslim" and "Jew" were merged under "Moroccan."

independence and many of them are still vitally needed. They represent the vast majority of the civil servants in the higher posts and with most training and experience. The total number of French civil servants in Morocco at independence was somewhat over 40,000.[51] To these administrators should be added about 10,000 Frenchmen who held even more crucial jobs in the public or semipublic corporations, such as public utilities, railroads, and port authorities. To fill these posts the new country had only approximately 3,000 well-qualified civil servants.[52]

Like the judicial convention, the formal settlement of the terms and procedures for technical and administrative aid from France was postponed by the rush of pressing business in the early months of independence and by the crisis of the fall of 1956. The convention was finally signed in February 1957, but the Moroccan government could not agree on how to execute its responsibilities under the convention. The problem was complicated by the Istiqlal's concern that they enter into their contracts without "spirit of domination" and with "exclusive service" to the Moroccan government.[53] The nationalist party also objected strongly to the minister handling the problem—a member of the Liberal Independent party. Once he was removed, criticism from the Istiqlal diminished rapidly, although the issue of "Moroccanization" became important. The delay in issuing contracts caused much apprehension among the French civil servants, and the new country probably lost many useful persons, especially among teachers.

Over the first year of independence French civil servants continued to work or leave at will. New Moroccan administrators were recruited and trained without central coordination or systematic planning.[54] The complete disapproval of the Protectorate regime in the Istiqlal program made it difficult for party leaders to acknowledge the necessity of keeping French civil servants and technicians. Having had little experience and no detailed information on the problems of Moroccan administration, the tendency was to postpone the issue. Though these shortcomings are understandable, it is important

---

[51] This is the figure given by Bouabid, *L'Action*, June 23, 1958, p. 9, and Balafrej, *ibid.*, July 21, 1958, p. 10.

[52] Balafrej gives the figure of 2,500 to 3,000 qualified civil servants. *Al-Istiqlal*, March 30, 1956, p. 2.

[53] *Ibid.*, January 18, 1957, editorial, p. 1.

[54] When the author interviewed officials of the Civil Service office in late 1958, they had not yet had a reply to their request of over a year before to the Undersecretary of State for Finance for the figures contained in Table 4.

to remember that the transition of the new country took place within these severe limitations, regardless of their source.[55]

These changes in the administration also took place during heated controversies among political parties and various events threatening public order, to which members of the Council of Government gave preference. Within the Istiqlal, policy toward the integration of French personnel does not appear ever to have been uniformly agreed upon. In the space of one week in the midst of the negotiations on the convention for technical and administrative aid, for example, the party supported contradictory policies. Si Abdelaziz Ben Driss, speaking at a party regional conference at Kenitra, claimed that France never intended to give Morocco her independence and that Morocco would not be free until aid was no longer needed. A few days later Allal Al-Fassi, speaking to the Amal Club of Casablanca, said that the Europeans in Morocco gave her "rich material and spiritual support" and that the Istiqlal had decided to do everything possible "to protect and defend the interests of the European guests of Morocco."[56]

At the end of 1958 there were about 15,000 French civil servants working in the Moroccan administration.[57] To these civil servants should be added an estimated 6,000 civil servants without tenure and about 7,500 administrators and technicians with the public and semi-public corporations. The total comes to slightly over 25,000 French technicians and administrators connected with the government. In late 1958 the plan for the "Moroccanization" of the civil service was not yet complete, though officials estimated that it would take from five to ten years to complete the task.[58] The initial effort was concentrated in the key offices of the government, such as the police, which is almost completely Moroccan, and communications, which claims to be three fourths Moroccan. Where more specialized skills are needed, as in finance, agriculture, public health, and public

---

[55] See the very critical, but penetrating article of Jean Lacouture, "Le Maroc à le conquête de lui-même," *Espirit*, June 1957, pp. 968-981. Particularly telling is his observation of the reliance of the Moroccan civil servant on the telephone rather than on written memoranda. This results in poor coordination and often ignorance of current business among the official's own staff.

[56] *Perspectives Marocaines*, no. 34, June 1957, p. 14.

[57] In July 1957, 18,000 were offered contracts, of whom about 3,000 declined. Lacouture, *Le Maroc à l'Epreuve, op.cit.*, p. 352. This figure was also given by Balafrej, *op.cit.*, although Bouabid placed the number between 12,000 and 14,000, *op.cit.*

[58] Interview with Naceur Bel Larbi, Director of Civil Service, Royal Palace, October 22, 1958.

works, progress undoubtedly has been much slower. Although the problem is seldom discussed publicly with much objectivity, officials do seem to be agreed that they will need between 4,000 and 5,000 French administrators and technicians in the government for the foreseeable future.

The Moroccan situation at the time of independence is probably best summarized by a special census of Moroccan civil servants at all governmental levels prepared by the Protectorate in the spring of 1955.[59] The survey showed a total of almost 18,000 Moroccans in the government, of whom only 2,000 were in the category of high civil servants. The effort to train more qualified Moroccan civil servants began late in 1957, with the establishment of an Arabic section of the National School of Administration. Early in 1958 regional training centers were initiated, which would provide introductory training for new candidates and improvement courses for presently employed civil servants. Small groups have also been sent to Paris for accelerated and regular courses at the French National School of Administration. About forty-five higher civil servants are trained each year by the National School of Administration. Only by costly improvisations like understaffing, on-the-job training, and reduced supervision, however, can Moroccan officials attain their goal of producing 2,000 qualified civil servants a year.[60]

Moroccan experience with the replacement and training of technical and administrative personnel contrasts sharply with her experience regarding judicial reform. The latter had not become an issue in the political system and reform proceeded quite smoothly. The new country probably had more lawyers than any other profession and many scholars of ancient and modern Muslim law. The reforms did not conflict with the goals of any group of Moroccans active in the political system, although there may have been isolated cases of resistance and tension. In many ways the problem of reorganizing the civil service has been the opposite. No well-planned program existed, nor was there time to make one until the second year of independence. The problem became a political issue between Morocco and France and among groups in the Moroccan political system itself. Although the explanation rests to some extent with

[59] "Fonctionaires du Protectorate Agents des Services Publiques de Nationalité Marocain," May 27, 1955, now with Statistical Service, Ministry of National Economy.

[60] This figure was given by Naceur Bel Larbi, Director of Civil Service, Royal Palace, in an interview, October 22, 1958.

the different character of the two reforms, it is also important to remember that the solution of these two problems placed different requirements on the political system as a whole.

A solution to the judicial problem was within the capability of the
existing political system. Morocco is predominantly Arab and Muslim. There was never any question among the nationalists of whether
or not the legal system was distinctively her own. The reforms were
harmonious with the aims of the King, the nationalist parties, and
other groups. Though it took some time to write the new legal codes
and to train judges, the implementation of the mechanism of the
judicial system did not directly or even indirectly conflict with
French interests in Morocco, once independence was granted. The
administrative problem was different, for there were many possible
optimum solutions and no clear-cut way of deciding which one
would be selected. As the paucity of published information indicates,
officials have reflected the ambivalence of the political system. The
problem had no distinctively Moroccan nationalist solution. French
experts were needed, but were distrusted by Moroccan officials and
discredited before the Moroccan public. Having no solution that was
sanctified by preindependence experience, the issue tended to become exceedingly controversial in the political system.

Separation of Whose Powers?

The phrase "separation of powers" has been used in many ways in
Moroccan political discussions, and probably reflects Moroccan indecision as much as French cultural influence. There are at least three
distinct meanings attached to the phrase. The first is the separation
of the judicial and other governmental functions. The second usage
is the reformation of the rural administration and its subordination
to a central Moroccan authority. The third form is in reference to
the roles of the King and other participants in the formal structure
of the government and, ultimately, in relation to the entire political
system. The royal household is a subject that is always treated with
meticulous circumspection by Moroccan politicians, but there are undoubtedly a variety of opinions concerning its proper role in the free
country. The sincerity of the King has never been questioned, although those differing from the King's views as to his proper role
became increasingly outspoken during 1958.

Under the Franco-Moroccan Agreement full "sovereign" powers
were bestowed on the King and no change was made in this legal-

istic basis for authority over the three years being discussed. As the political system developed and a well-defined central administration was formed, the more active participants began to question the efficiency of the administrative consequences of this arrangement. Outside of the formal structure of the government and administration, the supremacy of the King also had consequences for the Istiqlal and the whole political system. The influence of the King was not the same, however, when exercised in respect to the political parties as it was when he acted in the name of the nation. To say that the roles of the King were necessarily in conflict, even concerning the Istiqlal party, is an oversimplification. It ignores the ability of the party to maintain its solidarity, at least in the public eye, over three years when the King's proper position was a matter of dispute among many party leaders. The King did have certain advantages in dealing with the kinds of problems that Morocco faced in the early period of independence, but he certainly is not invulnerable. Depending on the time period, the setting, and the kinds of problems that confront the political system, either the King or the party may have the upper hand.

Before the formal agreement on independence was negotiated, the Istiqlal submitted in its congress that "no delegation of legislative powers can be made" and that the King remains the "sole depository" of Moroccan authority.[61] Quite possibly the party preferred that no delegations of authority be made to particular ministers while the minority parties were represented in the Council of Government. The indescribable rejoicing over the return of Mohammed Ben Youssef made it impossible, of course, to make even the slightest critical remark regarding the institutions of the new state. The importance of the King was affirmed dramatically in the spring of 1956, when the Moroccan Army of Liberation responded to his appeal after several unsuccessful attempts by political parties to subdue the fighting in the countryside. This success also served notice to the Istiqlal that the symbolic position that they had helped create for Mohammed V after World War II, not without certain benefits to themselves, was going to be a lasting center of influence in the new political system.

At meetings in Tangier and Madrid during the spring of 1956 the Istiqlal is reported to have discussed the party's new relation to the King. The Tunisian Neo-Destour newspaper, *L'Action*, attrib-

---

[61] *Al-Istiqlal*, August 17, 1956, p. 7, proceedings of December 1955 Congress.

uted the following observation to one leader: "It is in fact our party which has created the *mystique* of the exiled martyr, but this popularity is now a political reality which possesses an existence in itself and which the Istiqlal has neither the means—nor the interest—to oppose."[62] Apprehension among the more ambitious party leaders was very likely increased when the King put the Royal Army under the command of his son and the Sûreté virtually under the control of the Palace shortly after independence. By 1958 the main objections to the King's rule by the party's activist wing were his control of the police and the army. They were also impatient for the regime of the constitutional monarchy to be implemented. Though not immediately outspoken on the issue of Bekkai's submissiveness toward the King, they were very likely also disturbed by the precedent of complete deference to the monarch being set for future Presidents of the Council.

The Istiqlal was probably upset by the responsibility that the party would have in the popular eye while the operation of the government remained under the close supervision of the King. He had the buffer of the party to separate him from disputes and failures, but the governing party had no intermediary between itself and the populace. To provide itself with such a point of reference, the party looked toward elections and establishment of a constitutional monarchy. The Istiqlal had a predominant position in the Council of Ministers from October 1956, after some delaying tactics from the Palace. When the new courts were established, the party newspaper said: "It is necessary to add that the independence of the judiciary is only the first step toward the separation of powers, since there exists a third authority which is the legislative. . . . To proceed with this it is necessary to wait for the preparation of general elections, for the formation of a parliament which will represent the nation and promulgate laws in its name."[63] With the formation of a predominately Istiqlal government, the King took the precaution of establishing another hurdle between himself and the government, the Crown Council. The expansion of the office of the Secretary of the Government and the maintenance of the President of the Council's office within the palace grounds probably confirmed the fears of

[62] *L'Action*, April 2, 1956, p. 8. The spokesman was Ben Barka, but there is no reason to assume that reservations were confined to the progressive wing of the party. As *L'Action* also noted, Allal Al-Fassi could be considered "more royalist than the King" and had struggled alone in the 1930's.

[63] *Al-Alam*, October 24, 1956, Fr. Trans.

those objecting to a continuance of government by viziers."[64]

In the period leading up to the crisis of the fall of 1956, the Istiqlal talked of reinforcing the executive for an expected "government of action" and of abandoning the policy of "counterweights and dosages" in the Council of Government.[65] Among the progressive elements of the party there was particular concern over the lack of coordination and planning in the realm of economic affairs. Bouabid was among those objecting most strongly to the weaknesses of the "Ministry of Aix-les-Bains," as the first Council of Government was sometimes called. The "superministry" that merged supervision of all governmental economic activity was very likely a concession to him. To this new ministry was also added the Ministry of Agriculture in the Balafrej Council, but Bouabid's resignation in late 1958 suggests that these changes did not produce the kind of government that the party activists desired.

Changing the Council of Government did not help to clarify the relation between the King and his ministers. There were a few signs of discontent in the spring of 1957, when the Palace gained new prestige with the rapid and effective intercession of the Prince and Royal Army in the Addi ou Bihi revolt. There were reports of fears that the country was returning to a government based on "ancestral regime,"[66] but the institution of the monarchy was given new pledges of solidarity when the Tunisian Bey was removed.[67] Over the summer of 1957 the monarchy was also reinforced by bestowing hereditary right to the throne on Prince Moulay Hassan. In the fall a High Council for National Defense was formed which institutionalized the leading military roles of the King and Prince. The ability of the King to alter the institutional structure of the new country was, of course, unquestionable, but this fact very likely further inflamed

[64] Not including the large number of army officers working with the King and the Prince's army staff, the Palace had a staff of about 650 for government business in October 1958. (See Table 4.) With the formation of the Balafrej government both the Civil Service and the Information and Touring Ministries' staffs of 130 also came under the President of the Council and, thereby, under the King's more direct supervision.

[65] See the comment of *L'Action*, May 21, 1956, p. 8, asserting that no decisions were made in these meetings contrary to the King's wishes. There is, of course, no way to prove or disprove this.

[66] *L'Action*, February 13, 1957, p. 6.

[67] See the bitter attack on Bourguiba shortly after he removed the Bey, in the government-supervised newspaper, *Al-Ahd Al-Jadiid*, August 2, 1957, U.S. Trans. He was charged with being a dictator and most derogatory remarks were made concerning his betrayal of efforts for North African liberation.

Istiqlal leaders who felt that other important problems of governmental organization were being neglected.

Without some kind of popular mandate through elections or legal rights under a written constitution, the parties were helpless. After two years of independence the role of ministers was undefined and nearly all decisions had to be cleared with the Palace. There were signs that opposition parties were succeeding in using these ambiguities to undermine Istiqlal popularity. The increasing discontent was revealed for a moment late in 1957 by Mehdi Ben Barka, when he reportedly said that the future regime of Morocco would be a "socialist democracy." The haste with which the failure to mention the monarchy was corrected suggests how delicate the problem was.[68] A few weeks later Ben Barka presented an emphatic endorsement of constitutional monarchy before the National Assembly of Tunisia. An editorial also appeared in the party paper entitled "In spite of all intrigues our constitutional monarchy is a continuing creation."[69]

The role of the monarchy became central to Moroccan politics with the crisis of the spring of 1958. In what Lacouture described as "not a combat, but a dialogue," the problem unfolded as the Balafrej government was formed.[70] He wisely cautioned that it was not a question of the monarchy itself, "but the rhythm of its evolution and the ways leading to its liberalization." Taking the initiative in the drawn-out negotiations, the King issued a Royal Charter clarifying the future of the government: "National sovereignty is incarnated by the King. . . . We are going to build a regime of constitutional monarchy. . . . We will promulgate *a dahir* concerning the executive power defining the powers of the President of the Council, those of each minister, as well as the attributions of the Council of the Cabinet. The ministers, who receive their powers from Our Majesty and who are individually and collectively responsible before Us, will carry on the tasks confided to them. As for the legislative power, We withhold it."[71] With this document the King abandoned his role as mediator. The opposing argument was put by Ben Barka soon after the Royal Charter, in an editorial entitled "Let us Face Realities":

[68] See *L'Echo du Maroc*, January 11, 1958, p. 3. This source will be referred to hereafter as *L'Echo*.

[69] *Al-Istiqlal*, February 1, 1958, p. 3. He issued another statement on his return from Tunisia denying rumors of differences among the Moroccan leaders over the future of the monarchy. See *La Vigie*, January 31, 1958, p. 3.

[70] *Le Monde*, May 6, 1958, p. 5.

[71] *O.B.*, no. 2378, May 23, 1958, "Proclamation Royale (Traduction du message adressé par S.M. le Roi Mohammed V au people marocain le 8 mai 1958)," p. 805.

"It is important to leave the atmosphere of clandestineness which has not ceased to envelope the major decisions that engage the future of the country. . . . The directors of the party have sensed the necessity to specify, in a detailed program, the institutional framework which would permit the new governmental team to emerge from the vizierial system, a source of confusion and irresponsibility that has characterized the two preceding cabinets."[72] That this was not being accomplished under the Balafrej government to the satisfaction of the Istiqlal progressives soon became evident. In Bouabid's letter of resignation six months later he frankly stated the condition to his future participation: "To confer on the government sufficient and effective powers, consecrated by texts of law, in order to permit the executive to assume its responsibilities before H.M. the King and the country."[73]

Balafrej was compelled to try to neutralize these criticisms, which were probably more open within the Council of Government. Speaking to a conference of party secretaries, he admitted that the party had accepted office in the third government only with "some formal assurances" that it would be given "the necessary means to govern."[74] He added that the Council had not received these powers, nor had it been satisfied with the continued status of the police and Royal Army as appendages of the Palace. The King was apparently unwilling to make concessions that might have saved the Balafrej government. He did, however, explain why the elections and legislative reforms had been delayed before the National Consultative Assembly. The case of the party activists was strengthened when one of the more moderate party leaders, Abdeljalil, also admitted that the Council of Government had not received the necessary authority.[75]

There are at least two distinct relationships of particular importance involved in the transition of the monarchy. One is the relations of the King to the political system. The other is the relation between the King and the Istiqlal, which, in turn, is related to the political system as a whole. For the party the question has been whether or not it should continue to be dependent on harmonious relations with the King or put forth a greater effort to establish its own influence. Neither issue entailed conflict with the monarchy and

[72] *Al-Istiqlal,* May 18, 1958, p. 3.
[73] *La Vigie,* November 23, 1958, p. 1.
[74] *Al-Istiqlal,* October 18, 1958, p. 4. He made these statements in answer to questions and not as part of his speech.
[75] See quotations in *Le Monde,* October 21, 1958, p. 1.

it should be noted that, even after the split of the party, both Istiqlal factions continued to express complete loyalty. However, to allow itself to be merged with the King's following meant that the party would inescapably be limited to the course of action that Mohammed Ben Youssef chose. The progressive faction of the party may have skillfully used national politics to resolve a party problem, but they had also demolished nationalist solidarity.

Whatever thoughts a few of the most progressive politicians may have had concerning the institution of the monarchy, the King proved himself indispensable in subduing the tribal uprising at the close of 1958. In the early part of the period being discussed in this book, it was important to have a leader having the confidence of the French. The solidarity that Morocco did sustain is to a large extent the result of the mediation and consultation of the King, who could move freely among groups and individuals. He did not select the formal institutional structure that existed in Morocco in 1955, nor did he hedge in accepting responsibility for the future of the country when bargaining with the French. The very arguments that the Istiqlal constantly repeated concerning the advancement of the political system on the basis of some form of representative government can, of course, be used to justify his caution in making major institutional revisions before such a national consultation could be planned.

Problems of new governments accumulate more rapidly than new institutions can be designed to seek solutions. The political system must function while it is being modified. Both in the administration and at the ministerial level, alternatives are restricted by the few qualified persons. This is a problem in itself for a new nation, but it also is a quality of the political system that limits what can be done. It should not be precluded that the division of the party, difficult as it may make the immediate future of Morocco, may help to resolve the more difficult question of choosing and implementing new institutions. A second and related point is that influence directed along institutional channels is not necessarily a solution to many of the political problems of a new nation and often is not sufficient to solve problems of advanced nations. There must first be an agreement on the priority of the issues facing the nation and some popular understanding of the implications of the possible solutions.

In conditions of extreme social differentiation this may be difficult, and in Morocco this may have been almost impossible. The tendency has been for the political system to become increasingly divided into active and inactive segments as the problems of the country have become more complex. The national political system as a whole, thereby, becomes less capable of handling them. The political interplay of the factions of the Istiqlal and also between the Palace and the Istiqlal—often more in relation to the problems of devising a new political system than to national problems themselves—is evidence of this. In a political system of this kind the importance of the King should not be minimized, for he could play a dual role more easily than any other political leader. Although this may have antagonized some members of the Istiqlal, its contribution to the national political system may have been absolutely essential.

CHAPTER V

CITIZENS AND PRIVILEGES

Who Is a Moroccan?

A CRUCIAL problem for the development of a new nation is determining who will be its new members. At the time of independence Morocco included a large number of French, Spanish, and other nationals. Many Moroccans had cooperated in varying degrees in obstructing the struggle for independence. There was a variety of opinions regarding how many Moroccans should fall within some definition of collaborators or even if such an effort should be made at all. Some organized efforts have been made to punish individuals, though on the whole on a fairly restrained basis and without much publicity. Now beyond all documentation are the large numbers who were summarily dealt with by the resistance movement and enthusiastic crowds in the early months of independence. The question of citizenship also involves the more specific issue of what political rights exist for those who are fully acceptable by whatever criteria may be agreed upon and what opportunity will be given to them to exercise such rights. The handling of the entire citizenship issue provides further insight into the way in which the new political system of Morocco has developed. Until an agreed definition of a citizen can be found, all political action is severely limited.

Limitations on political action do not have the same implications for all political groups. Those groups already organized may have other means of communicating among their members or bringing them together in small groups. For the less active citizens the denial or restraint of the conventional civil or political rights of a free advanced nation may mean nothing. It should also be recognized that in a new country the loss of skilled administrative and technical help, while this discredits members of the previous regime, may crucially affect the operation of the new government. The question of membership standards for the new nation may directly relate to the emergence or the stifling of new political groups. Since the loyalty question easily takes on considerable significance in a new nation, great advantage accrues to the group whose past activity places them above criticism.

Probably the first problem of establishing the conditions and prerogatives of citizenship in a new country is the promulgation of a law on nationality. As in the case of the judicial reform, the work on the Moroccan nationality law progressed with very little publicity or discussion. The highly technical and specialized task was probably understood by only a few jurists in the new country. The question at stake, however, was as crucial to the future of the country as that of the purge. The loyalty issue was treated with great urgency and received much publicity, while the nationality law was left almost entirely to the Ministry of Justice.

No law had been written on the subject under the Protectorate and the last official document to mention Moroccan citizenship was the Treaty of Madrid in 1880. It simply stipulated that "Moroccan citizenship could not be acquired or lost." The question was complicated by the preindependence policy of the French to encourage some Moroccans to become citizens of France. There was also the difficult issue of possible linguistic and religious citizenship qualifications. Within Morocco there were large Algerian and bordering tribal groups, for whom some consideration was desired. The first public notice that work had begun on the nationality law was in December 1957. Nothing more was heard of the nationality commission until shortly after the formation of the Balafrej government, when a draft was presented for consideration by the Palace and the ministers. There were no indications that this basic piece of legislation was as controversial as other less fundamental laws. The official text, published in September 1958,[1] revealed the three major considerations in the drafting of the law. First, citizenship is a "purely political" relation to the state. Secondly, Morocco is not in a position to encourage an influx of new citizens because of demographic pressure, and thirdly, Moroccan citizenship is bestowed with certain qualifications that "safeguard national unity." The law distinguished between loss of citizenship, which can occur to any citizen, natural-born or naturalized, and forfeiture of citizenship, which may happen only to naturalized citizens. Citizenship may be forfeited for an offense against the King or royal family, a crime against the internal or external security of the state, or a crime carrying a sentence of over five years.

[1] *O.B.*, no. 2394, September 12, 1958, "Dahir no. 1-58-250 du 21 safar 1378 (6 septembre 1958) portant code de la nationalité," pp. 1492-1496. See also the explanation of the law by the Chief of Cabinet of the Ministry of Justice in *Al-Istiqlal*, August 23, 1958, p. 5.

The last chapter of the law provides that any person from a country where a majority of the population speaks Arabic or practices Islam may opt for Moroccan citizenship if he were living in Morocco at the time of the law's promulgation.[2] This is one of the first recognitions in Moroccan legislation of the primacy of Arab culture and also provides the opportunity for political sanctuary under Moroccan nationality for Algerians and others. The same chapter also includes a provision that persons living in territory adjacent to Morocco may opt for citizenship over the next year if they live within the boundaries which will be defined by decree in that period. This is perhaps the first recognition in law that Morocco does not accept the present frontiers—a fact which raises highly disputed questions in reference to Algeria, Spain, and France. At the time of promulgation the King was reportedly especially concerned over the tribes to the south bearing allegiance to him.

The nationality law is of interest in relation to the growth of the whole political system for its demonstration of the way in which basic legislation raises volatile issues and forces decisions that may later prove troublesome in their consequences. The same difficulty obstructs the formation of new institutions, which require similarly precise definition of procedures and qualifications. For example, this law and the Charter of Liberties constitute the first legal recognition of the institution of the monarchy. Previously it had rested only on Moroccan tradition and the authority bestowed on it during negotiations with the French. In the consideration of this and other laws, it is also noteworthy that only a minority of the Moroccan people were capable of reading and understanding such legislation. The influence that might be channeled through the legally specified procedures is almost insignificant in comparison to the operation of other aspects of the political system.

Purge: Who, When, and How Many?

In the early months of independence there was little discussion of a general purge, though comment appeared concerning the reorganization of the rural administration. The pattern was set by the King himself when he received Al-Glaoui in France and assured him that the past must be forgotten. Similarly in the early motions of the

[2] Or, alternatively, he may opt for Moroccan citizenship if he has had habitual residence in Morocco for fifteen years, been in the civil service for ten years, or been married to a Moroccan and in residence for one year.

Istiqlal the question of any kind of retribution for injustices during the preindependence period was avoided, but the party advocated the removal of officials of the puppet regime. As the regional administration was reconstructed, the most flagrant oppressors of the nationalists were removed, but no systematic attempt was made to define procedures or criteria for treatment of those accused of having collaborated with the Protectorate. So long as the country was torn by the war in the Rif and by other activities of the Liberation Army, it was difficult, if not impossible, to establish any coordinated plan.

The first clear expression of the need for a purge is found in the speeches of Balafrej and Al-Fassi during the National Council meeting in August 1956.[3] Though Balafrej referred only to "plots" against the country and the party, Al-Fassi elaborated on the "allies of imperialism . . . who have profited from the colonial regime and who have not been able to digest the results of independence." The National Council's resolution on purging the administration became more specific as it called for the removal of all "undesirable civil servants for reasons of their abuses or their anti-national conduct." These early protests were still concerned with the problem of converting the rural administration. Many officials known to have actively assisted in the exile of the King and the oppression of the movement still held their posts. These officials also obstructed the reorganization of the Istiqlal and its extension into the countryside.

The issue took on new importance in party statements during the delay between the National Council meeting and the formation of the second government. In a speech at Fès, Al-Fassi proclaimed that the party had fought for independence "in order to disencumber Morocco of traitors and feudals"[4] and his accusations were echoed in the party publications. The second government was formed, however, under conditions that precluded the internal strain that a thorough examination of the loyalty problem would entail. Bekkai's declaration on the formation of the new government made no reference to the problem, nor did the annual Speech from the Throne several weeks later, when the King reviewed the past year's accomplishments and the major issues of the coming year.

The problem was next raised in January 1957, after the King had left for Italy. During a speech in Safi, Al-Fassi claimed: "It is neces-

[3] *Al-Istiqlal*, August 24, 1956, pp. 7-10.
[4] *Al-Alam*, September 19, 1956, Fr. Trans. See also *Al-Istiqlal*, September 21, 1956, p. 3, an editorial on the role of the "neo-feudals" in the government.

sary that the people oppose traitors and conspirators. Liberation and purge cannot be separated."[5] If the Istiqlal charges had lacked credibility up to now, they were confirmed by the Addi ou Bihi affair. The revolt was not subdued until the Prince and the Royal Army occupied the province of Tafilalet, where Addi ou Bihi was governor. The incident reflects the contradictions inherent in such purification drives. Addi ou Bihi was fanatically loyal to the King, had resigned from his administrative post over the exile of Mohammed V in 1953, and had been kept in forced residence by the French until independence. His refusal to accept the administrative and legal reforms of the new state placed him in a position of rebellion that confirmed the Istiqlal charges of danger to the security to the state.

From this date the Istiqlal party continued to stress the conspiratorial threat to the new state. In *Al-Istiqlal* it was written, "The agents of division and subversion still circulate profitting from the official character they preserve in order to undermine the foundations of our young state."[6] These charges found apparent confirmation again a few months later when the sons of Al-Glaoui were arrested in Marrakech, though the precise circumstances of these arrests are not yet known. Although the King had fully forgiven Al-Glaoui before independence, the Istiqlal charged that the country was faced "with a dangerous conspiracy of reactionaries, anarchists and destroyers."[7]

A few days later the proposed purge was described by Si Abdelaziz Ben Driss, an *ancien* of the Istiqlal. During a party rally at Kenitra he identified three categories of Moroccan traitors.[8] They were supporters of "colonialism" in the preindependence period, like Al-Glaoui; those who were then following the "path of 'colons,'" some of whom might be expected to repent; and lastly those with an honorable past who had accepted "anti-patriotic principles" and were the most dangerous to Morocco's future. Perhaps with the arrests of the Glaoui family in mind, he claimed that the people were pressing for a "revolutionary purge," but that the more moderate Istiqlal preferred a "progressive purge." Soon afterward the trade-union newspaper claimed that the affairs of Addi ou Bihi and the Glaouis

[5] *Al-Alam*, January 18, 1957, p. 3, Fr. Trans. Similar declarations will be found in *Al-Istiqlal*, January 18, 1957, p. 3, in excerpts from his speeches in other cities in the south.

[6] *Al-Istiqlal*, February 9, 1957, p. 1.

[7] *Al-Alam*, April 28, 1957, Mohammed Tazi column, Fr. Trans.

[8] *Ibid.*, May 3, 1957, Fr. Trans.

demonstrated that the "confidence of the King and the Moroccan people had been poorly placed."[9] The trade unions called for the full revelation of the circumstances behind the Addi ou Bihi arrest, but not the Glaoui family arrests.

These events brought the first governmental action. A *dahir* gave the Minister of the Interior the authority to forbid property transactions by a limited number of persons, who were to be specified on a list established by decree.[10] This *dahir*, however, was only a stop-gap action from the viewpoint of the Istiqlal. The party asked for a more thorough examination of the problem before elections, which were being planned at that time to take place in the fall of 1957. Ben Barka warned against the effort of "traitors" who allegedly would take advantage of elections. Party officials agreed, "Traitors should not be permitted to return to the political scene in any manner . . . [or] those who were in the service of foreign interests and who were the most solid supporters of colonialism."[11] Actually the government proceeded much more slowly than the urgency of the Istiqlal statements suggested was appropriate.

The list of persons to have their assets frozen was not published until September 1957.[12] Though no announcement was made of the precise criteria of selection or who had applied them, the 193 persons were all directly related to the exile of the King in 1953 or to the regime established after his exile. The first group of twenty-seven persons were officials of the Palace during this period, the next twelve were leaders in the effort to revive the religious brotherhoods, and the rest were *caids* and civil servants, including the sons of Al-Glaoui, who had participated in the interim regime. This latter group did not include all the officials of the French-directed administration, but only those who had apparently been particularly objectionable in some unannounced way. If the list was intended to soothe Istiqlal fears, it failed completely, for the party reacted by asking when a second list would be presented and noting that the "omissions" from this list were generally recognized.[13]

[9] *Al-Istiqlal*, May 18, 1957, p. 3, reprint from *At-Taliâ*.

[10] O.B., July 26, 1957, no. 2335, "Dahir no. 1-57-236 du 22 hija 1367 (20 juillet 1957) soumettant à autorisation préabable certaines opérations mobilières et immobilières," p. 916.

[11] *Al-Istiqlal*, August 3, 1957, p. 4.

[12] O.B., September 6, 1957, no. 2341, "Dahir no. 2-57-1319 du 7 safar 1377 (3 septembre 1957) établissant la première liste des personnes soumises aux dispositions du dahir no. 1-57-236 du 22 hija 1376 (20 juillet 1957) soumettant à autorisation préalable certaines opérations mobilières et immobilières," pp. 1159-1161.

[13] *Al-Istiqlal*, September 14, 1957, p. 3.

The demand for further action was revived in the Istiqlal Youth Congress of late 1957. The young party members asked not only for a second list, but also for the speedy judgment of the accused, the publication of the procedures being used, and the extension of the purge to the Royal Army.[14] The party noted that the policy chosen by the King had been abused by "traitors," even though they had been given many months in which to mend their ways. These claims were accompanied by criticisms of the Liberal Independents and mark the prelude to the crisis removing them from the government. At the same time the U.M.T. started even more outspoken attacks on "agents of colonialism" and went so far as to name particular individuals who it thought should be removed. The trade union concluded, "The agents of colonialism are still more numerous in our country than we thought."[15] This was the first suggestion that the purge should include more than those who had committed offenses against the King or had made personal profit from the suppression between 1952 and 1955. The party now proposed to examine the loyalty of those who had allegedly opposed or obstructed policies or reforms of the new state since independence.

The Istiqlal's position was confirmed soon afterward by Driss M'Hammedi, the Minister of the Interior, who admitted that the purge was not complete.[16] He disclosed that the Council of Government under the supervision of the King was working on a *dahir* to define the "motives and causes" of the purge and added that the number to be affected would probably be under 2,000. He acknowledged the viewpoint, later confirmed by the King, that any purge should not be an "operation of vengance," but an "operation of safeguarding." The party was probably alarmed over the appearance of the Popular Movement at this time, which was charged with following in the steps of Addi ou Bihi. These fears were not confirmed by the King. In his Speech from the Throne for 1957 his only comment on the loyalty problem was a brief reference to "administrative measures against a category of persons who pursue activities threatening the internal and external security of the state," who would be brought before the Court of Justice.[17]

The King's visit to the United States and the hostilities around Ifni momentarily diverted attention from the purge issue, though

[14] *Ibid.*, October 5, 1957, p. 14.
[15] *Ibid.*, October 12, 1957, pp. 3-4, excerpts from *At-Taliâ*.
[16] *Al-Istiqlal*, October 12, 1957, p. 4.
[17] *Ibid.*, November 23, 1957, pp. 10-11.

the U.M.T. continued to write of the "vast assemblage of traitors" and the "resurrection of certain values that they [the U.M.T.] believed forever dead."[18] The charges of the Istiqlal underwent a subtle change toward the end of 1957, for the accused were no longer a limited number of persons who had committed specific acts against the King or the nationalist movement. The party defended the "memory" of Moroccans who had sacrificed their lives for independence and attacked "plotters" who were obstructing the "consolidation of independence."[19] In this way the charges of disloyalty were increasingly directed against opposition parties and the threat of subversion was portrayed as a contemporary danger. Meanwhile the government proceeded with much more restraint and the Minister of Justice disclosed in a meeting of Istiqlal officials that many of the accused persons had been transferred from the care of the Ministry of the Interior to his jurisdiction and that Addi ou Bihi would soon be brought to trial.

The delicacy of this task, for which the Istiqlal had waited so impatiently, was fully revealed in the events surrounding the trial of Driss Ben Bachir El-Riffi, accused of having been involved in French intrigue against the Liberation Army activities in eastern Morocco. Generally regarded as a test case for the more controversial cases of Addi ou Bihi and others, it was the first attempt to handle the problem of loyalty before the new Court of Justice, a special high court with authority to impose death for crimes involving the internal and external security of the state. The court met late in March 1958 and condemned to death not only Riffi but also two French officers and their interpreter, now in France. The entire episode ended with considerable embarrassment for both the French and Moroccan governments. The Moroccan Foreign Office hurriedly issued a correction while the matter was being considered in the French Council of Ministers. A few days later the verdict was annulled on a legal technicality, and even the Istiqlal admitted that the court was an "improvisation," though it defended its decision.[20] Although it was announced during the trial that Addi ou Bihi and sixty others would soon be brought before the Court of Justice, apparently further in-

---

[18] *Ibid.*, December 21, 1957, excerpts from *At-Talíâ*.

[19] See Ben Barka's signed editorial, *Al-Istiqlal*, December 28, 1957, p. 3.

[20] *Ibid.*, March 30, 1958, p. 3. Their criticism appeared before the verdict was reversed and noted that the court had been "instituted by His Majesty" without mentioning either the role of the Minister of Justice or the party in the events leading up to the trial.

dictments were postponed. Addi ou Bihi was not forgotten by the Istiqlal, which wrote during the tense spring of 1958 that "the accomplices of Addi ou Bihi prepare a reactionary coalition against those who organized and conducted the battle for independence."[21] The Riffi affair had apparently convinced the King that the issues raised in such trials would only disrupt the country during a period of delicate negotiations with France. Soon afterward the King appointed a Commission of Inquiry which was to meet privately.

The statute establishing the Commission of Inquiry[22] laid down the most explicit criteria for alleged subversion that had yet been suggested. Its jurisdiction was limited, first, to persons of "Moroccan nationality," though the *dahir* on nationality had not yet been promulgated, and, secondly, to the time period from December 24, 1950, to November 16, 1955. The focus of the inquiry thus remained that of loyalty to the King, for the first date is the day of his open break with Al-Glaoui and the latter is the day on which he regained his throne. Specifically falling within the law were acts of those who had "taken a major part in the preparation, execution or consolidation of the *coup de force* of 20 August 1953 . . . [or] committed acts of violence against the population or the resistants." The law thus added the crime of having plotted against the resistance, which was legal testimony to the continuing influence of the resistance. Further testimony to the influence of the resistance was the appointment to the Commission of two early resistance organizers, Al-Bachir Ben El-Abbès and Dr. Abdellatif Benjelloun. Though all the members of the Commission were members of the Istiqlal, there were no high party officials.

The president was Mokhtar Soussi, a member of the Crown Council, and the other members were M'Hammed Bahnini, Secretary of the Government; Abdellatif El-Filali, chargé of the judicial section of the Ministry of Foreign Affairs; and two lawyers of resistance background. That most of these men were closely associated with the Palace testified to the King's interest in supervising proceedings and conclusions. A further safeguard against repeating the fiasco of the Riffi trial was limiting the Commission to denying the accused their civic rights for from three to fifteen years and any property acquired by abuse of authority. The accused were limited to those whose assets were frozen in 1957 or who were to be designated

21 *Ibid.*, April 13, 1958, p. 3.
22 *O.B.*, April 11, 1958, no. 2372, "Dahir no. 1-58-103 du 6 ramadan 1377 (27 mars 1958) portant création d'une commission d'enquête," p. 625.

jointly in any one month by the President of the Council and the Minister of the Interior. They were entitled to representation by a Moroccan lawyer and might appeal to the King, though the hearings were not to be public. In his charge to the Commission, the King emphasized its administrative character and said that it did not represent a reversal of the general pardon he had extended at independence. Its purpose was to return property to those who had been unfairly deprived of it and to give some retribution to those who had suffered "certain misdeeds."[23] He stressed further that it should be free from "all spirit of revenge" and should apply in its proceeding "only the *dahir*." Whatever aspirations the Istiqlal, the trade unions, or—more difficult to know—the resistance might have had for a broader kind of purge, the King was clearly determined that it was to be restrained and specific.

From this time the purge was no longer a national issue except within the framework defined by the King. On the investiture of the Balafrej government the party recalled the urgency of the purge, but qualified its statements to a form similar to those of the King. During the Commission's work comment generally disappeared from party publications, though an unsigned letter in *Al-Istiqlal* asked for an official statement explaining the necessity for the Commission of Inquiry. The unknown correspondent claimed that the population was aware of only isolated cases in their particular regions and that more publicity would make known the true proportions of the "threat" to national security.[24] When one considers the self-explanatory character of the law appointing the Commission and the King's statements on the subject, it appears that the party may have been more interested in further propaganda than in resolving the problem with a minimum of controversy.

The King chose a propitious moment to release news of the results of the purge—the anniversary of his exile. With a few additions the punished were limited to those who had been included in the decree freezing the assets of alleged traitors in late 1957.[25] The

---

[23] *La Vigie*, April 5, 1958, p. 2.

[24] *Al-Istiqlal*, June 8, 1958, p. 2. The letter was headlined on the front page—a fact indicating that the paper's editors attached importance to it. The writer also charged that even while the Commission was pursuing its work "subalterns of colonialism" were being enrolled in the civil service.

[25] The list appeared in the press the same day from a communiqué of the Palace, *La Vigie*, August 20, 1958, p. 5. It was later printed in the *O.B.*, no. 2391, August 22, 1958, "Liste des jugements rendus le 16 août 1958 par la commission d'enquête instituée par le dahir du 6 ramadan 1377 (27 mars 1958)," pp. 1337-1340. See the analysis in *Le Monde*, August 21, 1958, p. 3, which is used in this paragraph.

sentences fell in three main categories and the worst offenders received multiple sentences. Sixty-nine persons, most members of Ben Arafa's immediate administration, had their goods totally confiscated, and sixty-eight others had their goods partially confiscated. The sixty-nine worst offenders were also condemned to fifteen years of national degradation, while a group of 179 minor officials received sentences of national degradation of varying shorter periods. There is no evidence that the Commission tried to extend the purge to persons who had committed acts against the resistance or other offenses during the King's exile. The King did not mention these results in his speech on the anniversary of his exile, nor did he refer to the subject in his Speech from the Throne in November 1958. His conduct after the announcement of the results, as before, suggests that he regarded the entire episode as one to be closed with a minimum of fanfare and to be forgotten as rapidly as possible.

This approach did not receive the approval of the party, which stated that the investigation should be extended to all "who destroy the authority of the state or who sow discord and disunion among the people." It objected to "weaknesses" of the measures taken against the charged. Although the Minister of the Interior was a member of the Balafrej government, the Istiqlal also asked if the minister had sent to the Commission the files of all those who should be judged and what means the Commission possessed to investigate other possible offenders. Coming from the more conservative leadership of the Istiqlal, the discussion emphasized how compelling and attractive the purge issue had become. The progressive wing was represented by Bouabid, who repudiated the work of the Commission by calling for an "extra-governmental" commission, which would reflect the opinion of the "popular mass."[26]

The demands for an investigation of specific offenses against the King before independence were difficult to distinguish from offenses that took place after independence. It was very tempting for well-established parties to encourage this confusion. If subversion since independence could be substantiated, opposition activity might be associated with it and, thereby, made difficult. Where the opposition could be associated with antinationalist activity in the preindependence period, it could also be discredited. If the field of accepted accusation was enlarged to include many possible offenses against the preindependence nationalist movement, the problem be-

[26] *Al-Istiqlal*, October 18, 1958, p. 4.

came almost unmanageable, as was learned in the trial of Riffi.

The progressive faction of the party had, of course, never made any secret of its eagerness to have Addi ou Bihi come to trial. That this trial was conducted in the midst of tribal uprisings is indicative of the risk that some party leaders were prepared to take. Istiqlal leaders were well aware of the possible implications of the trial, as a speech of Bouabid indicated: "The case of Addi ou Bihi demonstrates well that the foreign hand has not yet spared Morocco of all the plots that enabled foreign domination since 1905. . . . It is necessary that all these plots should be revealed and known to the Moroccan people. So long as Addi ou Bihi is not condemned, Morocco remains under the menace of other identical plots."[27] By late 1958 the tribal revolts had, of course, led many Istiqlal leaders to believe that new French and Spanish schemes were being carried out to disrupt the nation. Since these uprisings were also in areas where the Moroccan Liberation Army had been active, the issue risked casting doubt on the entire resistance, part of which was loyal to the Istiqlal. In his speech Bouabid acknowledged that certain resistance leaders might unconsciously be playing into the hand of foreign powers.

As the Istiqlal leaders had repeatedly claimed, the Addi ou Bihi trial did prove to have far-reaching implications. The testimony made it clear that Caid Lahcen Lyoussi had been involved in the Addi ou Bihi revolt and possibly had contrived with the French to provide arms.[28] Any doubts were dispelled when Lyoussi was relieved of his post as a Crown Councilor during the trial. Several days later he fled to the Middle Atlas Mountains and reportedly sought refuge with the Spanish. This struck very close to the Palace. Lyoussi had been given his high government position by the King and the trial of Addi ou Bihi had very likely been postponed with royal consent. The King followed his precedent of trying to keep a group of persons representing the Palace between himself and delicate questions. He appointed a "Special Council" of fifteen jurists, who swore out the warrant for Lyoussi's arrest and presumably would direct an investigation into his past associations.

[27] *Ibid.*, October 25, 1958, p. 5.

[28] *Le Monde*, December 24, 1958, p. 5. Part of the testimony involving General Cogny, commander of the French forces in Morocco at independence, appears in *Al-Istiqlal*, December 27, 1958, p. 4. If the charges are true that a thousand rifles had been delivered to the tribesmen with the collusion of the French commanders at Fès and Meknes, the affair may have been much more important than reports indicated at the time. It was also alleged that an attempt was made to get Spanish help in the Rif, where a coordinated rebellion was supposed to have taken place.

With the completion of at least the first phase of the general purge, investigations were limited more and more to the administration. Government ministries could always set up new criteria for acceptability, but action under these conditions excluded civil or criminal proceedings. In fact, it was never made clear whether the discharges and changes in the administration over the first three years of independence were supposed to involve loyalty or to be directed only at the problem of reorganization and efficiency. Though all ministries worked with severe shortages of skilled civil servants, they no doubt tried to eliminate persons known to have collaborated. Up to the third Council of Government there were few demands for a purge of specific ministries, except for the regional administration of the Ministry of the Interior.

Even the generally outspoken Istiqlal newspapers made only general reference to "traitors" and "feudalists" in the government and administration. Ministries were seldom named, except for those under the supervision of ministers from opposition parties. From August 1956 the ministries with the largest number of personnel were under Istiqlal direction, so that such criticisms might place party officials in the government in embarrassing positions, most of whom were on the party's Executive Committee. In June 1958 the party announced that 200 lower-ranking officials of the Ministry of the Interior were being released, "conforming to the line fixed by the Istiqlal party and by the government to purge the administration conforming to the directives of His Majesty the King."[29] A few days later the paper added that every ministry was now preparing a list of those to be purged and that the Ministry of Justice was particularly concerned.

Whether or not these charges could be considered as cases of loyalty is in question, although the Istiqlal seemed to want them to appear as such. They occurred while a major revision of the regional organization was in process and were distinguished from the Commission's work by the party itself. Another paper under party influence said that the purge was continuing in three parts: the work of the Commission; criminal cases such as Addi ou Bihi's, for those who had threatened the security of the state since independence; and an administrative purge for poor conduct or inefficiency at that time.[30] Further doubt originates from the fact that the first efforts in this new purge were made by the Minister of the Interior, Chiguer, a

[29] *La Vigie*, June 2, 1958, p. 1.
[30] Excerpts from *Al-Ahd Al-Jadid*, *La Vigie*, June 4, 1958, p. 2.

man known for his close association with the King. The Palace had consistently taken a lenient position on this problem and this minister had also been denounced by the Istiqlal as a weak party member at the time of his selection. By necessity or design, the Istiqlal, having once aroused interest in the purge, may have found itself compelled to continue this line of propaganda.

Civil Liberties for What?

The question of membership in the new state involves two important aspects: who will qualify as a member, and what privileges will be given to a member to distinguish him from a nonmember? Of most concern are those activities generally summarized as civil rights, though, of course, citizens also receive other benefits in the form of economic, social, and legal benefits. It should be clearly stated first that for a large proportion of citizens, who had felt the period of violence and disorder from 1952 to 1955, considerations of physical safety were probably more important than new privileges. How long such an epoch lasts is, in part, a function of the degree of disorder created during the struggle for independence and also the kind of goals given priority for the future. For the moment the question of how such goals are selected will be secondary to the way in which the individual citizen might directly engage in political activity under the protection given by civil rights. It should be clearly understood that this is only one way in which a member may exercise influence, and possibly a minor one in new states. An analysis that expected a new nation to conform in some spontaneous fashion to patterns of political behavior of advanced nations would be grossly distorted. On the other hand, the simple existence of advanced nations from whom the idea of an independent, modern nation is necessarily derived has certainly placed emphasis on the way in which such political systems operate and thus stimulated the desire to conform to such patterns to some extent.

Under the Protectorate all aspects of political behavior were under the decree powers of the Resident General.[31] Not only could he summarily impose martial law, but also suspend all the generally accepted rights of the accused under arrest and trial. Little attention was given in the colonial period to developing patterns of political behavior generally assumed to be vital in advanced nations. Further-

[31] See Rezette, *Les Partis Politiques Marocaines*, pp. 29-37.

more, the conditions under which Morocco has developed since independence have continued this pattern, regardless of the tradition set by the French. Not until early 1957 was the nation sufficiently ordered to permit the consideration by any universally applied criteria of the way in which individuals might participate in the political system. The military regulations, under which the new nation had existed since 1940, were abrogated two years after independence. Up to mid-1958 the new nation continued to regulate political action with the same laws that had been used against the nationalists before independence. Publications and organizations were forbidden and authorized under arbitrary controls by decree vested in the Residency since 1914, which had been transferred to the office of the President of the Council. Similarly, the authorization of new organizations or their disbanding was handled under Residency controls of 1914.

The use of this legislation is particularly interesting, for it was such abuses of the colonial regime that were one of the major grievances of the nationalists. Though it would be unfair to assume that these powers were perpetuated for the same reasons as when they were exercised under the Protectorate, it is important to note that political behavior during the first two years of the new nation's history was limited in the same way. On several occasions these powers were used by the Minister of the Interior to forbid meetings of political parties and to ban their publications. The circumstances within which the new country existed during this period may well justify this action, but it must also be admitted that for the large mass of the population the way in which political behavior was limited changed very little.

That those in positions of influence may have been in a dilemma on this question is suggested by the practically universal approval voiced for individual civil and political rights, although nothing was done. The origin of most claims for civil rights was the St. Cloud Declaration of the King, in which he proposed a constitutional monarchy. In his Speech from the Throne in November 1955 he stated one of three basic tasks of the new government to be "the creation of democratic institutions . . . within the framework of a constitutional monarchy granting to Moroccans of all faiths citizenship rights and the exercise of political and trade union freedom."[32]

[32] Landau, op.cit., p. 398.

These thoughts were echoed in the speeches of Bouabid and Bala-frej during the Istiqlal Congress of December 1955. Once Morocco became legally independent, the party's references to political and civil rights were noticeably more qualified. This lasted until the National Council meeting of the fall of 1956, when the party began its most outspoken attacks on the government and claimed a majority position in the Council of Government. At that time the party based its claim on its popular support and made some of its most fervent defenses of civil rights. The issue of individual rights was also championed in attacking those rural officials who were still obstructing the organization of the party. For example, Al-Fassi asked, "If the administrator does not believe in the rights of citizens, in the necessity of the play of general liberty, and if the laws permit authority to despoil these liberties, how are we to be assured that we live as free citizens in a free country?"[33] Shortly after the second Council of Government was formed, the party paper spoke again of "the respect of all liberties without which there cannot be a parliament or elections," but added its disapproval of persons who used these liberties to form "fake" parties.[34] Since the party placed great importance on the immediate formation of a Consultative Assembly, it had to recognize also the requisites of such an assembly, but it was at the same time reluctant to admit the full play of such rights in the formation of opposition parties.

The equivocal position of the Istiqlal on the question of civil and political rights is partially explained by arguments presented to the party membership in the *Internal Bulletin*. The experience of resisting the Protectorate had, the party acknowledged, established the habit of criticizing every governmental action. Before independence excessive criticism was useful to obstruct colonialism, but now, the party suggested, "Before we may criticize any action we must study it in every way and consider all of Morocco to be sure of its results."[35] The party may even have been sensing the aftereffects of the hyper-critical attitudes encouraged within its own organization before independence. Simultaneously, the party had to defend individual liberties, since one of the constant themes of its preindependence propaganda was the denial of civil rights. Although such rights did not yet have any legal basis in the new nation, the party claimed

[33] *Al-Alam*, August 28, 1956, Fr. Trans.
[34] *Ibid.*, October 30, 1956.
[35] "A New Mind for a New Era" (New Series), no. 2, February 1957(?), p. 2.

that the establishment of these liberties in the new country had infuriated the "colonialists" and their collaborators, who were now trying to destroy the country.[36] While the Moroccan citizen undoubtedly did have more personal freedom in independent Morocco than he had had under the Protectorate, he did not possess these rights by law and his political activity was governed entirely by Protectorate legislation. These weaknesses in the Istiqlal's policy were skillfully exploited by the opposition, especially while an opposition party leader was Minister of Information.

The King's Speech from the Throne of November 1956 reinforced his earlier position, and his inaugural speech to the Consultative Assembly the same month contains many references to individual liberties as prerequisites to representative government. The fragility of the new country's political system had been exposed with the Meknes uprising of late 1956 and for several months there was little talk of civil liberties. When the subject did arise again, later in 1957, it was usually accompanied with qualifications and reservations. It is possible that the Moroccan leaders had underestimated the complexity of a political system that guarantees the free exercise of certain rights and had oversimplified the task of setting up the array of rules and procedures prerequisite to such an intricate political system. It is also possible that they had, consciously or unconsciously, assumed that independence was the sole prerequisite for the harmonious interplay of millions of individuals in such a political system.

In a speech to the trade unions on May Day, 1957, the King announced that orders had been given to the Minister of the Interior to begin preparation for elections. The plan was presented to the Council of Government several months later and met with the apparent disapproval of the King. The Palace issued a press statement the next day stating that the King would personally see that all citizens participating in elections would receive the "necessary guarantees."[37] The imminence of the elections seems to have subdued the Istiqlal's enthusiasm. The party stressed the importance of avoiding "a sterile agitation to the detriment of constructive and perseverant action," without mentioning rights or guarantees. The reservations of the party were clarified later in the year when the Popular Movement began. In a signed editorial Ben Barka stated, "We are for liberties, but not for those which might permit traitors to regroup

---

[36] "Lessons from the Affair of Addi ou Bihi," *Internal Bulletin* (New Series), no. 3, March 1957(?), p. 1.

[37] *C.M.*, July 25-28, 1957, p. 1.

themselves."[38] As plans for elections were revised and improved, the problem of civil rights was raised again. In January 1958 regulations for the press and public associations were again considered by the Council of Government. The silence of the Istiqlal on these questions had given rise to sufficient doubt of the sincerity of its ministers on the Council to produce a public denial that the party discouraged guaranteed political rights.

Though an Istiqlal member was Minister of the Interior at that time, the party admitted that "one could not imagine a better police system for the disintegration of political parties."[39] The delay in promulgating *dahirs* on civil and political rights apparently was causing considerable embarrassment for the Istiqlal. The Democratic party had presented a petition to the King listing the alleged abuses of police powers under the Istiqlal Minister of the Interior. It also objected to the reported plan to give the minister authority to dissolve political parties without appeal for a period of two months. A counterproject reportedly presented by Bekkai was stopped by the Istiqlal ministers in the Council, while a proposal of the Liberal Independents was relegated to an interministerial commission, from which it never emerged. The situation became more intense with the burning of an office of the Liberal Independents in Rabat, which in turn provoked the destruction of an Istiqlal office.

Criticizing the Istiqlal on its most vulnerable policies, the opposition Democratic party also began a series of public rallies in the slums of Casablanca. When the French attacked Sakiet-Sidi-Youssef in Tunisia, the problem was rapidly reaching a climax and might have degenerated into mass violence. Again, as in 1956, international events created a situation in which the government felt that popular discontent was great enough to result in serious bloodshed. Referring to the Tunisian incident, the King instructed the Minister of the Interior to apply the existing legislation to forbid all public manifestations that might provoke disorder. Soon afterward the newspapers of the Democratic party were banned and it was forbidden to hold public meetings. During the Tangier Conference of the North African nationalist parties the newspaper of the Unity party was also banned after it printed opinions of the Democratic party leaders. Curiously, a Communist-oriented newspaper, *La Nation*, appeared during this period and the Communist party's Arabic

[38] *Al-Istiqlal,* December 28, 1957, p. 3.
[39] See the statement of Abdallah Ibrahim to the Party Inspectors' meeting, *Al-Istiqlal,* January 11, 1958, p. 7.

paper circulated more freely, though the party itself had been illegal since independence.

The circumstances of the fall of the second Council of Government are testimony to how important the issue of civil and political liberties had become over the preceding two years, though it was not the only major question involved in the crisis.[40] Through Bekkai the leading members of the Democratic party, Liberal Independent party, Unity party, and the still unauthorized Popular Movement presented a petition to the King asking for a law "guaranteeing and regulating the exercise of democratic and public liberties."[41] The petition submitted that, in the absence of any laws on the organization of political parties, press, or public meetings, elections could not take place. This position was reiterated by Bekkai during consultations with the King to form the new government. The evolution of the Istiqlal position on civil liberties during the month-long crisis is more difficult to follow, but represents a series of comments ranging from Ben Barka's abrupt reference to "healthy democracy" in its early phase to the definite commitment of Balafrej for the speedy preparation of a "Charter of Public Liberties" when he accepted the Presidency of the Council.

Ben Barka, after consultations with the King, stressed the necessity of implementing new liberties in a way that would "permit popular forces to mobilize the masses." In his words, liberty should be "constructive" and "instituted in Morocco in order to thwart imperialist intrigues and reactionary coalitions that camouflage themselves behind the so-called defense of democracy."[42] When Bouabid spoke some days later, he took a more definite position favoring "public and private liberties" with "permanent guarantees," but added that such liberties should not be used destructively.[43] As the question of civil liberties became a central issue of the crisis, the Istiqlal offered explanations of the suppression of such liberties over the past two months and the tardiness of the governments in which their party had had a majority to produce legislation concerning liberties. *Al-Alam* asserted that the party was quite willing that liberties should be guaranteed, but that they should not be used to produce anarchy or to be exploited.[44] This position was amplified by Ben Barka in a speech to party militants in Casablanca. He

[40] A good, brief catalog of all the issues involved is Jean Lacouture's article in *Le Monde*, April 17, 1958, p. 1.
[41] See *L'Echo*, April 17, 1958, p. 3.   [42] *Al-Istiqlal*, April 20, 1958, p. 3.
[43] *La Vigie*, April 23, 1958, p. 1.   [44] *Ibid.*, April 27, 1958, U.S. Trans.

claimed that "the agitations instigated for so-called liberties are only the warped plans of imperialists" and that the action of the government in suppressing the opposition parties was justified "to protect the people against the propagation of subversive ideas."[45]

The crisis came to a close, for the country if not for the Istiqlal, with the publication of a Royal Charter that specified: "Desirous equally to permit our subjects to exercise fundamental liberties and to enjoy the rights of man we guarantee to them the liberty of opinion, of expression, of assembly or association. This guarantee will be limited only by respect to the monarchial regime, the safety of the state and the imperatives of the general interest."[46] There was, however, some difficulty in obtaining Istiqlal endorsement for this Charter, and the subsequent statement of the dissatisfied elements of the party made only passing reference to this section of it. Once the new government had acted on the many problems postponed during the crisis, the King announced that the Commission on Revision of Legislative Texts was to write a *dahir* on public liberties by the twentieth of July. This placed the responsibility on the Secretary General of the government, Bahnini, rather than on an Istiqlal minister, though the draft *dahir* would be submitted to the Council of Government. The King's instructions recognized that elections were impossible without the full rights guaranteed by law, though subject to the "superior interests" of the country and to be used in a "constructive" way.

A month later the first draft of the Charter of Public Liberties was discussed by the Council of Government. This fact suggests that much of the work had been done over the preceding year. The proposed law was presented to the King early in August 1958 and final agreement was reached in the government over the next month. In comparison with work on similar fundamental legislation, work on the Charter of Public Liberties progressed at about the same speed. What is evident, however, is the rapidity with which a final draft was formulated, once the King decided to give personal attention to the problem. Although it may be controversial to what extent earlier progress had been hampered by the Istiqlal, it is clear that the King was able to have quick action taken, once he decided to do so. This was done, furthermore, at a time when the Istiqlal was showing signs of serious internal divisions and the Balafrej government was being

---

[45] *Al-Istiqlal*, April 27, 1958, p. 4.
[46] *O.B., op.cit.*

heavily criticized. The possibility should not be excluded that promulgation of this law was intended to reinforce the Balafrej government and to minimize the charges that the actions of the government had not resulted in the fulfillment of promises made by the King in May 1958.

As in the case of the announcement of the purge results on the anniversary of his exile, the King chose the dramatic moment of the anniversary of his ascension to the throne to issue the Charter of Public Liberties. The section on associations established that any organization whose purpose was to interfere with the territorial integrity or the monarchy of Morocco was illegal. Although the right of individual free association was granted without condition, any group wishing to levy dues or possess property had to be registered. The registration had to include the title of the group, its founders and officers, its headquarters, and the number and location of all affiliates. Special sections dealt with three categories of associations: political parties, foreign associations, and public-service groups.

A "political party" was any association whose activity "tends directly or indirectly, to make prevail the doctrine of the association in the conduct and management of public affairs and to assure it is followed by its representatives."[47] The financial restrictions on parties were extremely precise. All funds had to be of Moroccan origin. No funds could be used from a governmental source, and the occupation of its officials had to be specified. Parties might admit only Moroccans, but were forbidden to admit any military, police, or administrative personnel. For an offense regarding national integrity or the monarchy, a party could be suspended by decrees for two weeks, but might automatically resume activity if no action were taken in that period. Under a separate provision any association might be dissolved by decree for these same offenses, including any armed manifestation or paramilitary activity, but had judicial recourse.

Public meetings had to be announced one day in advance to the local pasha or *caid*, except for charitable, cultural, artistic, and sports groups. The conditions of keeping order at such metings were care-

[47] See *La Vigie*, November 26, 1958, p. 1 and pp. 6-7. It appeared later in the *O.B.*, no. 2404 bis, November 27, 1958, "Dahir no. 1-58-376 du 3 joumada I 1378 (15 novembre 1958) réglementant le droit d'association," pp. 1909-1912; "Dahir no. 1-58-377 du 3 joumada I 1378 (15 novembre 1958) relatif aux rassemblements publiques," pp. 1912-1914; and "Dahir no. 1-58-378 du 3 joumada I 1378 (15 novembre 1958) formant code de las presse au Maroc," pp. 1914-1919.

fully outlined. A long provision dealt with the procedure for dissolution of an armed mob, specifying different sentences for armed and unarmed persons and for those who departed after a set warning had been given. The press law required full information on officers, source of funds, and nationality of owners of any periodical publication. Scientific, technical, artistic, and professional publications were exempt. Under heavy penalty the director of a periodical was required to include within three days or by the next issue any corrections by a public authority concerning the content of an issue. Even heavier penalties required that any replies by a person mentioned in the periodical had to be printed in the same general location and type as the article provoking the reply. No charge might be imposed if the reply did not exceed twice the size of the original article.

Foreign periodicals printed in Morocco came under the same provisions, and those brought to Morocco in printed form might be forbidden by the President of the Council. The foreign press was further limited by the forbidding of any periodical "of foreign origin or inspiration of a nature to prejudice the national interest."[48] Foreign publications received the same punishment as domestic publications for provoking crimes; jeopardizing the internal or external security of the state; defaming ministers, civil servants, the forces of order, or the Royal family. The Minister of the Interior was permitted to confiscate any issue of a publication that might threaten public order, but all other procedures against publications were to be handled by the courts.

The political experience of the new country was reflected in this legislation in many ways. The careful provisions concerning foreign support of political parties and the foreign press were no doubt prompted by suspicion of schemes attempted by colonial powers, which suspicions were substantiated several times. The detail on the handling of armed mobs and the requirements of clear responsibility for public meetings recalled the Casablanca rallies of the Democratic party. They might also serve to restrain rallies for the Algerian nationalists and manifestations by the trade unions during labor disputes, both of which had resulted in clashes with police on several occasions. The participation of the unions and other pressure groups in political activity might also bring them under the broad definition given to political parties. All the organized groups of the

48 *Ibid.*, p. 1916.

new country were explicitly acknowledged in the selection of representatives for the National Consultative Assembly, which would seem
to have entailed their treatment as political parties under the law.

Like the nationality law, the Charter of Public Liberties further
institutionalized the monarchy, though it is interesting that the penalties for abuse of members of the Royal family were the same as
those for abuse of minor officials. The arbitrary powers of the Minister of the Interior appear to have been kept to a necessary minimum, with his authority generally limited by court-review procedures. The Istiqlal might suffer somewhat from the provision that
civil servants were not allowed to join parties, since the Istiqlal probably formed one of the largest groups of solvent, dues-paying members, although the large number of civil servants in sympathy with
the party would no doubt continue to give it local prestige. At the
end of 1958 there were no publicized test cases under the Charter
nor had parties begun to register under its provisions.

The problems of defining nationality, punishing collaborators, and
enacting legislation protecting political rights demonstrate several
important characteristics of the emerging political system in Morocco. The monarchy has been of key importance in focusing the
attention of the whole nation and of the parties on the need to provide fundamental laws for the political system. The King's activity
has been characterized by a willingness to forget past injustices and
perhaps even to minimize foreign threats to the nation since independence. Clearly the nationalists were consistently determined to
press the purge more firmly and generally preferred to magnify
crises. The Addi ou Bihi trial not only vindicated their alarm, but
also confirmed their claim to pre-eminence. The existence of the
new nation was in itself perhaps the most meaningful goal that was
universally understood by the Moroccan populace. Although it is
likely that the Istiqlal was guilty of opportunism, if one dwells on
the party's motivation, it should also be noted that the party was
trying to act on the national level by using terms and problems that
everyone understood. To seek influence is not immoral in the framework being applied in this book. It must be sought within the capacity of the members of the political system. To do so may set patterns of influence that bring difficulties in handling other problems
of the new nation.

The enactment of the Charter of Public Liberties is probably the
most important piece of legislation in the period covered by this

book, though its application now and in the years ahead will be the final test of its usefulness. Only the experience relating to the legal resolution of the problem can be considered here. The Istiqlal was certainly equivocal on the granting of political rights and on some occasions tried to confuse the issues of collaborators' treatment and citizens' legally protected sphere of political activity. It should also be recognized that if the party accepted the full preparation of the populace for informed participation in politics—a thing that is probably impossible—before seeking influence, it would very likely dissolve itself. Nevertheless, the formation of institutions in a new country opens new avenues for the exercise of influence in ways unknown to nationalists as well as to the population. The nationalists can use such institutions, but they must either use them on equal terms with other groups or try totally to discredit the opposition.

Underlying this difficulty is a more general problem of concern on the national level. In a new country it is difficult to bring individual influence to bear on specific issues and complex problems. For the vast majority of Moroccans the Charter of Public Liberties has meant and will mean little change in their political behavior in reference to the nation or to their local community. The opportunities and privileges that it offers will largely concern the small number of citizens who have a fuller understanding of national problems and who can utilize the existing pattern of influence to gain advantage under the law. A second general observation is that the Charter was introduced into the political system by an arbitrary decision of the King, though there was undoubtedly much sentiment in its favor among the population. The way in which existing problems have been solved is related to the way in which future problems probably will be solved—either by reinforcing existing political behavior or by suggesting new ways to act within the political system. To the political system as a whole the innovations that have been added by the Charter may not outweigh its confirmation of the basically arbitrary system of government Moroccans have known all their lives in matters of national concern.

The dilemma of the new nation is not merely that the individual abilities permitting considerable participation in politics are generally lacking. The nation must also deal with many problems in its early experience where the range of choice is fairly limited, if not predetermined. The technical details, as is the case in advanced political systems, remain largely in the hands of specialists and experts. The tendency may be to accept a low degree of participation and the postponement of more profound political reform in response to the immediate concrete problems facing a new country, as well as in response to the limitations of most of the citizens. Such an alternative may prove to be effective for a short period of time, but is certainly inviting attack from the advanced segment of the populace. In time it may provide grounds for charges of hypocrisy and authoritarianism against the original regime. In this way the short-run dilemma, which probably is only trying to operate with limited resources and under the pressure of time, paves the way for a crisis in the long run. The extent to which such a result is defensible depends, of course, on many factors and value judgments outside the scope of this inquiry. The general structure of the problem, however, should be appreciated by those observing new nations from the positions of highly developed and advanced political systems.

CHAPTER VI

VIOLENCE AND COERCION

Violence and Independence

FOR nearly three years, from December 1952 until November 1955, Morocco lived under conditions where the most common form of influence was the power over life and death. After the suppression of the Istiqlal a completely new organization, the resistance movement,[1] came into being. At the time of independence and for some months thereafter it was the strongest nationalist organization in the countryside. None of its leaders had been important in the pre-1952 Istiqlal, though many of them came from the lower ranks of the party. After two years of fighting and the formation of their own army they constituted an independent political element which still exists. Although a few of its members were given positions in the new rural administration, most guerilla fighters were not suited for civil service positions. The Istiqlal was not prepared to yield the victory they had gained after thirty years' effort to the relatively new arrivals, but the party was naturally eager to recruit as many of the resistance members as possible. The vast majority of the Moroccan people thought that independence meant not only the achievement of a new international status, but also the end of all the controls that had been placed on them by the Protectorate. The disorder and violence found in the early months of independence can be traced to three sources: the remnants of the urban resistance groups, the Liberation Army, and the popular impression that all political characteristics of the Protectorate regime would disappear immediately.

Isolated elements of the groups that were later to become the resistance had existed in Morocco since at least 1951. The leaders of the Istiqlal were generally aware of the existence of a body of opinion within the cells of the party favoring direct action, but the leaders refused to support such a policy. Not until the brutal suppression of the general strike in December 1952, was there any central or-

---

[1] Nearly all of the Moroccan terrorist organizations were interrelated in some way, but exact information is unavailable. Where the term "resistance movement" occurs only the general activity of organized violence is meant. The term "secret resistance" is used by Moroccans to refer to the urban resistance which was more closely interrelated. The Liberation Army will be specifically designated, although there were serious internal differences there too.

157

ganization of the resistance effort. A small committee formed in Casablanca began preparations early in 1953, but this group was discouraged by both the King and the Istiqlal, who still hoped that some reconciliation with the French could be arranged. Their reluctance to be involved in preparations for terrorist activity while trying to resolve the Moroccan problem without bloodshed and without the exile of the King meant that the resistants were almost totally unprepared when the King was exiled in August 1953.[2] In late 1953 terrorism was confined to the major cities, especially Casablanca, where the main targets were the French conservatives, who virtually ruled the country under the puppet King, Ben Arafa.

After the exile of Mohammed V no restraint was left on those qualified and willing to engage in direct action. The early leader, Zerktouni, organized the terrorist groups of Casablanca and later committed suicide when captured by the French.[3] In these early activities he was accompanied by Abdallah Senhaji, later to become chief of the Liberation Army in the Nador area; Dr. Abdelkrim Khatib, later a Liberation Army leader in the Rif; and three others who have now dropped out of prominence. With the King's exile this small committee in Casablanca made contact with the Provisional Executive Committee of the Istiqlal, whom they found still cautious even after all the leading members of the party had been arrested. The leaders of the Istiqlal committee were in contact with the resistants and from time to time met with Zerktouni or other terrorist leaders, but had no part in their decisions.

The early terrorist groups were organized in complete isolation from one another. One of the more successful, the Black Hand, managed to survive until independence and was directed by Abdelselem Bennani, later an official of the Istiqlal youth organization. Though these individual terrorist efforts occupied large numbers of French police and soldiers, they did not seem to have seriously impaired general French activity. The resistance was sufficient to create a stalemate, but could not enter into direct warfare with the French forces. For this an army was needed and the first steps to organize

---

[2] Moroccans are still reluctant to discuss the resistance. The Istiqlal has published only one historical article, *Al-Istiqlal*, August 23, 1958, p. 4, which is very general and ends with 1953.

[3] It is interesting to note that Zerktouni was a cell member of the Istiqlal selected to serve on a disciplinary committee to deal with other members charged with organizing terrorist activity. On this inquiry he made his first contact and became a member of the group. See *Al-Istiqlal*, June 22, 1958, p. 24.

one were taken in late 1953.[4] The resistance movement had been in contact with the Spanish zone from its early days and members about to be arrested by the police were smuggled to safety in the north. Though the urban terrorism continued until independence, from early 1954 on, the major effort of the resistance movement was the organization and training of the Liberation Army in the ex-Spanish zone.

The relation of the Istiqlal to the resistance movement at the time of independence is not entirely clear. The party itself was no doubt well aware that many of its best militants and particularly the most active youth were rapidly joining in the resistance.[5] Though the problem was out of party hands until late 1955, it was apparent that if the resistance continued long enough and the Rifian Liberation Army became sufficiently large, the party would simply no longer exist. Once the negotiations were actually under way the Istiqlal leaders also felt their responsibility for maintaining enough order to continue a national administration and desired to rebuild their party. The party directors, however, were not even agreed after the return of the King. Al-Fassi maintained that the resistants would cease fighting only when they were satisfied that certain "national reforms" were accomplished.[6]

Those in positions of responsibility, including both the King and the party leaders in Morocco, could not afford to take nebulous positions. The new government was confronted with serious problems of internal order stemming from the difficulties of reorienting the members of the resistance. Until the formation of the Royal Army and the Sûreté Nationale the new country was almost totally dependent on French forces to keep order. The popular discontent with these remnants of the Protectorate impaired their usefulness and in some instances only served to provoke volatile demonstrations. Under the threat of unnecessary bloodshed of both Moroccans and French, as well as the persistent demands of the nationalists for concrete evidence of independence, steps were taken to organize the army and the police.

In nearly every province there were signs of serious disruption and a series of bloody incidents. For a few months uncoordinated and generally irresponsible units of party police were organized, while

---

[4] Interview with Dr. Abdelkrim Khatib, Casablanca, July 3, 1958.

[5] See the account in *Le Monde*, August 12, 1955, p. 4.

[6] *C.M.*, December 10, 1955, p. 2, and Annex V. Interview of Al-Fassi by *Maroc-Presse*.

in other areas the government was forced to rely on the control of the French Army to prevent disorder and uprisings. The final dissolution of the urban resistance groups was accomplished by the Moroccan police, but only after many urban resistance cells had been literally shot down after engaging in racketeering and smuggling. Some terrorists and guerilla leaders were absorbed into the new Moroccan administration, but the elder nationalist leaders in exile and prison returned to take over the more important jobs in the government.

The first evidence of the kind of spontaneous and brutal violence that the new nation might experience after independence was the Oued Zem uprising of late August 1955. Up to the time of this incident the French Army occupation of the countryside had been regarded as effective, though the repeated French use of the tribes to bring pressure against the cities had enabled some Istiqlal infiltration and indoctrination. For reasons that have never been fully revealed a local tribe descended on the country village of Oued Zem and brutally killed nearly eighty Frenchmen and their families.[7] The tribe had a record of violence under the Protectorate and might very possibly have been especially susceptible to fanatical appeals. They were also members of one of the larger religious brotherhoods, the Cherkaoui, whose main center, Boujad, is near by. The French reaction was swift and ruthless. Three thousand troops were sent to the area immediately and the tribe was herded into a mountain valley. After an angry speech by a French general the tribe was strafed at random from the ground and air. A conservative estimate of the dead and wounded is five thousand. The affair increased anxiety in Paris over further delay in settling the Moroccan problem and alerted the Moroccan leaders themselves to the kind of primitive violence that could be unleashed in the countryside.

As the return of the King drew near there were more indications of the kind of problem that the new country would have in establishing order. One urban resistance group, the Black Cross, appointed itself as an agent of order and announced that it would punish anyone disturbing the peace during the King's arrival.[8] There was also a sudden rise in the number of attacks on offices of rural French administrators and French forester outposts. In the cities there ap-

---

[7] *New York Times*, August 27, 1955, p. 1.
[8] *C.M.*, November 21, 1955, p. 3.

peared units of party police of both the Istiqlal and the Democratic parties, who arrested so-called "impostors" of other spontaneous police units and gangs trying to extort money from the population at large. In the midst of the popular refusal to pay taxes, attend school, or end boycotts, the Istiqlal asked that "ceremonies end in order to check maneuvers of provocation" and that the people should be "on guard against thieves operating under the camouflage of nationalism and the resistance movement."[9]

In late 1955 the political parties took advantage of the enthusiasm of the crowds to begin to enroll members, but they do not appear to have fully realized how volatile popular sentiment was. There are few signs that they anticipated the problems of reorienting the resistance movement and establishing order as the French controls were withdrawn. Very likely it had been assumed that the return of the King and the nationalist leaders would be sufficient to produce calm and confidence. On the contrary, all the northern provinces remained in a chaotic state and the Liberation Army continued to fight. While the disorder may have lent a sense of urgency to these negotiations and neutralized French reluctance to make substantial concessions, it also meant that the new nation revealed itself as unable to keep order among its own people and that the organization of a new national government was postponed. Whatever advantage the Moroccans gained in the negotiations for the Franco-Moroccan Agreements was paid for dearly in delaying the development of their own internal political system.

The first sobering incident after the return of the King was the riot at Souk El-Arbaa du Gharb late in January. What began as a welcoming celebration for the governor of Rabat City ended in a fierce riot with at least four dead and thirty wounded.[10] The conflict occurred between militants of the Istiqlal and the Democratic parties, who had come from many of the surrounding cities for the occasion. Both parties were engaged in intensive recruitment efforts and both were eager to prove their exclusive nationalist character. It is quite possible that the affair had been used by partisans of one of the parties in an attempt to disgrace the other. Responsibility has never been clearly placed and probably never can be, for it was the result of the highly charged emotions and indeterminate situation then characteristic of the country.

[9] *Al-Alam*, January 5, 1956, p. 4, Fr. Trans.   [10] *C.M.*, January 24, 1956, p. 1.

The situation was especially tense in the large *medinas* of Casablanca, where the resistance had been the strongest. The governor of Casablanca, union officials, and the King visited the crowded *medinas* to reassure the populace. The King's message was repeated in a speech at the main mosque of Casablanca, where he said, "Independence does not signify the reign of license and anarchy, or the preponderance of particular interests; it does not signify insubordination or the refusal to pay taxes which are the condition of the life of the state and its activities in all areas."[11] Subsequent statements indicate the imminence of violence, and disorder continued at least until the summer of 1956. As efforts to rebuild political parties grew, there were repeated clashes between the "police" of the Istiqlal and the Democratic parties. One of the most frequent centers for sporadic party gunfights was Mohammedia, a workers' suburb of Casablanca. The disorder was sufficient for the governor to intervene as mediator between the local offices of the parties, but little more was heard of the conflict after the unexplained kidnaping of three of the Democratic party militants. Other incidents took place at Kenitra and Fès, where local leaders of both the Istiqlal and Democratic parties were assassinated.

Serious disorder also occurred at Marrakech in the south and Larache in the ex-Spanish zone. Since the Spanish government was slow to recognize the newly won territorial unity of Morocco, independence celebrations in the north were repressed with bloody repercussions. At Larache the pasha, Khalid Raissouni, was forced after Istiqlal attacks to flee to the Spanish-administered town of Ceuta. He had been known as the "Glaoui of the North" and a puppet of the Spanish. With less evident political overtones similar violence erupted in Marrakech during the independence celebrations. The crowds brutally killed at least fifteen members of Glaoui's entourage and administration.[12] As a result an Istiqlal official was made Minister of the Interior, though there is no evidence that the party was instrumental in the affair.[13] As with the Oued Zem incident it is possible that local party militants had excessively aroused public feelings over the Glaoui regime.

[11] *Ibid.*, February 8, 1956, p. 1, and Annex I.

[12] *Ibid.*, May 3, 1956, Annex III, lists the names of fifteen members of Glaoui's entourage; *New York Times*, May 4, 1956, p. 3, reported nineteen.

[13] From this time M'Hammedi replaced Lahcen Lyoussi. M'Hammedi, however, was not replaced some months later when the sons of Glaoui were arrested under even more mysterious conditions.

Urban Terrorism and the Police

The legacy of organized violence caused trouble for the new country until the summer of 1956. Urban terrorist groups were organized in an isolated fashion with elaborate devices of control and communication. The leaders admit that the members were mostly *gens du peuple* who found return to the routine of factories and shops difficult. With independence they were cut off from their network of supply and communication centers in the north. Several groups of terrorist cells continued to exist after independence without direction and also without purpose. The Black Hand was reportedly integrated into the new Moroccan police. Others were offered positions in the new rural administration, though often with embarrassing consequences. Probably the largest share of these severely tested patriots simply drifted back to their old jobs, but a few became the core of a series of gangs of racketeers. Those who were unable to adjust to a peaceful life received ultimatums from the police, which were followed by "liquidation" if their criminal actions did not stop.[14] These vestiges of the urban terrorist organization also became the target for Communist penetration. Moroccan officials admit that Communist infiltration in the propaganda committees of the resistance movement made some progress.

An example of the disintegration of the urban resistance was the history of the Black Crescent. Even before independence the Black Crescent was disavowed by the bulk of the resistance leaders, who put the populace on guard against the possible extortion that the group might practice.[15] The group reportedly organized its own army in the mountains and participated in a series of gunfights among competing mobsters in Casablanca. These fights ended with the arrest and escape of the man thought to be the head of the entire Casablanca terrorist organization, Ahmed Al-Hassan.[16] The Black Crescent continued to operate, however, and soon after these gunbattles issued a statement defending the national loyalty and honesty of their organization. After a warning from the Minister of the Interior the Moroccan police were sent against these patriots turned criminal. Although the Black Crescent issued a tract in Casablanca

[14] See Lacouture, *Le Maroc à l'Epreuve*, p. 165.

[15] The official character of this problem is testified to by the communiqué's being issued for the Liberation Army by the Secretary of State for Information. *C.M.*, February 25, 1956, p. 2, and Annex VI.

[16] See *C.M.*, April 15, 1956, p. 2, and April 16, 1956, p. 3. Like many other names used in the resistance, this is probably a pseudonym.

denying any Communist connection and again pledging their loyalty to the King, the government was apparently convinced that they were incorrigible. In a battle between the terrorists and special shock brigades of the Sûreté, the leader of the Black Crescent was killed.[17] Reports that the Black Crescent had violently differed with the Istiqlal over affiliations cannot be verified. Thus ended one of the most tragic episodes in the Moroccan struggle for independence.

The establishment of order in the new nation was the work of the Sûreté and the Royal Moroccan Army. The police force of about 10,000 men[18] and its modern equipment testify to both the efficiency and the cost of the Sûreté. The Director has been Mohammed Laghzaoui, a financial supporter of the Istiqlal since 1943 and also deeply devoted to Mohammed V.[19] The only existing legislation concerning the police force is a vaguely worded *dahir* issued shortly after independence in which the Sûreté is "attached" to the Ministry of the Interior.[20] The police were generally regarded as being virtually under the personal control of Laghzaoui and the King. Strenuous efforts were made to remove all French police from public view as rapidly as possible, and the Sûreté has set the pace of all other government offices in its "Moroccanization" program.

Like the work of the Ministry of the Interior, the work of the Sûreté is not open to public criticism and police acts are seldom questioned. On one occasion when police methods were questioned in the National Consultative Assembly, it provoked an explanatory statement from the Sûreté.[21] The monthly meetings of the high officials and area commanders of the police are always directed by Laghzaoui, apparently without supervision of any government agency. The police appear to operate as an autonomous organization responsible only to their Director and the King. This fact is also indicated by the frequent communiqués issued by the Sûreté

[17] *Ibid.*, July 28, 1956, p. 2, and July 31, 1956, p. 1. The Secretary of State for Information issued a statement after this incident admitting that the victims were members of clandestine terrorist gangs, but he denied that they had any political affiliation.

[18] The trade unions claim 11,000 members from the police. Interview with Mohammed Abdelrazak, Secretary, Federation of Electrical Workers, Moroccan Labor Federation, Rabat, May 27, 1958. No figures are officially issued by the Sûreté itself. The government payroll has 8,900 people listed under "police" in Table 4.

[19] See Rezette, *Les Partis Politiques Marocaines*, pp. 194-196, for his background.

[20] *O.B.*, no. 2274, May 25, 1956, "Dahir no. 1-56-115 du 5 chaoual 1375 (16 mai 1956) relatif à la direction generale de la sûreté nationale," pp. 476-477.

[21] See *L'Echo*, January 13, 1958, p. 4. The case involved the delay in providing medical care to an arrested man who had allegedly been mistreated while in police custody.

on their accomplishments, organizational changes, promotions, et cetera. Considering the circumstances under which the police were first organized, their self-regulating organization was probably necessary, though some system of accountability and inspection will eventually be needed. The Moroccan police pose another example of the problem of devising a political system that will not function in the same way as did its Protectorate counterpart.

The prestige of the police, as well as the inability of most Moroccans to use the legal checks or to participate effectively in political groups to express possible grievances, has no doubt restrained criticism. The close association of the Director with the King and recurring outbreaks of violence have probably also delayed more careful definition of the police role. The Istiqlal is generally regarded as having little influence among them. The police were initially organized with men from the resistance movement, who acquired their prestige quite apart from the Istiqlal and very possibly had long been dissatisfied with pre-1952 Istiqlal policy. Though the Director did much for the party before independence, he no longer holds an important position in the party.

The most extreme criticism of the police has come from the trade unions, or U.M.T. (Moroccan Federation of Labor). During the early months of independence the police were forbidden to join a professional trade union, and the *dahir* on collective conventions in mid-1957 officially sanctioned this ruling.[22] Discontent over the police up to the time of the formation of the Balafrej government cannot be traced, but several revelations were made during the crisis. At that time a motion of the National Consultative Assembly called for economies in security forces, better coordination in their use, and delimitation of the role of the police and other security forces of the Ministry of the Interior. A more outspoken and direct attack against central control was made by Ben Barka, who claimed that the Sûreté should "recognize the normal conception and the only logic of police which makes them the agent of execution of Government and of its regional representatives."[23] Whether this outburst resulted from police actions restricting party activity, government plans, or the selection of the new government is not clear, but there is no doubt that the more radical elements of the Istiqlal were unanimous in their disapproval of police administration.

[22] *O.B.*, no. 2339, August 23, 1956, "Dahir no. 1-57-119 du 18 hija 1376 (16 juillet 1957) sur les syndicats professionels," pp. 1110-1112.
[23] *Al-Istiqlal*, May 18, 1958, p. 3.

No changes were made in the organization of the Royal Army or the police to the end of 1958. Although there were many rumors of Laghzaoui's approaching departure, he remained Director of the Sûreté at the time of the formation of the Ibrahim Council. Since Ibrahim had been detained by the Casablanca police for questioning on his sources of income in September 1958, this was a particularly delicate situation. Although the Sûreté published the letter requesting the police investigation, the affair had cast doubt on Ibrahim's honesty that was not likely to be forgotten. During the fall the U.M.T. continued an outspoken attack on the Sûreté. The U.N.E.M. (National Union of Moroccan Students) Congress also severely criticized the police, especially for allegedly introducing an informer in its meetings.[24] There was almost no way of substantiating such charges, but the concurrence of Balafrej in the fall of 1958 indicates that the police had become a sufficiently controversial issue to prevent his keeping silent on the matter. In his address to the secretaries' conference of the Istiqlal he specifically referred to the police and the army as the crucial areas of government operations over which his government had lacked control.

The problem of establishing order and organizing police in Morocco demonstrates the difficulties of a new nation which has undergone some years of military occupation by a colonial power. The usual devices of civil rule had been discredited or had lapsed into disuse. Sophisticated political behavior was limited by the capability and experience of the population. In the early stages not only were many citizens fully capable of violence, but the population remained in an excited state in which mass violence could easily be unleashed. To cope with this threat the country needed to establish order rapidly and take measures to forestall further violence. To a certain extent the new nation had to cooperate with its past colonial ruler if the minimal agreements and cooperation necessary for the transition were to be obtained.

While the violence of the terrorists clearly delayed the development of the new political system, so also did the effort needed to reassure foreign powers that the lives and property of foreign nationals were safe. Violence had to be controlled even at the price of curtailing the activity of nationalist parties, who found it difficult to integrate the terrorist groups and to explain the necessity of police supervision. All this took place in a setting where the nationalist

[24] Motion of 3rd Congress, *Al-Istiqlal*, August 16, 1958, p. 16.

leaders were very likely unprepared and reliant on appeals that lost significance with the act of independence. The solidarity that was acquired during the struggle for independence was not automatically transferred to the postindependence setting. Even more important, the kind of solidarity that enabled the sacrifice of human life was not suitable to the development of a new political system prepared to deal with the problems of independence. If severe sanctions had been used indiscriminately, confidence of the citizens in their nation would have been destroyed.

An Army with No Country to Defend

Three armies were active in Morocco up to the end of 1958. Their transition presents in microcosmic form most of the important issues that have occupied the new country since independence. The Liberation Army was the product of the struggle for liberation in the countryside. From it has emerged the basis of a new political party, the Popular Movement, whose leaders and centers of strength are rooted in the areas where the Liberation Army was first active. The integration of this guerilla army into the Royal Army takes one through the most hectic phase of the establishment of order. Although organized by urban resistants to recruit and discipline troops it relied heavily on tribal loyalty to the King. The Royal Army has since been organized on similar lines of personal loyalty to the King. There are definite indications that this has been resented by the Istiqlal. The role of the French Army has also gone through a myriad of changes in the new country. At times it actually helped the new nation establish order and worked closely with the Royal Army. Its actions on other occasions have produced sufficient tension to destroy order, particularly in the border provinces along Algeria and the Sahara.

As the Liberation Army has undergone its many transformations since the first battles in the Rif Mountains on the eve of independence, its reception by the government has also changed according to the current relations with France and the internal situation in Morocco. While completely neglected by some of the Istiqlal leaders during the early months of the transition, it was constantly championed by Al-Fassi and was the instrument of his irredentist claims. In late 1957 and 1958 the Liberation Army again played an important role in the new political system as the problems of North Africa and the regions south of Morocco took on greater importance in

Moroccan politics. In this later epoch policy toward the French troops became more strict and their evacuation began. In many ways the manipulation of military force in the new nation reflected the crucial points of tension in the emerging political system.

The circumstances of the formation of the Liberation Army are not entirely clear and by this time are probably beyond accurate documentation. Enough is known, however, to help explain the difficulties of the merger of the irregular army and the Royal Army in the summer of 1956, as well as to suggest the origin of the Popular Movement. The early phases of the Liberation Army's existence also point up the Istiqlal's indecision on the use of violence. Late in 1953 the men planning the resistance had made contact with Moroccan elements in the French forces and might have been able to stage a bloody, if ultimately fruitless, uprising. Both Moroccan officers in the French Army and the Istiqlal leaders discouraged such a scheme that would only result in the needless loss of life, give more international sympathy to the French, and perhaps have precluded the formation of another army in a safe place, as was later done with the Liberation Army units in the Rif and Middle Atlas Mountains. A man known only by his pseudonym "Rachidi," Dr. Abdelkrim Khatib, and Abdelkrim Ben Abdallah, a known Communist,[25] were the early planners of the guerilla army. Rachidi was shot in a terrorist action in mid-1954 and remains noticeably absent in Istiqlal commemorative statements, which focus on Zerktouni, known to have been an Istiqlal militant.

Plans for an irregular army probably began at the first meeting of the Council of the Resistance in late 1953. Funds were already being collected from Moroccan workers in France and in Morocco from middle-class Moroccans who were known to have savings. At this time Ahardane, an ex-officer of the French Army and later governor of Rabat City, was asked to begin to recruit officers and non-commissioned officers of Moroccan origin in the French Army. Logistical preparations began during 1954 and a series of meetings was held in Paris in which the free leaders of the Istiqlal participated. The Council of the Resistance was in contact with Algerian revolutionaries. There is some evidence that it was hoped to coordinate the first battles of the Moroccan Liberation Army with new Algerian attacks in the Oran region, possibly to draw the aggressive Beni Snassen tribe near Oujda into the North African war and also, of course, to engulf Morocco in the battle for Algerian independence.

[25] Lacouture, *op.cit.*, p. 137.

Other tentative plans for uprisings at Berkane, in the midst of the Beni Snassen tribe, and in the Marmoucha tribal region were also abandoned by the leaders of the Moroccan Liberation Army late in 1954.

Moroccan troops were sworn into the irregular army to die on behalf of independence for all North Africa, as well as to fight for the King's return. There is no doubt that the new army received trained men from the Algerian Liberation Army and possibly material as well. In Cairo Al-Fassi participated in the North African Liberation Committee along with representatives of Algeria. Though it is quite possible that coordinated campaigns were postponed due to the relatively open terrain in northeastern Morocco or logistical problems, it is also important to note that no combat began in Morocco until October 1955, when plans for Moroccan independence were already under way.

In 1954 Istiqlal leaders began to play an important role in the resistance movement, though the movement itself was never the arm of a political party and always regarded itself as a separate organization. A distinctly Istiqlal terrorist group, also begun in Casablanca under Fqih Mohammed Basri, was active in smuggling endangered terrorists into the Spanish zone for the army's cadre.[26] Though the Spanish were reluctant to permit the Islah party to resume activity in their zone, they tolerated the landing of arms and the establishment of centers of training, supply, and operation.[27] The main training center, near Nador in the Rif Mountains, was under the direction of Si Abbès Messaoud, Abdallah Senhaji, and an Algerian.[28]

[26] *Ibid.* He also claims that this group was active in the fighting against the Black Cross after independence. Basri's Istiqlal background is most likely correct, since he later became one of the resistance representatives on the party's Political Commission.

[27] The major condition was that the Liberation Army troops were not to appear publicly with arms. The arrangement, of course, did much to establish Franco's policy of cooperation with the Arab countries. The attitude of the northern nationalists toward this aid is much like the ambivalence found in the earlier history of the Islah. The most common nationalist reference is that the new army was "tolerated" in the north, though it obviously could not have even been attempted without Spanish consent. Spain continued to play second fiddle to events in the French zone. For more information relating the Moroccan Liberation Army with the Algerian uprising of 1954 and Egypt, see Michael K. Clark, *Algeria in Turmoil: A History of the Rebellion*, New York, Praeger, 1959, pp. 83-84, 137-138, and Serge Bromberger, *Les Rebelles Algériennes*, Paris, Plon, 1958, pp. 72 and 91.

[28] The Algerian has reportedly since died in a French prison in Algeria after his return; Si Abbès was assassinated after Moroccan independence and Senhaji supported the Popular Movement. This further suggests the differences that existed between the Army and the Istiqlal. The Nador base is mentioned in Serge Bromberger's *Les Rebelles Algériennes*, Paris, Plon, 1958, p. 91.

This group started the preparation for combat in the spring of 1955 and was known as the "Coordination Commission." Above it was the "Committee of Revolution" under Dr. Abdelkrim Khatib, which maintained the crucial liaison with the agents and suppliers of the army outside Morocco.

The foreign network of communications, finance, and arms transport was largely in the hands of Istiqlal leaders. They were mostly second-rank leaders, with the exception of Al-Fassi in Cairo. The offices of the Istiqlal in Paris and New York were, of course, important, but the main pattern of support rested on Cairo, Geneva, Madrid, Tangier, and Tetouan. The agents in Tangier were Abdellatif Benjelloun, later Governor of Tangier, and Abderrahmane Youssfi, later on the Political Commission of the Istiqlal as a representative of the resistance. In Tetouan the main agent was Abdelkhalek Torres, the leader of the Islah. One of the most important agents of the resistance abroad was Abdelkebir Al-Fassi, a relation of Allal Al-Fassi, and most active in Madrid. Although the bulk of the Istiqlal leaders were freed in late 1954, they were too closely watched to do much for the resistance movement. Ben Barka met once with Si Abbès, but the available evidence suggests that their meeting was not a success. While there are indications that some nationalists might have been prepared to accept a compromise regarding the monarchy, there is nothing to show that the resistance ever wavered from its goal of the complete restitution of Mohammed V. Since the resistance movement was also devoted to liberation of all North Africa, it may well be that differences occurred over the best strategy for Algerian independence.

As the Liberation Army began to take shape in 1955 regional commands were established and the first steps were taken toward establishing units within French Morocco. By the fall of 1955 approximately 10,000 men were organized and trained, though the number of combat troops was probably nearer 5,000. The Rif segment of the army was the first to be formed, with units later organized in the Middle Atlas Mountains and in the Sous valley of Agadir. Abdallah Senhaji was in command in the western area of the Rif Mountains, between Tetouan and Nador and extending south toward Ouazzan and Karia ba Mohammed. Si Abbès was in command in the central Rif area to the north of Fès and Taza, including the strongholds around Boured, Taineste, and Aknoul.[29] In the north

[29] Each of these areas in the mountains had a subordinate commander. These

the men came mostly from the tribes of the central Rif Mountains. They had been known for their fierce fighting qualities since the uprising of Abdelkrim. In the Middle Atlas Mountains, the original center of organization was among the Marmoucha tribesmen in the region south of Taza, which was accessible from Algeria across the sparsely populated, arid plains of southeastern Morocco.[30] With arms and cadre brought in through Spanish Ifni some units were also established to the south.

All the units of the Liberation Army were near or bordering on the Sahara, possessed lines of communication and supply from Algeria or Spain, and, if simultaneously active, could create chaos in all the outlying regions of Morocco. Although the war probably strengthened the nationalists' bargaining position with France, it has never been clarified why the war began in late 1955. It is not even clear if the action was unleashed at the request of or in opposition to the nationalists in Rabat and Paris. Had the war been delayed another three or four months its purpose would have been completely in doubt, except to bring aid to the Algerians. Had the war occurred several months earlier when French procrastination was much more in evidence, its relation to the negotiations would be much easier to affirm. Whatever initial purpose the Liberation Army had beyond Moroccan independence was lost as the new nation took on responsibility for order and as the Royal Army was established.

As hostilities began in the Rif, Al-Fassi and Mohammed Al-Khadir, a leader of the Algerian National Liberation Front, announced the new plan for the liberation of all North Africa from Cairo.[31] A few days later Al-Fassi added that the war had been begun because the French were lagging in the fulfillment of the Aix-les-Bains promises. The decision does not appear to have been coordinated with the feelings of Istiqlal leaders in Morocco and France. Lyazidi hastily announced that Al-Fassi was in agreement with the solution to the Moroccan problem adopted at Aix-les-Bains, but that he had "expressed some reticence on the way in which the accords were put into effect."[32] Fighting continued in the Rif throughout

---

command posts were revealed first by Abdelwahab Laraki and soon afterward by the lists of the first Liberation Army delegation to visit the King. See also *L'Echo*, April 5, 1956, p. 1.

[30] *L'Action*, March 26, 1956, p. 8, asserts that arms were sent to this area by the Algerian revolutionaries.

[31] *Le Monde*, October 6, 1955, p. 1.

[32] Interview with *Le Monde*, C.M., October 15, 1955, p. 20.

the time of the return of the King and the early negotiations for independence. In January the French Army launched an offensive in the Rif area, but the Liberation Army forces easily took refuge in the mountains and Spanish zone beyond the reach of French troops.

Early in 1956 Al-Fassi announced from Cairo that "the Army of Liberation of Algeria and Morocco will cease combat when the Moroccan government becomes responsible for the security and defense of the country."[33] The statement testifies to the Algerian connections of the army, as well as the way in which it could exert pressure for more rapid concessions from the French. The King, however, denied that the threat posed by the Army of Liberation would be used as an argument in the forthcoming negotiations. He added later, however, that an appeal for order in the Rif would be made "when the negotiations have proved the total sincerity of France." He continued, "We can then isolate the true patriots from those who make themselves the instruments of occult forces."[34] His statements suggest that the new government did not feel capable of stopping the Rif war until it could produce evidence of substantial results from the negotiations. It also intimates that there might be trouble in pacifying the army, which later events showed to be true.

Throughout the early months of 1956 there were sporadic attacks on French outposts and rural offices of government agencies. The units of the Liberation Army in the Middle Atlas began to extend their activities eastward with new attacks near Khenifra and Khemisset. As the Liberation Army became more active it became a greater threat to the establishment of order in Morocco and more difficult to control. Plans for the integration of the Liberation Army in the new Royal Army did not go into effect until the signing of the Franco-Moroccan Agreement. The first delegations of Istiqlal leaders went into the Rif to make contact with army officials and to explore their terms for discontinuing the war. The exploratory talks by the Istiqlal leaders caused considerable confusion and disillusion among the guerilla tribesmen, who had expected to continue fighting for the liberation of all North Africa and did not understand the intricacies of party politics. Competition among the parties for the support of the Liberation Army also began at the time of the visit of these delegations. An *alim* at Qarawiyn, Abdelwahab Laraki,

---

[33] Interview by *France-Soir*, C.M., January 10, 1956.
[34] Interview with *Gazette de Lausanne*, C.M., January 21, 1956.

announced that an army delegation would soon come from the Rif under the sponsorship of the Democratic party. A few weeks later Laraki was assassinated outside his home in Fès.

In late March thirty chiefs of the Liberation Army voluntarily came to Rabat and met with the King. The agreement was that they would discontinue fighting on the appeal of Mohammed V, but would not yield their arms until certain that Moroccan independence was complete. So long as they were not molested by the French troops the cease-fire would be obeyed on the personal request of the King. When preparations were under way for the establishment of the Royal Army, they would leave the mountains and join in the defense of the King. At that time they were not associated with any political party. During their visit to Rabat they stayed with Caid Lahcen Lyoussi, a leader of the army in the Middle Atlas and later an opponent of the Istiqlal. Order was gradually restored, but the situation remained tense. Small bands of the army roamed the countryside and felt entitled to deal in their own way with remnants of the old rural administration. Final resolution of the Liberation Army problem was postponed until the first review of the Royal Army, when the first irregular troops were integrated. In the interlude the Istiqlal and the official press were conspicuously silent, though there were rumors that Dr. Khatib and other members of the Council of the Resistance were unsatisfied.

The problems of the transition of the Liberation Army were converse to those of the urban resistance. The tribesmen were quite content to become soldiers of the King and to preserve the loyalty on which their involvement in the national struggle had begun. The urban resistance leaders appear to have been estranged from society and reluctant to see their fighting force dissolved. Although some leaders of the army were reportedly enraged over abandoning Algeria, the tribesmen were prepared either to accept positions as ordinary enlisted men in the Royal Army or to flee to Algeria where they could continue fighting. The political background of the two organizations differed. The leaders of the urban groups were of mostly Istiqlal background, but the leaders of the Liberation Army in the field were not. The Liberation Army embodied an organized mass that could be transferred easily to party membership if it were properly handled and which, even more important, was from parts of the country where parties were organizing freely for the first time.

173

That the integration of the Liberation Army proceeded as well as it did is undoubtedly due to its loyalty for Mohammed V. Appeals continued to be issued by the Ministry of the Interior after the first Royal Army review. Shortly after the cease-fire, handbills indicating that units of the army might resist integration were circulated in the Taza region. Integration with the Royal Army was not universally accepted until the journey of the King into the troubled regions. The split in the leadership of the Liberation Army became public when the Ministry of the Interior condemned "colonialists and bandits" for disrupting order in the countryside, and contradictory statements were made by Al-Fassi and Dr. Khatib.[35] While the Istiqlal paper tried to maintain that those continuing opposition in the country-side were impostors and troublemakers, the Secretary of State for Information admitted in a press conference, "For the moment the Army of Liberation is not in the structure of legality."[36] He cautioned against accepting reports that the Liberation Army would continue fighting until Algeria was liberated. There were reports of incidents in the Middle Atlas and Oujda regions, but less activity in the Rif area after the delegation to the King. Amid complaints that the Algerians were receiving support from Beni Snassen near Oujda, French troops moved into the region in force and began intensive operations along the frontier.

Two months after formal independence the Moroccan government was still finding it much more difficult to establish control of the revolutionary army than had been anticipated.[37] The system of zones was organized, but the problem seemed to become worse as latecomers were loosely organized in the Middle Atlas region. As reports circulated of French plans to reinforce their border patrols to the south, tribesmen from the Middle Atlas began to infiltrate southward to form the core of the Liberation Army in the Sahara. In the face of renewed difficulties the King again received delegations from the Rif, Beni Mellal, and the Sahara[38] and plans were made for a royal visit to the remaining areas of confusion. Exploratory trips to Oujda were made by the Prince and the Commander of French Forces. Later the Prince met with Dr. Khatib and Abdel-

---

[35] See statement of Al-Fassi from Cairo, *C.M.*, May 15, 1956, p. 3. Dr. Khatib said: "The mission of the Army of Liberation is not yet ended. It will be only when North Africa is liberated, including Algeria." From *Al-Alam*, May 16, 1956, Fr. Trans.
[36] *L'Echo*, May 24, 1956, p. 1.
[37] See the comment in *Le Monde*, May 26, 1956, p. 4.
[38] *C.M.*, June 4, 1956, p. 1.

kebir Al-Fassi in Madrid. Not until the end of June, four months after independence, was order fully restored.[39]

In July 1956 General Cogny took over command of French forces in Morocco. A secret agreement was reached with the Royal Army for the disposition of the two armies in the countryside and especially in Agadir province, the base for French operations to the south of Morocco. Since Al-Fassi had made his first major speech claiming the Sahara bordering regions, including Colombe-Bechar, Tindouf, Mauritania, and Rio de Oro, before this agreement was made, there is little doubt but that this agreement with the French forces resulted in tension within the nationalist ranks. Al-Fassi suggested the growing confusion among units of the Liberation Army by denouncing those who were trying to create a "fake army" to confuse the people. The Istiqlal apparently refused to believe that there could be internal dissension in the Liberation Army. The party paper said that the new outbreaks were the work of a "secret hand" trying to divide the army and part of a plot to permit colonialism to resume its old position.[40] The discord was revealed with the assassination of Si Abbés Mesaoud, who had come to Fès to negotiate with the Prince for the integration of his troops. He was killed by a band of Liberation Army troops under a dissident, Si Hajjaj, who favored continuing the revolution.[41]

Since Si Abbés had forbidden organizers of the Istiqlal to enter his region of command and had distributed anti-Istiqlal propaganda among his troops, it is possible that he was assassinated to permit the party's expansion among the Liberation Army.[42] His death added to the demoralization of the army, which, in the absence of a clear chain of command in the Fès area, began the motions of an attack on the ancient capital of the region. The King immediately issued a statement of consolation on Abbés' assassination and the leaders of the Liberation Army were again summoned to Rabat.[43] Si Abbés' funeral was attended by the Prince, M'Hammedi, and Laghzaoui,

[39] See reports in *Le Monde*, July 1-2, 1956, p. 2, and July 3, 1956, p. 4. At this time there also occurred the first riots in Marrakech. Whether or not they were led by elements of the Liberation Army moving south is not clear, but it is certainly quite possible.

[40] *Al-Alam*, June 30, 1956, Fr. Trans.

[41] *L'Echo*, July 2, 1956, p. 1.

[42] See the comment of Lacouture, *op.cit.*, p. 144.

[43] The names of this group will be found in *C.M.*, July 3, 1956, p. 1. Of the five men, two are no longer in positions that can be located, while the other three men—Dr. Khatib, Ahardane, and Senhaji—are all in opposition to the Istiqlal.

while the King formed a new commission of liaison with the Liberation Army leaders. As French reinforcements arrived in the Foum Al-Hassan area of Agadir province, the last major drive to incorporate the Liberation Army in the growing Royal Army was undertaken under the personal direction of the King.

From July the bulk of the Liberation Army was disbanded. The combatants arrived in Rabat in groups of hundreds and even thousands, very likely accompanied by tribesmen who were not actual troops but were attracted by the offers made to the army and by the color of the occasion.[44] The troops were reviewed by the King, the Prince, and Dr. Khatib. In mid-July the King made a triumphant tour of the Liberation Army areas, starting with near-by Khemisset. He continued to the Fès region, the strong points north of Fès and Taza, and ended with merger celebrations at the Liberation Army center near Nador. An emergency mission of Balafrej to Paris had apparently received sufficient concessions to persuade the Liberation Army units that the minimum requirements for an independent state had been fulfilled. After the trip of the Prince and Dr. Khatib to the region south of Marrakech, organized fighting by the Liberation Army ceased in the interior and a new phase of the Liberation Army of the Sahara began. By this time the original leadership of the army had almost completely disintegrated.

About 6,000 tribesmen were reportedly incorporated in the Royal Army, while about 3,000 were given employment in the government, mostly in the police force.[45] Another 3,000 reportedly joined the Sahara Liberation Army south of Agadir,[46] which became the instrument of redemption for the irredentist advocates under Al-Fassi. Since only about 500 of the original Rif Army are estimated to have reached the south, it seems that, as the units of the Liberation Army infiltrated southward, they acquired more troops from surrounding tribes. During the migration the guerilla bands received aid from Istiqlal offices in the countryside and the gradual process of domination of the Liberation Army by the nationalist party began. The Council of the Resistance agreed to participate in the Istiqlal meetings of August 1956, but it was made very clear that they were independent and distinct from the party representatives.

[44] Lacouture, *op.cit.*, places the number of combatants at 6,000. Al-Fassi claimed that 9,000 guerrilla fighters had joined the Royal Army. *C.M.*, May 23-26, 1957, Annex VIII.

[45] *C.M.*, September 17-19, 1956, p. 1.

[46] *Le Monde*, August 30, 1956, pp. 1 and 4.

Though the Istiqlal repeatedly came to the defense of the Liberation Army, it never spoke in the name of the army.

The resistance and the party peacefully coexisted until late 1956, when it became apparent that the Liberation Army did not unanimously approve of the interference of a political party in its affairs, nor did it like the results of supporting the government. Most of the well-known Liberation Army leaders did not take positions in the party or actively oppose it. The two resistance leaders who joined the Political Commission of the party were Fqih Mohammed Al-Basri, organizer of the Istiqlal segment of the urban resistance in Casablanca, and Abderrhamin Youssfi, who was an agent of the Liberation Army abroad and not one of its leaders in the field. The party's control of the Liberation Army was not possible until it had been confined to the Sahara regions, where its supply and communications relied on Istiqlal support. Later is was to become more clearly the semiofficial tool of the party and, perhaps by default, of the government, since the campaigns around Ifni in late 1957 could not have been carried out without heavy logistical support.

The formation of the Royal Army created several delicate problems for the new government. Although one of the basic demands of the Liberation Army was the "total liberation" of the country, a new army could not be formed without aid from the French. In the first parade of the Royal Army were 500 French noncommissioned officers and an estimated $3,000,000 worth of French equipment.[47] While the Liberation Army could provide many troops, they were not trained in the procedures of a modern army. The officers of the Liberation Army were perhaps better qualified since many Moroccans had been commissioned in the French Army. A program was begun to train 1,000 new officers immediately in the French military school at Meknes, now given to the Moroccans. In the fall of 1956 more Liberation Army chiefs assembled for training as noncommissioned officers and more reinforcements were received after the merger of the French and Spanish zones.

Two Armies in Dispute

The formation of the Royal Army and the confinement of the Liberation Army to the border regions of the Sahara did not resolve

---

[47] *New York Times*, May 15, 1956, p. 3. In reply to questioning in the National Assembly, Bourges-Maurnory announced that 142 officers and 603 noncommissioned officers of the French Army were participating in the Moroccan Army in late July 1956.

the problem of military relationships in the new nation. In both internal and international politics controversies concerning the role of the Moroccan Army, Liberation Army, and the French Army persisted, although the latter was subsequently relegated to the realm of international affairs. During the difficult summer of 1956 there was considerable cooperation between the new units of the Moroccan Army and the French Army. In the Beni Ouidane valley a joint occupation proceeded with all three armies and agreement was reached for the movement of troops of all three armies around Foum Al-Hassan.[48] After the intervention of the King, Royal Army units were permitted to circulate in areas under Liberation Army control and arrest officers who were wanted for crimes.

In some ways the movement of the Liberation Army to the south was better advised than toward Oujda, where it would have handicapped government operations and could have been more easily neutralized by French forces in Algeria. The Liberation Army troops in Agadir remained fairly quiet over the summer of 1956, although the French undertook some operations to subdue the units moving southeasterly toward Figuig. General Cogny stated soon after these encounters that French troops intended to remain along the Algerian border, but he minimized the importance of aid being received by the guerillas from Algeria. Just as negotiations for the permanent military convention with France were about to open, the arrest of the Algerian leaders disrupted the French-Moroccan relations. With the riots at Meknes the French forces were moved into the interior in number. The crisis aroused the Sahara army and there were reports that the Liberation Army began obstructing the Royal Army below Agadir.[49]

The reorganization of the Liberation Army in the Sahara involved political maneuverings that are in themselves important for an understanding of the use of military force and Moroccan politics since independence. Though the government, of course, denied any connection with the Liberation Army units in the Sahara, the Istiqlal offices of Agadir, Marrakech, Ouarzazate, and Tafilalet provinces all had bureaus for the Sahara army.[50] Though it is not certain if the

[48] See the account of the visit of the Le Monde correspondent, June 11, 1956, p. 1. Royal Moroccan troops were transported to Foum Al-Hassan in French Army trucks. L'Echo, July 8, 1956, p. 1.

[49] Le Monde, December 29, 1956, p. 3.

[50] Interviews with Istiqlal party inspectors. It is interesting to note that the inspector in the most important region for control of the southern Sahara, Agadir, was Abdelaziz Ben Driss, an old friend of Al-Fassi from Qarawiyn days.

Sahara Liberation Army was wholly dependent on the Istiqlal, it received no official acknowledgment and was initially supported only by Al-Fassi. Early in 1957 he made a tour of the southern provinces and pronounced in one of his speeches: "Citizens, the battle of the Sahara has begun. The Istiqlal proclaims the debut of this battle and invites the people confident of their strength to engage themselves there. . . . The most important aid to offer Algeria is to open another front against colonialism in the Sahara."[51] Soon afterward skirmishes took place in Mauritania and the Liberation Army was reported to be encamped in the Draa valley. With these new incidents General Cogny stated that the French Army's mission was to seal Moroccan borders. More incidents occurred during the spring around Foum Al-Hassan, but French sources again acknowledged that the Moroccan government did not wish to associate with them.

During 1957 the Sahara Liberation Army continued to operate with the core of Middle Atlas troops that had been too late to participate in the fighting in the north.[52] As a result of its initial skirmishes and the agitation by the Istiqlal the new guerilla army grew to about 3,000 men. During 1956 the Istiqlal appears to have gradually established full control. The periodic skirmishes were probably necessary to maintain the spirit of men living under these conditions. Bands of Liberation Army men, probably led by Ben Hamou, were generally regarded as responsible for presenting the Moroccan officials with the arrest of the Glaoui family.[53] Ben Hamou, known to have been a leader of an Istiqlal-dominated faction of the Liberation Army, was a leading figure in the Ifni offensive in the fall of 1957. Before this campaign there were at least two purges of the Sahara army; this situation definitely left the Istiqlal in a leading position.

As preparations started it appeared that the mountain tribesmen of the Middle Atlas were not compatible with newly recruited desert tribesmen, who came from the Ait Ba Amrane tribe of Ifni. The Sahara army wished to maximize its solidarity and many of the Middle Atlas tribesmen were sent home, though they may also have been considered politically unreliable. There had already been several motions toward organizing the Berbers into a political movement opposing the Istiqlal, which would very likely include several Middle Atlas tribes. In November, after the first purge, the Popular

[51] *Al-Alam*, January 27, 1957, address to the Chiadma tribe of Safi province, Fr. Trans.
[52] See *Le Monde*, February 20, 1957, p. 2.
[53] *Ibid.*, May 4, 1957, p. 1.

Movement was announced. Among its leaders were Dr. Khatib, now inactive in the Liberation Army, and Ahardane, thought to be popular in the Middle Atlas regions. Their action again jeopardized the solidarity of the Sahara army and several of its high officers were dismissed under suspicion of sympathy with the Popular Movement. The final purge was definitely designed to put the Liberation Army under Istiqlal control, but this did not mean that the party could control the Council of the Resistance. The Council also had its own source of influence as spokesman for the large numbers of resistants who had returned to normal lives in Moroccan society.

Just as the transition of the Liberation Army reflected some of the tension in the Moroccan political system, so has the development of the Royal Army. There were no indications of party activity or any political indoctrination within the army except loyalty to the King, but the Istiqlal has criticized the army and allegedly attempted to increase the number of officers of strong Istiqlal leanings.[54] The King is the Commander-in-Chief and his son, Prince Moulay Hassan, became Chief of Staff. There is little doubt but that the Royal Army has functioned under direct supervision of the Palace. The monarch's position was made clear in the *dahir* creating the army, which specifically provided that the army was "placed under Our direct authority" and would participate "as We determine in the maintenance of public order."[55] The first Minister of Defense was a Liberal Independent and a close friend of the King. The minister's powers were never carefully defined and his authority was divided with the King, the Prince, and the Royal Cabinet.[56] During the first government crisis Zeghari, an independent and an even closer confidant of the King, became Minister of Defense and remained at the post until the fall of 1957. The Ministry of National Defense was not supervised by an Istiqlal member until the ministry's authority was strictly limited to preparing the budget for the ministry and the army, managing their finances, and directing the organization, equipment, and training of the army. Any proposals regarding the mission of the army were to be submitted to the King for approval.[57]

[54] See the comment of Lacouture, *op.cit.*, p. 143.

[55] *O.B.*, no. 2282, July 20, 1956, "Dahir no. 1-56-138 du 16 kaada 1376 (25 juin 1956) portant création des Forces armées royales," p. 765.

[56] See *O.B.*, May 11, 1956, no. 2272, "Dahir no. 1-56-096 du 9 chaabane 1375 (22 mai 1956) portant création du ministère de la défense nationale," p. 410.

[57] *O.B.*, November 23, 1956, no. 2300, "Dahir no. 1-56-175 du 4 rebia II 1376 (8 novembre 1956) fixant le compétence et les attributions du ministère de la défense nationale," pp. 1340-1341.

The close association of the Royal Army with the Palace has meant that whatever reservations existed concerning its mission or supervision were muffled and, if expressed, appeared in veiled form. Over the first year of independence there was almost no comment on the Royal Army. The few references that can be found in party documents on the "social and economic role" of the army suggest that some discussion was taking place of the possible nonmilitary duties of the troops. When the Istiqlal occupied the Ministry of National Defense the party paper announced that it looked forward to the end of "confusion" in the ministry and that a new *dahir* was being written for this purpose.[58] The law referred to was probably the *dahir* on the High Council of National Defense that appeared several months later. The powers of the Minister of Defense were not changed, but opportunity was provided for six ministers and the Prince to meet under the chairmanship of the King "to clarify . . . all questions touching the general policy of the defense of the country, the missions, the general organization and the employment of the Royal Armed Forces."[59] Other representatives could be included as needed, the *dahir* further explained, specifically the President of the National Consultative Assembly. Since the King was chairman, retained the power of convoking the committee, and directed the activities of its secretariat, the only modification of the pre-existing structure was officially to give voice in national defense to other ministers, but then only when the King chose to consult them. If this was the legislation to which the Istiqlal had referred, the Istiqlal got much less than it had anticipated.

The direction of the armed forces, like that of the police, involved establishing a network of understood institutional controls while a new country was undergoing reforms and was threatened by violence. Though agreed that the forces of order should have no active political roles, the Istiqlal leaders resented the highly centralized control that had persisted. However, for these services to play a neutral role requires not only a well-defined governmental structure (which in Morocco is not yet fully accomplished), but also a citizenry which can understand its individual rights and how these rights are protected within the given institutional structure. In view

[58] *Al-Istiqlal*, September 21, 1957, p. 3. There was also implied criticism of the earlier administration of the Army for continued reliance on French Army logistics and supply.

[59] *O.B.*, no. 2352, November 22, 1957, "Dahir no. 1-57-331 du 15 rebia II 1377 (9 novembre 1956) portant création auprès de S.M. le Roi d'un Haut comité de défense nationale," p. 1480.

of the use of the police and army to maintain order during transitional party quarrels that often involved the Istiqlal, it would be most difficult for the King to justify giving control to Istiqlal ministers. The Istiqlal leaders felt that they should be given authority in this field immediately and that the establishment of *dahirs* on individual rights and party activity could be issued later.

During the government crisis of May 1958 the motion of the Istiqlal-dominated Consultative Assembly called for more financial controls over the army and increased participation of the Royal Army in projects of "national and social interest."[60] The Royal Charter under which the new government was formed made no direct reference to the army or the police, but promised a *dahir* defining the powers of each minister. In the acceptance speech of Balafrej, however, the army was discussed at some length. He called for better integration of the forces in the northern and southern regions of Morocco, elimination of foreign cadre, new administrative texts, and more use of the army in social projects. The dissent from Ben Barka a week later, voicing the party's dissatisfaction much more strongly, compared the situation of the Royal Army to the "anomaly" found in the direction of the police. The open break of the more radical Istiqlal elements and the tribal uprisings in the fall of 1958 postponed action on this problem.

By the end of 1958 only the position of the French Army was clear. During the year France abandoned all her border posts and inland camps and left about 10,000 troops stationed around the major cities near the coast. The Moroccan Army of Liberation still showed signs of the difficult transition, though the tension was seen only among Istiqlal factions and was no longer a national problem. The guerilla forces in Agadir province and the tribes in French and Spanish territory to the south appeared to bear allegiance to the King and Al-Fassi. There were some units which continued their allegiance to Fqih Mohammed Al-Basri and the activist group of the party. Perhaps because of the absence of a more overriding issue, in August 1958, clashes occurred at Bou Arfa between elements bearing loyalty to these two Istiqlal factions.[61] The Liberation Army factions may also have been divided over how much and what kind of help was to be given to the near-by Algerian revolutionaries.

[60] *Al-Istiqlal*, April 20, 1958, p. 7.
[61] *Le Monde*, August 24-25, 1958, p. 3, and September 2, 1958, p. 3.

The position of the Royal Army as the arm of the Palace had been strengthened over 1958 by the successful occupation of Tarfaya province and by the tribal uprisings. Criticisms from the Istiqlal continued, and even the moderate Balafrej once noted that his government had not been permitted to change the governmental relationship of the army.[62] The most serious attack was probably the motion of the U.N.E.M. Congress calling the Royal Army an "army for display."[63] The students objected to its cost, the continued presence of foreign officers in its ranks, the failure to define the authority of the Chief of Staff and Minister of Defense, and—probably the most serious objection—the alleged presence of "antinational and antipopular" forces in the army.

These motions certainly represent the most extreme opinions on the army and only the opinion of the most progressive Istiqlal elements. Shortly afterward the King made his first public defense of the army and in his Speech from the Throne said, "We have placed them under Our high command in order to indicate the way to follow in the superior interest of the nation."[64] The tribal uprisings postponed any further controversy for the rest of 1958, but there was little doubt but that Mohammed V was determined to keep control of the Royal Army. When the Minister of National Defense was given full civil and military powers in the northern provinces during the Rif revolt, rumors spread that the King had made a concession on army control. A palace communiqué quickly ended this speculation by stating that this measure had been taken only to enable maximum efficiency in a special situation and "changes nothing in the principle by which the army is placed under the supreme authority of H.M. the King."[65] The critics of the army were most likely very glad not to have ultimate responsibility for the volatile situation in the north and the Middle Atlas. The ability of the Royal Army to restore order in these regions has no doubt stilled further criticism for some time.

The changes in the use of military force since independence demonstrated the new government's difficulty in dealing with highly organized and potentially extremely influential groups, either through their adherence to a political party or through their more direct participation in politics by the use of military force. The po-

---

[62] *Al-Istiqlal*, October 18, 1958, p. 4.
[63] *Ibid.*, August 16, 1958, p. 16.
[64] *La Vigie*, November 18, 1958, p. 6.
[65] *Ibid.*, October 30, 1958, p. 2.

sition of the Liberation Army was the least tenable, for its existence contradicted the proclaimed sovereign status of the new nation and prevented it from extending its own controls over large areas of the country. The Istiqlal's attempt to absorb the guerilla army met with stiff resistance from its leaders, who have since formed the core of a new party. At the time of the integration the action of the Istiqlal was harmonious with the needs of the new nation, though it is important to note that it was only the final appeal of the King that successfully concluded its activity. From that time the Istiqlal took a greater role in supporting the remnants of the Liberation Army, then in the Sahara, though the Istiqlal leadership does not seem to have been agreed on its purpose.

The role of the French Army is more difficult to evaluate, for in the first year of independence and to some extent in the second year the Royal Army remained dependent on French assistance. It was only after the first year that the demands for the evacuation of foreign troops began, when both French and Spanish intrigue cast doubt on their purpose. As the sole depository of Moroccan sovereignty and as the avowed chief of the integrated elements of the Liberation Army, the position of the King as Commander-in-Chief of the new Royal Army was inescapable. The result of his leadership has been that the army has been almost totally divorced from direct intervention in political activity, and also that the direction of the army remained under his personal care. Since the basic institutions and rules for the political system are still in the process of being formulated and political activity still takes place under highly restrained conditions, it is difficult to see how the army's control could have been assigned to others. Because of the limited usefulness of military force in resolving political problems over long periods of time, it is probably to the advantage of the emerging political system that the army has been held in check. Had the King been willing to use the army except in circumstances of imminent violence, it is quite likely that the degree of controversy and compromise that have taken place thus far would have been precluded. While the criticism of the Istiqlal may be based on the justifiable objection that the effectiveness of the government has been reduced due to the King's reluctance to delegate authority in other fields, it is difficult to explain how this restraint is objectionable in eliminating the use of military force in the new political system.

CHAPTER VII

RURAL ADMINISTRATION AND
THE TRIBES

The Reorganized "Bled"

ROUGHLY four fifths of Morocco's population live in rural areas, and from this segment come about two fifths of her national income.[1] In the early months of independence this important group of Moroccans was almost totally ignored. The pressing issues of the central government received most attention and funds were diverted for the formation of the services needed for the government. Some changes have gradually been made in the system of administrative rural control left by the French and Spanish Protectorate, but many high Moroccan officials admit that the system changed very little in the first three years of independence. The French civil controllers and indigenous-affairs officers departed, but much the same authority was placed in the hands of their Moroccan counterparts. With the exception of judicial powers that have been delegated to the Ministry of Justice the entire rural administration is centrally directed by the Ministry of the Interior. Its actions both in Rabat and in the countryside have been subject to much criticism, but in the absence of any system of public accountability such charges are difficult to evaluate. That serious blunders were made in the first year of independence is undoubtedly correct, though it must also be acknowledged that many efforts were made to improve rural administration.

From the viewpoint of the emergence of the new political system, the most important function of the Ministry of the Interior is its part in bringing the tribes into contact with national political life. It is through the officers of the rural administration that the populace as a whole received its first day-to-day impressions of the new government. To the extent that the administration followed the pattern of highly centralized, authoritarian control which characterized the French and Spanish systems, the people very likely saw little difference between independence and colonial rule. The ameliorating conditions have been, of course, that the present agents of authority

---

[1] "*Bled*" means "countryside" in Moroccan Arabic and is commonly used to refer to outlying regions. Historically Morocco was divided into the *bled al-makhzen* and *bled as-siba*, country of the Sultan's government and country of dissension.

have been selected by a popular King and are generally regarded as men interested in building a strong, independent Morocco.

The tribal structure remains the basic way of life in much of the countryside,[2] though there are tremendous variations in the strength of the tribal system among different regions. In areas of the High Atlas, tribes remain virtually untouched; while in parts of the coastal plains, tribal habits have become virtually forgotten and are treated as part of a romantic past. Tribes are, nevertheless, the basic unit for the administration in the countryside and their economic and political institution, the *souk*, or market, will form the basis of the rural commune. As the communes are developed, the tribes, whose system of rule by popular council, or *jemaâ*, is extolled by even the most progressive politicians, will begin to play a more important role in making decisions affecting the central and regional government. Eventually they will participate in some form of indirect election of a regional and, later, a national representative body. In early 1959 regional geographic units were still outlined by tribal boundaries, and regional officials were assigned to tribes or several tribes. Even the Istiqlal based its rural organization on the tribes. Independence may have actually reinforced the solidarity of those tribes bearing historic loyalties to the King. Independence alone has by no means meant their automatic dissolution.

Under the French Protectorate there were approximately 600 tribes, to which are now added roughly 100 more tribes from the Spanish zone.[3] The French administration had divided the tribes into increasingly larger units called circles, territories, and regions. The regions of Rabat, Casablanca, and Oujda were under civil control, and the remaining four regions, Fès, Meknes, Marrakech, and Agadir, were under military control. In the north the Spanish, centering their administration on the coastal ports, used five centers: Larache, Tetouan, Alhucemas, Chaouen, and Nador. The French civil controllers and indigenous-affairs officers operated largely at the level of the territory and circle, with Moroccans retaining the traditional posts of *caid, khalifa,* and sheikh, under close supervision. The *caid* was historically the representative of the King over a certain tribe or

---

[2] The word "tribe" is generally frowned upon by present-day Moroccans, though it occurs frequently in government and party publications. Many nationalists contend that the tribal system was about to collapse at the turn of the century and was artificially revived by the colonialists. Whether or not this is the case is somewhat beside the point for the present analysis.

[3] Estimate based on the *Carte des Tribus,* Institute Géographique National, Annexe du Maroc, Rabat, 1958, and *Morocco 1954, op.cit.,* p. 47.

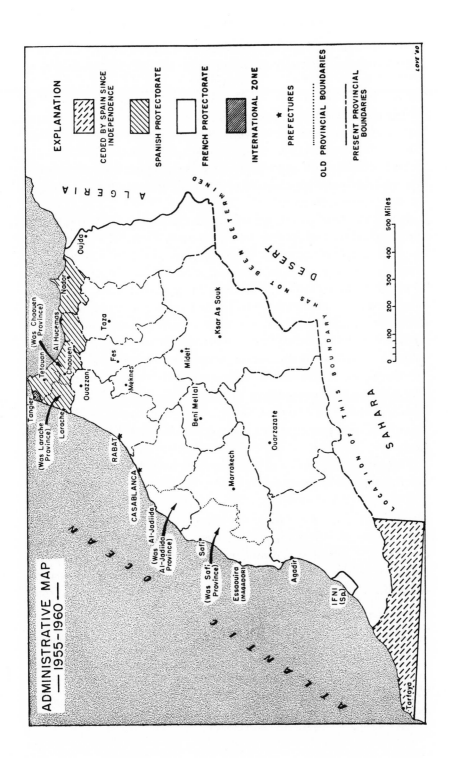

ADMINISTRATIVE MAP
— 1955 – 1960 —

EXPLANATION

CEDED BY SPAIN SINCE
INDEPENDENCE

SPANISH PROTECTORATE

FRENCH PROTECTORATE

INTERNATIONAL ZONE

★   PREFECTURES

·········· OLD PROVINCIAL BOUNDARIES

——— PRESENT PROVINCIAL
BOUNDARIES

LOVE '60

ALGERIA

ATLANTIC   OCEAN

Tangier

Tetouan

(Was Chaouen
Province)

Al Hucemas

Chaouen

Nador

Oujda

Ouazzan

Fes

Meknes

Toza

Mideit

Ksar As Souk

(Was Laroche
Province)

Laroche

RABAT

CASABLANCA

Al–Jadiida

(Was Al–Jadiida
Province)

Safi

(Was Safi
Province)

Essaouira
(MAGADOR)

Beni Mellal

Marrakech

Ouarzazate

Agadir

IFNI
(Sp.)

Tarfaya

DESERT

HAS NOT BEEN DETERMINED

LOCATION OF THIS BOUNDARY

SAHARA

0   100   200   300   400   500 Miles

tribes, though he might also have assistants, the *khalifas*. The tribes were divided into sections, including a number of villages, or *douars*, each of which might be supervised by a subordinate delegate, the sheikh for the section and the *moqaddem* for a single *douar*. The larger towns, even in military areas, had some civil municipal structure under a pasha and civil controllers, while the larger cities had fully elaborated, French-run municipal governments. Although the French and Spanish supervisors have been replaced by Moroccans, approximately the same system of rural administration has been used in independent Morocco.[4]

Under the new government the regions became provinces, which had reached the number of twenty by 1959. Even before the liberation of the Spanish zone the King reorganized the French zone into thirteen provinces: Rabat, Meknes, Fès, Taza, Oujda, Tafilalet, Ouarzazate, Marrakech, Agadir, Safi, Mazagan, Chaouia, and Tadla. The additional provinces were formed from the larger territories formerly included in the French regions. Each province and the cities of Rabat and Casablanca had a governor and an assisting secretary general.[5] After the integration of Tangier and the Spanish zone and the formation of the second Moroccan government, a new *dahir* was promulgated establishing nineteen provinces, adding Tangier, Nador, Larache, Tetouan, Chaouen, and Alhucemas or Rif provinces,[6] and also governors for the cities of Meknes, Fès, and Marrakech.

Except for the addition of Tarfaya province below Agadir in 1958, the rural administration remained much the same for the first year and a half of independence. This number of provinces was unwieldy, but the new nation needed to centralize control in the early period of independence. The few skilled administrators allocated to the provincial administration were able to keep personal contact with the entire area under their control. With the return of Mohammed V the entire existing structure of minor officials, from

[4] For more details on the colonial administration, see *Morocco 1954, op.cit.*, pp. 43-49, and Ayache, *Le Maroc: Bilan d'une Colonisation, op.cit.*, pp. 84-95.

[5] See *O.B.*, no. 2252, December 23, 1955, "Dahir de 16 décembre 1955 (ler joumada I 1375) relatif à l'organisation provinciale," p. 1871. During the period studied there was no standard usage of provincial names. The following names were used interchangeably: Midelt, Tafilalet and Ksar As-Souk; Rif and Alhucemas; Beni Mellal and Kasba Tadla; Chaouia and Casablanca.

[6] *O.B.*, no. 2296, October 26, 1956, "Dahir no. 1-56-133 du 8 rebia I 1376 (13 octobre 1956) modifiant le dahir du ler joumada I 1375 (16 décembre 1955) relatif à l'organisation provinciale," pp. 1335-1336.

caids down to *moqaddems*, was in disrepute and under attack. Until new minor officials could be trained and while serious threat of violence remained it was considered necessary to have high-ranking officials in close contact with the populace of smaller areas.[7]

Next to ministerial posts the positions as governors are probably the most highly coveted jobs in the Moroccan government. The governors are appointed by *dahir* of the King and are the most important agents of the Minister of the Interior. Their political affiliations are generally followed with great speculation, especially their standing with the Istiqlal party. The northern provinces, for example, were originally governed by high officers of the Army of Liberation who chose to integrate their troops quietly into the Royal Army. Their inexperience and occasional abuse of office led to the trial of one, the removal and transfer of others. With the lack of qualified civil administrators, military training has been relied on heavily.

In some provinces, such as Agadir, Fès, and Oujda, men generally acknowledged as more favorable to the Istiqlal than their predecessors have replaced earlier appointments, though the governors are very likely much too busy to participate in party politics except by convenient acts of oversight or possible favorable appointments. None of the top-echelon leaders of the parties have chosen jobs in the rural administration; they have preferred to remain in Rabat in ministerial positions. Given the conditions that inspired the early provincial organization of Morocco there was little need for detailed legislation on gubernatorial powers, relations between superior and subordinate officials, and procedures of accountability. One highly general *dahir* has been passed, but does little to define carefully the duties or authority of the governor.

The only systematic presentation of the organization of the rural administration has been a volume prepared late in 1957. As summarized in Table 5 it listed positions for 735 officials, of which only 574 were filled. A new rural office was improvised shortly after independence, known as the *supercaid*, who managed the *caids* and subordinate officials of a circle. His function appears to have been similar to the old civil controller and indigenous-affairs officer. Each *supercaid* supervised roughly four *caids*, though the number of *caids* to any particular circle varies with the local tribal structure. As the

[7] This was plainly stated as the rationale for the first geographic division in the communiqué announcing the reorganization of provinces in mid-1958, *La Vigie*, August 12, 1958, p. 1.

TABLE 5

Number of Posts for Rural Officials (Filled, Vacant, and Total Posts in December 1957, with Ranks)[a]

Posts	Filled	Unfilled	Total
Prefectures	40	4	44
Governors, staff, and			
pashas of provinces	76	14	90
Supercaids	62	10	72
Caids	249	37	286
Khalifas	147	96	243
Total	574	161	735

[a] *Livre des Commandements*, Rabat: Ministry of the Interior, 1957.

figures suggest, the number of vacancies in the rural administration increases in the lower echelons, with the most unfilled positions occurring among the *khalifas*. Since the number of assigned *caids* averages about three tribes per person, it is quite possible that the quality of supervision also deteriorates sharply in the lower echelons. In the absence of sufficient trained persons willing to take these lower positions, the many rumors of injustice and arbitrariness at the lower level of tribal administration take on increased credibility. There was no statute on the duties and authority of the lower rural officials, although they were forbidden to add a percentage onto the *souk* transactions for their personal income; this practice had been a major abuse of the Protectorate's lower rural administration.[8]

The transition of the rural administration is summarized in Table 6, which gives the dates of appointment of the governors, pashas, *supercaids, caids,* and *khalifas.* The table does not indicate how many previous occupants there may have been for these positions, but only the date of the last appointment as of the end of 1957. The trend toward the early organization of the coastal provinces, Rabat, Chaouia, Fès, and Meknes, is evident. In regions more distant from the capital, where order was restored later, positions were filled or new appointments were made only toward the end of 1956. The problem of proper tribal supervision is again suggested by the predominance of unfilled posts in provinces where the tribal structure is stronger, such as Meknes, Taza, Alhucemas, Tafilalet, Agadir, and

[8] *O.B.*, no. 2267, April 6, 1956, "Dahir no. 1-56-047 du 7 chaabane 1375 (20 mars 1956) fixant le statut des caids," p. 342.

TABLE 6

Dates of Appointment of Rural Officials
(from December 1955 to December 1957 by Quarters)[a]

	1956				1957				No Date Given	Un-filled	Total
	1st[b]	2nd	3rd	4th	1st	2nd	3rd	4th			
Prefectures[c]	9	13	3	4	5	3	–	–	3	5	44
Rabat	8	4	8	3	4	12	1	7	1	6	54
Chaouia	7	5	–	9	5	7	2	9	5	7	56
Marrakech	1	–	3	37	5	1	8	1	1	–	57
Fès	14	2	3	7	2	4	1	2	–	13	48
Meknes	5	6	3	4	7	1	2	1	–	14	43
Taza	3	–	8	6	4	4	3	2	5	15	49
Kasba Tadla	2	6	3	10	5	3	2	1	2	9	43
Safi	4	5	–	9	5	1	8	2	1	4	39
Al-Jadiida (Mazagan)	2[d]	2	1	12	3	3	–	2	1	2	28
Tafilalet	3	–	1	1	13	1	4	6	–	20	49
Agadir	10	1	18	3	1	1	1	–	2	12	49
Oujda	7	1	7	7	–	2	3	7	–	2	36
Ouarzazate		1	10[e]	5	4	1	1	1	1	11	35
Tangier		–	–	–	–	1	–	–	3	–	4
Tetouan		–	5	–	–	–	–	–	6	2	13
Larache		1	7	1	–	–	1	–	2	9	21
Nador		–	14	2	–	–	–	–	–	14	31
Alhucemas (Rif)		–	10	–	–	–	–	–	2	11	23
Chaouen	1	1	4	–	2		–	–	1	6	15
Total	76	48	106	120	65	55	37	41	36	161	735

[a] *Livre des Commandements*, Rabat: Ministry of Interior, 1957.
[b] Includes December 1955.
[c] Prefectures include the cities of Rabat, Meknes, Fès, Casablanca, and Marrakech.
[d] One man serving as *supercaid*, pasha, and *caid*.
[e] One man serving as *supercaid* and *caid*.

Ouarzazate. Some of the provinces, like Agadir and Marrakech, where there were difficult problems of establishing order, show lumps of assignments as the reorganization became possible. In the northern provinces nearly all appointments were made shortly after the integration of these provinces and left virtually untouched since that time. Despite the frequent criticisms of the rural administration the total appointments each month suggest that a sustained effort has been made to assign, transfer, or remove officials, with the possible exception of the northern provinces.

Among the twenty-four governors in the provincial division of late 1957, seven had participated in the resistance. Their youth suggests their possible lack of training or experience, for they range from 29 to 48 years and have an average age of 39. The *supercaids* are even younger, ranging from 23 to 47 years, with an average age of 33. Though no official studies of their background have been released, the Istiqlal paper reported that 37 of them are either teachers of various kinds or minor officials from the Protectorate.[9] The omission of any information on the other officials tends to substantiate reports that many of them have had little or no training; this is especially true among members of the resistance. In the early months the rural administration was handicapped by the use of the resistance fighters, some of whom were even illiterate, and the rapid promotion of minor interpreters, secretaries, and assistants of former French rural officials. The Ministry of the Interior, however, like all other government functions, was conducted with severe limitations of personnel. Excessively rapid or numerous dismissals would very likely have simply meant the collapse of the rural administration. To provide the needed training and reorientation, with French help the ministry organized a *"caid* school."

The major task of the school has been to impress the new officials with their role as supervisors and planners, rather than arbitrary agents of authority in the Protectorate tradition. Emphasis was placed on fairly rudimentary administrative procedures such as census-taking, evaluation of resources, and design of simple community-improvement projects. Instruction also emphasized developing the skills needed to encourage participation in the rural-commune scheme. The rural officials attended school one week of each month over a period of four months, in order to avoid disrupting their work. Throughout the course the officials have lectures on administrative law, accompanied with one week each of general orientation, social problems, agriculture, and, lastly, economy and finance.[10] The school was started in late 1956 with approximately one hundred officials attending over the academic year in three groups. The government hoped that about 150 more officials would have passed through by the summer of 1958.

The officials have been spared none of the rigors of academic study; they take a four-hour exam and short oral exam upon the conclusion of the series of lectures and panels. The results of the

[9] *Al-Istiqlal*, December 28, 1957, p. 10.
[10] See the abbreviated schedule of the first two weeks of the course in *Al-Istiqlal*, January 11, 1957, pp. 6-7. For more details the plan is available, *Cours de Perfectionnement*, Center for Moroccan Orientation, Rabat, Ministry of the Interior, 1957.

examinations have been transmitted to the Minister of the Interior and have resulted in changes in rural assignments. Since many of the introductory lectures were given by high government officials the school affords an opportunity for some political indoctrination by parties, which was in evidence in at least two of the published lecture summaries.[11] The main focus of the course rested, however, on the development of the basic skills needed by a local administrator and the cultivation of his understanding of governmental services. As the presence of eighteen *supercaids* in the first group suggested, the course was designed in response to a real need to train even higher-ranking rural administrators.

The renovation of the rural administration presupposed a clear definition of its new organization and goals, but received little attention until 1957 and no action until 1958. Thirteen provinces and two prefectures were included in the new plan, which would reduce the number of high rural officials by one half. The announcement of this plan admitted that the first division had followed the lines of the colonial administration in order to compensate for the lack of low-level administrators and to facilitate strong central direction.[12] The new plan was designed to form economically viable units of the provinces, to eradicate distinctions between the north and south, to give more provinces access to the sea, and to "eliminate the tribal spirit." When the new division was being studied, it was reported that subordinate to the reduced number of governors would be seventy-two "subprefects," corresponding to the *supercaids*, or circle chiefs, who would, in turn, supervise 720 rural and urban communes.[13] When the plan was announced two months later, no comment was made on coordinated administrative changes and no appointments were made under the new structure until early 1959.

In the south the new provinces suggested a return to the larger "regions" used by the French Protectorate. Marrakech included Safi, and Casablanca included Al-Jadiida (Mazagan), while Agadir, Tafilalet, and Ouarzazate were left virtually the same. The most notable change was merging the small northern provinces with larger neighboring ones. Nador was incorporated in Oujda, Alhucemas (Rif) province in Fès, and Chaouen, Tetouan, and Larache were merged into a single province under Tetouan. The northernmost

[11] "Les Institutions Démocratiques de l'Etat," *Cours de Perfectionnement, op.cit.,* and "Exposé sur l'Information," *ibid.*

[12] *La Vigie,* August 12, 1958, p. 1.

[13] *L'Action,* June 16, 1958, p. 14.

town of Rabat province, Ouazzani, was also put under Tetouan, while the inaccessible town of Moulay Bouazza in Rabat province was put under Meknes. Tarfaya remained a single province partly because of problems of communication and also because of the continued reliance on military administrators in border areas. The five city governors were reduced to two, Casablanca and Rabat, which now will also include neighboring Salé.

Politics Comes to the Countryside

Though the statutes governing the rural administration were not completed by the end of 1958, the various Ministers of the Interior since independence had made it clear that new standards of conduct were expected. Shortly after the return of the King, the Minister of the Interior issued a statement announcing that justice would no longer be in the hands of the rural administrators and that the custom of taxing the population periodically for the elaborate entertainment of visitors would be discontinued. When one considers the disruption of the countryside by the Liberation Army and the crises produced by movements of the French Army until the fall of 1956, changes seem to have been made reasonably fast. Though many of the agents of authority in the countryside may have been of doubtful loyalty or opposed to the Istiqlal in 1956, it must be remembered that the government was totally unprepared for the transition and also that the people were unreasonably optimistic as to the changes independence would automatically bring. Though there were repeated addresses from the King[14] as well as explanations by the Minister of the Interior, trouble occurred in the early months of independence where officials of the old regime remained in office.

Until order could be restored under Moroccan auspices it was difficult to engage in any systematic overhaul of the rural administration. As Table 6 shows, the tendency was to establish acceptable municipal administrations first. Regional governments were reconstructed with the establishment of the governor's office, and work continued downward. The King made the new standards of the rural administration clear and also emphasized the purely administrative function of the new *caids* and *khalifas* as the judicial reform made progress. In the summer of 1956 he decided that no gov-

[14] For example, see the King's speeches at meetings of rural authorities. Lacouture, *op.cit.*, pp. 151-155.

ernors, *caids,* or minor officials would be allowed to appoint members of their family to positions of authority. A further preliminary reform was ordered in the fall when the King directed that a complete inventory of the rural administration be made, including specifically how each official was paid and how much land he owned or had acquired while in office. The continued disorganization of the administration of the countryside was revealed by the King's reiteration in late 1956 that rural officials were responsible to the Minister of the Interior, who would be in charge of distributing any ill-gotten lands.

The rural problem was probably first clarified in the late fall of 1956 at the second meeting of the governors with the King and M'Hammedi. The Minister of the Interior admitted that up to that time the emphasis of the administration had been on restoring public order, but that from that time on more work would be done on reform of administrative techniques and improvement of the rural economy. The King defined the new role of the administrators, saying, "Today we are alone responsible for our problems, for our destiny; the governors should not forget that they are the representatives of the central power, to directives to which they should conform; they should not forget, moreover, that they have a role to play as educators in their administration."[15] At the same time plans were announced for increased agricultural credits, the *caid* school, and the collectivization of land seized by officials of the old regime.

The conversion of the rural administration was especially important to the Istiqlal and the U.M.T., both of which had been virtually excluded from activity in the countryside since 1952. Though cells of nationalists existed in some towns of the countryside, the party had never been able to establish a full organization among the tribes. With independence this opportunity was presented to all political groups. The Istiqlal repeatedly blamed officials of the old regime for restricting its efforts, even though the Ministry of the Interior was directed by an Istiqlal member from mid-1956. The Istiqlal's new rural offices sent delegations to the Palace, and the U.M.T. gave the King its views on the pending appointments in various regions. The Istiqlal Congress of December 1955 called for complete reorganization of the powers of the rural administration and a statute defining their method of recruitment, promotion, and control. During the National Council meeting in August 1956 Allal

[15] *C.M.,* October 11-14, 1956, p. 3, and Annex VIII.

Al-Fassi charged that during the short period in which the Ministry of the Interior was under Lyoussi free rein had been given to treasonous intrigue, but that since M'Hammedi had taken the post these offenses had stopped.[16] It seems that he was expressing the solidarity appropriate for the occasion, since attacks on the rural administration continued incessantly throughout the summer and fall of 1956. He had given a more accurate appraisal shortly after independence when he admitted that the tribes constituted a problem since the *bled* was ten years behind the urban areas.

The transition of the rural administration placed the nationalists in a difficult position. The disorder in the interior of the country was evidence that Morocco could not manager her own affairs. Trained officials did not exist and no doubt many of the existing tribal chieftains were under French influence. The party could not avoid taking issue when its organizational efforts were being obstructed. Many officials also wrote to the party concerning the conflict of party membership and government service. The Executive Committee of the party issued a special communiqué in the summer of 1956 assuring members who were rural officials or members of the police or army that their party positions were in no way incompatible with government service.[17] However, in acknowledgment of the need to keep party policy and governmental duties distinct, they were advised not to take offices in the party. Though there was no general legislation on the political conduct of civil servants until the Charter of Public Liberties in late 1958, the members in such positions were cautioned at that time that no personal considerations should ever influence their conduct. Whether or not this was the case was almost impossible to determine.

For the party the rural problem was probably not so much that the tribes objected to party affiliations of officials, as that the tribes did not understand the difference between the government and the party. The directives given to rural sections of the party were to explain the meaning of a central government under independent status. For most tribesmen the King, government, and Istiqlal were to some extent identified, so that whatever errors were made by rural officials were to the detriment of the party as much as of the new government. If *caids* of the old regime remained in place momentarily or if unskilled new officials arrived to replace them, explana-

[16] *Al-Istiqlal*, August 16, 1956, p. 7.
[17] *Ibid.*, June 15, 1956, p. 3.

tions were more difficult for the party organizers working on the scene than for the government officials remaining in Rabat. In many ways effective action by the party was confined to the same channels as those used by the government itself. Like the government, the Istiqlal concentrated on obtaining the higher officers of the rural administration. There was no way for the central office of the party to cope with the individual shortcomings of the rural administration with any more facility than could the Minister of the Interior himself, for whom it was a process of first assigning responsible and credited higher officials.

A typical case is the sustained Istiqlal criticism of the governor of Taza. The party papers accused him of handicapping the organization of the party and of seizing party offices.[18] Though a government spokesman who belonged to the party denied that friction was as serious as party papers reported, he added: "I am certain that the ancient administrative spirit still exists among some *caids*."[19] The same day an Istiqlal delegation arrived from Taza to petition the government, while an attack was also begun on the governor of Tafilalet. Criticism was intensified during the crisis leading to the formation of the second Bekkai government. Allal Al-Fassi complained over the orders of the Minister of the Interior forbidding rural officials to attend Istiqlal rallies in the Fès area,[20] and there appeared notices of continued opposition to Istiqlal organizers by some *caids* of Marrakech.[21] In public opposition to the Istiqlal Minister of the Interior, Al-Fassi spoke of efforts of the rural officials to retard the work of the party and the trade unions.

With the formation of the Bekkai government of October 1956 the Istiqlal predominated in the Council of Government, and the Democratic party refused office. From that time there was much more comment on the abuses of the rural administration in the Democratic party's papers, while criticism almost disappeared from the Istiqlal papers. Over the summer and fall of 1956 Democratic party officials in the countryside had been mysteriously kidnapped in quite large numbers, mostly in the north, and in Rabat and Chaouia provinces.[22] These disappearances have never been adequately ex-

[18] *Al-Alam*, July 27, 1956, and July 31, 1956, Fr. Trans.
[19] Press Conference, Abdallah Ibrahim, Secretary of State for Information, *C.M.*, August 1, 1956, p. 1, and Annex II.
[20] *Al-Alam*, October 1, 1956, Fr. Trans.
[21] *Ibid.*, October 18, 1956, Fr. Trans.
[22] See account in *Rai Al-Amm*, September 15, 1956, Fr. Trans. That these were regions where the resistance was strongest is probably not pure coincidence.

plained, nor was the possible complicity of rural officials in these events ever eliminated, even though incidents continued throughout 1957. A *caid* near Tsoul reportedly had nine members of his family working in minor official capacities, while there were many incidents of officials' obstructing the work of the party. In Es-saouira (Mogador) the pasha allegedly permitted the police to disperse a parade of party youth,[23] in Goulimine the *caid* arrested party officials returning from a meeting,[24] and in Taza one of the *caids* was blamed for inciting the crowds sufficiently to cause the lynching of a party official.[25] Like the Istiqlal reports, the Democratic party reports cannot be verified, nor have they been commented on by the Ministry of the Interior. They are sufficient in number, however, to justify the conclusion that there was still considerable abuse of the rural administration in 1957. They also strongly suggest that some rural officials of resistance background participated actively in the suppression of the Democratic party, though no evidence is available after the banning of the party papers early in 1958.

In the early months of independence the problem of establishing order precluded any well-organized effort to integrate the tribes. The first major appeal to the countryside was the campaign of Caid Lahcen Lyoussi in the fall of 1956, which was promptly followed by the tour of Allal Al-Fassi. Their activity reflected the first major division of political opinion on the role of the countryside in national politics. Its full implications were never allowed to develop at that time, partly because of the international crisis of October 1956 and also because the King disapproved of a split that might revive a Berber-Arab differentiation. To refer to the controversy of the fall of 1956 as a Berber-Arab division would be an oversimplification and would give undue credit to the efforts of the Protectorate to foster this differentiation. In some respects it was the first time that tribes participated in the new political system on the national level, though in only a passive role. Involved in the activity was the conviction of some leaders that the countryside was being neglected in favor of the organized urban population and that the position of the King was threatened by the Istiqlal. The tours of Lyoussi and Al-Fassi are also the prelude to the formation of the Popular Movement, which emerged a year later over similar discontent with the policy of the Istiqlal.

[23] *Ibid.*, July 11, 1957.
[24] *Ibid.*, May 31, 1957.
[25] *Ibid.*, May 11, 1957.

Caid Lahcen Lyoussi, a devoted friend of the King and chieftain of the large Ait Youssi tribe of the Middle Atlas, resigned after the uprisings in Marrakech early in May 1956. Shortly afterward the Secretary of State for Information held a press conference censoring Lyoussi for a recent speech at Sefrou where the Istiqlal was criticized.[26] Lyoussi released a correction at the same time and maintained that his speech had been misinterpreted. The dilemma of Lyoussi's position, and that of anyone attempting to organize rural opinion, was that any rural political activity could be compared to colonial tactics. This does not necessarily mean that there are no differentiations between the urban and tribal population which might suitably form the basis of a political movement. Given the history of the Berber *dahir* of 1930, the difficulty of constructively channeling rural opinions, and the lack of any institutional procedures to bring these opinions to bear on the governmental problems concerned, even the best-intentioned rural agitation was likely to be easily identified, rightly or wrongly, with colonialism.

In an interview in the Democratic party paper soon afterward, Lyoussi revealed the dilemma of starting a rural political organization.[27] He argued that the sole means of unifying Morocco was to discontinue all political parties and to rally around Mohammed V. This statement was an admission of the difficulty of organizing the countryside and also conflicted with the King's wish to remain apart from organized political groups. Lyoussi supported extending orthodox Muslim law to all the tribes. His only specific proposal was to call for the withdrawal of French troops, which, in view of this proposal's popularity two years later when it was actively pursued by the Istiqlal, may have had considerable appeal. From the viewpoint of the emergence of the new political system the important revelation was the tacitly admitted difficulty of converting rural opinions into meaningful form in the new nation.

Several months later Lyoussi renewed his activity among the tribes. His experience and the Istiqlal reaction is of importance not so much because the event led to easily identified changes in the existing government, but because of the revelation of the problems of bringing

[26] *C.M.*, June 15, 1956, p. 2, and Annex V, Press Conference of Abdallah Ibrahim. He also objected to the accounts, appearing in the foreign press, of trouble between Berbers and Arabs. The Moroccan government is extremely sensitive on this issue. The reporter for *France-Soir* was expelled in August 1958 for his accounts of unrest among the tribes.

[27] *Rai Al-Amm*, June 27, 1956, Fr. Trans.

the rural populations into contact with the central government. Late in August Lyoussi assembled several hundred Berber leaders and *caids* in the Middle Atlas Mountains. His speech was again an attack on partisan politics and called all political groups to unite behind the King. He added that "some parties" were undergoing a decadence due to their internal divisions, lack of program, and refusal to accept criticism. In his opinion the civil servants pertaining to such parties had displayed "fanaticism" in the execution of their duties and the local representatives an "arrogance" in their interference in local government to the advantage of their parties. The origin of discontent was most succinctly put in his charge that such parties "forget that the largest part of the inhabitants of our country are of the country; that the element that has produced the glory of our country is of the country; . . . and (that) it is contrary to the interests of the people to confer all political, social and economic responsibility to some men who ignore all the tribes and the countryside."[28] The beginnings of a political movement were demonstrated soon afterward, when a Middle Atlas group sent a telegram to the King testifying to their faith in the leadership of Caid Lyoussi.

In September, Lyoussi continued his tours with an entourage of officials known for their devotion to the King and also known for their opposition to the Istiqlal.[29] A meeting of several thousand Berber tribesmen took place near Beni Mellal and was followed by other rallies around Kasba Tadla. There was also a meeting in solidarity with Lyoussi among some Rif tribes, and there were reports that activity inspired by his appeal had begun near Marrakech. His efforts were allegedly stopped at the request of the King, who did not want the Berber-Arab issue to be resurrected. Also, at this time the "Berber Tract Plot," linking French officials with propaganda activity among tribesmen, was revealed by the Moroccan police. Since the government was undergoing an attack from the Istiqlal rural leaders, any tribal discord might justify the party's accusations or provoke serious incidents of violence. As events worked out, it was the arrest of the Algerian leaders by the French and the Suez crisis that did just this.

The Lyoussi affair demonstrated not only that the tribes could be appealed to outside the framework of the Istiqlal and the rural ad-

[28] *C.M.*, August 26, 1956, p. 1.
[29] *Ibid.*, September 1, 1956, p. 1, and Annex III. The groups included Addi ou Bihi, the son of Abdelkrim, and several others implicated in the revolts of late 1958.

ministration, but also that such an appeal was an extremely delicate question to introduce into the new political system. The potentiality of this appeal was suggested by the Istiqlal reaction, which was, in fact, a tacit admission that the tribal problem was a very real one in Moroccan politics and that tribal support was considered very important by Istiqlal leaders. Al-Fassi immediately proceeded to make one of his most extensive tours of the countryside and probably his longest visit up to that time in the Middle Atlas Mountains. A week after the Lyoussi rallies, Al-Fassi visited the same tribal centers.[30] His speeches were devoted to long historical analyses of the common historical and religious background of the Arabs and Berbers, which paradoxically acknowledged the existence of the latter as a distinct group. The success of the trip was tarnished by an attempt to assassinate the "Leader" near Boulemane.[31] It is doubtful if this tour brought the party the hoped-for dividends, since it is still weak in the area. Nor did the campaign of Al-Fassi serve to silence Lyoussi, who spoke to a group of Middle Atlas *caids* at the palace the next month. He again denied any interest in fomenting discord between the countryside and the cities and pledged full loyalty to the King.

There is no way of evaluating to what extent the Istiqlal dominated the rural administration. An experienced government official, who is not an Istiqlal militant, has estimated that approximately eighty-five per cent of the rural officials are members, five per cent members of the Democratic party, and ten per cent remain independent of any political affiliation. The more important consideration is to what extent officials favor parties in their day-to-day activities. Many of the rural officials have probably accepted Istiqlal membership simply because the government or the local population were heavily Istiqlal. It should not be forgotten that the Istiqlal organization is fairly new in the countryside and, therefore, is itself in the course of establishing its reputation among the tribesmen. The abuses that do occur are as likely to reflect on the party as to act in its favor. Even those officials who are active Istiqlal members must

[30] The tribal centers were also areas of Liberation Army activity: the Ait Youssi tribe, Sefrou, Ain Aicha, Boulemane, Immouzer du Kandar, Khenifra, Karia be Mohammed, and Ghafsai. See *Al-Istiqlal*, September 28, 1956, p. 3.

[31] *Al-Alam*, September 25, 1956, Fr. Trans., reports that thirty-four bullets were sent through his vehicle without wounding him. His courage enabled him to continue to Boulemane and give his address as scheduled. This escape from death very likely did much to enhance his mystical reputation among the tribesmen. It is curious that some Moroccans would attempt a political murder of a martyr, which the French never did. This is perhaps further testimony to the political inexperience of the rural politicians.

also retain a degree of impartiality in their role as representatives of the Ministry of the Interior and the King. Local party officials confirm the view that the party finds its local administrative rapport best in the areas of the country where it has had strength for some time before independence.

The small posts to be offered in the *douars* and *souks* could provide only a small sinecure for only a few local party militants.[32] The rural administration since independence has at least impressed the rural citizens that they now live under a political system where agents of authority can be changed for abuse of office and where supervision is exercised by a government having popular approval. Such a simple change from the Protectorate as being able to move about freely is no doubt welcomed and is not without political significance. Difficult problems continue to exist in finding trained persons, and Moroccan officials admit that educated youth are reluctant to go to remote distant posts. That abuses continue is suggested by the number of removals, but there also seems to be an attempt to promote and transfer rural officials in a rational manner. Over the past two years it appears that a fairly well-qualified body of higher officials has been assembled and that future emphasis will be put on perfecting lower echelons.

Although by 1959 the new rural administration had brought small relief from the oppressions of the Protectorate system, it had also opened the countryside to other forms of political contact. The rural officials may be for the present a somewhat less authoritarian version of the French and Spanish administration. But a most important contribution to the political education of the tribesmen will be the implementation of the rural commune system. In the meantime, the desires and expectations of the rural population are also known through the political parties working among the tribes. The methods and results of the party activity in the countryside may be controversial, but to the extent that the rural administration has not filled the rural expectations or has confirmed rural dislike of central government, tribesmen and peasants looked to other means of expressing their discontent. This is probably the most crucial aspect of the political transition of Morocco, for it is in the introduction to several means of expressing political opinions and forming expecta-

[32] Since so many posts remain unfilled, the party may not have been too successful in finding militants willing to isolate themselves in remote parts or possibly in convincing the Minister of the Interior that their men should be appointed.

tions that the population of the new state comes into contact with the new political system. It is also the first step in breaking down the tribal system. The incidents with Lyoussi and the rural organization of the Istiqlal were only alternative ways of bringing tribal politics into relation with national politics.

Problems in Distant Provinces

At the provincial level of organization serious difficulties have existed in at least three cases, Agadir, Oujda, and the northern zone as a whole.[33] The province of Tafilalet might have joined this category, but the suppression of Addi ou Bihi's local rule by the Royal Army early in 1957 avoided such an eventuality. Though poor communications and lack of personnel are partially responsible for the difficulties encountered in all these cases, the immediate circumstances vary considerably. Misguided as he might have been, Addi ou Bihi was fanatically loyal to the King. There was never any question of the province's seceding from the country or becoming the object of hostilities that the new country could not control. The cases of Agadir and Oujda involve both external and internal circumstances, but in the opinion of the Moroccan government, and certainly of the Moroccan people as well, involve the future existence of the new country. In this way they are typical of the overriding questions of national existence that preoccupied the new nation in the first three years of its independence.

The Agadir question was concerned mostly with the French. The port of the province had been expanded under French rule far beyond its present needs, in anticipation of exploitation of the southwestern Sahara. During 1956 large numbers of French troops were moved to the area as the Moroccan Army of Liberation moved toward the desert. This was done in consultation with the Moroccan government and, at least at times, in coordination with the new Royal Army. Readily accessible from the north by only two roads, the region had become a French-built southern outpost. The French

[33] This is excluding the very controversial case of the Tangier. Its international status was relinquished in the fall of 1956 and the Moroccan government has since proceeded to extend national regulations to the ex-international area. The attention that the protests of the foreign and Moroccan residents received as their privileges and businesses were affected is interesting testimony to the advantages of organization and education in national politics. It is probably fair to state that the artificial economy and political anomaly of Tangier, which unavoidably faced adjustment, have received disproportionate concern as a national problem.

autonomy in the region was accompanied with considerable Moroccan autonomy, which was based on the enclave of devout Muslims of the Sous valley. The Istiqlal following among the orthodox Muslims of the region had been established by visits of local *ulema* to northern Islamic institutions and by migration of surplus population to northern cities, where they were open to indoctrination in urban slums. The first Istiqlal inspector for the province was one of the earliest members of the nationalist movement and a colleague of Allal Al-Fassi. This fact suggests the difficulty the party may have had in the region. In the summer of 1958 the party was just beginning to organize towns and villages outside the city of Agadir.

The party, like the government, had been delayed by the French troops and the Liberation Army. At the time of the Meknes riots and the arrest of the Algerian leaders the French government was especially concerned over the isolated group of French nationals to the south and sent military reinforcements into the area. Agadir was particularly vulnerable to any campaign of the Moroccan Liberation Army in protest against the Algerian arrests or in coordination with new campaigns by the Algerian Liberation Army. The French fears were very likely not entirely unsubstantiated, though evidence is meager. Certainly the Royal Army was not yet capable of defending the local inhabitants at that time. Five Algerians had been arrested for complicity in the Meknes riots and the sympathy of the Moroccan Liberation Army for North African liberation was well known.

During 1957 the new country did not press for French evacuation of Agadir. The silence of the Istiqlal leaders, except Al-Fassi, on the irredentist claims to the south seemed to indicate that the government was content to allow the entire question of the defining of southern borders to rest for the moment. French concern was again denoted when high officials of the French Embassy made a visit to the province shortly after the Meknes affair. The Moroccan government took the precaution of publicizing that this was with the permission of Rabat and in harmony with the government's desire to rebuild close relations with France after the Meknes riot. The signs of apprehension from both governments was very likely based on real problems in Agadir. The King generally appointed Royal Army officers in the most troublesome provinces. The first two governors here were Royal Army captains and were apparently able to keep order, probably with the help of the French troops. Only two months after a governor with strong Istiqlal loyalties was appointed the Ifni war began to the south.

During 1957 Al-Fassi's drive to regain the southern regions gathered momentum. He made several visits to the southern provinces where he exhorted them to combat to regain the vast desert stretches toward French West Africa. During this period the governors probably helped keep the remnants of the Liberation Army in the Draa valley supplied, but out of action. Since the guerillas there at that time were supposed to be largely from Middle Atlas tribes, they were probably disposed to follow the directions of the then still unknown, but active, leaders of the Popular Movement.[34] This situation of mutually reinforcing common background and loyalties was disrupted in the summer of 1957, when a new governor was appointed and the irredentist campaign had reached national proportions. The reorganization of the Liberation Army in the Sahara began as relations with the French proved desperately fruitless. The new governor was from the Ait Ba Armane tribe to the south of Agadir and around Ifni, from which area new Liberation Army troops were supposed to have come when the Middle Atlas elements, suspected for their loyalty to the Popular Movement, were sent home. The new governor was generally regarded as extremely sympathetic to the Istiqlal, and evidence of his yielding to Istiqlal interests in the province after his appointment confirms this view. In November 1957 the Ifni war began.

There is no way of estimating how long the Moroccan government had been resisting pressure for this resort to war. Nor is there any evidence but that the government concurred in Al-Fassi's view. By the end of 1957 French and Spanish procrastination might have convinced the government that a small war might be helpful in getting attention for the myriad diplomatic problems which had been stagnating for nearly a year. The offensive may also have been an official or spontaneous attempt to help the Algerians, since the F.L.N. began its first major Sahara campaign in October 1957. The announced intention of the French government to exploit the Sahara alone had implications that were even more serious for Morocco than for the Algerian revolutionaries. The war, with the subsequent assertion of Moroccan claims to the south by the King himself,

[34] It is probably not justified to speak of the loyalty of a tribe in contemporary politics, since many of them were completely urbanized and belonged to the Istiqlal. However, those in the Liberation Army had come from outlying sections and were related to the Middle Atlas Liberation Army effort of Lyoussi.

tended to reduce Agadir's importance in internal politics and no doubt ended whatever doubts there may have been about Istiqlal strength in the area. The problem of governing Agadir province was resolved by its becoming a national emergency, which, in turn, removed the province from questions of internal politics.[35]

The problem of establishing the regional government in the easternmost province of Oujda was also laced with international considerations. In Oujda the issue was even more laden with risk to the new country. If a war were to start in that province, it would be most difficult to restrict it. There were large numbers of Algerians in the north, units of the Moroccan and Algerian Liberation Armies to the south, and many extremely aggressive tribesmen to the east, who had been active in the Rif Moroccan Liberation Army. Tribesmen and peasants had suffered from the closure of the border between Oujda and Oran because they relied heavily on seasonal migration to the farms around Oran to supplement their income. The fact that the region between Oujda and Oran is ruggedly mountainous down to the sea made it appropriate territory for smuggling arms to the Algerian revolutionaries and for counterterrorist efforts by the French Army or local French civilians.

Though no information is available on the quantity of aid being given to the Algerian revolution by Morocco, the bulk of this material passed through Oujda province for transport across the border between Oujda and Oran or along the desert border to the south. There are, of course, numerous sheltered coves along the northern coast where material can be unloaded. The main supply and training center of the Moroccan Liberation Army was in the vicinity of Nador and was reportedly supported by skilled guerilla soldiers from the F.L.N. The Istiqlal also has old roots in Oujda. The mining industry was brought under Istiqlal influence by the late 1940's. Oujda was also the only Moroccan city that staged a violent demonstration when the King was exiled.

Moroccan regional administrators have probably had a higher mortality rate in Oujda than in any other province—an indication of the problems of government there. The eastern part of the province

[35] There is another local source of tension, also derived from French efforts to give Agadir a certain amount of autonomy. Much of the foreign business of Agadir is controlled by Demnati, a merchant of whom little is known. His attempt to start a bank for the area with foreign capital was denounced by Al-Fassi as a veiled form of colonialism. The Agadir earthquake has, of course, put the province's entire future in doubt.

was still held by the Moroccan Liberation Army in early 1956 and there were fears of new disorder among the Beni Snassen tribesmen. The restoration of order was undoubtedly encouraged by the appointment of Bekkai as the first President of the Council, for he comes from this tribe and arranged a reception of the tribesmen by the King early in 1956. About a week after appointment, the first governor was killed in a mysterious accident in the eastern part of the province. The circumstances of his death have never been explained, though it is quite possible that more militant elements of the Liberation Army resented the pacification effort of the new government. A few weeks after independence there were successful attacks on government offices to seize arms, and the pasha of the city of Oujda was wounded in an assassination attempt. The Commander of French forces in Morocco made frequent inspection trips to the province. Although the violence may have been in reaction to this display of French interest, it was probably the presence of French forces that forestalled more serious uprisings.

Over the summer of 1956 there was at Oujda at least one conference of the Prince, the Minister of National Defense, and the French Commander. By fall the situation seems to have become extremely precarious and there were frequent reports of impending mass violence, mostly over the restrictions on Algerian nationalist activity by French forces. The major adjustment in the province's administration was made just a month before the arrest of the Algerian leaders. Had it been postponed, there may well have been a demonstration in Oujda that would have far surpassed the violence around Meknes in October 1956. Rabat decided to appoint a new governor in September, Si Mohammed Ben Amar Hamidou. The fact that he had been a leader in the Liberation Army suggests that his appointment meant concessions to the Moroccan guerillas and to the Algerian revolutionaries. Shortly after the new governor was installed, the King made his official entry into the city of Oujda and his first visit to the province.

As in several other cases, the presence of the King very likely was crucial in solving the problem of Oujda province. His visit alone made it much more difficult for local elements, who might have been willing to start a major uprising, to act among the local Moroccans. An attempt was made to impress the local population with the benefits of the new government by distributing some land to peasants[36] and by opening a new irrigation dam, which had been built, of course, under the Protectorate. The King's speech[37] at the official welcoming ceremonies recognized the highly volatile situation in the province and testified to Moroccan moderation on the Algerian problem over the first two years of independence. He praised the members of the Liberation Army who had accepted integration into the Royal Army and promised land and jobs to those who returned to their villages. He asked the people to respect the French troops in the province, but noted the religious, ethnic, and geographic ties of "North Africa as a whole." Independence for Algeria was not specifically endorsed, but he noted: "All that touches Algeria has profound resonances in Morocco as much in reason of the intimate lines and affinities which exist between the two peoples as in reason of their geographical adjoinment. That is why the return of peace in Algeria remains for us a major preoccupation." The province remained, however, extremely sensitive to relations with the F.L.N., and each Algerian crisis meant another threat to Moroccan hegemony in the area.

The threat in Oujda is not confined solely to Moroccan sympathy and support for the Algerians across the border. There is a large number of Algerian refugees displaced by hostilities along the border regions and left jobless by the loss of seasonal migratory labor. The number is generally placed at about 50,000,[38] though Moroccans often claim double this number. When tension mounts over the future of Algeria, as happened in the summer of 1958, the province is endangered. After the rebellion of the French Army in Algeria, the Moroccan Ministers of National Defense and the Interior and the Director of the Sûreté went on a special inspection tour of the province. An impressive review of the Royal Army was held, though it was never clear whether the Moroccan government was more concerned over a French invasion from Algeria or over disorder among alarmed Algerians in Oujda.

In the rash of violence that spread over Morocco in late 1958 many of the most serious incidents occurred in this province. A terrorist attack of unknown source took place in the refugee camp at Berguent, where several women and children were killed. The radio

[36] Lacouture, *op.cit.*, p. 65. Lacouture is firmly of the view that the province would have been lost if the Moroccan government had allowed the situation of the summer of 1956 to continue.

[37] His speech at that time appears in *ibid.*, pp. 137-139.

[38] See the estimate of Lacouture, *ibid.*, p. 64.

tower at Oujda was blown up and a French espionage and counter-terrorist group was thought to have been involved in arrests of French personnel at the Dellidja mines.[39] Probably in connection with the increased agitation of the Popular Movement, at least three attacks were made on Istiqlal officials in the eastern part of the province, the area of the Beni Snassen tribe. Seven persons were wounded in the town of Berkane, near the city of Oujda, when a bomb was set off in a crowd during celebrations of the anniversary of the King's ascension to the throne. Though there were many other violent encounters in the fall of 1958, the large number in Oujda province indicated that it remained one of the most volatile areas of the country.

The northern provinces were probably the most difficult to integrate. The problem of local government was complicated, as in the two cases above, by Spanish reluctance to make concessions. Morocco's acceptance of the Spanish provincial structure in the north, designed for supervision by sea communication from Spain, is evidence of the new nation's unpreparedness. Not until mid-1958 were new boundaries outlined that would orient the northern provinces toward Rabat and establish new provincial capitals in close communication with the southern areas. The major obstacles to the integration of the ex-Spanish region are obvious. The north had had Spanish administrative, educational, and financial systems. All the special training of administrators, all public notices and regulations, and all communications were in Spanish. The poverty of Spain meant that the level of general education and economic development was markedly lower in the north. With the exception of the area around the city of Tetouan nearly all the north still possessed an intact family tribal structure, which in some areas was among the least modified in the whole country.

The integration of the northern region was initially delayed by Spanish reluctance to recognize Moroccan independence after the French Agreement of 1956. The entire area from Tetouan to Oujda was occupied by the Rif segment of the Liberation Army, which did not fully agree to the merger with the Royal Army until summer. The provinces of Nador and Alhucemas were armed strongholds of the resistance, which had extensions through tribes southward

[39] See the accounts in *Le Monde,* October 8, 1958, p. 2, and October 9, 1958, p. 3. The mine was in the peculiar position of crossing the border so that persons wishing to enter Morocco or Algeria illegally could pass through with the cooperation of the mine's authorities.

into the ex-French zone north of Fès and Taza. After independence the new administrative appointments were almost entirely from the leaders of the Liberation Army. They lacked experience and were very likely skeptical of, if not opposed to, the dissolution of the guerilla army. As shown in Table 6, nearly all these changes took place in the last half of 1956. There were only three changes over the next year, and roughly one half of the posts remained empty. In four of the northern provinces the original governors proved incapable and had to be removed. One of them, Si Abdellah Senhadji, was indicted on criminal charges and later became the leader of the uprising at Alhucemas late in 1958. The government later admitted that poor administration had contributed to the tribal revolts.

During the fall of 1956 emergency allocations were made for needy families in the north, especially those of the Liberation Army troops. A national drive was begun to raise relief funds for distribution in the north. There was little improvement over the next year apparently, for in the fall of 1957 a second relief drive was held and nearly the same amount of funds were once again distributed. The new government seems to have gone as slowly as possible with the integration of the north over the next year. This was undoubtedly due to its own limitations as well as to its awareness of the potentially hostile situation that could arise in the old Spanish zone. In a summary of educational progress in the fall of 1957 the northern zone was still carried as a single separate figure, with the note that no detailed figures on the schools there yet existed.[40] Examination of the personnel folders of the 4,000 civil servants of the old Spanish administration did not begin until March 1958. A merger of the two civil service systems could not begin until the withdrawal of the peseta, which was not done until February 1958.

The monetary procedures for replacing the peseta with the franc had been discussed intermittently with the Spanish throughout 1957. Neither party appears to have been eager to reach an agreement and the Ifni war further postponed an agreement.[41] The accord for the retreat of the peseta was finally signed during a lull in the fight-

[40] "Recensement des Elèves des Etablissements d'Enseignement du Maroc," Rabat, Ministry of National Education, November 10, 1956.
[41] Franco agreed in principle to the withdrawal of the peseta in July 1957. *C.M.*, July 4-7, 1957, p. 1. He also signed commercial, administrative, and cultural conventions at this time. The question was not settled, however, regarding the exact procedures and controls for this delicate monetary switch, which was the subject of controversy over the next six months.

ing with Spanish and French troops in the south.[42] With the monetary merger a whole new field of controls and regulations began in the north. New taxes, licenses, and fees came into effect. Within a month there were petitions for relief and special controls to keep down the cost of living. One of the first measures—which suggests how desperate the situation had become—was to fix the price of bread. Many of the tribesmen are said to have relied on smuggling and drug traffic, which became increasingly difficult, to supplement their income. In the city of Tetouan the depression resulted in many workers' being laid off and in subsequent strikes. This situation meant not only local unemployed, but also serious repercussions in the countryside, where large families were very likely dependent on checks from relatives in the city.

The experience with the integration of the north is important not only as a problem in administrative reorganization, but also as background to the uprisings in the north in late 1958. The government never officially admitted serious apprehension over the administrative and economic disorganization in the north. Long before the uprisings, however, efforts were being made to redress the situation. The problems of the north could not be solved without advancing its entire system of roads, telephones, schools, farming methods, et cetera, to a level comparable with that of the south. The long-run needs for general development of the north could not be met within the time limits imposed by the political system. There were at least four extended inspection visits over the first eight months of 1958 by the Minister of Public Works.[43] A symbolic effort was begun over the summer of 1957 with the Unity Road project of the Istiqlal, but this only scratched the surface. A special commission was started for development of the northern provinces, but a decade's work could not be completed in one year.

The Tribal Revolts of Late 1958

The tribal disorders of late 1958 are related to both the weaknesses of the rural administration and the rise of the Popular Movement. They were also partially the result of poor administration and of the difficulties of communicating with the tribesmen. The gov-

[42] See Le Monde, January 15, 1958, p. 5.
[43] For example, see notices in La Vigie, January 2, 1958, p. 1, and L'Echo, February 25, 1958, p. 2. These trips were not simple tours of Tetouan, but sessions were held with engineers and technicians in the most remote towns of the Rif Mountains. Many of these same towns were involved in the uprisings at the end of 1958.

ernment was well aware of the hazards of delaying the formation of closer ties between the countryside and the capital, but it lacked resources and plans. Just before the outbreak of violence in the more inaccessible tribal regions, the government passed a series of stringent regulations concerning the possession of arms and imposed stiff penalties by military courts for illegal possession of arms. Very possibly the police and the Royal Army had indications that serious violence was threatening, though they may have been taking general precautions because of events in Algeria or as a consequence of the incident at Bou Arfa. Local officials were probably aware of the increasing tension during the summer of 1958, but nothing official appeared in government statements. Rabat could hardly have been ignorant of the depletion of tribal food reserves over the summer so that many areas were at a near-starvation diet level by fall. The occasional removal of a rural administrator for corruption or inefficiency also suggests that the central government was at least informed on the shortcomings of certain rural officials.

The first incident took place at Ajdir when leaders of the Popular Movement decided to move the body of the assassinated Liberation Army leader, Si Abbès, to a memorial shrine in the mountains of the Gzennaia tribe north of Fès. The local authorities intervened and were humiliated; Ahardane and Dr. Khatib of the Popular Movement were arrested. The disorder seemed to have been quietly overcome. The government made no further moves, but the arrest of the leaders of the Movement resulted in two of their lieutenants' starting small revolts with bands of armed tribesmen. Ben Miloudi led a group near Oulmes and Moha ou Hammou led another band in the Tahala region of the Beni Ouarain tribe.[44] The government's reaction to these two guerilla groups revealed a clear priority for restoring order.

Royal Army troops were dispatched promptly to surround and disarm the Miloudi forces. The Oulmes area is to the immediate east of Rabat and is occupied by a large tribal confederation. The government took decisive action against Miloudi and rapidly restored order in the nearer area. The uprising did not spread and the suppression of the Miloudi group terminated the disorder around Oulmes. In contrast, the government chose not to intervene so rap-

---

[44] The latter incident was not reported as serious until a week later and was repeatedly discredited in government statements, though Moha ou Haddou was still at large in the Beni Ouarain tribe at the end of the year. For the early comment see *Le Monde*, October 24, 1958, p. 2.

idly in the Tahala area or in a less threatening minor uprising near Rich in Tafilalet province.[45] Though positive relationships are hard to draw, it is interesting to note that in Tafilalet and Rabat provinces and in the area of the disputes in particular, the Istiqlal had a good basic organization, though perhaps lacking strong popular support. In the Tahala area, where the uprising continued into 1959 and the government postponed sending troops for three months, the party has only two small offices, on the edge of the almost impenetrable mountains of the Beni Ouarain.

During this first period there were also indications of trouble in the northern provinces of Alhucemas, Nador, and Taza. The government suspected that Spanish intervention was clandestinely taking place from her still-occupied outposts on the coast. Balafrej went so far as to complain officially about the release of arms to dissidents in the north, for which concrete evidence later appeared. Ahmed Lyazidi, the Minister of National Defense, was given full civil and military powers in the three provinces and conducted an investigation. The concentration of authority alone suggested that the local administration was weak. *Al-Alam* recognized that there were deeper problems of a "social and economic order" in the area. Further recognition of administrative difficulties and implied recognition of tribal interests was the appointment of an army officer of Rifian origin as governor of Taza.[46] Passive resistance was widespread. Villages were deserted, roads were blocked, and Istiqlal offices ransacked. Though no official statement was made, there was little doubt that the tension in the Rif region was much more serious than the skirmishes with Popular Movement bands.[47]

The King's part in restoring order in the north testifies further to his key importance in the political system. His first direct intervention was to broadcast an appeal for order in the local Berber

[45] The Rich uprising never became serious and appears to have been a small band loyal to Addi ou Bihi, the ex-governor of the province. The first public note of this dispute, thought to have started with about fifty men in October, was found in January. See *Le Monde*, January 8, 1959, p. 5.

[46] *Ibid.*, November 4, 1958, p. 3. Captain Medboh is one of a group of highly experienced governors coming from the Royal Army. He had been governor of Ouarzazate, Nador (at the time of the removal of Senhadji) and Rabat (on the removal of Ahardane).

[47] At this juncture in events, as throughout the stages of the uprisings of late 1958, the local press was replete with assurances that the disorder was terminated. At this time, *Al-Alam* noted that there was a "general improvement" and *Al-Ahd Al-Jadiid* claimed that the troubles had disappeared and were due only to "foreign propaganda" and subversive forces, although fighting continued for two more months.

dialect during Lyazidi's investigation. The widespread character of the discontent was revealed when the King received a large delegation of Rifian tribesmen. The Palace was undoubtedly worried lest more serious violence be touched off during the approaching anniversary of the throne celebrations. The tribesmen expressed their resentment over injustices committed by local administrators and their discontent because of the small number of their own tribesmen who had been made officials. The veterans of the Liberation Army in the delegation felt that they had not received sufficient recognition in the government and that more opportunity of direct contact with the King would result in great satisfaction among their colleagues. The King responded: "All the injustices that have been reported will be repaired. All legitimate rights will be satisfied. Return to your tribes in tranquility and without fear. Transmit to your brothers our paternal solicitude. Transmit to them equally our order: that each return to his village since we have given our instructions that no one should be troubled."[48] Even though the King's appeal was not completely successful in preventing further conflict in the Rif area, it is difficult to imagine any form of influence that might have been more effective.

The second phase of the uprisings was ushered in by the detonation of a bomb in the midst of a crowd at Khemisset during the Anniversary of the Throne celebrations. The new disorder in the regions near Rabat could have revived the fighting which had been so successfully ended in the Miloudi affair a month before. Although an isolated act of terrorism, the bombing killed one and wounded forty-eight persons. Two days after the bombing, the King received a delegation of local tribesmen, who expressed their "indefectible faithfulness" to the Throne and condemned the use of violence. The national holiday was marred with similar acts of terrorism and violence in Oujda and Taza provinces, while there were other reports of more serious trouble around Alhucemas and Nador. The uprising of the Beni Ouarain tribe in the Tahala area continued, though two false reports were made of Moha ou Haddou's having been arrested.

Although the isolated terrorist acts probably had some antecedent in party struggles, the northern provinces soon revealed much deeper sources of tension. A second official investigation was conducted by Abderrahmin Aneggai, which involved studying the

[48] *La Vigie*, November 12, 1958, p. 1.

grievances of the 900,000 persons in the provinces of Taza, Nador, and Alhucemas. The visit of the Royal Committee brought temporary calm to the region, and violence diminished for the second time while Aneggai was in the Rif. His report marks the end of serious violence, including isolated cases outside the troubled areas, until the uprisings of early January 1959. Popular attention may have been diverted by the crisis over the formation of the Ibrahim government and the growing split in the Istiqlal, both of which were becoming public at this time. The stimulus for the attacks that the arrest of the Popular Movement leaders, Ahardane and Dr. Khatib, may have provided was also relieved. Their trial had been postponed twice during the second period of trouble, and during the inquiry in the Rif they had been provisionally freed. Their release also suggests that the investigation may have found that the arrest of the tribal leaders had multiplied the government's problems.

The results of the Aneggai investigation[49] were conveyed to the King early in December. This marked the end of the second period of disorder and the beginning of a second interlude of relative calm. The difficulties in Taza province were said to have a "political aspect" and probably referred to the band of guerillas under Moha ou Haddou. The provinces of Alhucemas and Nador had more serious trouble arising from their integration with the south and the shortcomings of rural officials. The report is a very revealing official commentary on the problem of establishing a national political system where the range of social differentiation is extremely wide. The palace spokesman stated that, especially in Nador and Alhucemas, the populace felt that "the benefits of independence were not dispensed to them as largely as in the southern zone." Certain "exactions" were denounced by the tribesmen, who accused officials, from sheikh to governor, of malpractice.

The tribesmen and peasants were uniformly agreed on the failure of local administrators to gain the confidence of the people and to understand local problems. This lends some credence to reports that many administrators had been sent to the region who had no knowledge of the local Berber dialect or customs. The report stressed the need for "honest and just" administrators who understood the tribesmen and who came from the same region if at all possible.

---

[49] All quotations and information on the report are taken from *La Vigie*, December 9, 1958, p. 1, and December 10, 1958, p. 4. The latter was an official communiqué from the Palace on the inquiry.

Most revealing was the admission that the first three years of independence had left the tribesmen with the feeling that "they were not participating in the general direction of the country." Equally revealing was the recommended solution, though probably only intended as a stopgap to more effective action. "Ministers and undersecretaries of state or their immediate collaborators" were urged to visit the region frequently and make direct contact with the populace. Among the suggestions of the tribal delegations was the need for local officials to leave their offices and to seek solutions locally where possible. The investigation also concluded that local administrators should give up party affiliations and that political parties should cease "interfering in the administration or in judicial affairs."

With a knowledge of the serious grievances of the rural population and of Popular Movement activities to bring these grievances into focus, it is surprising that the government decided to proceed with the trial of Addi ou Bihi. The Istiqlal, however, had been demanding his trial for some time and might have thought it would be an effective object lesson to the tribesmen. The trade unions were also insistent and the new government of mid-December 1958, under Ibrahim, one of their closest associates, gave them new avenues of action. There were practically no indications of further clashes with the tribal groups in late December, though the bands operating under Popular Movement leaders were still intact in the mountains north and south of Taza. During the interlude before the third violent epoch there were a few isolated acts of violence in the cities, where pro-Algerian sentiment had been aroused over the fast of the arrested Algerian leaders in France. These events, however, were almost certainly part of the continuing problem of regulating Moroccan-Algerian relations. Perhaps more pertinent to the rural discontent was the apparent pardon of Ahardane and Dr. Khatib, who were permitted to go to Madrid in mid-December. As organizers of the Liberation Army in the Rif they were familiar with the Spanish officials concerned with the region and might assist in seeking a settlement to the alleged Spanish interference in the north. They returned toward the end of December, but subsequent events proved that any proposals to ameliorate Moroccan-Spanish differences had failed.

The trial revealed that Addi ou Bihi and Lyoussi had been the witting or unwitting agents in a French scheme to arouse tribesmen late in 1956. The third period of violence began as Lyoussi took refuge with his tribe in the Middle Atlas Mountains. Although there were indications of renewed trouble throughout eastern Morocco, the most serious region remained the Rif north of Taza and the Beni Ouarain strongholds to the south. The centers of resistance threatened to join and cut off the eastern part of the country from Rabat or to spread westward around Fès. The King made a last appeal to the tribes to cease passive resistance and to return to their villages. The easternmost area around Nador remained calm, but resistance continued where strong tribal leaders were active. The ex-*caid* and ex-Liberation Army officer, Si Akchouch, continued to lead the Gzennaia tribe; Ahmed Mezziane was announced to be leading the Beni Ouraighel; and Moha ou Haddou remained in the mountainous refuge of the Beni Ouarain tribe.[50] This made the environs of Alhucemas the focal spot of the uprising, where Senhadji continued to be the main agitator.

Early in January 1959 the rebels began operations to seize the port of Alhucemas, which was virtually surrounded by the dissident tribes and undefended by Moroccan troops. The Prince led an expedition of 20,000 Royal Army troops to subdue the insurgents, although the King's appeal appeared to have separated the general tribal discontent from the party-inspired maneuvers. During the campaign evidence was obtained that the Spanish authorities had conspired with the rebel leaders and provided arms for some of their men.[51] With the threat of larger-scale foreign intervention stopped and the port of Alhucemas secured, the Royal Army turned to restoring order in the Middle Atlas. In late January operations were begun to establish army posts throughout the troubled regions and to capture the still active leaders, Moha ou Haddou and Akchouch.

The experience of the new nation with administration of the countryside provides further examples of the problems of independence and of the ways in which solutions are sought. It would be easy to compare the 1958 revolts with the differentiations used by the Protectorate. The rural-urban and Arab-Berber distinction functioned very differently under French and Spanish rule. The formation of the new nation provided a new point of reference of both analytic and concrete significance. Obviously the differing ways of life did not change magically, but these differences were now to be

---

[50] See *Le Monde*, January 8, 1959, p. 4.
[51] See the charge of the Prince, *New York Times*, January 10, 1959, p. 9.

harmonized within a totally new framework. The troubles of the first three years of independence do not justify earlier policy or confirm its assumptions, which were after all designed within the French or Spanish political system and were designed primarily to suit the needs of France or Spain. There is probably no more insidious risk to an understanding of a new country than allowing the colonial framework to transpose into analysis after independence.

The colonial powers did leave institutions for regional administration, which have been used in roughly the same form in the new country. The renovation of the system was impossible in the first hectic year of independence and was not actively undertaken until 1958. With the important exception of separating the judicial system from the regional administration, the rules and procedures remained much the same. There is much evidence that personnel limitations reduced initiative and effectiveness at lower echelons. The implications for the emerging political system are important, for it is quite possible that the central authority of the new nation may have appeared arbitrary and less efficient than the old colonial regime. To the extent that the development of an advanced political system requires the ability to use institutional forms of influence, the new country may have even lost ground. Not only were the officials of specific, concrete institutions less effective, but the people's confidence in the efficacy of such institutions may have deteriorated.

The development of the rural administrative system also provides evidence of the way in which coercion and violence operated under the new political system. It is difficult to estimate to what extent the use of coercion was necessitated by material aid given by foreign powers or by tension generated as societal groupings found change difficult. Where traditional relationships did come into conflict with the needs of the new nation, the King was almost always able to effect a solution without the use of coercion. In the cases where the Royal Army has been used—in the Tafilalet revolt and in the uprisings in the northern provinces—there was substantial evidence that aid had been given by the ex-colonial powers. The presence of foreign arms in these regions does not preclude, nevertheless, that coercion might not be in use in other parts of the country. Comparison is impossible because the new country has been understandably reluctant to provide detailed information on points of tension and details of administration where tensions have not been nationally known.

CHAPTER VIII

INDEPENDENCE AND THE ISTIQLAL

Transition and Conflict of Leadership

LIKE the new nation, the Istiqlal party has undergone a major reorganization and reorientation since independence. That these changes have produced tensions and differences of opinion is not surprising, though the party tried to sustain the appearance of a solid front until late 1958. When one considers the size and prestige of the major nationalist party, it was equally to be expected that the problems of its political reconstruction would be similar to those encountered by the nation as a whole. The constantly repeated claim of the Istiqlal that it was the sole true representative of those who struggled for independence was in many ways quite true, but it also proved to be equally true that the same leaders had differing conceptions of how national affairs should be conducted. Like the relationship between Rabat and the country, the relation between the central headquarters of the party and its members displayed difficulty in defining and giving priority to goals. They both lacked trained personnel and had occasional personality clashes. Like the nation itself, the Istiqlal party benefited greatly from the mass enthusiasm immediately following independence, but later found that these high expectations could also be a source of dissension and the basis of a differentiation of groups within the party. The Istiqlal had problems in developing harmonious, stable relationships with the trade unions and the resistance movement. The party also displays sensitivity to criticism, reluctance to admit conflict within its ranks, and hesitance to release precise information on internal affairs.

The party has gone through three major organizational phases, which correspond roughly to the more easily distinguished stages of the country's development since independence. The first dates from the return of the King in November 1955 to the National Council meeting of the Istiqlal in August 1956. During this period the party enjoyed the momentum derived from the liberation itself, but also began to define its new organizational needs as a party in a new political system where it by no means monopolized influence. Between late 1956 and early 1958, the present organization of the

Istiqlal was constructed while differences both within the party and among other groups in the nation began to be expressed more sharply. During this second period the party made its major effort to train cadre and to extend its rural organization. On the central level continued attempts were made to integrate within the party framework what party leaders called the "centrifugal forces" within the party. The third stage of the Istiqlal's development was roughly from the formation of the Balafrej government in May 1958 to the split of the party early in 1959. During this period the party was immobilized and unable to make decisions regarding its own re- form or national affairs. Differences of opinion on national problems became so great that many party leaders left the Executive Com- mittee or appealed to the public in opposition to more conservative party leaders. In some respects the Istiqlal became the victim of the political system that it had done so much to make possible.

Even before independence there were respectable nationalists who differed with the party. Since then group interests have been even more distinguishable. The Istiqlal itself does not claim to represent them all, but it has tried to have all important groups closely asso- ciated with the party and to present a common program with them. The Moroccan habit of referring to the Istiqlal as simply *"al-hizb,"* or "the party," indicates the familiarity of the Istiqlal in the minds of all Moroccans. Perhaps the best definition of the role of the Istiqlal with independence comes from *Al-Alam*: "The party is a means of political, social and cultural education. It is a true school where the human being learns to serve his country and his fellow patriots. . . . A party can be democratic only if it disposes a well- defined program of action that is beneficial to the community. . . . For a party to be irreproachable, it should not accept in its ranks the adversaries of its antagonist, since the symbol of a political group is not like diplomatic negotiation where one exploits another to arrive at his ends."[1] Emphasis on the educational role of the party is important and is manifested in the party's illiteracy and feminist groups. It suggests the less consciously pursued role of the party in introducing many members of the nation to participation in poli- tics on a national scale. The latter part of the *Al-Alam* statement suggests the continued emphasis of the Istiqlal on complete loyalty of its members. It is perhaps in this way that the Istiqlal departs most markedly from the general conception of a political party, for it attempts to attribute to itself a purpose and a solidarity that is ir-

[1] December 29, 1955, Fr. Trans.

reproachable by anyone outside the party. There is a reluctance to admit that the party is just another element of the political system. The party, however, does not argue this case so much in terms of its actual function, which may be unclear even to itself in its full magnitude, but tries rather to transfer this preeminence to its doctrine. As the party has discovered, to be above dispute and at the same time to participate in the responsibilities of government is not easy.

The basic organizational unit is the cell, above which are ranged subsections and sections. The sections and their subordinate groups are divided among seventeen regions, which are each supervised by an inspector and a regional committee. The central organization of the party consists of the Executive Committee, the Political Committee, and the various types of service commissions that function in Rabat. The supreme authority of the Istiqlal is the party's Congress, but this Congress is, in fact, relatively unimportant in party affairs. In the period of this study the only Istiqlal Congress was held in December 1955. In late 1955 the party found itself in a difficult position. Its leaders were heavily involved with problems of the new government, its following was poorly organized and, like the nation itself, it lacked a clear-cut program. Istiqlal leaders will now admit that the Congress of 1955 was improvised. The bulk of its work was very likely done in the special committees of old party militants. There is no evidence of dispute of the motions of the Congress, which followed closely the introductory speeches of Balafrej and Bouabid. Since Morocco was still in the throes of celebrating the King's return and many of the party militants were still in prison, there is no doubt but that the delegates were hastily assembled.

In view of subsequent party policy the three motions on "general party policy" are of particular interest. The party placed the irredentist goal very high, but did not call for unification. Secondly, it "reaffirmed its faith to the principle of constitutional monarchy and its determination to see a democratic regime guaranteeing the rights of the citizen and individual liberties installed in Morocco." Lastly, it approved the Speech from the Throne, but recorded doubts concerning the French declaration of October 1955, which had stressed "interdependence."[2] The general motions reveal the continued stress on independence as conceived during the Protectorate, i.e., the King, the territory, political and civil rights, and fully affirmed liberation from any colonial claim. The subsidiary motions of the Congress are extremely general and simply review the obvious

[2] See *Al-Istiqlal*, August 17, 1956, p. 5.

tasks of the new nation. Perhaps significant by way of omission was the low priority given to economic problems that the country was almost certainly to encounter or to controversial international issues, such as Algeria. These goals and territorial unification predominated in party policy statements three years later, but the emphasis on individual rights was dropped.

The 1955 Congress took place under strained circumstances. The differences of opinion among the members of the Executive Committee had already been exposed during the negotiations for the return of Mohammed V. Allal Al-Fassi had retired to near-by Tetouan during the Congress and soon afterward departed for Cairo, where he remained until March 1956. The Leader of the party had been incensed over the results of the Aix-les-Bains Conference and returned to a self-imposed exile until the Franco-Moroccan Agreement was signed.[3] This exposure of weakness during the formation of the first Council of Government very possibly prevented the party from claiming more seats. Though limited by the disorder in the countryside, the reorganization of the party was led by Balafrej, the Secretary General, Ben Barka, and a handful of party militants.

With the return of Al-Fassi the Istiqlal took a more aggressive position. He entered Morocco after a series of meetings of the Executive Committee in Madrid and Tetouan, in which the problems of the Army of Liberation, the merger of Islah and the Istiqlal, and the relationship of the party to the King and government were reportedly discussed.[4] The Leader acknowledged that the party had participated in the first Council of Government at a "sacrifice," but that it was prepared to govern alone if asked. Similar opinions were expressed by the Istiqlal youth, whose conference in Fès voted in favor of the formation of a "homogeneous government." This was a crucial period for the Istiqlal, for not only did it encounter the problem of resolving its relationship with the Army of Liberation, but also it experienced a second occasion of publicly reported conflict among its leaders. Torres, the leader of the Islah, allegedly differed strongly from the views of the Istiqlal on the way in which the Rif combatants should be calmed and on the future of Spanish-Moroccan relations, particularly regarding the disposition of the northern Khalifate.[5]

[3] L'Action, April 2, 1956, p. 8.
[4] See the account in ibid., April 2, 1956, p. 8.
[5] See C.M., March 20, 1956, p. 5, and Annex IX. Later reports also appeared in L'Action, April 9, 1956, p. 8.

Dissatisfaction with the first government appears to have accumulated over the summer of 1956 as the need for an organizational overhaul became increasingly apparent. With independence the party no longer had an unchallenged claim to nationalist fervor, for both the resistance and the trade unions could maintain with considerable justification that they had made sacrifices as great or perhaps even greater than the party over the preceding three years. While the Executive Committee continued to represent the views of the party, there was no way in which it could also claim to represent the separate organizations of the new nationalist groups. Though the Executive Committee was technically elected by the party Congress, it obviously continued as a body of more or less coopted elders, as demonstrated in Table 7. The leaders of the party recognized the

TABLE 7

Continuity of Istiqlal Leadership from 1929 to 1958[a]

	1929	1934	1937	1944	1945	1956	1958
Allal Al-Fassi	x	x	x	exile	exile	x	x
Ahmed Balafrej	x (in France)		x	x	x	x	x
Mohammed Ouazzani	x	x	x	exile	PDI	PDI	PDI
Omar Abdeljalil	x	x	x	x	x	x	x
Mohammed Ghazi	x	x	x	x	x	x	x
Mohammed Lyazidi	x	x	x	x	x	x	x
Boubker Qadiri	—	x	x	—	—	x	x
Mohammed Al-Fassi	— (in France)		b	b	b	x	x
Abdelkrim Benjoulloun	—	—	—	x	x	x	x
Mehdi Ben Barka	—	—	—	c	c	x	x
Abderrahmin Bouabid	—	—	—	c	c	x	x

1929: Committee of National Action
1934: Among signatories of *Plan of Reforms*
1937: Executive Committee
1944: Among signatories of *Manifesto of Independence*
1945: Executive Committee
1956: Executive Committee
1958: Executive Committee

[a] Sources include: Interview with Lyazidi, July 31, 1958; Mehdi Bennouna, *Our Morocco: The True Story of a Just Cause*, p. 145; Comité d'Action Marocaine, *Plan de Reformes Marocaines*, p. 11; Rezette, *Les Partis Politiques Marocaines*, p. 287; *Manifesto of Independence, Istiqlal Party Documents*, pp. 3-5.

[b] Member of high-level Istiqlal group of Protectorate civil servants, which was kept clandestine from other membership.

[c] In influential positions in party. Ben Barka was secretary to Balafrej for the Executive Committee. Bouabid was party organizer in key center, Salé.

danger of the dispersal of party influence among the three groups and formed the Political Committee to give the unions and resistance a voice in party policy. Gradually the functions of the Executive Committee and the Political Committee were reversed. The former became simply the spokesman of the party in the latter committee, which represented three distinct organizations. The Political Committee was enlarged to about forty members by 1957, including the Istiqlal member of the Crown Council, representatives of the parallel organizations of the party, i.e., youth, feminists, et cetera, and all ministers of the government from the Istiqlal regardless of whether or not they belonged to the Executive Committee. By 1958 each of the three groups passed down to its members the decisions of the Political Committee through their own executory agent similar to the Istiqlal's Executive Committee.

The change in nationalist leadership and the need to endorse a program suitable to all three groups led to the National Council meeting of August 1956. The purpose of the Extraordinary Congress of 1955 is difficult to discern, except perhaps as a rallying session for the available militants and some reinforcement for the leaders' views during negotiations with the French. The purpose of the 1956 meeting is clear. The party needed to set a precedent for the newly innovated Political Committee, to explain the new party organization with inspectors and subsections, and to prepare to claim a majority of the ministries. The committee to draft the new unified program included the young leaders, Ibrahim and Ben Seddik, who later became the Istiqlal's severest critics. Undoubtedly their proposals were subsequently submitted to the executive organ of each organization before the National Council was held, but the way was prepared for more effective merger and close policy coordination among the three nationalist organizations.

By the time of the National Council meeting, the central organization of the Istiqlal had been organized under Balafrej, who had been Secretary General since 1944. Mohammed Lyazidi occupied the post of Assistant Secretary General and Boubker Qadiri was made Inspector General. An eleventh member was added to the Executive Committee to represent the Islah, Abdelkhalek Torres, though he was frequently absent due to the ambassadorial positions he held, first in Madrid and later in Cairo. Central support to the party organizers was provided by four commissions: Administrative,

Press and Information, Discipline, and Orientation and Program.[6] The first commission supervised the training of cadre, assisted in making arrangements for party meetings, and provided central liaison for the regional inspectors. The second supervised the external propaganda of the party. The third acted as a court of last resort when cases of expulsion or disciplining were forwarded by the inspectors or regional committees. The last handled the publication of internal party propaganda, including the *Internal Bulletin* of the party.

The National Councils of the resistance and of the U.M.T. participated as distinct organizations in the meetings of August 1956, and their motions were separately published.[7] Al-Fassi paid tribute to the three distinct groups in the battle for independence, which, he claimed, "have never ceased to have a complete unity in orientation." He added, "The natural lines which unite these three forces are such that nothing in the world could break them."[8] The General Motion of the National Council was not much more precise than that of the Extraordinary Congress, though new emphasis was placed on the need for a purge, administrative reorganization, and solution of economic problems. Political suggestions were much less in evidence, though Al-Fassi spent some time outlining the party's suggestions on rural communes. The major point of the meeting was the demand for a "homogeneous government," though the Council of Government was not changed until the crisis of October 1956 and even then contained several opposition-party members. It was probably the Algerian crisis that prohibited convening the Congress which the Council voted to hold the last week of December 1956.

In practice it appears that the party Congress has served to rally party membership on occasions when popular manifestations can be expected to improve the party's position. The Congress envisaged for late 1956 was very likely planned to reinforce the Istiqlal leaders' objections to the first government, but was not held after the change of government had already been forced in October 1956. Though the Congress is supposed to be held every two years at least, there was no further public discussion during 1957. It was not until early 1958, when there were new proposals on internal organization, that a Congress was announced for the fall of the year. At the same time studies

[6] Interview with Mehdi Ben Barka, President, National Consultative Assembly, Rabat, November 8, 1957.

[7] See *Al-Istiqlal*, August 24, 1956, pp. 4-5.

[8] *Ibid.*, pp. 7ff.

were under way in party headquarters for the reorganization of the central committees, which had become unwieldy over the past year and whose functions were becoming vague as the Political Committee grew in importance.[9] The increased activity of opposition parties over the preceding year also made a Congress appropriate as a show of strength and solidarity. Then too, the internal divisions of the party leadership that had been exposed publicly over the formation of the Balafrej government could be smoothed over in a Congress. If the Congress of September 1958 had taken place as planned, it seems clear that it would have served, like previous national rallies, to endorse changes that had already begun and to accept a program whose content was already decided on.

The changes in the central direction of the Istiqlal that were under consideration were to improve the integration of the unions and the resistance at the head of the party, possibly to pave the way for a merger of the three organizations. A group comparable to the Political Committee was to have become the supreme executive organ of the party, unions, and resistance, though each organization was to remain distinct for the time being. The new group was to elect the party's Executive Committee and thus give the unions and the resistance a direct voice in the party's internal affairs. The regional inspectors were to report directly to the integrated Political Committee, and the Inspector General presumably was to be abandoned. The plan would have done much to destroy the collegiate leadership of party elders and it is important in understanding the central problems of the party, which erupted during the formation of the Balafrej government. Not only has the Istiqlal been obligated to reconstruct its own organization, but it has also had to maintain good rapport with two organizations outside its ranks if it wished to retain its position as the most influential party. The party risked losing its predominant position among those who fought for independence if either the unions or the resistance established a party. Because of considerable overlapping of membership the Istiqlal would very likely have lost many of its most active urban members. Given the policy of the unions, the Istiqlal would also have lost its position as the vanguard of nationalism.

A second conflict also occurred between the Islah and the Istiqlal leaders in late 1957. The problem centered on the composition of

[9] These plans were announced by Ben Barka in his report to the inspectors' meeting following the Tangier meeting of the Executive Committee. *Ibid.*, March 1, 1958, p. 4, and March 8, 1958, p. 3.

the regional Istiqlal committee in Tetouan and led to reports that Torres was considering reconstituting a separate party for the north.[10] How the reconciliation was effected has never been explained, but soon afterward the incident was smoothed over to the satisfaction of Torres and the Istiqlal. The disputes in mid-1958 were more serious, for they threatened the kind of break in the entire Istiqlal organization that the Political Committee had been designed to prevent. Due to conflicting views over economic and foreign policy the leaders of the party most closely in touch with the U.M.T.—Bouabid, Ben Barka, and Ibrahim—differed strongly with the program under which the Balafrej government agreed to take office. The trade union and resistance representatives on the Political Committee felt strongly enough to boycott its meetings and virtually broke away from the Istiqlal, though they hesitated at first to start a new opposition party.

As Istiqlal leaders admitted, this rendered the Political Committee a useless organ. It also set off a series of actions in open defiance of the party leadership, now once again concentrated in the Executive Committee. Though a committee had been provisionally constituted for the organization of a 1958 Congress, it was dissolved.[11] The relatively passive role of the Congress is suggested by the ease of postponement as the internecine struggle became bitter.[12] The internal crisis was further revealed in the publication of a speech of Ibrahim criticizing the "intellectual *bourgeoisie*" in *Al-Istiqlal*, which was followed with the summary disappearance of the paper. Boucetta and Douiri, representing the more conservative faction of the party, made an attempt to continue the journal, but their nocturnal seizure of the paper's offices was stopped.[13] When the paper reappeared, Mohammed Lyazidi was editor in place of Ben Barka. With the revival of the paper there was no further publicity on the crisis, though neither did any evidence of a solution appear.

[10] Most of the reports appeared in the Democratic party and Tunisian papers. See *L'Action*, June 24, 1957, p. 7, and July 22, 1957, p. 6.

[11] The members of the committee were: Benjelloun, Qadiri, Bouabid, Ben Barka, from the party, and Ibrahim, Ben Seddiq, and Basri of the unions and resistance. Interview with Mohammed Lyazidi, Executive Committee, Istiqlal party, Rabat, July 31, 1958.

[12] The postponement was announced in *La Vigie*, August 28, 1958, p. 2. See also *Le Monde*, July 10, 1958, p. 3.

[13] *Ibid.*, July 1, 1958, p. 16. An excellent analysis of the crisis by Lacouture will be found in *ibid.*, July 2, 1958, p. 3.

The seizure of the newspaper was possibly the most important turning point in the struggle over party leadership. The agreement, apparently reached in July, to bury antagonisms until a party Congress could be held, was broken. Ben Barka's use of the party newspaper for an attack on the conservative leaders forced his resignation as editor and nearly resulted in his expulsion from the party.[14] Bouabid reportedly intervened to save Ben Barka's membership, but the balance that had enabled the Congress planning to get under way was lost. The full intrigue in the inner circles of the party will never be known, but a second reconciliation was attempted in September 1958. The party leaders were shocked to see factions of the Liberation Army fighting one another at Bou Arfa and, as was discovered in the conference of party secretaries in early October, there was a momentary consensus over the failure of the Balafrej government to receive the ministerial authority promised by the King. Late in September the Istiqlal released a communiqué stating that a Preparatory Commission had been formed to plan a party Congress for the anniversary of the Independence Manifesto of 1944, January 11th.

The reconciliation of the diverging interests of the leading nationalist groups may have been facilitated by Bouabid, who was certainly the only spokesman of the progressive group in the government. He seemed to play a moderating role and had already persuaded Balafrej to remain in office in late August. In any event the Executive Committee agreed to meet with its bitter critics, Ibrahim, Ben Seddiq, and Al-Basri, late in September to select the Commission. The composition of this crucial meeting is an indication of the significance of the Political Committee, which had not functioned, of course, since the walkout of the above three men when the Balafrej government was formed. The Preparatory Commission included Mohammed Abdelrazak, Mohammed Mansour, Mohammed Bennani, and Kacem Zhiri.[15] They were, respectively, a leader of the trade unions, a resistance leader, a party official of conservative leanings, and the Director of Radio Maroc, who was thought to be progressive but remained with the conservative element after the party split. The composition of the Preparatory Commission was clearly a concession to the dissenting elements of the party, though presumably its conclusions were to be submitted to the Executive Committee and the three opposition leaders.

[14] *Ibid.*, January 27, 1959, p. 7.
[15] *Al-Istiqlal*, October 18, 1958, p. 3.

The Preparatory Commission was given three fairly well-defined tasks: to prepare a new set of internal party statutes; to agree on the agenda of the Congress; and to make the material preparations for the Congress. The first task apparently included deciding how delegates for the Congress were to be selected, although the announcement also specified that they would be selected by election in a way to be "determined later." Since the Congress would provide an irrevocable endorsement for the motions to be presented and might play an important part in selecting some officers, this selection process was clearly the most crucial question of the preparation. The qualifications for voting in the selection of delegates, the supervisory procedure for such elections, and the system of representation might well determine which faction of the party would successfully emerge from the Congress. There seemed to have been agreement that not every member could vote, but that some standard of party militant should be used. The number of qualified voters would determine how many delegates participated from regions of different loyalties and, most important, might affect urban representation, which was favorable to the trade unions and progressives in many instances.

If the existing organizational structure of the party were used to hold the vote or if the inspectors were given supervisory powers, it was likely that more conservative preferences would be reflected. It was also quite possible that many trade union members did not join in the activities of party organization, but participated through their union alone. The system anticipated by the activist faction was that all qualifying as members through party, trade union, or resistance participation would be allowed to vote. Delegates were to be chosen by neighborhood meetings outside the regular organizational structure of the party on the basis of one for every thousand members. The conservative group may well have expected that a strictly popular selection process, especially where members of aligned nationalist groups were allowed to participate freely, would jeopardize their rural strength and might be abused in the cities. The new nationalist organizations, the U.M.T. and the resistance, were under the influence of the radical leaders. Although Al-Fassi may have had some influence among parts of the Liberation Army in the Sahara to the south, the urban resistance and Liberation Army units nearer the Algerian border were probably loyal to Al-Basri.[16]

[16] This does not necessarily contradict the opinion expressed above that the Liberation Army was under Istiqlal control. When the party leaders could agree

The selection system outlined above was unanimously accepted by the Preparatory Commission, according to the progressive members, but did not receive the assent of the Executive Committee and the three factional leaders. The seriousness of the differences among party leaders is indicated by this failure to agree even while acts of violence were being directed at the party. In early November the printing plant of *Al-Alam* was unsuccessfully bombed and a party organizer at Oujda was assassinated, possibly by Popular Movement militants. Shortly after these attacks, an Istiqlal office in the Old Medina quarter of Casablanca was bombed without damage. This could have been done either by urban resistance elements loyal to the Popular Movement or by followers of Al-Basri hoping to express resistance dissatisfaction with the Balafrej government. Internal conflicts and disapproval of the Balafrej government had reached such proportions by this time, however, that even external attacks on the Istiqlal could not revive its old solidarity. On the contrary, toward the end of November there is evidence of stepped-up agitation by the progressive group. Bouabid submitted his resignation, and this produced the downfall of the Balafrej Council; Ben Barka abandoned the Executive Committee.[17] Though it was not known until the complete split of the party, the entire central organization of the party was in the hands of those loyal to Al-Fassi and Balafrej from the end of November 1958.

The circumstances surrounding the failure to hold the Congress of January 1959 reveal much of the difficulty that had delayed holding a Congress and also shed some light on the more general problem of instituting representative government. The Preparatory Commission made no statements until the day when the Congress was supposed to have been held. The problem of intrigue in the political systems of new countries is demonstrated in the total absence of any signs, not to mention official statements, of the difficulties encountered by the Commission until its failure had become undeniably obvious. On the day before the Congress was to be held, the resist-

---

on the mission of the army, which they appear to have done successfully up to August 1958, there was no conflict of loyalty. The Bou Arfa clash took place three months after the open disagreement of Istiqlal leaders and probably resulted from their anticipation of a test of their strength, such as this selection would have been.

[17] See his statement in *La Vigie*, January 27, 1959, p. 2, after Al-Fassi announced the expulsion. Ben Barka stated he had not participated in the Executive Committee for three months. The last recorded participation was his speech to the inspectors' meeting of November 20. *Al-Istiqlal*, November 29, 1958, p. 5.

ance and union delegates on the Commission revealed to the press their account of why no plans had been made. The opposing members replied in a statement that included some correspondence with the party's Executive Committee on the problem.[18] The Commission appears to have been at an impasse since early December, when the trade unions had published an extremely critical piece on Balafrej and when the various groups within the party began campaigning for support during a preparatory census of party membership.

Many of the charges and countercharges cannot be substantiated, but between them a fairly clear picture of the obstacles to the success of the Committee can be formed. The members favoring the progressive opinions of the party revealed, first, that work was stopped over the question of how delegates were to be selected for the Congress. They noted that agreement had tentatively been made that one Congress delegate would be elected for every thousand members, but added that the Commission members of the conservative orientation also wanted to permit "about a hundred" delegates to participate as party "notables," without being elected. These men would undoubtedly be mostly old Istiqlal militants, who would be loyal to Al-Fassi and Balafrej and who might not be elected because of their retirement from everyday activities of the party. The second charge of the progressives of the Commission, which cannot be positively verified, is that the other members of the Commission refused to meet after the fall of the Balafrej government in late November. A letter from the conservative faction implies this, but does not admit that they refused to participate. They stress the trade unions' attack on Balafrej and allege that it was part of a planned campaign, in cooperation with the resistance, to discredit the Istiqlal Old Guard.[19] There may have been an abortive attempt to capture the Istiqlal organization while the conservative leaders were occupied with the formation of a new government. The critics of Balafrej may have hoped to force his resignation—which actually happened two days after the attack in *At-Taliâ*—and to acquire prestige of office in the internal party struggle.

According to the two members of the Commission representing the Istiqlal viewpoint, the union and the resistance delegates repeat-

[18] All these statements appeared in *Al-Istiqlal*, January 17, 1959, pp. 4-5.

[19] The planned nature of this attack is also indirectly supported by their letter. The distribution of leaflets and meetings with activist supporters began on November 30, 1958, followed up with the attack of the Balafrej government in a full issue of *At-Taliâ* on December 2, 1958.

edly refused to arrange a meeting to reaffirm the Commission's mission after the attacks on Balafrej. It is not clear why the representatives of the critical faction had agreed to sign the request for clarification when it was probably known to them, or would have been easy for them to ascertain, that Ben Seddiq and Al-Basri would not reply. There are two possible explanations of importance. One is that the leaders of the critical group decided that they could not win a contest where Congress delegates were freely elected and purposefully produced the impasse. The second is that their wish to discredit the Balafrej government, with which all the leaders of the activist element had been associated since spring, overrode their desire for a Congress. The calculation may thus have been that the Congress could be delayed while the attack on Balafrej was made and held later with the added support they would have with one of their own leaders in office as President of the Council. In either case, the opposition group may have been agreed among themselves to provoke a split of the Istiqlal if their aims were not accepted.

Conjecture on the failure to proceed with the Congress is not so important as the demonstration of the difficulty of making decisions in a new country. The Istiqlal and its associated groups probably include the most advanced segment of the population, which has more skilled, devoted leaders than any other similar segment. Even so, the delicate synthesis of nationalist forces around the Political Committee failed. A last-minute attempt was made to bring the factions together in a committee of Al-Fassi, Ben Barka, and Bouabid when the Ibrahim government was formed.[20] Its purpose was to reconstitute the planning committee for a party Congress and to agree on the way in which the criticisms of the activist group in the party press could be ended. According to the progressive group, Al-Fassi refused to consider a reorganization of the Executive Committee, which would probably have given the dissenting leaders a voice in party direction. To achieve such a synthesis would almost have made the party equivalent to the national political system for the most active political participants.

Reconstruction of the Party Cadre

Until early 1959 the tribulations of the Istiqlal's leaders generally took place in isolation from the mass of the members. No doubt rumors of these differences filtered down, especially in urban sec-

[20] *L'Avantegarde*, February 16, 1959, p. 8.

tions of the party, but communication on the whole has been carefully controlled and there was no way in which a member could express himself on these differences. The party was understandably anxious to preserve its own solidarity and a common front with the other nationalist organizations. The main working link between the base of the movement and the central offices in these efforts has been the inspectors. Their areas of authority are divided by centers of population and ease of communication and do not conform to either the old or new provincial boundaries. Their arrangement reflects the historic areas of popularity and organization. Of the seventeen inspectorates, eleven correspond roughly to the first provincial lines, though exceptions are made to place more accessible circles under nearer inspectors in bordering provinces: Agadir; Midelt; Ouarzazate; Oujda, with an assistant for Nador and Alhucemas; Safi; Al-Jadiida (Mazagan); Tetouan, including Chaouen; Tangier, including Larache; Fès, with an assistant in Taza; Meknes; and Beni Mellal. The other six inspectors are located in the major cities, where their area is divided as follows: in Casablanca one for the city and one for the agricultural plain of Chaouia; in Rabat one for the city, Kenitra, Salé, and the tribal regions south of Rabat and another for the plain of the Gharb; in Marrakech one for the city and the north of the province and another for the south.

The inspectors convene once a month at party headquarters in Rabat for two and occasionally three days. Their meetings are chaired by the Inspector General, who conducts the session on internal party problems. They also hear a political report which usually is given by Al-Fassi or Ben Barka. From time to time other Istiqlal ministers participate and give reports on the activity of their ministry, especially Balafrej, Abdeljalil, and Ibrahim until his departure from the government. These reports are not passively reviewed, but are open to questioning and debate. The inspectors are expected to meet with the sections roughly once a month and explain the subject of the central meetings, which often concentrate on current problems or accomplishments of the government. At the same time the inspectors are perhaps in closer touch with the base of the party than most of the Executive Committee and can pose the doubts and needs of their area. The inspectors also usually supervise elections in the sections and subsections, where the list of nominations is, as a rule, first submitted for their approval. In cases of discipline or expulsion the report is submitted to the inspector before final action is taken.

The inspectors' most important function is organizing new sections and subsections, reviewing the admission of new members, and supervising the submission of reports by the subordinate levels of the organization.

Thirteen inspectors were under arrest or in prison during the struggle from 1952-1955,[21] so that it is quite possible that the party, at least on this level, was not in close touch with the resistance. Many inspectors had been arrested three or four times, several of them during the Fès riots of the 1930's. The inspectors represent a surprisingly orthodox Muslim group, if one can judge from their education. None attended schools in France or even French-operated schools in Morocco. Only three speak sufficient French to enable them to have communication in that language, though they may understand French. Six of the inspectors attended the Muslim university of Qarawiyn at Fès and one the similar university of Moulay Youssef at Marrakech. Of the remaining nine, four were educated in village Koranic schools, four in the Arabic-speaking free schools sponsored by the party, and one in both types of school. With the exception of the inspector at Fès, all those who attended a Muslim university did so before World War II and were active as students in the prewar struggle of the party. It is probably not coincidence that the university-educated inspectors, having the longest history in the party and also most rapport with the old militants, occupy the historic strongholds of the party: Fès, Gharb, Al-Jadiida, Rabat and environs, Marrakech city and north, Oujda, and Agadir.[22] These inspectors plus those in Tetouan and Meknes, both historic centers of party activity, have membership in the nationalist movement from before World War II. Though a young militant, active in the early resistance, was inspector at Casablanca and a young Qarawiyn graduate at Fès, all the other inspectors whose party membership dates since the war were found in regions where the party has been freely active only since 1955.

In addition to the activities of the inspectors, a major contact with the base is the frequent trips of members of the Executive Committee to the countryside. These trips are perhaps the only, and by no means a highly reliable, indication of which leaders cultivated most

[21] All biographical data has been compiled from interviews with sixteen of the party inspectors. The inspector at Tangier was the only one not interviewed.

[22] While the latter area may not have been uniformly well-organized before 1955, the party has historic lines to the strongly Muslim Sous valley of Agadir.

influence in the base of the party.[23] The frequency, timing, and areas of these trips give some indications of organizational weaknesses. The trips also demonstrate the continued importance of the well-known, martyred leading figures. While the leaders may be quite capable of running a large organization with a minimum of personal contact, the Istiqlal base still places a high value on the rallies and speeches of the heroes of the party, very likely a higher value than they place on the routine, less colorful contacts with the inspectors. It is not surprising that the most frequent visitors, Al-Fassi, Ben Barka, Qadiri, and Lyazidi were all persons free from the responsibilities of government. The Istiqlal ministers, in fact, made no tours in 1957 aside from brief appearances at party meetings or national celebrations near Rabat or in one of the other accessible cities.

By far the most active rural campaigner in 1957[24] was Al-Fassi. His travels were concentrated in areas of party strength, though undoubtedly people came from many miles to hear him. In the early part of the year he visited areas of Democratic party strength most seriously affected by the poor agricultural year. His fall excursions were definitely into the regions where the Popular Movement was reported to have a following. His speeches are in no way organizational discourses, but long (often two hours), addresses on the history of the Istiqlal, its solidarity with other nationalist groups, and, above all, the Sahara. Their content is important, in that, next to the speeches and visits of the King, this is probably the most direct, forceful account the people of the countryside receive concerning the activities, goals, and problems of Morocco. The other tours of party officials take on much less dramatic proportions and are usually described as "conferences." They appear to have a more organizational intent, especially in the case of Ben Barka, who made relatively frequent, but brief, trips for regional conferences of party secretaries.

[23] There is considerable speculation in the more rarefied atmosphere of Rabat about who "controls" the Istiqlal organization. In fact, there is probably no one who controls it, but several who have closer contact than others. This speculation attributes both a selfishness to Istiqlal leaders and a sophistication to its members that is exaggerated. It also lightly dismisses the long experience of the common struggle for independence and tends to assume that differences among nationalists in Rabat are similar to quarrels among Western politicians.

[24] A survey has been made from party documents of all rural visits during 1957, from which this paragraph is written.

Like the country, the party has been handicapped by the lack of cadre. Efforts to ameliorate the situation have been directed by the central headquarters of the Istiqlal. To the extent that this training has been successful, which is most difficult to measure, the new personnel have provided more central control. At the time of independence the Istiqlal found that many of its former section leaders and regional officials who possessed a basic education were needed in the new government and provincial administrations.[25] The Istiqlal was, no doubt, eager that its members occupy government posts. It was probably also faced with a problem similar to that of the resistance, where those who had made continuing, great sacrifices looked upon independence as the end of their struggle. The subsequent personnel training program went through two phases.[26] The initial phase was immediately after independence, when the party first realized that it was seriously handicapped by the lack of skilled militants. At that time both Balafrej and Ben Barka were devoting all their time to the Istiqlal and planned the first cadre schools in the spring of 1956. Only a few secretaries and instructors of existing sections attended short courses in the Rabat school, which does not appear to have done more than confirm the need for more trained militants and to have provided some experience for the design of the later school.

With the reorganization of the Istiqlal in late 1956, the first large-scale effort was made to train cadre in a centrally held school. The origin of the students, which is found in Table 8, is interesting, for it indicates the areas from which the party could draw militants and also the areas in which more trained militants were needed. The party itself was restrained by the lack of order in the summer and fall of 1956, as is suggested by the relatively few members coming from the disturbed areas. The large number coming from Beni Mellal, Oujda, Midelt, and Marrakech reflected the need for cadre in areas where the party had a nucleus of workers which it hoped to build up into a stronger organization. The cities were apparently, as one would expect, relatively well staffed, for Fès and Rabat were

[25] The Istiqlal maintains, of course, that they were all asked to leave their party functions to assist the new nation. This is not entirely clear, for it is equally possible that party workers who had been participating for ten years in the middle echelons now felt entitled to more secure and remunerative positions, which are offered by the Moroccan civil service.

[26] Except as otherwise noted, all the information on the cadre training effort comes from an interview with Mohammed Benchekroun, Party Headquarters, Rabat, March 4, 1958, and from data later compiled by him for this study.

TABLE 8

Istiqlal Cadre Training Program in 1956 and 1957[a]

Late 1956: Central School, Rabat	(Two weeks)	Summer 1957: Regional Schools	(One month)
Beni Mellal	70	Oujda	70
Midelt	80	Rabat	60
Oujda	60	Kenitra	200
Marrakech	60	Boujad	180
Agadir	20	Khouribga	40
Casablanca and Chaouia	40	Meknes	42
Al-Jadiida and Safi	50	Ksar As-Souk	10
Ouarzazate	20	Midelt	10
Northern Zone	30	Safi	35
		Marrakech North	40
Total	430	Marrakech South	84
		Fès	157
		Casablanca	50
		Ouazzan	40
		Khemisset	40
		Total	1058

[a] Interview with Mohammed Ben Chekroun, Secretary, Administrative Commission, Party Headquarters, Rabat, March 4, 1958. The inspector at Al-Jadiida (Mazagan) reported that 80 militants from his region also attended cadre school in 1957; this did not appear in Ben Chekroun's list.

not included and the Casablanca group had only ten. Like many of the addresses of the leaders of the party, the courses show the same reiteration of basic principles of the Istiqlal, elementary explanations of party organization, and introduction to the structure and services of the new government.[27] Furthermore, they derived much of their persuasiveness from the lecturers, who were nearly all members of the Executive Committee, high Istiqlal government officials, or well-known *anciens* of the party. Beyond the level of central direction and inspection of the party, the level of preparation and general education was extremely low.

The 1956 courses were hastily organized and conducted in the midst of other crises. Several of the inspectors of the party voiced the opinion that the Rabat school in 1956 accomplished little beyond basic indoctrination. The party had not operated freely for a sufficient time to identify the most promising militants; those attending

[27] See the outline of one series of lectures in *Al-Istiqlal*, October 12, 1956, p. 4.

were, therefore, selected largely on an ex-officio basis. Since the structure of the party was at that time in the course of being changed, it is also quite possible that the party did not receive the maximum benefit because it did not place them geographically and organizationally where they were needed most. Largely under the impetus of Ben Barka, a second series of party courses were planned for the fall of 1957. For this series, held in regional centers of strength, as shown in Table 8, selection was more carefully conducted. The inspector and the regional committee reviewed the possible candidates and considered their promise, level of formal education, and previously held offices. The courses were arranged in part to provide leadership for the growing membership, but also to fill gaps created by the continued drain of skilled personnel by the government.

The content of the courses remained basic indoctrination and "general culture," in the party's words. Leading party figures were still used, but more for the introductory and concluding addresses. While the 1956 school lasted for only two weeks, the 1957 courses went on for a month of lectures and conferences. A fourth of the militants came from the Rabat region, where the party was poorly organized in the south, and a fifth from Beni Mellal, where the Middle Atlas was only spottily organized. The large number from Fès may be explained either by the large number of educated militants who have come from there to work in the government or by plans to develop popular strength in the poorly organized Taza region. The Istiqlal has tried ever since 1957 to establish regular cadre schools in each region of the party, but not with uniform success. The regions of Rabat and Gharb can naturally use the facilities and materials already assembled for the initial schools. Casablanca, Safi, Chaouia, Marrakech, and Meknes planned to conduct their own courses over the summer of 1958, but the other regions either had no plan or else expected to continue using the centrally organized courses. The most advanced regions are probably Casablanca and Marrakech, where plans had been made to conduct cadre courses at the section level with materials sent out by the inspector.[28]

The role of the trained cadre in establishing a harmonious and effective relationship between the central office of the Istiqlal and the base of the movement is most important. The major communi-

---

[28] It is interesting to note that the two inspectorates with the most advanced programs to train militants were centers of dispute when the party split. This confirms Ben Barka's importance in cadre training and also suggests that the schools were influenced by him.

cation device is the *Internal Bulletin* of the party, which the inspectors are responsible for sending to each cell. Since independence the *Bulletin* has been first a weekly, then a bi-weekly, and, since January 1957, a monthly. The party relied on its trained instructors and secretaries to use this publication to sustain a direct relationship between the directors and members. The Istiqlal has been aware that the complex organization and large membership, separated from the leaders by inspectors and two levels of committees, could result in a passive, disinterested base. In his speech to the National Council meeting Al-Fassi acknowledged that bureaucracy could lead to stagnation, but added that the inspectors had been functioning over the previous three months "without creating any obstacle between the central administration and the sections."[29]

The most important problem in organizing the base of the Istiqlal has been the procurement and placement of militants. The effort of the cadre school has not been sufficient to provide one alert, ambitious party member for each cell—the optimal situation. Many of the militants of the party have been attracted to government positions, and some of the older militants may now feel that independence signifies the end of their struggle. The new role of the Istiqlal as both a political organization and a means of social action requires just the opposite. Its political appeal must now be established under competitive conditions, without the unifying quality of a struggle for freedom. The social reform encouraged by the party, and relying on its organization to some extent, requires an even more efficient organization. It must deal with larger numbers of people, most of whom probably have a lower education than the early Istiqlal members and many of whom have only the vaguest conception of a nation and its problems. Ben Barka, probably the best-qualified commentator on the party organization, estimated that the Istiqlal had only 250,000 active, well-informed members. These were persons who read the party *Bulletin* regularly or had it read to them; were willing to spend a large part of their leisure in party-sponsored projects, such as reforestation, school construction, and literacy courses; and made every effort to pay their dues. He estimated that the militants of the party did not exceed five per cent of the members, or about 80,000 to 90,000 persons. These are members who are capable of organizing local activities and of explaining and defend-

[29] *Al-Istiqlal*, August 24, 1956, p. 9.

ing the Istiqlal's national activities and who, of course, make sacrifices of both time and income to fulfill their party obligations.

The militants are occupied mostly as cell instructors—positions requiring more knowledge of the party and organizational technique than the elected cell officers. They are, of course, also the persons that the inspectors guide toward responsible positions in the upper hierarchy of the region. Many are also occupied with youth activities. The distribution of the more promising and talented militants is a major problem of the internal structure of the Istiqlal. Some leaders do not feel that the young, more active militants were actually receiving important positions; this may be part of the explanation for the "regrouping" of cells. Being generally the ambitious and devoted members, the militants probably exhibit the same tendency as other educated, capable persons in their preference for work in the cities and for contact with important party officials. The number of party militants who can understand orders, give clear instructions, and plan party functions is probably considerably under the 80,000-90,000 figure. The shortage of skilled cadre helps explain the frequent visits of high party functionaries and the monthly liaison between inspectors and subordinate committees.

In response to the lack of well-qualified cadre the Istiqlal began "regrouping" its cells. The previous quota of twenty-five members, frequently exceeded, was lifted to one hundred early in 1958. Where the party was well organized, four or five old cells were merged into the new cell. Where the party was poorly organized, the members were grouped in larger numbers. This regrouping permitted more effective dispersion of cadre and more direct contact between the members and cadre. Groups of about a hundred were able to participate in the general activities of the party and to maintain personal contact with the cell officers. It was hoped that the plan would provide opportunities for the more promising and more devoted members, whose potential had sometimes been isolated in the small cell or lost under poorly qualified officers. Groups of a hundred also enabled the segregation of the more devoted, active members in specialized activities of the party at the cell level, which should gradually alleviate the need for cadre. Since the cell instructors were formerly distributed at the rate of one to four or five cells, they now were distributed one to each larger cell, where their efforts could be concentrated more easily on the active membership. The full transition to the "group system" probably required several months, with the cities being the most easy to convert. It began with Ramadan 1958, but was discontinued with the increasing party tensions over the spring of 1958.[30]

The split of the Istiqlal provided some further insight into the role of supervisory structure of the party. The confinement of the dispute to central party figures for nearly a year testified to the importance of leadership and the submissiveness of the members. The tactics of the opposing groups revealed reluctance to provoke a division until the acting group could be fairly certain of having the support of the inspectors and the militants, who apparently would bring the members with them. In December 1958 the criticizing faction apparently did not control the central organization of the party and used their own organizational structure to reach the party cadre. It was later revealed that resistance offices and trade union bureaus were responsible for distributing handbills and holding small rallies in late November 1958. The maneuver had apparently attempted to reach the base of the party and failed. Not only did it lack the support of the inspectors and militants, but some militants sent reports to the conservatives in Rabat. The author's interviews with the inspectors confirmed their loyalties when the split took place. In the early weeks of the split only two inspectors were expelled, Abdelhai Chami of Casablanca and Mohammed Habib of the southern region of Marrakech.[31] Casablanca was, of course, strongly influenced by the trade unions and Chami was once the assistant editor of *Al-Istiqlal*, with Ben Barka. The case of southern Marrakech is more interesting since it was Al-Glaoui's stronghold up to independence. The party had been ruthlessly excluded from the area and the population freely exploited by the feudal ruler. Perhaps more than in any other region, the party organization had been built up from nothing since independence.

The activists were not alone in making an appeal to the militants. In the course of December the considerable party activity by the Al-Fassi group denoted the extent of the controversy in the party, even though it had not yet become known that a split was imminent. Al-Fassi must have known that he could depend on his old friends from before the war who were inspectors. This group in-

---

[30] See *Al-Alam*, April 12, 1958, U.S. Trans. The "group system" clearly carried the imprint of Ben Barka's organizational ideas and perhaps his ambitions. There is no doubt that it would do much for the Istiqlal, but the conservatives might have been very happy to have the easier-going elder cadre in control.

[31] See Istiqlal communiqué in *La Vigie*, January 27, 1959, p. 2.

cluded the inspectors of Rabat city and the south of the province, Al-Jadiida, Tetouan, and Agadir. His prestige in Fès, as well as the predominance of his religious colleagues in the upper ranks of the party there, assured it that he would keep this historic Istiqlal stronghold. His appeal to the militants seems to have been made in a series of party conferences in mid-December 1958.[32] The men giving the talks at these conferences cannot all be identified, but seven of the eleven meetings had one or two discussion leaders known to be loyal to Al-Fassi and Balafrej. The two most important towns, Mohammedia and Kenitra, were assigned to pro-Balafrej officials who had refused to participate in the Ibrahim Council. Several of the others were division chiefs in the Ministry of Foreign Affairs, who also left the government with Balafrej. There were no participants associated with Ben Barka. The conferences dwelt on the advances made under the past government and ended with an appeal for unity in the face of "artificial or forged" divisions that might be inspired by "colonialism or its partisans." The meetings confirm the importance of direct contact and are also a manifestation of the increasing concern of the pro-Balafrej group. Most of the participants had seldom taken an interest in the internal affairs of the party before this time.

For practical purposes it may be fair to conclude that the party was already split as of December, since both factions were using their own organizational channels and their own colleagues to work within the party. As in the case of the impasse of the Preparatory Commission for the Congress, each element excluded consideration of the opposition's viewpoint from its presentation. The conferences demonstrated that the conservatives were able and willing to combat the radical group. The effectiveness of the exclusion of the critical element on this occasion may have confirmed opinions that the party would have to be split. The opposition was excluded from using the party organization after the dispute of early December. The conservative leaders' renewed interest in internal party affairs was again in evidence during the celebrations of the Independence Manifesto on January 11th. All of the party celebrations were provided with speakers from the conservative group.[33] This was the second occasion on which the Ben Barka group had been excluded. Like the opposition parties, they may have begun to sense that they could be exterminated by default if they could not reach the mass through some supervisory party structure.

---

[32] *Al-Istiqlal*, December 20, 1958, p. 5.   [33] *Ibid.*, January 17, 1959, p. 5.

With independence it is to be expected that a nationalist party will lose some of the solidarity and discipline it enjoyed while in opposition to a colonial power. The growth of membership alone required a more clearly defined supervisory organization. A bureaucracy's guiding hand was needed even more when opposition parties could organize. The system of inspectors was, in part, a response to this need, but the party was limited in its selection by the large number of skilled organizers drawn into the government. The lack of any statutory regulation of new party officials suggests the degree of improvisation in their appointment, the difficulty of making decisions in the central machinery of the party, and the submissiveness of members. The system of inspectors, who were in a position to handle as peers local leaders of the trade unions and the resistance, might have resolved the difficulty if the leadership problems of the party had been solved. The schools for training cadre of the party could also have made a large contribution toward eliminating conflict among supervisors and among members of the three organizations, if agreement had first been reached on what were the respective roles of the three groups. In the final analysis, however, the split of the Istiqlal requires consideration of the political system as a whole. Other aspects of the political system did not stand still for Al-Fassi and Ben Barka to settle their differences and constantly presented new problems that accented and multiplied the internal party differences.

How National Is the Istiqlal?

The Istiqlal was the largest single political organization in Morocco. In many respects its experience since independence presents in microcosm the difficulties of national political action in a newly established country. The quality and quantity of members differed greatly in different regions. The organization of the base varied with the period of time which the party had had to organize since the establishment of order and also with the varying stages of social progress of different regions of Morocco. To devise a single plan that would produce uniformity from such diversity was almost unimaginable. The fundamental structure of the organization of the base, therefore, changed among inspectorates, while the most important adjustments, designed specifically for needs manifested after two years' experience, only began in 1958. When one is given the limitations of participation and the problems at the central office of the Istiqlal, it is not surprising that most of these adjustments have been imposed from above with little or no popular participation. The procedure of organizing cells, sections, and subsections continued at different rates and with varying success in the seventeen inspectorates of the party since late 1956. Any quantitative study of the organization is almost immediately outdated, but trends and structural differences can be fairly carefully documented to the party split.

Before any new organization could start, the Istiqlal had to establish one extremely important new distinction in the minds of its members, especially in view of the opposition to the party among some administrative officials. The Moroccan political system at the time of independence required that the party define the difference between itself and the government and the administration. During the struggle for independence this distinction was self-evident to members at all levels. In July 1956 orders were dispersed both through the Ministry of the Interior and through the Istiqlal that local officials of the government had no right to hold political meetings.[34] The party evidently experienced some difficulty with officials who organized or spoke in favor of political groups in the name of the party without being members of the party. Party regulations stressed that correspondence was to be kept from governmental channels and that even high officials known to be loyal to the party were not to be accepted as suitable agents for party business. Such an elementary distinction was probably not clear to the base of the party. Furthermore, it should be remembered that the King was the key symbol in the preindependence political experience of Moroccans. It was very likely more difficult to explain to a party member the new meaning of the party apart from the King than the new meaning of the government, now under the King's direction.

The Istiqlal leaders were fully occupied with the negotiations in late 1955 and early 1956, while many of the militants remained in prisons until their administration could be turned over to the Moroccan government. The war in the Rif and the disorder in other parts of the country also retarded the party's reorganization. Even the most rudimentary inventory of party membership, cadre, and resources was impossible until mid-1956, when the new inspectors and beginnings of the subsection system began to restore some order within the Istiqlal. It is commonly related that many persons in the

[34] See *Party Regulations*, Rabat, *Istiqlal*, 1958, p. 13.

exultation of independence joined every political party or group that had favored the King, some carrying cards from the Istiqlal, Democratic, and Communist parties simultaneously. In the rejoicing, nationalist fervor could not only be abused in individual cases, but some groups, possibly in good faith, started to organize in the countryside Istiqlal party offices that were later disowned by the national office.

The new organization had to be reconstructed entirely, from the supervising committees down to the base. Except for the remnants of Istiqlal militants in the major cities, nearly everything had been lost during the three years of violence. The countryside had never been well organized except for some of the larger towns and areas of special strength prior to 1955.[35] Thus, as the Istiqlal leaders approached the problems of independence on the national level, they also found what were very possibly even more ominous problems within the party. The urban strength had been decimated by violence and many young urban militants were committed to the resistance group. In rural areas the Army of Liberation remained the most active organization, while the new administrators of the independent government were by no means consistently favorable to the party. To the mass of the Moroccan population it had been the resistance and the Liberation Army who had played the most active role in the struggle and who were the obvious vanguard for the nation's reconstruction. These two organizations had existed outside the party's ranks for three years of battle and continued to do so over the first three years of independence.

Since independence, one of the most important membership problems of the Istiqlal has been limiting membership, rather than enrolling members. With limited numbers of skilled militants the party might actually have been overrun immediately after independence. Rapid, indiscriminate recruitment permitted many to join who were unable to participate in party activities, hastily recorded on the party rolls, and even disloyal to the party. To engage in organized political action presupposes certain powers of self-discipline and understanding. Even after independence the Istiqlal also wished to keep some customs of its clandestine past, including in the party regulations that "members will not discuss party affairs

[35] Interview with Mohammed Lyazidi, Executive Committee, Istiqlal Party, Rabat, January 10, 1958. Some of the larger towns where small cells had existed in the countryside were Azrou, Khemisset, Sefou, and Khenifra. See Julien, op.cit., p. 109, for examples.

with outsiders."[36] While flooded with new applications in 1956, the party also had to reenlist the members of the pre-1952 organization, whose records and location were largely unknown.

The sketchy regulations issued in 1956 demanded a background investigation for members who joined in 1952 and withheld their right to vote in party affairs until they became fully qualified members.[37] In the rush of events of 1956, the party continued this admission procedure, which also required only recommendation by two members to become a nonvoting member. The party apparently completely lost count of membership by late 1956, since the entire membership records of that year were discarded and new cards were issued to all members starting in 1957. Though never publicized, it was also agreed in the National Council meeting to conduct a minor purge of the party and to adopt a system of probationary admission. It was later admitted that many "undesirable" persons had joined in early 1956 under the simple recommendation procedure, which was brought under control by having new names submitted to the local party committee and then to a regional committee on membership before the candidate could be accepted.[38]

Any discussion of the total membership or membership trends should, therefore, take into account the potential saturation of the organizational capacity of the Istiqlal. Head-counting is not nearly so important in a new country as the ability to accomplish a given task regardless of the number of heads involved. The contribution of the Istiqlal to the new country has, of course, to some extent consisted of familiarizing large numbers of persons with the basics of political participation, but its most substantial and immediate contributions have been specific projects accomplished with a selected group of members supervised by trained cadre. With this qualification, the number of Istiqlal members alone is significant largely as it substantiates the Istiqlal's claim of being the most popular political party, which has never been in doubt since independence and which is also a distinction of limited significance. In 1958 the Istiqlal had approximately 1,600,000 members, distributed as indicated on Table 9. This is very likely a reduction in the earlier membership of the party, which may have reached 2,000,000 in 1956 and may have dropped below its present membership in 1957. Membership in the

[36] *Party Regulations, op.cit.,* p. 11.
[37] *Ibid.,* p. 11.
[38] *Al-Alam,* August 31, 1957, "Where Are We?" U.S. Trans.

TABLE 9

Istiqlal Sections and Subsections by Inspectorate (with Ratios of Popular Strength and Organizational Strength per Subsection)[a]

Province[b]	Population (nearest thousand)	Members (nearest thousand)	Section	Subsec.	Pop./ Subsec. (nearest hundred)	Memb./ Subsec. (nearest hundred)
Rabat (2)						
City	115[c]	30[d]	1	10	11,500	3,000
Salé and Kenitra	170	40[d]	2	8	21,200	5,000
South and Banilieu	131	20[d]	3	72	1,800	300
Gharb	724	200	13	89	8,100	2,200
Subtotal	1,140	290	19	179	6,900	1,600
Chaouia (2)						
Casablanca	550[c]	100	1	18	33,900	5,600
Chaouia	691		9	61	} 8,300	1,100
Beni Mellal	[e]	90	3	22		
Subtotal	1,241	190	13	101	12,300	1,900
Beni Mellal	366	20	10	94	3,400	200
Safi						
City	84	20[e]	1	5	16,800	4,000
Province	581	80[e]	21	57	10,100	1,400
Subtotal	665	100[d]	22	62	10,800	1,600
Marrakech (2)						
City	203[c]	23	1	12	16,900	1,900
North	457	107	12	114	4,000	900
South	411	95	18	111	3,700	900
Subtotal	1,071	225	31	237	4,500	900
Al-Jadiida	426	120	7	120	3,700	1,000
Oujda						
City	90	20[d]	1	5	16,000	4,000
Province	309	70[d]	14	29	10,600	2,100
Subtotal	399	90	15	34	11,400	2,600
Rif and Nador[e]	536	10	5	23	23,300	400
Midelt	307	60	31	149	2,000	400

TABLE 9, continued

Province[b]	*Popu-lation (nearest thousand)*	*Members (nearest thou-sand)*	*Section*	*Subsec.*	*Pop./ Subsec. (nearest hundred)*	*Memb./ Subsec. (nearest hundred)*
Fès						
City	265[c]	70[c]	1	40	6,600	1,700
Province	539		10	66	} 7,000	1,300
Midelt	[c]	100[c]	2	11		1,300
Subtotal	804	170[c]	13	117	6,900	1,400
Meknes						
City	140	30[c]	1	8	17,500	3,700
Province	329	50[c]	31	52	6,300	600
Subtotal	469	80	32	60	7,800	1,300
Taza[e]	376	50[c]	11	49	7,700	1,000
Ouarzazate	381	70	24	119	3,200	600
Tetouan and Chaouen						
Tetouan City	111	30[c]	1	10	11,100	3,000
Provinces	296	50[c]	2	22	13,400	2,300
Subtotal	407	80[c]	3	32	12,700	2,500
Tangier and Larache	449	80[c]	4	15	29,900	5,300
Agadir and Tarfaya	Not yet well-organized					

[a] The figures given for sections and subsections are those collected in the interviews with respective inspectors. Some corrections have been made in their data according to the latest tabulation given by Mohammed Benchekroun, Secretary, Administrative Commission, Party Headquarters, Rabat, April 7, 1958.

[b] Cities have been listed separately to demonstrate the urban characteristics of the party. Some provinces have two inspectors; this is indicated by the number in parenthesis and by the space in the listing below provinces.

[c] City population figures exclude foreign population.

[d] The willingness of the inspectors to give membership figures varied considerably. Estimates have been based, as needed, on membership figures of other inspectors having similar organization, indicated when the total figure is marked with a "d." Where only the division between urban and rural membership is marked "d," an estimate has been made only of the division itself and not the total.

[e] In several instances provincial circles are exchanged among inspectors in the adjoining provinces. Two circles of Chaouia come under the Beni Mellal inspector, two of Fès under the Midelt inspector, while Taza's inspector is considered an adjoint of the Fès inspector, although he covers roughly equal territory. Rif province is actually split between the Tetouan and Oujda inspectors, while Nador is entirely under the latter. Under the new provincial boundaries the discrepancies between administrative areas of the party and the Ministry of the Interior are reduced, but no map had yet been issued by the end of 1958.

cities, where the Istiqlal possessed a reasonably good organization from the moment of independence, has remained fairly stable. Considering only the large cities distinguished in Table 9, the Istiqlal had about 350,000 urban members. If allowance were made for membership for smaller cities and the many towns, a more accurate estimate could be made of the urbanized membership of the party, which might be as much as half the total membership.

Leaders of the party are naturally reluctant to admit that the party has lost members at any time since independence. In the cities they have probably not lost large numbers, though they must work there in harmony with the more convincing appeal that can sometimes be made by the trade unions. It is very likely that active urban members are largely youth and middle-class Moroccans. The workers, many of whom officially belong to the party, probably tend to concentrate their attention on the unions, which bring them concrete benefits and can appeal to occupational solidarities. The large fluctuations of membership have occurred in the countryside, where occupations are seasonal. The worst loss was probably suffered in 1957, when harvests were extremely poor and near-famine conditions existed in some parts of the country. Membership reached its lowest point in early 1957, perhaps down to a million, and was halved in many rural towns. In 1958 it was probably kept from regaining the uncontrollable proportions of 1956, when whole tribes were sometimes sworn into the party.

Like total membership, cell figures have varying significance. Thus, in regions where the Istiqlal is well-organized cells have about twenty-five members; in regions where the organization is new, but progressing well, cells tend to have about fifty members; and in regions where organization of the party is still rudimentary cells may include as many as four hundred members. The party has been compelled to adjust its lower-level organization to the social structure, educational level, and militants available in the various regions of the country. Each cell elects a secretary, a treasurer, and an assistant for each of the two officers. An effort has been made to have at least one literate officer per cell, known as the instructor. To some extent the best-trained militants have been segregated by the system of instructors. Though they are formally elected by the cell, they are required to be literate in order to fulfill their obligation of reading the *Internal Bulletin* to the cell and giving literacy lessons. If possible, they have attended cadre school or are experienced members of the party. Though this is not explicitly admitted, the inspector appears to rely heavily on the instructors in his supervision of the base of the party and probably has had the most important voice in their selection. Most inspectors admitted that they had only one instructor for every four or five cells, even in areas where cells ranged up to several hundred people.

The tendency was to have most members per cell in rural areas where cadre was lacking, where members have sometimes been indiscriminately admitted, and where the party utilizes the tribal structure. In the cities, where more experienced members are available both for cell and superior offices, the cell can be kept down to a more manageable size. The more efficient urban organization is also indicated by the ability of the middle echelons of the party to supervise larger numbers of cells in the cities, almost two hundred to a subsection in Casablanca and almost sixty in Marrakech.[39] In rural areas, conversely, the number of cells organized under a subsection drops to as low as four. Actually in areas where the party was just beginning to organize, such as in the south of Rabat or south of Meknes, the cell may be a meaningless unit and the organization may be limited by the subsection committee iself. The organization sequence in new areas is definitely from the top downward, stemming from small groups of militants established first in the villages, or *douars*, of the new area.[40] Under the direct supervision of the inspector the organizing committee is qualified as either a section or subsection committee, usually on the basis of at least one section to each administrative circle, and the other new groups are assigned subordinate positions. Cells are developed only after a year or so of instruction and training.

The extent to which this ideal organizational structure is achieved is difficult to measure precisely, but it is most nearly approximated in the cities. Indicative of the party's organizational flexibility is the absence of any set of regulations on the details of this system.[41]

[39] These figures have been calculated from the interview with the inspectors of the cities or regions mentioned.

[40] The main areas of expansion of the party in early 1958 were southern Rabat, southern Meknes, and inland around Es-Saouira (Mogador) where the members of "organizational committees" were respectively 26, 26, and 18. In Table 15 for simplification they have been included with the sections and subsections according to information from Mohammed Benchekroun, Interview, April 7, 1958.

[41] See *Party Regulations, op.cit., passim.* It is, of course, possible that the high officials of the party do possess such a complete set of rules and chose not to divulge them. In view of the frankness with which high officials of the party did discuss the present organization, this seems unlikely. The reason for the outdated and incom-

The entire system of subsections is not even mentioned in the party rules. The procedures are much like those of the preindependence period, and very likely most members are unaware of the significance of the organizational expansion of the party. Under the new system the three officers of each cell form a subsection committee. The cell committees from the defined area or the subsection committee elect seven of their members as the subsection group officers. From the seven officers at the subsection level two are selected as delegates to the section committee. The section committee, in turn, selects one member to sit on the regional committee, working with the inspector at the regional headquarters. Since the elections at the section level are generally personally supervised by the inspector and the results of all elections of the region are submitted to the inspector for approval, the degree of central control is probably high. Except as provided by National Council or Congress meetings, there is no further central representation of the membership. The organization is designed almost entirely to enable central headquarters to direct the membership in the fulfillment of goals defined by the Executive Committee and the Political Committee. To the extent that the headquarters is concerned with opinion among the base of the party, it is dependent on the monthly meetings of the inspectors in Rabat.

An estimate of the development of the Istiqlal organization since independence is complicated by the introduction of the subsection late in 1956. At the National Council meeting of 1956 there was no representation from Beni Mellal or Ouarzazate, while Marrakech had relatively small numbers of delegates, but all had strong organizations in 1958.[42] If the regions of Fès, Meknes, Rabat, and Chaouia are selected as the historic strongholds of the party, it is notable that, whereas they constituted over half of the delegates in August 1956, by 1958 they included only about a third of the sections and subsections. Perhaps more significant were the characteristics of the 1956 delegates. Approximately two fifths of the delegates were in the thirty- to forty-year-old age group and most of them had probably joined the party between 1941 and 1952. Another two fifths were in the age group of twenty to thirty years, the

---

plete regulations is probably simply that those who need to know them are verbally instructed, while the base of the party is not concerned or very interested. The proposed Congress of January 1959 was to have adopted a new set of regulations.

[42] *Al-Istiqlal*, August 31, 1958, p. 3, gives geographical origin, age, and recruitment dates of all delegates.

bulk of them also probably joined before the 1952 suppression. Only seventy-one delegates (eleven per cent) had joined the party since the resistance began in 1953. The progressive party leaders may have been correct in complaining that the base of the party was in the hands of *ancien* cadre. In 1956 the new elements of the party were clearly excluded, although many of them may have been better qualified for organizational work and more highly motivated. The figures also support the proposition that the Istiqlal had an "old" organization in comparison to the unions and the resistance. Those who had engaged in the struggle for independence for ten to twenty years were probably more likely to be content with the patronage and prestige that the party had acquired and to neglect the organization itself.

The Istiqlal of 1958 showed self-evident differences in its organization when evaluated simply by the geographic distribution of its offices and the number of members under the inspectorates, given in Table 9. Thus, in areas of long-standing strength, like the Gharb plain, membership probably approached a third of the population. In areas where the party did not possess nuclei of strength before independence but where it had a good organization, like Midelt or Ouarzazate, the proportion of enrolled population dropped to a fifth. Where the party's basic organization was in its preliminary stages, like the Rif, Taza, and Nador areas, membership was much lower than a fifth of the population. Membership figures alone, however, are likely to be misleading. To influence a hundred dock workers in Casablanca may give the party considerably more influence on the national scene than to have enrolled a hundred agricultural workers in the Gharb.

At the same time, of course, the Istiqlal is engaged in the mobilization of previously isolated areas and, in particular, making some of the first efforts toward politicization of tribes. It is the double action of the party, both as a contender for influence in Rabat and as a vehicle for social change for the population as a whole, that entails a careful evaluation of membership figures. The Istiqlal participates in the political system in the cities and more advanced rural areas much like a political party in an advanced country. At the same time it must consider and, to some extent through its own activities, promote basic social adjustments. Indeed, its continued claim to preeminence rests to a large extent on its ability to demonstrate its capacity for a role beyond that of a conventional contender for influence in Rabat. In this regard the 1958 organization of the party revealed a remarkably effective job of integrating and also organizing the southern regions of Ouarzazate, Marrakech, and Midelt, where the French Protectorate had nearly cut off all pre-independence contact with the central government.

There were some areas of noticeable weakness in the distribution of Istiqlal sections and subsections. Some areas had only small organizing committees and still lacked a substructure of cells or subsections. These were the more retarded areas of the country that are accessible from existing positions of party strength: southern Rabat province, where twenty-six committees are at work; Meknes province, where twenty-six rudimentary committees are working to the south along the highway to Beni Mellal and also north of Meknes city; and lastly among the large tribal confederations around Es-Saouira (Mogador) where eighteen organizing committees are working. The second group of weak areas were those regions where no Istiqlal organization has yet penetrated or where it is limited to small groups in the towns, probably composed mostly of merchants and townspeople. These regions were the most inaccessible by highway and were characterized with the strongest remaining tribal structures, some of them virtually out of contact with the rest of the country. Such areas were the forested area between Oulmes and Khenifra; the entire Ait Youssi tribal region from Sefrou south to Midelt; the tribes on the northern slopes of the High Atlas Mountains roughly between Beni Mellal and Midelt; the large Beni Snassen tribe in Oujda province; and most of Nador and Rif provinces or the central Rif mountains. Two special cases are Tarfaya and Agadir provinces. The former became a part of Morocco only in mid-1958 and remained largely under Army administration. The party organization in Agadir actively began only in the spring of 1957 and was again discontinued during the Ifni crisis.

The rest of the Istiqlal organization in early 1958 falls into three groups using two standards of measurement: the number of members per subsection in each inspectorate and the number of population per subsection in each inspectorate. The reasons for devising these indices are threefold: the subsections are evidence of full articulation of the Istiqlal's model organizational scheme; their establishment denoted the existence of sufficient experienced party militants to extend the membership of the party to the countryside in strength; and the differentiations established correspond roughly to the major different states of social advancement to which the party must adapt itself, excluding, of course, the most retarded areas as yet relatively untouched by the party. A section committee can easily be established by a mere handful of militants and, as their locations suggest, are situated mostly in the larger rural towns where a small group can be assembled without having any significant base in the surrounding countryside. The cell is unsuitable for a basis of calculation simply because it varies so widely in size and exhibits no consistent characteristic in the different situations confronting the party. Reliable national figures on size and number of cells are also difficult to obtain and seem to exist only where the more efficient inspectors have taken a particular interest in cell development. Using the indices suggested, the three groups that result conform to the historic pattern of Istiqlal expansion, the accessibility of the countryside, and the differences in social structure of the various parts of the new nation.

The first group is formed by the nine cities listed in Table 9. In each city the Istiqlal was sufficiently centralized and possesses cadre trained well enough to organize thousands of members under a single section. The historic urban basis of the party undoubtedly remains. There were from ten to twenty thousand citizens for each subsection, much more than could possibly be organized by the rural party structure. The party thus appeared to function in the cities like a party in advanced nations, depending on the more efficient communications of urban life, on experienced party workers for specific demonstrations requiring mass support, and on the more specialized parallel organizations of the party who find their center in the cities. The subsections had from three to four thousand members under their supervision, more than those supervised by any other sample of the party's organization. This is consistent with the generally higher quality of education found among urban members and the larger numbers of experienced party members to become responsible cell officers, essential to managing the large number of cells needed. For example, the party inspector of Casablanca estimated that he has two thousand experienced party militants, enough to provide one for over half of the cells in the city. Within these ratios there are two exceptions of importance. The population ratio in Casablanca of nearly 34,000 to a subsection seems high, though this is probably not a sign of weakness when one considers the strong union organization of the city. The population ratio in

Fès was considerably less—about 7,000 population per subsection; this is probably explained by the reluctance of the ancient Istiqlal stronghold to break with the traditional party organization. Even before World War II Fès had an intricate system of neighborhood, or *quartier*, committees, which have very likely been kept for sentimental reasons.

A second category was formed by the seven more-advanced rural areas surrounding these cities. The inspectorates of the Gharb, Chaouia, and Al-Jadiida comprise the most productive and modernized agricultural regions. Oujda province has both a large modern irrigation project and considerable mining activity. Fès, Tetouan, and Meknes regions are also partially intensively cultivated and old party centers, though there are some fairly isolated tribes. The tribal structure still existing in much of southern Meknes was being organized by the twenty-six groups and actually placed Meknes province in a border-line position between this stage of Istiqlal organization and the weaker one next described. What might be called the well-organized countryside had a population ratio of from six to ten thousand, with the most advanced areas of the Gharb and Chaouia a bit below this ratio and less uniformly advanced areas, like Oujda and Tetouan, a bit above.

In all these areas the sections have a well-developed group of subsections, sometimes as many as ten or twelve. Many of the larger towns in these areas figured in the history of the Istiqlal before independence and very likely contained large numbers of militants. The membership ratio is from one to two thousand members per subsection, with the Gharb, Oujda, and Tetouan having slightly more. If the figure of cell membership in these areas is arbitrarily put at from fifty to a hundred, the result is a requirement of from ten to twenty militants for each subsection. The need could probably be fulfilled considering the history of party activity in these areas and the effort at cadre training since independence. The numbers of members per subsection indicates both well-developed, rural organization and also one adjusted to the limitations on communication and the slightly lower level of education probably found in the more modernized agricultural regions. With the exception of the more isolated parts of Tetouan, Oujda, and Meknes provinces there is little indication that the organization has been designed to conform to tribal structures.

The third category established by the ratios are those where the party has had to rebuild from very few preindependence strongholds and with almost no penetration of the countryside before 1955. In Beni Mellal, Safi, Marrakech, Midelt, Rif, and Ouarzazate provincial areas the party has had some following in the large cities, especially in Marrakech. In these more newly organized areas the tendency is to build a much heavier organizational superstructure, which lacks the popular base found in the above two categories. Whether or not the militants working in this organization were of the same quality as others is not clear, though considerable effort at cadre training has been made in the newly opened territory. The concentration of available cadre in the dispersed organization's upper levels has probably left few militants at the cell level, which was almost meaningless in some of the new areas. In this group the population ratio was from two to four thousand per subsection, with exceptions for Safi and the Rif-Nador sector. The inclusion of some of the eighteen organizing committees in the Safi-Es-Saouira region as subsections has also distorted the figures somewhat. Like Meknes, the Safi area borders between this and the above category of organization, with its northern area fairly well organized and the small groups without substructure scattered over the south. The twenty-four thousand persons per subsection in the Rif-Nador regions reveals the extremely retarded organization of this area, which would be even more apparent if the twelve weak subsections at Targuist had not been included.

The most striking feature of the organizational structure in these cases was a membership ratio of from two to nine hundred persons per subsection. With some qualification for the more retarded Rif-Nador area and also for parts of the Safi area, these might be termed regions with basic organization. The party has advanced beyond the initial penetration phase of the small organizing committees, for nearly all sections have been developed with some subsections. But the organization appears momentarily arrested, with the subsection network as its basic structure. The six rural areas considered have almost one half of all the subsections in the country. Cadre is sufficient to man a large number of subsection committees, but not yet sufficient to expand cell development and, thereby, membership. This fact was confirmed by the small number of members per subsection and by the inspectors of these regions who admitted that cells often run to four hundred persons. Actually the cell was probably not important, since control and supervision were exercised by the large number of subsections, which are in much closer proximity to one another than their counterparts in more highly organized areas. The third category is predominantly Berber regions that were cut off from the party under the French administration. The tribal structure is still relatively strong. The practice of the Istiqlal has been to establish, first, the small committees to demonstrate the advantages of the party and, no doubt, provide small favors to initiate rapport. The few capable persons are quickly absorbed into the subsection committees and membership is limited to those able to fulfill the basic responsibilities of a member.

The contrast between the organization of the Istiqlal in the advanced rural areas and more retarded areas, still possessing considerable tribal structure, is further explored in Table 10. The intent here is only to demonstrate the general linguistic characteristics of the Istiqlal itself. Language differences do exist in Morocco and the consequent problem of communication cannot be ignored, as the party itself has recognized in its strong support for the literacy campaigns. Until such time as linguistic uniformity is achieved, the Istiqlal like any other national structure in Morocco will have to cope with two languages.[43] For the approximation all urban party centers, including cities and large towns, have been included as Arabic-speaking, while the rural circles have been divided. The proportion of sections to population is about the same in Arabic- and Berber-speaking regions—an office for roughly every 10,000 persons.

The percentage of population that has joined the Istiqlal is smaller in the Berber-speaking areas: thirteen per cent as compared to nineteen per cent in the Arabic-speaking areas. A subsection in Arabic-speaking areas has about eight thousand members as compared with about five thousand in Berber-speaking areas. The more advanced organization of the Istiqlal existed in the Arabic-speaking areas, where each section had slightly less than six subsections per section, including the organizing committees. The membership ratio trend in Table 9 is confirmed by the language differentiation. The Berber-speaking areas are entirely rural and largely in the third category of organizational progress described above. A Berber-speaking subsection has under seven hundred members, while in the Arab-speaking areas a subsection averages over eleven hundred, or almost twice

[43] This is somewhat of a simplification, for there are at least three distinguishable Berber dialects: Rifian in the north, Chleuh in the south, and Middle-High Atlas area dialects.

TABLE 10

Estimated Linguistic Differentiation of the Istiqlal and Comparison
to Rural Administrative Organization[a]

Province	Arabic					Berber Dialect				
	Pop. (th.)	Admin. Units[b]	Sect.	Sub-sec.	Memb. (th.)	Pop. (th.)	Admin. Units[b]	Sect.	Sub-sec.	Memb. (th.)
Oujda	264	4	11	22	60	135	1	4	10	30
Midelt						307	5	31	149	60
Tetouan-Chaouen	407	6	3	32	80					
Fès	752	6	12	107	160	52	1	1	10	10
Taza	184	2	7	33	30	192	3	4	16	20
Meknes	246	3	22	18	40	223	3	10	42	40
Ouarzazate	111	1	7	38	25	270	2	17	81	45
Chaouia	1050	8	10	79	160	191	2[c]	3	22	30
Beni Mellal	175	2	5	53	10	191	3	5	41	10
Marrakech	659	4	14	110	125	412	3	17	127	100
Mazagan	426	6	7	120	120					
Rif-Nador						536	8	5	23	10
Rabat	907	8	13	109	180	233	2	6	70	20
Safi-Es-Saouira	398	4	12	42	60	267	1	10	20	40
Tangier-Larache	449	6	4	15	80					
Agadir-Tarfaya	(incomplete)									
Total	6028	60	127	778	1130	3009	34	113	611	415

[a] Contemporary officials are extremely loath to discuss this distinction. The location of party units was known from the interviews with the inspectors and with Ben Chekroun, April 7, 1958. The administrative units were known from the *Livre des Commandements*, Rabat, Ministry of the Interior, December, 1957. Those that are predominantly or almost completely Berber-speaking were determined from a linguistic map used prior to independence for training indigenous-affairs officers and by advice of rural officials. Since the generally accepted preindependence figure was slightly over half Arabic-speaking, any bias here is in favor of Arabic and allows for literacy efforts, et cetera, since independence. All cities and towns listed in the *Livre, op.cit.*, are assumed to be Arabic-speaking.

[b] They are cities, towns (pashas), and circles (*supercaids*).

[c] These two circles are the ones held under the Istiqlal inspector at Beni Mellal, which kept the predominantly Berber regions under the same inspector. The party offices in Fès province directed by the inspector in Midelt do not include an entire circle, but only several tribes.

as many members. Like Morocco as a whole, the party has been affected by the language differentiation. The tendency has definitely been to organize most effectively among Arabic-speaking Moroccans. The progress made in the Berber-speaking areas, where the Istiqlal was practically nonexistent up to 1955, is excellent considering the limitations of cadre, social differences, and the difficulties of organizing until order was restored.

The Istiqlal's clandestine habits have been preserved most strongly in its financial structure. Since the educational standards are low, records may be very poor. In the struggle for independence many subsidiary sources of income were added to dues from members, so that only central records are complete. The party's monetary difficulties are revealed by the great detail given to the handling and use of money in the regulations. Actually much of the organization in new areas has probably been at a loss financially, particularly in depressed areas. The party rules of 1947 and 1945 specified that local sections could keep one fifth of their income for expenses. The rather sketchy 1955 rules raised this amount to thirty per cent, and were more emphatic about the necessity of paying dues, which were raised to one hundred francs a month.[44] The party has also received large donations from wealthy merchants and industrialists, which are kept confidential. If one accepts the membership figure of 1,600,000 and assumes that a tenth of the members pay dues regularly, the party would have an income from dues alone of sixteen million francs a month, or slightly under half a million dollars a year. Party officials at the central level maintain they have no idea how many pay dues. The poor are exempted, seasonal workers are asked to pay only during employment, and those belonging to unions pay only half the Istiqlal fee. This, of course, eliminates half the possible income from all trade unionists, who are probably the largest segment of regularly employed members. Nevertheless, even a modest estimate of the Istiqlal's income amounts to a formidable sum of money for a Moroccan organization. To this regular income should be added consideration of resources that potentially include the fortunes of nearly all wealthy Moroccans, who have made and continue to make large donations for special causes and emergencies. The Istiqlal has no money to waste, but neither is it handicapped by lack of funds.

[44] See *Party Regulations, op.cit.*, pp. 4, 8, and 10 for financial provisions.

The Shattering of Nationalist Solidarity

The split of the Istiqlal in late January 1959 provided a new source of documentation on the internal relationships of the party and a test of the comparative strength of the Old Guard and dissident factions. Many of the implications derived from the organizational reforms suggested by Ben Barka were much more clearly outlined and put into practice in the new National Union party. There was a general testing of loyalties, which proved that Al-Fassi was still an influential figure, that the causes he had expounded over the previous two years were probably more persuasive among the base of the party than had been generally conceded, and that his grass-roots campaigning was very likely another demonstration of the importance of direct contact in political communication in a new country. The entire episode is also striking evidence of the confusion of national and party politics in a new nation, the restricted participation in party politics in many areas of the country, and, above all, the incalculable advantage of possessing an organization where opposition is scattered. Only the initial stage of the division can be considered within the space limits of this book. That the nationalists could afford to differ in early 1959 is in some respects testimony to the political progress in the first three years of Moroccan independence.

Ben Barka announced the decision to form the "true" Istiqlal party on January 25, 1959.[45] Balafrej, the Secretary General of the Istiqlal, was in Europe at the moment and remained there. This tends to confirm the opinion that his position in the party was largely symbolic and that he had no crucial role to play in the day-to-day operations of the party. It was the Leader of the party, Al-Fassi, who rushed to Rabat and supervised the counterattack from Istiqlal headquarters. Nearly all his closest collaborators in the following weeks were old associates from Fès, or Balafrej's junior colleagues from the previous Council of Government. In the party as a whole, activity during the early stage of the split was confined to the larger towns, cities, and modern agricultural areas. Nearly all the party organization in the second and third categories of organizational development was hardly mentioned in the national press. There un-

---

[45] *La Vigie*, January 26, 1958, p. 1. For the first months of its existence the new party had no commonly used name. When it underwent a reorganization in the fall of 1959 the name "National Union of Popular Forces" (*L'Union Nationale des Forces Populaires*) was adopted.

doubtedly was much discussion among members and organizers in the newer regions of party activity, but the first concern of Ben Barka and Al-Fassi was to consolidate their positions in the key urban centers. Just as the membership in general and the more removed segments of the party in particular seemed to have had little influence on past party activities, so during the split was there little evidence that what local groups decided had much influence on the central authority claimed by Ben Barka or Al-Fassi. Where regional or local committees of the new party sprang up, there is little doubt but that the organizing hand of the trade unions and Ben Barka's group had been at work. The split is practically totally devoid of any behavior commonly associated with spontaneous individual political participation.

The Executive Committee of the Istiqlal, which had been the sole central authority of the party since late November, was not affected seriously. Ben Barka and Bouabid were the only Committee members who were associated with the critical group. Ben Barka was immediately expelled, but Bouabid's position remained ambiguous. He did not participate in the meetings to organize the new party and his position in the Ibrahim government, which was supposed to be without party alignment, may have restricted his action. Perhaps the most significant indicator of Al-Fassi's strength and the prevalence of conservative opinion in the higher echelons of the party was the unanimous support given him by the party headquarters[46] and the top officials of the Istiqlal Youth. Ben Barka had even been prevented from establishing control of the Administrative Commission over the previous three years, although he was generally acknowledged to have been the most active organizer. That some youth leaders of the party decided to remain neutral refuted the frequent assumption that the younger party leaders of the progressive group had more appeal among young Moroccans. Several popular and prominent young men, like Douiri, Boucetta,

[46] The motions and communiqués discussed in this subsection of the study are nearly all reproduced in the issue of *Al-Istiqlal*, January 31, 1959, pp. 3-5, after the split. The statements of Ben Barka and other information will be noted, but activities at central headquarters are all documented from this source unless otherwise specified. For readers who might be unfamiliar with the politics of underdeveloped nations, it should also be mentioned that the appellations "conservative" and "radical" seldom have the same meaning in new countries that they have in industrialized nations. They are used here for convenience, but their connotations should be restricted to the material presented or implied in this book.

and Tahiri, remained with the Al-Fassi faction, although the elder nationalists definitely predominated in the conservative group.

In addition to Ben Barka, those immediately expelled were Ben Seddik; Al-Basri; Driss Medkouri, the Assistant Inspector of Chaouia; Houcine Hajbi; Ahmed Ben Bilou; and Thami Ammar, the Minister of Agriculture in the Ibrahim government. All these men were alleged to have taken part in the founding meeting of the Democratic Istiqlal. Although Ibrahim and M'Hammedi were not present, they were undoubtedly well informed about what was being done, and their past activity in opposition to Balafrej left little doubt as to their ultimate loyalty. The new government had been formed, according to the King, on a personal capacity and without party alignment. This was the basis for charges by Al-Fassi that some government ministers were showing preference for the Ben Barka group. He also cast doubt on the possibility of fair elections under the nonparty government. The strange aspect of this argument is, of course, that the old Istiqlal leaders never expressed any doubts or concern over the abuse of authority when they dominated the Council of Government. Furthermore, every Istiqlal Council of Government since independence had expressed complete confidence in its ability to hold elections without favoritism. Although there were several ministers who were sympathetic with them on the Council, the Old Guard appeared to have just discovered the value of safeguards against administrative abuses and electoral disadvantage.

Balafrej's supporters had begun to object to the Ibrahim government before the party split. The party had taken great pains to make it very clear that Ibrahim took office without the support of the Istiqlal. The party had criticized Ibrahim before the party split for permitting Lyoussi to escape, for weakness during the devaluation of the French franc, and for the failure of his foreign policy. The foreign-policy attack was the most surprising, for Ibrahim had been in office only one month and Balafrej had set all the precedents from which the new government worked. When Al-Fassi accused the new government of "carelessness" in diplomacy "vis-à-vis important national problems such as the Sahara, the frontiers (and) the financial and economic dependence of Morocco," he was actually accusing his colleague Balafrej and the uncommitted minister, Bouabid. Such distinctions were completely lost in the barrage of charges and counter-charges that began with the split. The reformed Istiqlal made the same omissions in its statements. Political irresponsibility was not a new phenomenon, for the opposition parties had consistently acted and been treated the same. It is a characteristic of politics in general in the new country and can be explained only by more general consideration of the operation of the political system. Nevertheless, it was surprising to see how quickly the nationalists, who were once above such squabbling, could behave like any minority party.

With the party split Al-Fassi was given unspecified emergency powers. The slogan of the campaign against the dissidents was "Barrier against Fascism," which suggests the passions aroused and the firmness with which opinions had been formed apparently for some time. The inspectors met three days after the split and gave a vote of confidence to Al-Fassi. The Political Committee was no longer a policy-making group, but served as a coordinating mechanism to combat the Ben Barka group. It also provided an avenue of expression to the elements of the resistance that were loyal to Al-Fassi and a device to represent the trade unions that broke off their affiliation with the U.M.T. The appointment of long-time party militants, Abdeljalil and Ben Driss, as inspectors in Casablanca and Marrakech indicated that the threat in these two cities may have been more serious than the Istiqlal admitted.

The struggle to attract the militants and members of the base of the party began immediately. On the second day of the split Al-Fassi announced that Committees of Action and Vigilance were being appointed at the central office and at each regional inspector's office. Though not made explicit, their purpose seems to have been to detect agitation by the Ben Barka forces and to consolidate the membership where inroads had been made. At the same time Al-Fassi announced that a purge of the party would be needed. For this purpose he appointed Purge Committees in each region. The power to expel members associated with Ben Barka was apparently delegated to the inspectors, since notices of expulsion bearing their names appeared soon afterward.[47] The only other comment of organizational significance was the announcement by Al-Fassi that the long-postponed and controversial Congress of the Istiqlal would take place in two months. The selection of delegates and agreement on agenda for the proposed Istiqlal Congress probably went smoothly, since the stumbling blocks to the one proposed for January arose entirely from differences between the two factions.

[47] See *La Vigie*, February 1, 1959, p. 2, and February 3, 1959, p. 3.

The controversies over the future affiliation of the existing Istiqlal local organizations were confined to urban centers in the first stage of the split. Kenitra was an example of this type of controversy. It was a city with strong trade unions because of its large military base and light industry, but it also had many early affiliations with the Istiqlal before independence. There had been some violence there in the former few months of tension, and fighting broke out between party factions during the split. Khouribga was also the scene of party violence. It had a history of serious labor discontent, and the province of Chaouia was reported to have many minor administrators from the resistance. Another heated dispute took place at the rural town of Beni Mellal, where supporters of the two factions quarreled over the disposition of the party office. Since no fights occurred in cities where the organization was firmly in the control of one or the other faction, it appears that disputes were more likely where the forces were equally divided by the dispute. There were no violent exchanges in Casablanca in the early period of the split, where Ben Barka and the trade unions seemed to have dominated the organization. Similarly, in Fès where Al-Fassi was dominant, the local organization was the first to send wishes for his success, even though meetings were held there by Ben Seddik. After the first round of the split, the Old Guard Istiqlal had done better than was generally expected, but they still faced many problems in the towns and villages as the Ben Barka committees expanded their activity. The future of the National Union depended heavily, of course, on the policies of the King and on the ability of the old Istiqlal to reinvigorate itself.

The Istiqlal of Al-Fassi probably had to keep the system of inspectors and sections, whether or not it was effective and appropriate. Party organization was one of the latent causes of the division. The inspectors had certainly proved themselves an effective device for control during the initial attack. It is also doubtful if the system of Ben Barka, based on regionally autonomous groups in a federation, is likely to work much differently in practice. In the bitter exchanges following the split Al-Fassi commented, "You know we have endured a tribal system," when asked about Ben Barka's organizational plan. He went on to defend specifically a more highly centralized organization on the basis of the small size of Morocco and the desire of all true nationalists to subordinate their interests to the national office.[48] The organization of the Istiqlal was clearly

---

[48] This seems to confuse the requirements of good propaganda with good organiza-

suited for a party where there are a number of experienced and venerable militants. But the experience of the Istiqlal also showed that both the opinions and selection procedures of inspectors made it difficult for new ideas and new militants to establish themselves in the party.

The system did not appear to provide much room for the increased capability for political participation of party members who progressed with the educational and social change of the new country. Ben Barka may have charged with some accuracy that cells and sections had "fallen into a state of lethargy" and the militants of the party had "withdrawn into themselves."[49] This statement was not made until the party split, but it revealed deeper differences concerning the organization of the party. The view of the Al-Fassi group is perhaps indicated by their desire to have about a hundred historic militants of the party participate in the Congress without election by the base. Both factions of the Istiqlal were, of course, aware of the importance of young militants and disciplined mass action and made appropriate allowances, but there were major differences over the importance that these sources of party strength should be given in the entire party structure.

The amorphousness of the Istiqlal program, as well as that of other parties, makes it difficult to trace any policy changes that accompanied the split. Al-Fassi repeated with new emphasis the old claim of the party to preeminence among the nationalists. The leaders of the Istiqlal faction, who had been exiled and had fought with the Old Guard group over the previous ten years, were promptly associated with "colonialists and their partisans." But after having spoken in unison for three years the new parties seemed to find it difficult to disagree with each other. The program of the National Union can perhaps be anticipated from the demands of the trade unions and dissident party members over preceding months, but the Al-Fassi faction has little new to offer. In October 1958 his party looked as if it might be opposed to the King, when Balafrej, Abdeljalil, and Bouabid jointly criticized the monarch's refusal to make concessions to the Balafrej government. In the three intervening

---

tion. It should be remembered here that the new provincial administration had been announced, with the admission of the shortcomings of an overcentralized structure for this purpose. Though a political party is not the same, the ethnic and geographical differences that suggested the administrative setup also hold for a political party.

[49] *La Vigie*, February 2, 1959, p. 3.

months, it became the party most closely allied with the King. There were many events outside the differences in the party that account for this, but the split made it definitive and probably inescapable for the future. All the statements by the Al-Fassi faction stressed the King and Islam. The specific content of the proposals are as vague as the motions of earlier meetings, but much more outspoken on the crucial role of the King and the importance of religion.

The national problems were simply listed as always: evacuation of foreign troops, liberation of the Sahara, unification of North Africa, social justice, et cetera.[50] The three main principles of the party were listed as "faith in Islam, faithfulness to the Fatherland and attachment to the King." By referring to the action of the opposition as a "heresy," Al-Fassi implied that they represented a program and beliefs in conflict with the religion of the people. There were other indications that the Old Guard would try to give to the counterattack a meaning "of a defense of Islam and tradition against 'secular materialism,' if not of monarchial faith against revolutionary spirit."[51] Clearly the Istiqlal did not feel the need to issue new goals in the circumstances of the split, but concentrated on preparing the most appropriate arguments against the Ben Barka group. The tactic was indicative of the frequently found tendency of Moroccan political leaders to seize on the most nearly universal appeal to extend their influence and to mobilize mass opinion. Al-Fassi also charged that the new party was in collusion with "financial interests" and in "an alliance between ancient feudalism and modern feudalism."[52] The additions to the program of the Istiqlal seemed to have been entirely in anticipation of the future struggle with the reformed Istiqlal. For this combat Al-Fassi was evidently prepared to use every form of influence available to him.

The experience of the Istiqlal provides much insight into Moroccan political behavior as a whole. Since the party encompassed a large share of the most active and best-prepared members of the nation, it was certainly not typical of the national political system. If one views the experience of the Istiqlal more generally and in relation to the political system as a whole, it may be quite possible that the leaders of the party could not have made decisions or exercised their

[50] See *Al-Istiqlal*, January 31, 1959, p. 3.

[51] From editorial of *Le Monde*, January 29, 1959, p. 1.

[52] See *Le Monde*, February 1, 1959, p. 2. There is some evidence that the radical group had been in contact with the Popular Movement before the split of the party and might be using these contacts to explore their common interests.

influence in another way. The means of persuasion and the range of subjects that can be handled by the population as a whole are very limited. Certainly for the questions of the internal party organization there were few men outside the upper echelon of the party who understood all the implications of the organizational structure, both to the party and in reference to national politics. To reveal the source of discontent and explain the differences that did exist would be to risk dissolution of the party. This is, indeed, what happened when the paralysis of the central governing body of the party finally forced the issue into the public.

Perhaps the most striking evidence of the problem of mass participation in politics in a new country is the uniformity with which the membership of the Istiqlal followed the older leadership. In the early phase of the split, at least, it was only a matter of a few persons, very likely in personal touch with the contenders for whom they worked, trying to seize a few party offices. The members of the party did not meet after the crisis, nor is there much evidence of any concern about the split among the mass of followers. In the towns it was undoubtedly a favorite topic of conversation and speculation, but people did not act. They waited for the leader of their particular loyalty to act or to set in motion a scheme to capture the local party organization.

There are several implications of this episode that are important to a full analysis of the influence structure of the new nation. All political parties reflect to some extent the major political issues and problems of the nation concerned. Their ability to resolve these questions within the party is a question of both the internal relationships of the party, if agreement can be reached as to how to demarcate "internal," and the national political system. In advanced countries there are often weak parties, but they are gradually reformed or dissolved where the political system as a whole operates smoothly. If the generalization may be made that this interaction is on the whole to the benefit of the advanced country, then the deficiency of the political system of the new nation is more easily explained. There is no point of reference in the national political system of Morocco or similar new countries that compares to political systems within which parties in advanced countries work. For the Istiqlal leaders there were no problems of elections, of recognized system of patronage, or of multiplicity of group interests to lead them out of their dilemma. Where the level of education is so low and the national problems so complex, this is likely to be the case even where several parties are found in a new country. The Moroccan political system is not likely to change very much in its over-all characteristics with the formation of the Democratic Istiqlal.[53]

The Istiqlal used all the four forms of influence briefly introduced before: charismatic, institutional, coercive, and traditional. The appeal to religion and the fatherland involved charismatic influence. At the base of the party the organizational activity on a tribal basis utilized traditional influence. There is fairly well-substantiated evidence in this and other chapters that the Istiqlal has, from time to time, resorted to coercion. The organization itself is, of course, a means of exercising institutional influence. The use of institutions within the party bears further comment here. As one treats the Istiqlal apart from the national political system for a moment, one sees that the use of institutional influence in the party helps clarify problems of its use in the more general framework. It is important to note the difficulty of using institutions even in the more advanced setting provided by the party membership. Organizational questions alone certainly do not explain the insurmountable differences between Ben Barka and Al-Fassi, but they are a reflection of very different approaches toward the use of an organization. Both men recognized the value of solidarity in the party and must have had a wide area of agreement to have managed to work together so long.

What is an appeal in an organization is, however, also a form of influence when more generally treated. Ben Barka seems to have preferred increased reliance on institutional influence in the organization; this is revealed in his concern for training militants and "regrouping" the cells. The Political Committee scheme is also a manifestation of this, although it has much wider ramifications in the entire political system. To follow Ben Barka's course of action meant placing certain limits on the use of other kinds of influence or, perhaps more accurately, abstaining from their use. As the tension and

[53] This entire line of reasoning could also be done by using simply organizational terms, within the framework of the party alone. This would mean treating the national political system as a limiting factor rather than the focus of analysis. Since the unit of analysis being used here is the nation, this course has been purposely avoided. For immediate needs of policy makers the more confined approach is probably sufficient, but may be misleading where predictions are desired for long periods of time. As is so commonly the way in analytical systems, one makes his choice and pays the price in terms of the kind of predictions that can be made. If one is given the prescientific stage of theory formation in the social sciences, it is unlikely that any single theory is about to be formed that is sufficiently elaborated to make any prediction desired, even though the same data may be used differently in two different theories.

eventual split of the Istiqlal demonstrate, there appear to be certain combinations of influence for certain purposes or to deal with certain problems that are unstable or ineffective. The Istiqlal apparently did not have sufficiently well-defined channels for the use of institutional influence to permit the organizational changes under consideration to be accepted or rejected. These implications will be further explored later, but it may be noted here even as developed in an organization.

CHAPTER IX

THE MOROCCAN LABOR MOVEMENT

Growth of the Labor Movement

THE Moroccan labor movement is the second largest group claiming a national role in Moroccan politics. Despite some internal tensions, the Moroccan Federation of Labor (U.M.T.) remained the only union organization until late 1958. Though it represented only a third of the membership of the Istiqlal, the Moroccan Federation of Labor enjoyed certain advantages in political activity. For the most part its members were concentrated in urban centers; this fact facilitated communications and supervision. The industrial and commercial occupations of most members introduced the workers to organized behavior and provided experience that many Istiqlal members never had. By its working-class composition the U.M.T. possessed a ready-made appeal for post-independence solidarity. The obviously oppressive economic conditions and abuse to which Moroccan laborers had been subjected over the preceding thirty years were of immediate concern. The practical lessons that union leaders could draw from the experience of advanced countries were much clearer and more easily adaptable to a new country than in the case of the more complex political situations of the Istiqlal. Though free union organization has been one of the distinguishing characteristics of advanced countries, there was no "colonialist" heritage attached to union purposes or methods.

As a result, the U.M.T. has enjoyed a double life as nationalist spokesman and also as working-class spokesman. Where specific interests of the workers were involved, the union could halt all economic activity. Where national problems were at issue, the U.M.T. could speak with almost more legitimacy than the Istiqlal itself. Through the Political Committee of the party the union leaders had a direct voice in Istiqlal policy formation and in questioning Istiqlal ministers in confidence. On the governmental level the U.M.T. was, however, not limited to its Istiqlal associations, but was directly represented on a number of important commissions and planning bodies. Although crucial to the transition of the economy, the U.M.T. was not forced to commit itself to either governmental or party decisions. With a tendency to put forward the most progressive proposals the U.M.T. escaped the responsibility of putting them into operation and could not be cross-examined. This was a particularly important advantage to the union during the transition period, when many decisions were made on the basis of immediate needs of the country and when many controversial decisions were avoided in order to smooth relations with France.

The contribution of the union to the development of the new country was, nevertheless, considerable. Regardless of their natural organizational advantage the workers constituted a crucial group whose expectations and needs had to be represented and fulfilled as much as was possible. More than any other group in Morocco the U.M.T. succeeded in gaining legal and social benefits for its members. Appropriate credit must be given to the men who had the understanding and skill to bring to bear on labor problems. Few leaders of other organized groups progressed as well or had such explicit, persuasive plans. Though the U.M.T. represented only a minority of Moroccans, it included the vast majority of employed Moroccans. Strikes could have been used with political effect, but union leaders exercised restraint. The union leaders understood that no redistribution of existing wealth would noticeably ameliorate the workers' conditions; such a vitally needed change in conditions would require sizable increases in total national production. They were aware of the difficulties entailed in enlarging social services, training skilled workers, and attracting investment to Morocco. To these ends they have given invaluable cooperation to the government, although they have held somewhat different opinions from the government as to the ideal role of the government in the economy.

Though some of the U.M.T. criticisms of the government, especially in the area of foreign policy, have been severe, the union's contribution to the smooth functioning of the political system should not be overlooked. In the absence of articulate public opinion, defined institutions, and multiplicity of organized groups, national politics may tend to become increasingly isolated from the citizens of a country. Opinions that are held by large numbers of people outside the nation, as well as alternative methods of dealing with internal problems, may easily be ignored. In becoming the most outspoken critic of the Moroccan government, the U.M.T. probably helped prevent the procrastination and complacency that could have made national government a meaningless device in Morocco. Nor should the colorful and often controversial arguments of unionists be lightly dismissed. Such arguments present positions and problems concerning the Arab world and the Communist countries which no new nation can push aside. The way in which the union appeal has been made should also be considered in relation to the limitations bearing on any political group that is sincerely interested in increasing popular political participation. If the transition is to be made from autocratic government to some form of representative government, or even respected national government, the citizens must begin to participate in some limited way. This is not to deny that the U.M.T. has sometimes exploited favorable situations, but its own occasional irresponsibility is increasingly controllable by the play of a political system that it is helping to develop.

The Istiqlal's claim to preeminence among Moroccan national organizations is no doubt justifiable in view of its thirty-year effort for independence, but the U.M.T.'s position is also strong and in some ways more persuasive. During the years of oppression the workers were economically more vulnerable than many of the prominent Istiqlal leaders, who solicited and received large donations from wealthy Moroccans. Lacking national or regional prestige, the workers were also more vulnerable to police control and brutal suppression. Although French trade unions had existed in Morocco since 1936, Moroccans were not legally permitted to join them until after World War II. During the brief period of harmony with the Communists after the war, the Moroccan offices of the French C.G.T. began to organize Moroccans. Other French unions were not receptive. Communist activity was especially strong among the miners and dock workers.[1] In recognition of the growing Moroccan membership under the C.G.T., an affiliate was set up in 1950 under supervision of French Communists, but run by Moroccan union leaders. The large demonstration of Moroccan laborers in Casablanca on May Day, 1951, revealed their growing strength and may have caused French officials to step up plans to suppress all nationalist activity. With the tension between the Communist and free worlds during the Korean War there were many reports of increased attempts to associate the Moroccan workers with Communism in order to justify

[1] In 1948 one of the first strikes of Moroccans occurred when all the Moroccan officers of the miners' federal of the C.G.T. were imprisoned. The secretary general of the federation was sentenced to life at hard labor. *Al-Istiqlal*, May 4, 1956, p. 5.

destroying the nascent labor movement.[2] In 1952 May Day demonstrations were forbidden, and in December of that year a sympathy strike took place over the assassination of Farhat Hached, a vigorous union leader of Tunisia.

Contacts between the Istiqlal and the union leaders had no doubt multiplied in the period from 1947 to 1951. Just as the union leaders needed a unifying appeal like independence, so did the Istiqlal need the mass support and strategic strength of the urban laborers. Moroccan union leaders were no happier being run by French Communists than by any other French organization. Discontent on nationalist grounds appears to have multiplied some time before the 1952 crisis. Communists are reported to have received increasingly cold receptions at union meetings during 1951, while nationalists of undoubted Moroccan sentiment became more popular.[3] The Istiqlal reportedly intensified its efforts to organize workers' cells, whose discussions were oriented to the particular social and economic problems of the laborers. One of the explanations often given by Moroccan officials for the brutal suppression of the 1952 sympathy strike is that the union leaders had made the decision to renounce C.G.T. sponsorship. In late 1952 the Moroccan unionists were certain that they influenced the majority of the C.G.T. members and could seize control of the organization. This forced the C.G.T. to recognize the possibility of an independent Moroccan union, or to permit the Central Committee of the C.G.T. for Morocco to be taken over by Moroccans and, thereby, lose C.G.T. French membership in the Protectorate.[4] The Communists are alleged to have chosen the first course, which indirectly gave international recognition to Moroccan nationalism and was an anathema to Protectorate officials, especially in Casablanca. To forestall nationalism as much as Communism among the workers, the Casablanca strike of 1952 was mercilessly suppressed.[5]

Though the Istiqlal was unable to reorganize until the return of the King, the union leaders, many of whom had been released with the Istiqlal leaders in late 1954, were able to present the Protectorate

[2] For example, see *France Observateur*, November 15, 1951, pp. 6-8.

[3] Claude Bourdet, "La crise marocaine," *Espirit*, 19 année, no. 176, February 1951, pp. 281-282.

[4] Lacouture, *Le Maroc à l'Epreuve, op.cit.*, pp. 299-300.

[5] U.M.T. officials now claim that the French Communist members of the Central Committee wished to avoid the sympathy strike, which was held on the insistence of the three Moroccans on the Committee. Interview with Seddiki Said, Press Officer, U.M.T., Casablanca, February 13, 1958.

with a *fait accompli* that could not be undone. A small committee of union leaders was formed clandestinely in February 1955 and made contact with the pro-Western union international, the International Confederation of Free Trade Unions (I.C.F.T.U.). The leaders were Maghjoub Ben Seddik and Taib Bouazza, who remained secretary general and assistant secretary general of the U.M.T. The small group of organizers knew that the Resident General was planning a new *dahir* on union organization which would give authorities special powers of supervision, control of finances, and approval of officers. In March another clandestine meeting was held in Casablanca. It was decided to affiliate with the free-world international and, thereby, gain its world-wide influence both for the nationalist cause and for the protection of the Moroccan workers. Forty-five delegates were assembled and twenty-two regional committees were announced unexpectedly.[6] Regional offices were set up at Casablanca, Oujda, Kenitra, Rabat, Safi, Marrakech, and Fès, with a reported membership of 20,000 by May Day, 1955. The unions were, of course, still closely watched by the French police, but the basic organization of the most advanced industrial areas of Morocco was completed while terrorism continued. Paris remained the center of the unionists' agitation, though dues were collected in Morocco and some efforts were made to aid victims of violence. The French administration recognized the new union in late 1955, but excluded agricultural workers.

The U.M.T.'s advantage over the Istiqlal was not entirely due to the facility of organizing workers already segregated by their occupations and factories. The unions were organized nearly six months before the Istiqlal. Most of the Istiqlal leaders were still occupied with Franco-Moroccan negotiations in the early months of 1956 when the U.M.T. had an estimated 400,000 members.[7] Even before the King returned, the U.M.T. claimed to have no political functions, but nevertheless was represented during negotiations with France and frequently consulted on internal affairs. It also spoke up freely throughout the negotiations and was generally able to make

[6] *Le Monde*, March 22, 1955, p. 5. At the time discussions were still continuing in Paris on how to permit the unions to be revived safely, *ibid.*, p. 1. The first warning had been an appeal to the Resident General submitted in January 1955, *L'Express*, March 26, 1955, p. 5.

[7] The same estimates are given in "Ou en est le Maroc," *L'Afrique et l'Asie*, 3è trimestre, no. 35, 1956, p. 29, and in an interview with Mohammed Abdelrazak, Secretary, Federation of Electrical Workers, Moroccan Labor Federation of Rabat, May 27, 1958.

decisions much faster than any political party. The union began a training school for organizers in December 1955, six months before the Istiqlal began training cadre. While rapidly expanding in the French zone, where its basic framework already existed by late 1955, the U.M.T. undertook expansion into the Spanish zone, heretofore cut off. A month after the Franco-Moroccan Agreement was signed there were fifty-six unions organized in the Spanish zone, and a U.M.T. conference of over a hundred delegates was held at Tetouan. At the same time the union was organizing the outlying parts of the French zone, especially the mines. Eight months before the demise of Addi ou Bihi, Ben Seddik flew into the Midelt area to settle labor riots over his early organization of the mines in Tafilalet province. From the moment of independence the workers had a single purpose and a unified leadership, which the mass of Istiqlal members lacked.

Union leaders expressed the same sensitivity concerning internal differences of members or leadership as did the Istiqlal. There were early indications of such difficulties in 1956. Late in July the general treasurer of the U.M.T. was arrested in Casablanca, allegedly for the abuse of union funds.[8] As in most cases of corruption involving government or private individuals, nothing more was heard of this case until the treasurer and another U.M.T. critic, Mohammed Jorio, were expelled from the union several months later. Jorio's importance is today minimized by the U.M.T., but his earlier activity in the union movement suggests differently. When he was Ben Seddik's right-hand man in Rabat they jointly reviewed a massive labor demonstration in the capital shortly after independence. Bouazza and Jorio directed a mass meeting of Rabat workers after the King's return. Over the summer of 1956 Jorio had formed the Free Confederation of Moroccan Workers from the elements of the Rabat workers loyal to him and had given the by-laws of the new union to the governor of the city.[9] The new union grouped many of the more skilled workers of the city, who led a demonstration before the royal palace demanding legal recognition. These more articulate workers expressed their attachment to "the defense of the material and moral interests of all workers without political or foreign influence on the sacred principles of syndicalism."[10]

[8] *C.M.*, July 30, 1956, p. 3, and *Le Monde*, August 1, 1956, p. 4.

[9] They were, of course, never accepted. Perhaps by poetic justice the new union was rejected through Ahardane on the basis of the same arbitrary rules concerning new associations as were later used to forbid Ahardane's Popular Movement a year later and to remove him from office.

[10] *Courier du Maroc*, November 25, 1956, p. 1.

The minor schism was apparently encouraged by the depressed condition of many skilled trades in Rabat, especially among construction workers. The workers also objected to the close association of the U.M.T. with the Istiqlal in the effort to change the Council of Government over the summer of 1956.[11] Faced with specific causes for internal dissension, the subsequent U.M.T. inquiry dwelt more on the national repercussions of the incident. The U.M.T. announced that it would study "a situation created by anarchist elements" whose propaganda "tends to trouble public order and to lead the workers to commit acts contrary to the supreme interests of the nation."[12] After preliminary inquiries by the Minister of the Interior, the King himself came to the rescue of the U.M.T. He stated, "His Majesty disapproves of the discord among the workers [and] he encourages them to express their claims and opinions on the side of the U.M.T., which has demonstrated itself capable of assuming the defense of the rights and interests of the working class."[13] The determination of the Istiqlal and union leaders to suppress the affair quickly and effectively may have been reinforced by the support reportedly given the schism by the opposition Democratic party. In relation to the national political system the affair is most important as an example of the tendency to rely on nationalist or universal appeals to resolve internal crises and also to avoid inquiry into more profound causes of discontent. That this was done is not only evidence of the continuing importance of an appeal in terms of national solidarity but also of the difficulty of making a public appeal in other terms. The tendency of the union movement to be preoccupied with political problems continued and was in even greater evidence by 1958.

The problem facing the Moroccan union was formidable. The existing labor force had never been fully employed, Moroccans lacked the skills and knowledge for the operation of much of the economy, and the country had to establish confidence to attract capital. The decline in economic activity began several years before independence, probably beginning in 1952.[14] Most directly affecting the unions was the extremely serious condition of unemployment. The official figures

[11] There were later reports that it was also related externally to disputes among international union organizations, see *Tangier Gazette*, December 7, 1956, p. 1.

[12] *C.M.*, November 22-25, 1956, p. 4.

[13] *Al-Istiqlal*, December 7, 1956, p. 5.

[14] See *L'Evolution Economique du Maroc, op.cit.*, pp. 13-15, and "Morocco," *Structure and Growth of Selected African Economies, op.cit., passim.*

are incredibly low and make no allowance for underemployment, though this was a chronic problem even before independence. Even so, official unemployment doubled in the last six months of 1956 and has remained at about 30,000 since then.[15] This estimate is based on the unfilled requests for employment at the placement bureaus of the government, and thereby it includes urban workers with some skill. It is more significant if judged in comparison to the figures for 1954 and 1955, when registered unemployment was about 1,000. A more realistic estimate of unemployment is probably about 200,000, the figure most often cited in official speeches. It is frequently estimated to be as high as half a million, when allowance is made for those who have crowded into slums and seek perhaps one day's labor a week by soliciting in the streets. A more meaningful estimate of both unemployment and the progress of the U.M.T. may be formed from the 1952 census figures on the active population, placed at just under three million for the south.[16] Agricultural occupations included about two million. This left an urban active population figure of about one million. At least one of every five able, urban laborers is unemployed and probably two out of five. Since rural families often depend on members in the city, the misery of unemployment is multiplied many times over.

Given this difficult situation, the U.M.T. has exercised restraint, but has also occasionally produced labor disturbances for what seem to be predominantly political motives. The U.M.T. and the Istiqlal jointly increased criticism of the government during 1956 when the Democratic party was still in the government. Their objections rapidly decreased after formation of the predominantly Istiqlal government in October of that year. The new government took over at the time of a crisis in relations with France, when the unions no doubt felt restraint. Even so, the change in the official number of collective conflicts was large, being about fifty a month during 1956 and then dropping suddenly in November 1956 to a fifth of this amount.[17] Comparable figures for 1958 are not available, but the increase in labor disputes was easily noted after the dispute over forming the

---

[15] These figures are by the Bureau of Placement and include only registered workers who are now unemployed. *Le Maroc au Travail*, Rabat, Ministry of Labor and Social Affairs, 1958, pp. 87-88. Since Moroccan independence was under discussion in early 1955 and the Franco-Moroccan Agreement was signed in early 1956, the increase in unemployment coincides with the Meknes massacres and not independence alone.

[16] *Ibid.*, p. 17. Note the qualifications of this chart, excluding much of mining, railroad, and public works.

[17] See *ibid.*, p. 148.

Balafrej government. The former Minister of Labor and Social Affairs, Abdallah Ibrahim, refused to participate in the Balafrej cabinet and is known to be a close friend of Ben Seddik. Both of these men have made speeches vigorously attacking the policy of the Balafrej government.

Over the summer of 1958 the rash of strikes led to violence on one occasion and nearly to violence on another—something which had never before happened. The first incident took place over the release of some workers from a rug factory in Rabat; this action produced the first general strike of free Morocco. The dispute was not settled, and several weeks later a small riot at that factory necessitated police intervention. The tendency of the U.M.T. to exaggerate the importance of the dispute and to use a general strike in Rabat over the incident drew careful criticism from the Istiqlal—the first time the U.M.T. was publicly reprimanded by the party.[18] The second incident occurred in Casablanca during the popular resentment over the Algerian referendum. During the picketing of a factory riots took place between the police and the workers, when the U.M.T. demonstrated with some 10,000 laborers. About fifty workers were wounded and several officials of the U.M.T. detained. Bouabid, the most important mediator of union views in the government, made a special trip to Casablanca to investigate the dispute and a U.M.T. delegation was received by the King. The Ministry of the Interior issued a statement assuring workers of the right to strike, but also defending the right to enter the factory for those who wished to continue working.[19] The disputes were evidence of the growing discontent of the union leaders with the policy of the government and also their ability to create incidents that could seriously jeopardize the order and economy of the new country.

Despite these increasingly bitter attacks on the government, the voice of the unions has been much greater than superficial examination would suggest. Up to the time of the Balafrej government the U.M.T. was represented on the Council of Government through Ibrahim. It has always had a sympathetic spokesman in Bouabid. Union delegations can, of course, have access to the King as they wish and have often been consulted by him on particular problems. The U.M.T. has been allowed ten of the seventy-six seats in the

[18] *Al-Istiqlal*, June 8, 1958, p. 5.
[19] *Petit Marocain*, September 26, 1958, p. 4, making reference to the Charter of the United Nations and the Moroccan penal code in the absence of any Moroccan legislation of union strike procedures. The dispute raised the whole problem of picketing and closed-open shops, not yet covered by union legislation.

Consultative Assembly, where all union officers participate and Ben Seddik is Vice-President. Other important government organs on which labor representatives sit are: the Superior Council for the Plan and its commissions; the Commission for the Formation of Professions; the Labor Courts; the Bureau of Placement; the Central Commission for Prices; and the committees of the Fund for Social Aid. When one considers the membership and the representation accorded other groups, one sees that the U.M.T. is widely recognized and well informed on governmental matters of general interest and of direct concern to labor. In a government where administrative decision and special commissions are the most commonly used methods of regulation and planning, the role given to the U.M.T. is unquestionably great. In the absence of a well-defined institutional decision-making process, committees and high civil servants make the day-to-day decisions of government, while the most important decisions are reserved to the King and his cabinet. The unions have access to or are specially consulted by nearly every important authority. However, in the present state of the working class the influence which the U.M.T. has had in these organs and its contribution to the national welfare is probably appreciated by only a small number of the workers. Since the union leaders have been unable to enjoy the full benefit of their recognition in the new nation, direct participation probably has become increasingly attractive. Though its immediate goals may be more easily distinguished than those of the Istiqlal, the U.M.T. has probably also had similar problems of maintaining solidarity and interest which increased participation in national politics might revive.

Labor's Strength and National Politics

Like other organizations the unions have lacked cadre and have undertaken special training programs. The U.M.T. possessed an initial advantage from its reservoir of cadre trained before 1952 by the C.G.T. About one hundred and fifty militants have been selected for special training, though the labor exchanges, which also provide U.M.T. office space in each large city, also give general instruction to promising young unionists. Like similar Istiqlal courses, the U.M.T. cadre school lasts two weeks and is strongly supported by high officials of the union.[20] The organizational problem of the

[20] See the outline of the schedule and interviews with candidates. *Al-Istiqlal*, March 16, 1957, pp. 6-7, and May 25, 1957, p. 5.

unions is, of course, simplified by the concentration of Morocco's industrial and commercial structure in a few large cities. Approximately one half of all industrial and commercial establishments of the country are in Casablanca;[21] this fact enables close supervision of a large segment of the workers by the directors of the U.M.T. themselves. Nearly three fourths of the industrial and commercial personnel work in the four cities of Rabat, Safi, Meknes, and Casablanca. This fact has undoubtedly simplified the leadership problem for the U.M.T. and probably permitted more central control than has been found in the Istiqlal.

Prior to independence the union was forced to organize small, industrial cells supervised under regional groupings, but the trend since independence has been to form national federations. In 1958 federations had been formed for twenty-six occupations or governmental ministries, which included roughly two fifths of the U.M.T. membership, or 200,000 workers. With the exception of agriculture, these federations include the most important sectors of the Moroccan economy and the bulk of the civil service. As listed in Table 11,

TABLE 11

Membership of the U.M.T. by Federations and Local Unions in 1958[a]

Federations—25			
Government		*Industrial*	
Public Works	20,000	Mining	30,000
Post, Telephone & Telegraph	5,000	Electricity	5,000
Public Health	5,000	Railroads[c]	8,000
Education	15,000	Ports and Docks	11,000
Agriculture (rural agents)	5,000	Tobacco[c]	2,000
Finance	3,000	Transport	32,000
Municipalities	10,000	American Bases	6,000
Justice (clerks)	3,000	Fishing	20,000
		Hotels	10,000
Subtotal	66,000		
		Subtotal	124,000
Government Services		*Services*	
Police	11,000[b]	Banking	2,000
Customs	3,000	Motor Fuels	3,500
Firemen	1,500	Bakers	3,000
Exportation Company	1,000	Free Schools	1,500
Subtotal	16,500	Subtotal	10,000
	Total in Federations	216,500	

[21] *Le Maroc au Travail, op.cit.*, pp. 20-21.

TABLE 11, continued

Local Unions—39			
Urban		*Rural*	
Tangier	3,000	Khemisset, Rabat	3,000
Casablanca	200,000	Had Kourt, Rabat	1,000
Agadir	10,000	Ouazzan, Rabat	1,500
Mohammedia (Fedala)	12,000	Sidi Kacem, Rabat	4,000
Khouribga	10,000	Souk Al-Arbaa	1,000
Kenitra	25,000	Berrichid, Chaouia	3,000
Salé	2,000	Boujad, Chaouia	2,000
Safi	12,000	Ben Slimane, Chaouia	3,000
Tetouan	10,000	Benamed, Chaouia	1,500
Al-Jadiida	5,000	Al-Gara, Chaouia	1,500
		Settat, Chaouia	3,000
Subtotal	289,000	Berkane, Oujda	4,000
		Beni Mellal, Beni Mellal	5,000
		Fqih Ben Salah, Beni Mellal	6,000
		Kasba Tadla, Beni Mellal	2,000
		Essouira, Safi	3,000
		Al-Hajeb, Meknes	1,600
		Khenifra, Meknes	2,000
		Ksar As-Souk, Tafilalet	3,000
		Midelt, Tafilalet	1,800
		Taza, Taza	1,500
		Azrou, Fès	2,100
		Azemmour, Safi	2,000
		Sefrou, Fès	1,000
		Arcilla, Tangier	1,500
		Nador, Nador	1,500
		Alhucemas, Rif	2,000
		Larache, Larache	3,000
		Ksar Al-Kebir, Larache	3,000
		Subtotal	70,500

Total in Local Unions   359,500

Total U.M.T. Membership   576,000

[a] Interview with Mohammed Abdelrazak, Secretary, Electricians Federation, U.M.T., Casablanca, May 27, 1958. The provincial designations for the regional divisions for 1956-1958 have been used here since the new map had not been publicly released.

[b] The police were not officially unionized as of late 1958, but were included as a federation by union officials, as indicated here.

[c] Some of the unions included as industrial or service type might be called governmental. Railroads and tobacco are government enterprises. The free schools, an old Istiqlal project, are now supervised under the Ministry of National Education.

over 300,000 workers are organized in local unions. The variety of occupations included and the geographical scattering of the locals probably make them less important than the separate, centralized federations. The system of representation is similar to that of the Istiqlal and, also like the Istiqlal, the delegates have seldom changed since independence. The last Congress of the U.M.T. was the clandestine meeting of March 1955. A National Council meeting was held in December 1955, at the time of the Istiqlal Congress, and another in August 1956, at the time of the Istiqlal National Council. Regulations provided for one delegate for every fifty members for each federation or local, with a maximum of five delegates. Such rules meant that the large unions would be severely underrepresented in the Congress and, furthermore, these regulations made no adjustment for the unions' financial contribution to the U.M.T. The Congress is supposed to be convened every two years. Plans for a Congress in August 1958 were postponed for apparently the same reasons as were the Istiqlal Congresses.

The central organs of the U.M.T. are the Administrative Commission of twenty-one members and the National Bureau of nine members of whom the latter are elected by the Congress. Actually, changes have been made in the absence of a Congress and, as in the case of the Istiqlal, it is most unlikely that a Congress would reverse or oppose a decision of the leaders. The importance attached to the various unions is partly revealed by those represented on the National Bureau: railroads, mines, electricity, public works, education, municipalities, agriculture, and two delegates from local unions of Casablanca. The National Council includes the central officers of the federations and representatives of the locals and of agricultural unions, which up to now have remained simply the rural locals.

The U.M.T. is officially a service arm of the independent unions; it represents them on government matters, training cadre, and printing the unions' daily Arabic newspaper. Legislation requires that all officers of unions be Moroccans; this law has had the effect of abolishing the old French unions.[22] As the close supervision of the meetings of the unions suggests, it seems unlikely that any important decisions are made without consultation with or previous clearance from the U.M.T. As in the Istiqlal, this strong supervisory authority no doubt extends to the collection of dues and election of officers, though the

[22] O.B., no. 2339, August 23, 1957, "Dahir no. 1-57-119 du 18 hija 1376 (16 juillet 1957) sur les syndicats professionnels," pp. 1110-1112.

leaders are very sensitive about any suggestion that unions are dominated by the U.M.T.[23]

Dues are a hundred francs a month and the U.M.T. officials claim that members purchase an average of nine stamps for their union cards each year. Like the Istiqlal, the U.M.T. is reluctant to publicize its financial system, but a rough estimate can be made. Since most industrial and government workers have regular incomes and are under regular supervision by union officials, it is probably reasonable to estimate that 300,000 persons pay dues at the suggested rate. This gives the U.M.T. an income of approximately $600,000 a year or slightly more than that of the Istiqlal. This amount in excess of the Istiqlal's is even more likely because of the party's arrangement of charging half-dues to union members. Union officials claim that members are expelled if they do not pay their dues for two or three months. This penalty probably varies considerably among unions and industries. Where the U.M.T. is strong, failure to pay dues may mean losing one's job. Where work is seasonal or uncertain, local union officials are probably much more lenient. The check-off collection system has been rejected because it might give the government leverage over the unions in some cases and also because it might be considered as a tax by union members. The U.M.T.'s argument denotes both suspicion of the government and conformity to the level of understanding of its members.

The rural influence of the U.M.T. is considerably less than its urban influence. In a country where roughly four fifths of the population are in the countryside, the unions may find their importance increasingly diminished as the rural population becomes more active. The vast proportion of the rural population consists of small landowners. The Ministry of Labor conservatively estimates that there are 88,000 regularly hired farm workers,[24] of whom about three fourths are concentrated in the intensively farmed regions of the Gharb, Chaouia, and Doukkala plains and Meknes. The original *dahir* on union organization exempted farm workers, though many

---

[23] See Ben Seddik's reply to this inquiry in Lacouture, *op.cit.*, pp. 303-304. U.M.T. officials are not clear on this point. As the Istiqlal leaders will say that the central party headquarters makes decisions of "national" concern, so the union leaders submit that matters concerning all the "working class" are reserved for final judgment by the U.M.T. central organs.

[24] *Le Maroc au Travail*, *op.cit.*, p. 29. The most common estimate is that about one million families occupy five million hectares of arable land, while about one hundred thousand families are supported by about one million hectares of land owned by French and Moroccan large landowners.

labor agreements were made in the early months of independence under Protectorate legislation. Full property rights were not extended to rural unions until the law on union formation in mid-1957, which gave the unions not only corporative status but also opened up the possibility of using the unions as a device of collective agricultural enterprise.[25] The Table of Union Membership (Table 11) suggests that approximately 70,000 rural workers are now organized,[26] but it is not possible to judge if their solidarity and support of the U.M.T. approaches that of the large urban unions. The U.M.T. is now working to provide rural workers with vacation rights, warnings before layoffs, annually limited working hours, seniority rights, and minimum work rights in the event of bad-weather layoffs. Thus far legislation has provided them with daily hour limits, minimal working conditions, maternity benefits, and accident benefits similar to those of urban workers, but not the family allowances and state insurance of urban workers.[27]

The most controversial area of union organization has been the civil service and the forces of order, particularly the police. One of the first public attacks made on a high government official was over an attempt to prevent the U.M.T. from using the new labor exchange in Kenitra in the summer of 1956. Both Bekkai and the Secretary General of the government, Bahnini, were bitterly criticized by the U.M.T. for allegedly delaying the formation of the civil service unions having equal rights with other workers.[28] Early in 1957 the question of union rights for civil servants was raised again with less vehemence when the law on professional unions was being studied. During the work on this *dahir* the U.M.T. proposed a single civil service federation and appealed eloquently for equal treatment of all Moroccans. But the *dahir* on professional unions proved to be far short of U.M.T. desires. While it provided that "unions can be

---

[25] *O.B.*, no. 2339, August 23, 1957, *op.cit.*, pp. 1110-1112. The *dahir* specifically provides for rental or purchase of machines, fertilizer, seed, plants, animals, and feed as union property.

[26] The figures of Table 11, if biased, favor the rural union membership. Several of the rural locals are not in agricultural regions and are probably mostly town workers not included in federations. The frequent claim of the U.M.T. to 200,000 rural unionists is undoubtedly an exaggeration, as demonstrated by its own figures and announced goal of recruiting 100,000 rural workers.

[27] Interview with Mohammed Abdelrazak, Secretary, Federation of Electrical Workers, Moroccan Federation of Labor, Casablanca, May 27, 1958.

[28] See *Al-Istiqlal*, October 12, 1956, p. 10; October 26, 1956, p. 5; and October 19, 1956, p. 5. This intense attack coincided with the effort of the Istiqlal to replace the Democratic party ministers in October 1956 and diminished after the change of government.

created among civil servants,"[29] nothing was said concerning their right to strike or to encourage the formation of a single, governmental federation. In a press conference the Minister of Labor, Ibrahim, confirmed that no strike privileges had been extended to civil servants and that the problem would be handled in a forthcoming *dahir* on the civil service itself. Such a *dahir* had not appeared by early 1959, but a decree was promulgated in February 1958, forbidding civil servants to strike.[30]

The professional union *dahir* also barred unions from the "forces of order," which include the *gendarmerie* of the Ministry of the Interior, the Sûreté National, and the Royal Army. This was an even more serious defeat than rejection of a single union organization of civil servants. The police had already been organized in a federation and were still considered as one by the U.M.T., although officially the union had been dissolved. Not only are the police one of the largest groups of easily organized and well-paid civil servants, but many of them come from the urban resistance, as do many workers, and very likely they could be made into one of the strongest unions of the U.M.T. It is perhaps in acknowledgment of the working-class loyalties of the police that their union formation has been discontinued. The U.M.T. has constantly made vigorous attacks on the administration of the police. It once made the ominous comment that the police supervisors "might oblige us to combat them with the same vigor as we have the Protectorate."[31] During the labor unrest of the summer of 1958 the intervention of the police in both Rabat and Casablanca inflamed these feelings. These events were accompanied by the detention of Ibrahim, one of the most outspoken critics of the Balafrej government, for questioning on his sources of income. He was reportedly released only after the intervention of the Palace and he published a vehement open letter to Balafrej in the union paper.[32] In early 1959 police still joined the U.M.T. individually through local unions.

The U.M.T. has always been prepared to criticize the government freely despite its close association with the Istiqlal and the ministers

---

[29] *O.B.*, no. 2339, *op.cit.*, p. 1110.

[30] Interview with Naceur Bel Larbi, Director of Civil Service, Rabat, November 22, 1958. Union officials still claimed that government workers could strike. Hachimi Bennani, the U.M.T. chief for Rabat, in an interview, September 26, 1958, submitted that the successful walkout during the general strike of June 5, 1958, proved this.

[31] Quoted from *At-Taliâ, L'Action*, June 10, 1957, p. 6.

[32] See *Le Monde*, September 23, 1958, p. 5.

from the party. It supported the Istiqlal against the Democratic party ministers in the first Council of Government and directed its criticisms particularly toward Boutaleb, the Democratic party's Minister of Labor and Social Affairs. The U.M.T.'s detailed rejection of Boutaleb's proposed Labor Code is testimony to the excellent preparation of the union leaders.[33] Although the Labor Code had been endorsed by the King, it was flatly rejected in favor of separate legislation on various union problems. The unions objected most strongly to clauses giving the Minister of the Interior the right to dissolve unions where public order was threatened and they insisted that any restriction of union rights must be done through the Ministry of Justice and appropriate courts.[34] Since then individual pieces of legislation have been agreed upon, establishing a system of labor courts, basic union rights, collective conventions, professional unions, and minimum wages. Other laws are administered by the Ministry of Labor to inspect working conditions and to control child labor and women's working rights. The U.M.T.'s insistence that it have complete authority over the selection of workers to be hired or released has evoked charges of veiled "imperialism" from the largely French-owned factory managements. Machinery for negotiating collective conventions was stalemated for a whole year[35] when the government intervened to form a Superior Council for Collective Conventions to establish industrial patterns for the conventions. The new Council received the blessing of the King, who attended its first meeting, but it was soon paralyzed by the controversies of late 1958.

Criticism by the U.M.T. has by no means been limited to comments about conventional union activities. Though the U.M.T. maintains that its political role is concerned only with advancing working-class interests, the union has frequently attacked individuals in the government and has freely expressed its opinions on nearly all major national issues. That the U.M.T. has behaved rather like a union of an industrialized country may suggest a very similar national role for it. This would be a reasonable conclusion if Morocco possessed a political system comparable to that of an advanced na-

[33] See particularly the letter of Bouazza, *Al-Istiqlal*, October 27, 1956, p. 3.

[34] See, for example, the letter to the Secretary General of the government, *Al-Istiqlal*, October 26, 1956, p. 5. In this respect the unions asked for and received rights that had not yet been given even to political parties. The *dahir* on civil liberties and right of assembly to cover party behavior only began to be studied in the summer of 1958.

[35] The Ministry of Labor review, *Le Maroc au Travail*, published in April, 1958, noted only rural collective conventions and gave no completed conventions for urban unions or federations.

tion. Actually, neither political nor economic affairs are so specialized in Morocco, where the few large organizations tend to hold a disproportionate influence not only over their own members, but also in their unilateral capability to exercise influence on the national level. A more obvious analytical error is to impose criteria of popularity in evaluating such groups in new countries. A less apparent one is the similar assumption that the members themselves participate individually in politics in a way comparable to union members in advanced countries. For this reason the constant reiteration of the patriotic devotion of the workers and frequent tributes to the King in union speeches and documents have special significance. The detailed objections and claims of the U.M.T. are probably not understood by most laborers, but they do know the meaning of nationalist fervor. The specific disputes are disassociated from nationalist slogans, but major policy differences are accompanied with assertions of the sacrifice and patriotism of the working class. The subtle difference that erupted in the summer of 1956 is evidence of the increasing tensions of the preceding three years, which came to a head in the formation of the program of the Balafrej government. To trace how this division occurred is easier than to explain how the split could have been avoided.

The basic differences between the U.M.T. leaders and the elder Istiqlal chiefs were evident from the time of independence. Shortly after the Franco-Moroccan Agreement Ben Seddik declared: "For us it is now a matter of establishing in this country a concrete democracy, the essential condition of effective independence. Not a formal and judicial democracy, but a real democracy, based on equality of classes and a just division of wealth. Above all it is a matter of putting to an end the oppression and the exploitation which is characteristic of the colonial regime and of definitively liquidating the after-effects of an irrational economic system, based on privilege and exploitation."[36] Immediately after independence it was agreed that only by increasing total production could living standards be raised. Since active and effective leadership of the unions was a reality, it was only a question of time as to how long the U.M.T. would permit others to shape Morocco's political and economic future. The first breakdown took place in the fall of 1956 when the U.M.T., like the Istiqlal, found its expansion blocked in some areas by conservative rural administrators. The National Coun-

[36] Al-Istiqlal, March 30, 1956, p. 8.

cil meeting of the summer of 1956 called for an austerity policy and more governmental direction of economic development.[37] Although on the whole these statements constituted merely a protest document, the motions left no doubt about the U.M.T.'s more aggressive economic program, which included state operation of firms closed since independence, nationalization of mines and railroads, and new regulations on prices and wages.

The King's reluctance to change the Council of Government only a few months after independence unleased an intensive attack, which was one of the most eloquent portrayals of the activist opinion among the nationalists. In a letter to Bekkai, Ben Seddik wrote: "It is sclerosis which is the threat to our administration. That which, until lately, personified the Protectorate (has it not, in fact, all the powers?) has not been able to resolve itself to adapting to the new times. . . . The menace thus remains. It is necessary to avoid it by putting at the disposition of their original administration those, happily of small number, who wish to edify the new Moroccan administration on the volcano of the ancient Protectorate."[38] With the change of government in October 1956 the union softened its criticism. The importance of increasing production, replacing French industrial cadre, and designing an economic plan were stressed. As the concrete accomplishments of the U.M.T. multiplied in the spring of 1957, emphasis was put on the need for a purge, objections to foreign troops, and insistence on the complete "reorientation" of the economy: "The working class, which knew the necessary price at the moment of armed revolt is still the first line of defense against plots. It has known to make the effort needed to increase productivity, whose level has not satisfied the owners of firms. It has known to be flexible in its vital claims in order that malintentioned types cannot use these claims as a pretext to suspend commercial or industrial activity and paralyze the country. In spite of all this the situation has only become worse."[39]

The predominantly Istiqlal government during 1957 did not escape U.M.T. criticism, though labor disputes were much less frequent than in 1956. The government was criticized for failing to give priority to training Moroccan skilled labor, to "Moroccanize" the administration, and to detect plots from abroad to preserve economic and military privileges of the Protectorate. By 1958 the U.M.T.

[37] *Ibid.*, August 24, 1956, p. 5.   [38] *Ibid.*, October 12, 1956, p. 10.
[39] Quoted from *At-Taliâ, ibid.*, March 9, 1956, p. 5.

seemed convinced that "a vast plot [had] actually been prepared against Morocco by foreign powers."[40] May Day, 1958, came in the midst of the crisis during the formation of the Balafrej government. The King reaffirmed his belief in the importance of the workers' being organized in a single movement and outlined his intention to work toward a complete system of social security, but he cautioned the workers that production must be maintained and that, in order to attract investment, all foreign property in Morocco should be respected. The crisis of early 1958 continued to worsen and the U.M.T. went into full opposition to the Balafrej government. The opinion of the discontented union leaders was probably best summarized by Ibrahim: "The end of the Protectorate has marked the beginning of independence, but independence is not liberty. In effect, if the responsibilities of power are in our hands, if theoretically the means of combat which we have are more important . . . , if in different areas we have obtained nonnegligible success, it remains no less that our economy, as under the Protectorate, is in the hands of others and our currency is subordinated to another currency; it remains that the vital sectors of Moroccan economy are under foreign bondage, that the national administration is directed by non-Moroccans, the physical energy of the nation is dissipated, the standard of living lowers day by day, while foreign troops occupy the country and daily defy its wish, and that schemes repeat themselves and build up to install here a new Protectorate."[41] Though speaking to young militants of the U.M.T. youth organization,[42] this statement included most of the reforms that inspired U.M.T. opposition over the summer of 1958 and the eventual split of the Istiqlal. The vast majority of the workers probably did not understand such complex economic problems, nor did the U.M.T. itself publish any detailed plan as to how Ibrahim's goals might be achieved. Nevertheless, this does not obviate the fact that the appeal could be made effectively in the new political system and that these goals continue to have considerable meaning for many influential and articulate political participants.

[40] *At-Taliá* editorial, *Al-Istiqlal*, January 18, 1958, p. 5.

[41] *Ibid.*, June 22, 1958, p. 8.

[42] The U.M.T. has its own youth group outside the Istiqlal youth groups. Officials estimate it at 10,000 (interview with Seddiki Said), but it is probably nearer 5,000. It is concentrated mostly in the cities and probably one half in Casablanca. This labor organization of a large group of the most active urban youth is, of course, another way in which the urban organization of the Istiqlal is reduced and made dependent on U.M.T. cooperation. The party probably also loses many potential party workers also.

The international policy of the U.M.T. also suggested both its willingness to dissent from the official line of the government and its reasons for such dissension. The difference was one of timing more than ultimate policy, for Morocco has evolved over two years a foreign policy similar to that advanced by the U.M.T. shortly after independence. Through its contacts with the Tunisian and Algerian unions, shortly after the Franco-Moroccan Agreement, the U.M.T. proposed more coordinated support for the Algerian Liberation Front and common planning for economic development of North Africa. By the end of 1956 the U.M.T. had opposed the unloading of French military supplies and troops in Morocco. At the same time plans began for a confederation of the North African unions, which materialized in the Tangier unionists' conference late in 1957. In 1957 the U.M.T. extended its objections to foreign troops by refusing to unload American air-base supplies. In the course of these events the unions were committed firmly to Algerian independence and the expulsion of all foreign troops, while the official policy was still one of firmness and negotiation. The policy of nondependence, which was devised in late 1957, tacitly recognized the demands of the U.M.T., though the union leaders remained very critical of the Ministry of Foreign Affairs.

In 1958 the fight over Ifni, the Sakiet affair in Tunisia, and the "13th of May" uprising in Algeria played into the U.M.T. hand. The U.M.T. leaders were active in the Tangier meeting of the three North African nationalist movements and became more outspokenly neutralist.[43] As conditions in the Arab world worsened with the Lebanon occupation and the Iraqi revolution, the U.M.T. policy was increasingly vindicated. The union was particularly critical of the Foreign Ministry over its slowness in recognizing the new Iraqi government. The ill-timed and poorly announced transfer of an American air base to S.A.C. produced new demands to evacuate foreign troops. Morocco's adhesion to the Arab League and recognition of the Algerian government-in-exile followed the lead of union policy, though these events came about only after two years of crisis and futile negotiation. The U.M.T. could point with some justification to its foresight and clairvoyance as contrasted with the hesitancy of more conservative opinion. That the unions did not have the re-

---

[43] See their reaction to Gaillard's Mediterranean Pact plan in *L'Action*, March 17, 1958, p. 11, and to the European common market, *Al-Istiqlal*, February 8, 1958, p. 3, editorial from *At-Taliâ*.

sponsibilites of the King and the government in the transitional period is easily overlooked in retrospect and very possibly not understood by many Moroccans.

Labor Solidarity Bows to Politics

There had never been any doubt of Ben Seddik's preference for the more progressive wing of the party. How successful the U.M.T. National Bureau had been in propagating its opinions among union members, however, has never been clear. Over the summer of 1958 the strikes took on increased political significance within the party structure, since the U.M.T. was not giving the Balafrej government as much cooperation as it had given Bekkai. The departure of Ben Seddik and Taib Bouazza from the Political Committee in May 1958 provided grounds for wide speculation concerning the formation of a new leftist party. The usual assumption was that such a new party would carry with it the membership of the trade unions. The large amount of unemployment had obvious repercussions on the strength and persuasiveness of the U.M.T. There were also some historic trouble spots, like Khouribga, Djerada, and Casablanca, which were distinguished largely by their early industrialization and early union organization. The curious aspect of the U.M.T. split was that trouble began among these workers.

Available evidence suggests that the dissension within the trade-union movement was not over any fundamental policy disagreement, but over the way in which its internal affairs were conducted. An almost ironical feedback of the extension of institutional influence among the workers via trade-union organization was that apparently they developed an understanding of institutional procedures and resented unfair manipulation of the union. The split of the U.M.T. among the Casablanca port workers before the Istiqlal split further substantiates this conclusion. Injustices by the union organization were the major grievances, although with the division of the Istiqlal there were many accusations of political abuse by union officials. Not too surprising was the large number of Rabat unions, many that had been involved in the Jorio split of 1956, who were the first to leave the U.M.T. in early 1959. In these cases and also generally in cases throughout the country, it was usually the small minority of highly skilled workers who took the opportunity to leave the U.M.T. They were, on the whole, workers having higher standards of living, more skill, and probably more education than those who remained with the U.M.T. in the first round of the division.

The first U.M.T. split took place in Casablanca, the historic center of Moroccan union activity. Many of the events coincide with major points in the general governmental crisis of the fall. For example, Ibrahim was detained at the time of a threatened strike in Casablanca of all municipal transport workers and was released at the same time as the U.M.T. and the Istiqlal agreed to submit their differences to a party congress. Of less doubtful political significance, however, is the marked increase in strikes after the detention of Ibrahim and the publication of his acrimonious attack on the government in the U.M.T. newspaper. Shortly after this affair two serious strikes of the superphosphate workers and the marine workers of Safi began. Each strike increased the bitterness between the forces of order and the U.M.T. The police intervened forcefully in the Safi strike, as had been done in Rabat the preceding summer. The U.M.T. charged that there were forces of division working in the nationalist movement, whose purpose was to promote mass disinterest in politics and to leave the way open for a political savior. This was only the beginning of a humiliating attack on the Balafrej government, but by late October 1958, when the full attack was made, the U.M.T. may easily have been more concerned over its own solidarity than over the policy of Balafrej.

There was only a small warning of the internal trouble. The U.M.T. had held a meeting of all union officers shortly after the formation of the Balafrej government. The main theme of the meeting had been that workers must remain vigilant against "maneuvers and provocations of colonialist capitalists, whose purpose is to sow seeds of division and doubt within the working class." Ben Seddik spoke of a "vast plot fomented by capitalism to destroy the U.M.T.," but this was certainly not a new charge.[44] With the advantage of historical hindsight, it can now be said that it may have been that the leaders of the union were not only concerned at this time with planning a campaign against Balafrej, but also with signs of unrest in their own ranks. In late September there were several serious clashes between police and strikers in Casablanca. Bouabid intervened personally at the last moment to avert a strike of the port workers, but his effort proved fruitless. Simultaneously, there were two violent

[44] *Al-Istiqlal,* June 1, 1958, p. 7.

clashes with the police at striking factories in Casablanca, where over a hundred workers and police were hurt.

The scale of these incidents as well as the threat of tying up the vital port of Casablanca led to a meeting between union officials and the King. These incidents also evoked the Istiqlal's second public disapproval of the U.M.T. The party criticized the irresponsible use of the strike, saying: "These incidents, which are multiplying all over Morocco, transform the least significant social conflict into an open conflict between the forces of order and the workers. . . . The right to strike includes as a corollary respect for liberty to work. To wish to impose one's wish by brutality is a proof of weakness. . . . The workers should themselves make the distinction between syndicalist action with a view toward the realization of just claims and sterile agitation, which, in sapping strength at the same time saps all chance for the improvement of the country."[45] This general position had been supported by the government also, which had intervened with Bouabid in the labor crises of late September. The official spokesman of the Ministry of the Interior suggested that there might have been some foul play. He stressed the guarantee against violence and arbitrary rule given to all people by the government and added: "Each individual in a modern country is, at all times and absolutely, free to choose between work and strike. He should not be uneasy on this subject, nor submit to constraint or, the most important reason, to conditions on his free choice."[46] The Ministry stated that both judicial and police methods would be used to see that this guarantee was preserved, which, in effect, removed the official sanction that had been given to a single union organization. The firmness of the government no doubt infuriated the union leaders, but the provocation for the government's action was not revealed until the Casablanca port workers' dispute.

The port dispute began over a simple controversy concerning the firing of a single worker in September 1958. Over the next two months it multiplied into a full-scale battle between Old Guard and progressive forces of the Istiqlal.[47] The controversy began in mid-

[45] *Ibid.*, October 4, 1958, p. 14. It is probably only fair to mention here that the Istiqlal had not made this complaint on other occasions when coercion and violence worked to its advantage.

[46] See *La Vigie*, September 26, 1958, p. 1.

[47] It is probably only due to the party conflict that a full account is available, and the extreme circumstances under which it was publicly discussed suggest that the less-heated conditions formerly prevailing might very easily have kept abuses from public notice. There are three major articles on the dispute in *Al-Istiqlal*, as well

September when the workers objected to hiring a port worker of foreign nationality. The protest was presented by the leader of the opposition group in the U.M.T. Port and Dock Workers Federation. The U.M.T. ordered the firing of the dissident union member; this order, in turn, unleashed the demand by the entire federation for a new union election. It is claimed that a majority of the members met at the federation's office to demand a new election, which was impossible because the U.M.T. refused to supervise such an election, as was required. A strike began the next day and continued for three days as protest against the arbitrary action of the U.M.T. Several men on the picket line were wounded, allegedly by laborers sent by the U.M.T. to break up the strike and by the repulsion of nonstrikers trying to enter the dock area on U.M.T. orders.

The U.M.T. next officially requested the workers to return to their posts, but they refused to obey. Ben Seddik even went to the port and promised before a hostile crowd of laborers that new elections would be held. The government's position was explicitly of double intention, for the government was also determined to allow the workers loyal to the U.M.T. and willing to work to enter the docks. The U.M.T. National Bureau agreed to the new secretary proposed by the majority, and the strike was ended. But two days after work was resumed, the U.M.T. announced that it had rejected the secretary elected by the majority of the workers because he was of partial French parentage. During October the representatives of the protest group appealed to the supervisor of docks, but under existing regulations nothing could be done legally without the U.M.T.'s assent. The U.M.T. had legality on its side for the moment and received official assurance that its men would be permitted to work under the ruling of the Ministry of the Interior. The excluded workers had no legal recourse and proceeded to petition the governor of the city of Casablanca and the King to intervene on their behalf. If the U.M.T. had been content to discontinue its struggle with the opposing faction, it could have had the official support of the government and might have recruited enough new dock workers to replace the dissenters.

---

as many short items from local newspapers. The material from the party newspaper is from October 4, 1958, p. 14; December 6, 1958, p. 14; and December 27, 1958, p. 14. They are, respectively, a chronology of events, a letter from Douiri in reply to an attack in *At-Taliā*, and a letter from the new port workers' federation shortly after it was organized.

In the meantime, the bitterness between the Balafrej government and the U.M.T. worsened. There was also a strike of textile workers in Fès, and the officers of the Khouribga miners' union were replaced as signs of dissension in the U.M.T. ranks appeared there. The U.M.T. launched a new attack on the "traitors" at the port, expelled the leaders of the opposition, and blamed the discontent again on foreigners trying to impinge the U.M.T.'s reputation. The government then decided to conduct an official inquiry into the dispute, and the opposition workers held a rally to demonstrate their strength late in November 1958. Approximately two thirds of the dock workers attended. The U.M.T. introduced in the meeting about five hundred loyal workers from other factories. Several people were wounded in the resulting scuffle, when the U.M.T. tried to disrupt the meeting and threatened violent retaliation against any workers trying to split the longshoremen's federation. The official inquiry apparently proceeded as planned and in mid-December an autonomous federation of dock workers was formed. The U.M.T. attack on Balafrej was immediately extended to include all the ministers loyal to him. The convergence of events at this moment also resulted in Ben Barka's departure from the party's Executive Committee. The lines for the party split were firmly drawn.

The dispute among the Casablanca dock workers had, of course, been replete with charges of inefficiency, neglect, and abuse. These cannot be substantiated, but the sheer fact that a majority of the workers were sufficiently aroused to carry out the scission lends some credence to their grievances. The extreme measures to which the U.M.T. went to prevent the split in its ranks also suggests something of the tactics it may have used to maintain unity. There were no more signs of tension in public until the split of the party. Early in the party split Balafrej hinted that there might be discontent within the U.M.T. rank and file. The Old Guard of the Istiqlal may well have anticipated trouble with the U.M.T. for at least a year and, therefore, may have been trying to martial some labor support. The leaders of the Istiqlal said little about splitting the union movement immediately after the Istiqlal schism. When asked about starting autonomous unions, Al-Fassi replied by attacking the U.M.T. for not holding its Congress as announced and for not having had elections for the National Bureau since 1955.[48] Since the Istiqlal could

[48] *Al-Istiqlal*, January 31, 1959, p. 9.

be criticized on the same grounds, this would not have been a very strong criticism in a less volatile political atmosphere. The U.M.T. was obviously the most important group in the new National Union party. The ensuing exchange is of interest not only as it reveals the heretofore concealed differences within the labor movement, but also as it demonstrates the fragility of such organizations in a rapidly changing political system. The ruthlessness with which the one-time nationalist "comrades" of the Istiqlal and the U.M.T. engaged in this new struggle is also extremely important evidence on the operation of modern nationalism and on the problems of transition in new countries.

In the early phase of the party split, the Istiqlal accused the leaders of the U.M.T. and Ben Barka of having "personal ambitions" and derided the radical Istiqlal faction for considering themselves better than the party from which they sprang. Both these propositions are of doubtful meaning in a situation of political turmoil, and the latter can be questioned on historical grounds. The party also denounced rumors that the King was preparing to reiterate his position in favor of a single labor organization, although the Istiqlal had been pleased to have this done when the party had been supported by the U.M.T. A week after the party split the Rabat section of the Teachers Federation of the U.M.T. announced its decision to become an autonomous union. They were followed by the laborers of two factories in Casablanca and the phosphate miners of Khouribga. The departure of the entire free schoolteachers' group from the U.M.T. was not too surprising, since the schools were originally financed and staffed by the Istiqlal. In the case of the Khouribga miners there was a long history of difficulties between the U.M.T. and the local workers. Each of these schisms was accompanied by a petition revealing alleged malpractices and neglect by the U.M.T. The small autonomous unions were free, of course, to reorganize under the *dahir* on professional unions and to enjoy all the governmental benefits that had been channeled through the U.M.T.'s National Bureau.

A week after the party split the old Istiqlal formed a Committee of Liaison and Coordination to coordinate the new autonomous unions. The U.M.T. was denounced as "antinational and antisyndicalist" for allowing political interests to take precedence over workers' needs and for having denied the workers participation in union decisions. The party also made a big point of the omission of Article 87 from the Moroccan version of the International Labor Code,[49] which the Minister of Labor and Social Questions had submitted for ratification in 1957. The omitted article guarantees the workers against prejudice as a result of union activity and complete freedom in selecting or constituting a trade union. Since the new President of the Council, Ibrahim, was Minister of Labor and Social Questions when the Labor Code was ratified, the charges also reflected on his execution of office. The Istiqlal did not explain, however, why they had permitted this oversight two years previously or, alternatively, their ignorance of a matter which they now claimed to be of crucial importance to the labor movement.

The new committee for the autonomous unions was formed under Istiqlal sponsorship and, of course, could have used this provision to advantage. It continued Al-Fassi's accusations concerning the un-democratic features of the U.M.T., which it promised to rectify immediately. The composition of the committee gave some clues as to the source of union discontent. Five of the ten members were from mining enterprises. Four of these five were leaders of newly formed autonomous unions of workers for the Cherifian Phosphate Office, a semipublic corporation with large holdings around Khouribga. The enterprise was one of the oldest industrial establishments in Morocco, having been formed early in the Protectorate by the first Resident General. Its miners were among the first Moroccans to undergo industrialization and its French director had come under heavy criticism from the U.M.T. in 1956. Although a Moroccan director was appointed in 1957, signs of labor unrest had continued to appear among the phosphate miners.

The other autonomous unions formed in the first phase of the division of the nationalist party were mostly from mining, teaching, and a few factories of Casablanca. The miners' unions of Bou Arfa, Djerada, and Kachkate (Louis-Gentil) joined the Khouribga union in denouncing the U.M.T. Four more teachers' unions also succeeded in the second week of the crisis. One union of agricultural workers and several more Casablanca factories also joined the committee of autonomous unions. The construction workers' union of

[49] See *O.B.*, no. 2363, February 7, 1958, "Conventions adoptées par l'organisation internationale du travail, Dahir no. 1-57-294 du 23 joumade I 1377 (16 décembre 1957) portant ratification de conventions adoptées par l'organisation internationale du travail," pp. 235-256.

Rabat, which was the core of Jorio's strength in the trouble over the summer of 1956, also left the U.M.T. It is difficult to make an accurate estimate of the total number of union members that the U.M.T. lost over the split. While there was no evidence that a mass exodus would take place, several of the largest and more prosperous federations, mining and teaching, had been affected. From figures in Table II, a generous estimate might include all the free schoolteachers, one half of the marine, mining, and dock workers and the regular teachers, plus one fourth of the Casablanca workers in local unions—a total of 84,500 workers. Even if this amount is put at about 50,000 workers, or roughly a tenth of the U.M.T. previous membership, it is clear that the autonomous unions were able to play an active part in Moroccan politics.

The positions of the two Istiqlal factions in early 1959 presented curious contrasts. The Old Guard Istiqlal favored a centralized party organization with a supporting, decentralized union organization. The new National Union was organized along regionally autonomous lines, but insisted on the necessity of a single, strong labor movement. To some extent the different policies were dictated by the circumstances, although they also implicitly confirm more general differences in the views of Al-Fassi and Ben Barka. In the Leader's opinion there was no sign of doubt concerning the primacy of the party and its paternal relationship to the labor movement. Though it may be argued, as in the case of the King's popularity, that the Istiqlal made vital contributions to the rise of the Moroccan labor movement, the Istiqlal could not prevent the growth of an urbanized working population. The party had the choice of accepting or rejecting the laborers, who had received their political initiation under French auspices and from French union officials over the preceding decade. The elder members of the Istiqlal were separated from the workers in much the same way as they were separated from the young generation that joined their party after World War II. The young men of both the Istiqlal and the U.M.T. put their faith in efficient organization and derived satisfaction from the accomplishment of concrete goals. They were much more "of this world," less reliant on religious appeal, and much less tolerant of status based on historical precedence or social position.

This interpretation is not necessarily contradicted by the way in which the U.M.T. split. The free schoolteachers were almost unquestionably sympathetic to the more conservative faction. The schools were founded in the 1930's by the elders of the Istiqlal and financed by them until independence. Most of the teachers probably had some religious training at an Islamic university. Many Moroccan teachers in the national school system were also from the pre-independence era and revered the scholarly leaders of the original Istiqlal elite. The case of the defecting miners and dock workers was more complex, for it would be natural to expect the laborers who had been organized for a longer time to favor the more radical and ostensibly more modern Istiqlal faction. To understand their departure it is necessary to consider the startling contrasts in social advancement among the population of a new country. These workers shared the teachers' chronological precedence in the nationalist movement. Their twenty years of experience as organized or semi-organized labor groups had given them an understanding of union procedures that was very likely superior to that of most other workers. More than most laborers, they were subject to arbitrary controls under the Protectorate and worked under particular hazards that encouraged them to develop more political maturity than did less vulnerable workers. The U.M.T.'s central authority and use of the trade unions for bargaining on the national scene resulted in neglect of the miners' and dock workers' specific grievances and frustration of their ability to handle their own affairs. The advanced workers' affinity for the elder Istiqlal group is not derived so much from fundamental agreement on program or values, but more from their disinterest in politics as a union function. The ability to distinguish national politics from laborers' needs placed them outside the range of appeal of the activist group and within the range of the more relaxed party elders.[50]

In reference to the national political system, much the same holds for the division of the trade unions as for the Istiqlal. Overlooking the specific organizational differences represented by the two groups,

[50] With the almost complete lack of information regarding Communist affiliation among the workers, the possible reorientation of Communist strength in this split cannot be carefully analyzed. It is interesting to note, however, that the workers staying with the Old Guard and the teachers in particular are generally considered to have been the main target of Communist infiltration. The teachers have frequently met Communist organizers and militants among their French colleagues. The miners and dockers were the first to be allowed to join the C.G.T. before independence. The split of the party may have meant some loss of influence for Moroccan Communists and placed the groups most closely affiliated with Communism in the Old Guard party.

one sees that the issue of the split of the workers was fundamentally one of how institutional influence should be exercised. The development of the U.M.T. since independence and the progress made in guaranteeing workers' rights was immeasurably greater than that of the political parties' progress on behalf of the general population. This is partially demonstrated by the split of the U.M.T. before the party split took place, which was done within a framework of legislation and political procedures outside general political activity and actually built up by the U.M.T. The workers were, of course, aware of the national political tension as their respective capacities and position permitted. But they had also made spectacular concrete gains since independence and were probably reasonably certain that it was the U.M.T. that had enabled them to do so. The U.M.T. leaders derived considerable strength and also took on new vulnerabilities by bringing their members more directly into national politics. If their views had not been quite so extreme and if the composition of the membership had been more homogeneous, the split might not have taken place. The national goals which the union leaders derived considerable strength and also took on new vulnera-national terms, which was magnified almost irrationally as signs of tension in union ranks grew. The institutional procedures which the U.M.T. had built up and trained laborers to use were eventually used to divide the union.

Like the Istiqlal, the U.M.T. also faced certain difficult problems in sustaining solidarity within the range of social differentiation of Morocco. The leaders had a knowledge of trade-union regulations and procedures which the bulk of their membership probably did not share. The advantageous settlement of local labor disputes and the achievement of concrete local benefits were likely to be appreciated, but the contribution of the U.M.T. to the over-all institutional progress of the nation was probably less clear. To influence all the workers, the U.M.T. needed compelling and persuasive national goals more than a union organization does in an advanced country. The U.M.T. invoked the unblemished record, endless sacrifice, and resistance record of the workers as often as the Istiqlal, if not more often. The nation lacked national institutions within which the U.M.T. could make its position more explicit, but the U.M.T. had its own institutions that enabled internal tensions to manifest themselves. With only a partially developed national network of institutional influence the unions evaded procedures of accountability. The experience of the Moroccan labor movement is important testimony to the effects of uneven institutional development in a new country and the ability it may give a relatively small group to participate forcefully in national politics. It is even more important as testimony to the difficulties of using such influence on the national level while dealing with the day-to-day problems of a new nation.

CHAPTER X

OPPOSITION POLITICAL PARTIES

Nationalists Without a Party

OVER the first three years of Moroccan independence there were five opposition parties: the Democratic party, the Communist party, the Liberal Independent party, the Popular Movement, and the National Union. Among them is found a variety of forms of opposition and a variety of origins of discontent. They reflect historical divisions of the independence movement prior to liberation, illuminate Communist tactics in new countries, and indicate the first political rumblings of a discontented rural population. Their popular strength is not great, but their activities have evoked a strong reaction from the Istiqlal. Their legal role has never been clear, and until late 1958 their activities were governed by Protectorate legislation. The confusion and hesitancy not only indicated the indecisiveness of the government, but also the difficulty of establishing a role for criticism in the new nation. The Istiqlal had difficulty in explaining procrastination and occasional ineffectiveness to its own followers. Even within the Istiqlal opposition created more embarrassment and resentment than clarification. The uncertainties raised by opposition activity contributed to the split of the party. Even if opposition took a form that was harmonious with the issues and limitations confronting the new government, or the major political party, the problem of how it was to be expressed remained. The King was largely above criticism, while the Istiqlal ministers proceeded under his supervision and in response to the initial problems of the transition.

The tendency has been for criticism to dwell on international affairs. The government has seldom released detailed information on internal affairs, and available information was often too complex to be understood by the large proportion of Moroccans. The simplified form into which the opposition had to put its criticisms made international issues attractive. It also tended to create an impasse rather than an alternative, while it risked the stimulation of inflamed popular opinion that so easily erupts into violence. The setting of a new nation permitted the opposition to engage in a kind of opportunism, also found in the Istiqlal. Goals were sometimes completely reversed or patently impossible suggestions were made. Without effective means of cross-examination or without a check on potential hypocrisies by the members themselves, political parties may become a hazardous luxury or perhaps a meaningless squabble. Since the small parties lacked the organization, personnel, and access to government of the Istiqlal, they were even more tempted to rely on mass meetings and emotional appeal. The opposition was possibly more sensitive to public opinion than was the Istiqlal, which had the militants and opportunity in the government to form rather than follow public opinion. The surprising similarity of the programs of the opposition was partially a manifestation of this circumstance, which was evident not only in the goals of the minor parties but also in criticisms presented by the U.M.T. and the Istiqlal dissident group.[1] In a social setting where political participation was limited and problems were oppressively obvious, all the opposition sounded strangely alike.

However, the usefulness of the opposition should not be lightly dismissed. In several instances the Democratic party was instrumental in revealing local administrative abuses that might otherwise never have received attention. The ambivalence of the new government regarding the entire issue of the opposition is itself a question that has long merited attention. With a few exceptions the opposition groups managed to keep a certain amount of popular concern focused on this problem. Some provision eventually had to be made for opposition political groups, even if it was only the frank admission that they had no useful purpose. Actually, the efforts of the small parties to expose cases of arbitrary use of authority by rural officials and the police may have served to make the government cognizant of malpractices that might otherwise have remained unknown. One of the most serious problems in the development of the new administration has probably been the establishment of known procedures of accountability for minor officials, without which further institutional progress would have been difficult. Some of the critics' arguments presented real alternatives and no doubt represented segments of public opinion that very likely would otherwise have been ignored.

In the study of the emerging political system in Morocco the reaction of the Istiqlal and the King to the opposition groups was often more instructive than the actual policies and actions of the small

[1] See the similar comment by Lacouture, *Le Maroc à l'Epreuve, op.cit.*, p. 166.

303

parties. The Istiqlal generally refrained from comment on the opposition through party channels, though it enjoyed other advantages from its influence in government. When the party did launch an attack, its content revealed a sensitivity to criticism comparable to the official reaction to criticism from the foreign press. Istiqlal restraint was partly due to the difficulty in dealing with criticism on the party level while participating in the government and also to an awareness that sophisticated replies would not reach the persons for whom the opposition originally fashioned their objections. The Istiqlal reaction was, thus, an admission that any unrestrained minority party could be extremely effective in undermining the popularity of the major nationalist party. Like the original appeal of the opposition, the Istiqlal had to phrase its reply in terms that would reach the population and that would be persuasive. This can lead to a barrage of increasingly exaggerated positions and more highly generalized slogans until the forces of order intervene, as was the case with the outlawing of the Democratic party early in 1958. The political system as a whole could not respond to minor differences of opinion, which lacked persuasiveness and meaning, but it was also insufficiently developed to construct compromises over large differences of opinion, which might end in violence.

During these years the King has tried to remain the mediator in the disputes among Moroccan political parties. His inclusion of the Democratic party in the first Council of Government and later the ministers of the Liberal Independent party in the second Council of Government gave them considerable prestige and a claim to a national existence that would otherwise have been difficult to establish. The important posts given to the Democratic party in the first government could be justified by the party's efforts to hasten the King's liberation. The Liberal Independents were given controversial positions, the civil service and the army, in which the Palace had a particular interest. The King has been devoted to his loyal friends, even at the risk of criticism, as was demonstrated by his continued display of confidence in the leaders of the Popular Movement after their party had been officially banned. Though both this new party and the Democratic party were in disrepute with the Istiqlal in early 1958 and had been officially disciplined by the Ministry of the Interior, Mohammed V continued to acknowledge them and consulted them during the cabinet crises of April and May 1958 and on other occasions. His actions were no doubt motivated by his repeatedly stated desire to lead Morocco into some form of representative government and also his conviction that every effort should be made to preserve national harmony. This theme is found in many of his speeches, but was most emphatically stated during a special visit he made to the Consultative Assembly in mid-1957: "The members of the National Consultative Assembly should be convinced of the idea that we are all, King, government and people, in the same boat. There is no distinction among the different members of our Moroccan community. . . . They should . . . choose between two attitudes: to give strong support to the government, its action and its policy or to criticize it well. But in this case their criticism should be the stamp of honesty, of sincerity and of disinterest. It should be, in addition, constructive and accompanied with suggestions tending to present another policy and to demonstrate that it could give concrete results. . . . We have put you on guard . . . against negative criticisms that only lead to confusion. The country requires the mobilization of all its energy."[2]

The statement reflects the tolerance that enabled the opposition to exist and helped sustain its prestige under attack from the Istiqlal. Whether or not the information and institutions are available for them to play a useful role in the future is doubtful. With the problems of a minor party within the Moroccan political system during these early years of independence, it is further questionable if they would have chosen to be limited to this role even if the opportunity had existed. Since even the Istiqlal found itself fatally divided in trying to follow the King's advice, it is doubtful if any minor party would have survived while restraining itself in such a well-tempered fashion. The Istiqlal replied to the opposition when its governmental policies were sharply attacked or when its organization was seriously jeopardized. The superiority it enjoyed both through its contacts in the government and through its large organization tended to make further effort unnecessary and possibly hazardous because it might have drawn attention to the opposition. If the opposition parties have not confined themselves to the careful role suggested by the King, it should also be acknowledged that neither has the Istiqlal. The party had to appeal to Moroccans in roughly the same way, often with extremely emotional arguments that were far removed from the current problems of the country. Aside from the advantage of being

[2] *C.M.*, June 10-12, 1957, p. 1, and Annex II. The Democratic party is represented in the Consultative Assembly.

in the government, the Istiqlal was left with much the same way of exercising influence as the opposition parties.

On one occasion it was even suggested that it was conceivable that the Istiqlal might carry its actions to the point of violence, which has so frequently taken place over minority party activities. Significantly, this was in the summer of 1956 when the Istiqlal was waging an unsuccessful battle to gain control of the Council of Government. Speaking to the National Council of the party, Al-Fassi noted: "Happily, the clandestine organization of the resistance movement still exists. Its directors, who listen to me here, are among those most aware of the responsibilities that fall on them. They have not been tardy in putting an end to the dealings and pretentions of impostors and pseudo-patriots."[3] Though the Istiqlal has not been placed in the role of the opposition for long, it was possible, at least from August to October 1956, that it might be placed in such a position, had not the crisis of the Algerian leaders occurred. (It is important to note that when placed in the position of a small party in early 1959, the Istiqlal tended to behave similarly again.)

The Istiqlal's apparent disinterest in the problem of opposition parties also changed when discussions on elections began in the spring of 1957. Again the Istiqlal's claim to preeminence was threatened, though certainly not seriously, by a development of the country's institutions. Although the Istiqlal had probably lost some members in early 1957, nothing suggested that opposition parties had grown sufficiently to be a real electoral challenge. The party, however, was most cautious and wrote: "Experience proves that the first elections in a country recently liberated from foreign tutorship are always the occasion of diversions for the purpose of creating a sterile agitation to the detriment of constructive and persevering action which alone permits perfecting the liberation."[4] The statement may hold considerable truth, but it also reveals the reluctance of the dominant party to yield in even a limited way to the wishes of the minor parties.

In considering the Istiqlal's attitude toward opposition activity, however, it is important to note that elections establish the existence of an opposition in a most irrefutable way and presume that the opposition will have some protected means of expression. The party's

---

[3] *Al-Istiqlal*, August 24, 1956, p. 7ff. He later specified that such conditions now only existed in Taza and Tafilalet, regions where the party was being actively opposed by the new governors.

[4] *Ibid.*, July 20, 1957, p. 1.

response to the Popular Movement raised similar doubts as to the legitimacy and loyalty of the opposition: ". . . Responsible for destiny of our country, we will not release it to adventurers or politicians without scruples under the fallacious pretext of free political play. Also we will always make the distinction . . . between a true political party and a movement of anarchy and division."[5] Commentary of this kind has generally been accompanied with renewed allegiance to the King and tributes to the sacrifices of the party that have enabled the open political activity now allegedly being abused by the opposition. Frequently opposition groups have been belittled as "political clubs" or associated with colonialism. The stress of the Istiqlal on the need for continued solidarity has not been entirely without reason, but it has also resulted in the opposition parties' being confined to the same position in independent Morocco that the Istiqlal had under the Protectorate.

The Istiqlal presented an explanation of opposition parties and their responsibilities in the cell *Bulletin*. Adhering quite closely to the suggestions of the King, the party admitted that ". . . the opinion of a popular minority can help in achieving the general interest if it cooperates with the government in exposing the realities of the problems which the government is considering."[6] The last phrase was especially important, for it is the problems that are postponed and the laws that are not yet written which may be of primary concern to the opposition and that may also be best suited to extending the influence of a small party. The tendency to admit the existence of opposition parties and then to exclude them from any meaningful role was elaborated in the party's explanation of the "conditions" for "constructive opposition": "1) The opposition must have a defined program based upon a certain policy different from the aim or program of the government. . . . If the opposition party is unable to have a different policy, then it should not be an opposition party because the country will not gain anything. 2) The opposition must have its own methods for realizing its program. It may be easy to put forth a program or create a policy, but it may be more difficult to find the necessary means with which to achieve this. . . . 3) The opposition must be constructive . . . not using hard words that impair respect for the opposition. . . . 4) The opposition must be the product of general elections. . . . If the opposition is just depending

---

[5] *Ibid.*, November 2, 1957, p. 3.
[6] "The Government and the Opposition," no. 6, June 1957(?), pp. 1-2.

on a group of persons pretending to be a party and no opportunity has been given for the people to express their opinion toward them, they cannot be a real opposition. . . ."[7]

These criteria placed very hard conditions on the opposition and, indeed, might be considered somewhat unrealistic. In general form, most of the major problems of the new country were self-evident. The means for seeking solutions to these problems and the ways in which they might be brought to bear on any one problem were often limited. Since the priority given to goals and to the allocation of resources tended to be determined by the most pressing problems and by conditions imposed from abroad, the role of the opposition was even further restricted. That all this was extremely hard to convey to the average Moroccan was evident from the Istiqlal's own propaganda. The last qualification was undoubtedly the most restrictive, for elections had not been held (up to 1960) and the Istiqlal itself has expressed reservations on their advisability at the present time. In the absence of any legislation protecting minor parties or civil rights until late 1958, it is difficult to see how an opposition party could have been much more than a "group of persons." The Democratic party enjoyed semiofficial existence, the Communist party remained illegal, and the other parties had no official recognition until 1959. Their leaders and members had no collective rights or duties under law and as individuals were subject to serious handicaps in dealing with the government and the police.

The Democratic party was probably the largest and best-organized of the opposition. The Secretary General, Mohammed Al-Ouazzani, was one of the leading nationalists of the Protectorate. The party's roots extend back to the first nationalist activity of the early 1930's, a fact which gives it prestige and invulnerability that other parties do not enjoy. The split between the present elders of the Istiqlal and Al-Ouazzani took place in 1937, when Al-Fassi was selected as Secretary General of the nascent movement.[8] The personal dispute among the nationalist leaders continued to divide them after the World War, and in 1946 Al-Ouazzani founded the present Democratic party. In this early period the party was heavily influenced by Pan-Arab policy, derived from Al-Ouazzani's close association with

[7] *Ibid.*, pp. 1-2.

[8] See Rezette, *Les Partis Politiques Marocains*, pp. 101-103. There were twenty-one members at the Fès meeting of the Committee of Moroccan Action. Al-Ouazzani was of the opinion that Al-Fassi's background from Qarawiyn University and his inability to speak French would handicap the movement in dealing with the Protectorate.

Arslan, and, paradoxically perhaps, by intellectual "modernist" opinions derived from the French educational background of most of its early leaders. Though the Democratic party favored independence, it was willing to negotiate some kind of interim compromise.[9] A plan asking for independence in gradual stages over ten years was submitted to the Resident General in 1947. The party's conciliatory attitude was discouraged by General Juin, and by 1950 it adopted a program of full independence under Mohammed V. The Democratic party escaped the suppression of the nationalists in 1952. Since it had not developed the organization of the Istiqlal, it was little threat to French hegemony.

Al-Ouazzani fled the country and worked largely in Egypt and the Spanish zone until his return to Morocco at the end of 1956. In his absence the party was supervised by Abdelkader Benjelloun, an extremely capable lawyer of Casablanca, who helped defend arrested terrorists during the resistance period. The Democratic party was in an enviable position. The Spanish were prepared to make concessions to the Democrats in their zone to balance the Islah party and to irritate the French, while the party was still permitted to meet in the south.[10] Their privileges in the French zone enabled them to carry on some propaganda and also made them a potentially useful vehicle for Istiqlal and terrorist survival.[11] As independence drew nearer, the Spanish withdrew their support of the Democratic party in the north.[12] Like Istiqlal party members in the resistance, the Democratic party probably participated in the resistance on a nonparty basis. Not until independence did party affiliations in particular terrorist groups take on significance. The frequent assertions by the Istiqlal that the Democratic party did not participate in the resistance are probably also a product of the postresistance period, since accounts can be found of Democratic party members' being arrested for terror-

[9] Before the King became a leading symbol of the nationalist movement, the Democratic party was reportedly in favor of some type of republican government. See *ibid.*, pp. 161-162, and Pierre Parent, "Trente-Sept Ans de Maroc," *Espirit*, 21e année, February 1958, p. 211.

[10] See Rezette, *op.cit.*, pp. 230-233.

[11] See Rezette's comment on the "colonization" of the Democratic party by the Istiqlal in 1953. If this occurred, it was probably done more by the resistance movement than the Istiqlal and may have been the origin of Democratic party influence in the resistance in its early stages, *op.cit.*, pp. 358-359.

[12] *Petit Marocain*, June 16-17, 1954, p. 1. The Spanish had reportedly hoped for a separate independence movement in the north under their aegis and supported by the Arab League. The Moroccan nationalists apparently rejected this scheme at about this time.

ist activities.[13] The Democratic party leaders joined with the Istiqlal in 1955 to protest the King's exile and firmly opposed the French plan for a compromise solution.

Being a smaller party, the Democrats could make decisions more quickly than the Istiqlal, and announced their program in November 1955, a month before the Istiqlal Congress. The members recruited in the midst of the enthusiasm and confusion before the Franco-Moroccan Agreement were not well indoctrinated or organized. Though the Istiqlal was undoubtedly better known nationally, it is important to note that independence opened up completely new possibilities quite unrelated to contribution or to sacrifices during the struggle for independence. The Democratic party had participated with the Istiqlal in the negotiations, and its representatives had received roughly the same amount of publicity. Equal recognition had been given to both parties during Bekkai's negotiations for the formation of the first Council of Government, and the Democratic party received considerably more posts than its pre-1952 strength would justify.[14] The resistance and preindependence record of the parties was not clear and still remains obscure in important details. In the emerging political system the behavior of the twenty years before the repression was extremely distant and further blotted out by the virtual military occupation from 1952 to the end of 1955. In the well-known epoch leading up to the return of Mohammed V both parties had played important parts and both had been given his blessing.

The subsequent recruiting activity demonstrates that both parties were acting in a setting where problems were as yet poorly defined, where the government remained largely under the directions of the King, and where persuasiveness could easily deteriorate into violence. The competition of the parties became the struggle to see who could claim most members in the least time. For this struggle both parties lacked organization, but the Istiqlal had the advantage of a larger

[13] See *La Vigie*, April 10, 1954, p. 1, where seven party members were arrested. The police reportedly found evidence of the continuing close relations of the Al-Ouazzani and the Egyptians in documents discussing support from Egypt and the Muslim Brotherhood.

[14] There is some evidence that the Democratic party experienced the same misgivings as the Istiqlal over the distribution of cabinet posts. Unlike the Istiqlal, it did not feel compelled or perhaps was unable to air these views as the Istiqlal did in its Congress. During the formation of the cabinet there was some rather frantic travel to and from Tangier where Al-Ouazzani stayed. He later felt it necessary to deny that the Democratic party had objected or that it was divided over how to distribute cabinet seats.

number of militants and the cooperation of the U.M.T., which had an organizational framework in place. Frequent gun battles took place before the end of December 1955, and the Democratic party formally complained over the coercive recruitment methods of the Istiqlal. Tension increased as mass meetings were organized in Casablanca, Meknes, Fès, and Rabat. Apparently the breaking point was reached toward the end of January 1956, with the bloody clash of the two parties at Souk Al-Arba. A new round of accusations and counteraccusations began, in which the Democratic party protested the "fascist methods" being used by the Istiqlal. With the encouragement of the King a truce was made, but incidents of violence began again as soon as the Franco-Moroccan Agreement was signed. Democratic party militants were beaten up, its party offices burned, and new gun fights broke out as the terrorist organization was gradually assimilated into the parties.[15] The climax of these events was the assassination of the Democratic party leader of Fès and *alim* of Qarawiyn University, Abdelouad Laraki.

A second attack on the Democratic party began during the integration of the Spanish zone. In this area the Islah party, which had merged with the Istiqlal, was poorly organized and confined mostly to Tetouan. With the gains that it had made under Spanish rule, the Democratic party was very likely on roughly equal ground. The generally stronger appeal of Pan-Arabism in the north might also have worked to the Democrats' favor. The determining factor was not the program of either party, but the efforts of the still active remnants of the Liberation Army, possibly under Istiqlal influence. At least seventeen party militants disappeared over the summer of 1956.[16] They have not been heard from since and no explanations have been offered by the police. The same has been the case with subsequent acts of violence against Democratic party militants from Tangier, Taza province, and other areas. Although some of the missing persons had doubtful pasts by nationalist standards, no party has a monopoly on virtue. The Istiqlal did nothing, but protested violently in 1958 when its militants were irresponsibly abused. The kidnapings are more important as a revelation of how influence tends to be used in conditions of uncertainty and irresponsibility than as evidence of injustices that may have taken place in the new nation.

[15] For example, see *C.M.*, March 7, 1956, p. 3; March 14, 1956, p. 3; April 19, 1956, p. 2; April 22, 1956, p. 2.
[16] See first notice in *ibid.*, August 2, 1956, p. 2; the total was announced at Tetouan on August 30, 1956, *ibid.*, p. 2.

It is the difficulty of conducting open, accountable political activity that is significant in analyzing how the new political system has developed. Both parties were no doubt eager to recruit members and increase participation in the new political system, but neither had a clear conception of how popular expression could be used.

Like the dominant party, the Democratic party relied heavily on its top leaders in its early organization. At least one attended nearly every initiation of a new office. The party lacked the large number of well-qualified leaders that the Istiqlal had, and during its participation in the government there were few first-rank leaders free to devote all their time to the party. The tendency seems to have been to rely more on large rallies in the larger cities, where the Democratic ministers could easily appear. Like all minor parties the Democratic party never developed a national organization comparable to the Istiqlal. A survey of party documents reveals that most of the offices are in the cities: Casablanca, Fedala, Mazagan, Oujda, Meknes, Fès, Safi, Rabat, Salé, and Marrakech.[17] The rural regions of Democratic party activity are clustered. The ancestral home of Al-Ouazzani in the Gharb, which bears his name, is the center of one area of strength. A few offices are scattered south of the Rif Mountains and as far east as Fès. A second region of considerable activity is Chaouia province, where offices were founded at Settat, Khouribga, Benahmed, Oued Zem, and Boujad, which merges with another consistently organized area of neighboring Beni Mellal province, with offices at Kasba Tadla, Fqih Ben Salah, and Beni Mellal. Another cluster of offices is found around Midelt, where Itzer, Rich, and Ksar As-Souk have offices. The rural organization of the party had clearly relied on the ancestral and tribal connections of party leaders, which exist in each case of rural strength.

The membership of the Democratic party is certainly no more than a tenth of that of the Istiqlal—probably about 150,000.[18] During 1956 the dominant personality of the party, Al-Ouazzani, remained abroad traveling in Egypt and Syria and occasionally making trips to Tangier. In the absence of Al-Ouazzani, direction of the party rested with Abdelkader Benjelloun, who was also occupied with his government duties. The Political Bureau of the party, comparable to the Istiqlal Executive Committee, met from time to time with Al-

---

[17] *Rai Al-Amm*, Fr. Trans., from December 1, 1955, to June 30, 1956.

[18] Officials of the party claim more members than the Istiqlal, which is impossible. Indeed, all their exaggerations make it impossible to accept as credible much of their interviews. This is the same estimate as that of Lacouture, *op.cit.*, p. 158.

Ouazzani in Tangier, but on the whole the leadership of the party in 1956 appears to have been weak. The organization of the party on a national scale was delayed and perhaps prevented by the repression that began over the spring of 1956. At a National Council meeting early in August 1956, 127 sections were represented. When the Istiqlal decided to demand more cabinet posts, the Democrats called a second Council the same month and held rallies almost weekly in different areas of the country. With the North African crisis of late 1956, the sequence of high-level maneuvering followed by bursts of popular activity was curtailed for all parties. Soon afterward, Al-Ouazzani chose to return to Morocco and was received by the King early in 1957.

Lacking cadre and with distracted leadership, the party used dramatic devices to get popular support and curious alliances with other groups to bolster nationalist claims. Like other parties the Democrats sought to extend their influence in the ways and within the limitations presented by the society. To establish a national party in Morocco entailed organizing new adherents in areas where the political behavior of advanced nations is meaningless. The Istiqlal had the advantage due to its larger number of militants, the help received from the U.M.T. and the resistance, and the publicity it received in the government. The Democratic party opened its newspaper to national figures having rural influence, including Addi ou Bihi, Lahcen Lyoussi, and Dr. Khatib.[19] The Democratic party became the advocate of a "Democratic Front," which Lyoussi also advocated in his meetings with the Middle Atlas tribes. The Council of the party included a "motion" of the tribes in its conclusions and the party's leaders acknowledged their confidence in Lyoussi.[20] In Morocco's political history the Front is not important, but as the kind of tactic needed to spread the influence of a political group it is revealing. Over the rallies of the weeks before the first change of government, it was presented as the union of all forces loyal to the King and favoring "true democracy." The attempt of the Front to increase Democratic influence in the countryside by aligning tribal leaders and to neutralize the Istiqlal's appeal on the grounds of national solidarity was cut short by the international crisis. How the party tried to do this is important, though it may well be doubtful that it would have been successful even if freely continued.

[19] See interviews in *Rai Al-Amm*, August 1, 1956; June 27, 1956; and July 18, 1956, respectively, Fr. Trans.
[20] *C.M.*, August 21, 1956, Annexes II and VI.

The formal organization of the Democratic party is much like the Istiqlal, but lacks the refinement of the subsection—an indication that it has considerably fewer members to handle. The initial indiscriminate recruitment caused similar problems in both the Democratic and Istiqlal parties. In the summer of 1956 the Democrats formed provincial federations which were to be supervised by an inspector from the central office. The basic unit was a cell of about twenty members, whose directors in a given area combined to form a section council.[21] At this level the section council elects a secretary and treasurer. All these officers from a given area form the provincial bureau, where the process is repeated to choose two representatives of each provincial bureau for the National Council. For the Congress all the officers of the sections and all the members of the provincial bureaus are convened. Like the Istiqlal the Democratic party has held no Congress between the first reconstruction of the party in 1955 and the end of 1958. The Congress elects the Political Bureau of the party, which has included the same ten members since independence. Although the party started a cadre school in March 1957, it is unlikely that the school has reached the goals claimed by party leaders. As in the case of the Istiqlal, the emphasis is on general education and party indoctrination.[22] During 1958, without public meetings or newspapers, the organization seriously deteriorated and many party offices were closed.

The program of the Democratic party has surprising similarities to that of the U.M.T. Though the comment on labor problems is different, on other internal problems and on international affairs both critics have demonstrated the advantage of being in opposition where procedures of accountability are still poorly defined. Though perhaps neither the Democratic party nor the U.M.T. fully appreciate the dilemmas facing the new government, both their programs demonstrate the temptation to use dramatic issues in a way that will promote an organization. This is even more pronounced in the case of the Democratic party, which has reversed its position on several issues in trying to anticipate changes in opinion or to exploit international problems since liberation. This tactic, of course, occurs in advanced political systems too, but not in the same way. The Moroccan

[21] Interview with Abdelhadi Boutaleb, Political Bureau, Democratic Party, Casablanca, January 20, 1958, and the following organizational data.

[22] See the course outline in "Programme général provisoire de la première session des dirigéants de Casablanca," Secretariat Générale du Parti Democrate de l'Independence, Casablanca, February 4, 1957.

minor parties made policy changes in a peremptory way and with no apparent consideration of the rank and file, rather than from a reconsideration of party policy over a long period of time or in response to gradually changing interests or views of members.

The most striking example of this sort of tactic is the economic policy of the Democratic party, which is also the one involving technicalities and qualifying diplomatic conditions not likely to be understood by most Moroccans. In his speech to the National Council meeting of late August 1956, Abdelkader Benjelloun, then the Minister of Finance, maintained that sacrifices would be needed to obtain the foreign capital essential to Morocco's economic development. This policy was reaffirmed in the National Council meeting of May 1957, where it was added that the United States was the sole country able to fill Morocco's needs. A few months later, when Morocco accepted its first major loan from the United States, the party expressed fears that "national sovereignty and independence" were being jeopardized. In the fall of 1957 negotiations began for the survey and development of Moroccan oil resources by an Italian firm. The party's reaction was to suspect the company as a tool of "American high finance" that was trying to monopolize Arab oil supplies.[23] This kind of policy formation is not an exclusive characteristic of the minority parties, for cases of less marked changes can be found in the history of most Moroccan political groups, including the Istiqlal. The rapid reformulation of expectations with independence made it difficult to govern in response to popular wishes and to sustain popular interest in less dramatic but possibly more important goals. The opposition was not restrained like the Istiqlal, which had to provide at least nominal support for the Council of Government. Unchecked by responsibility or informed members, the opposition was easily tempted into opportunistic and disruptive tactics that lacked consideration of the long-run needs or of the present limitations of the new nation.

The advantage of the minority party in a new country is clearly in evidence in many other situations where the Moroccan government has been slow to act. They are all issues involving considerable

[23] *C.M.*, September 23, 1957, pp. 6-7. The Mattei oil deal was completed in 1958 after the party was silenced, so its reaction is not known. The agreement by the Minister of National Economy was published, *La Vigie*, July 27 and 28, 1958. The conditions for oil exploitation were defined by law in a special issue of the *O.B.*, no. 2369 bis, July 24, 1958. It was generally considered to be one of the most generous oil exploitation agreements in the Arab world.

popular sentiment, such as Algeria, foreign troops stationed in Morocco, relations with Egypt, establishment of "territorial unity," and "Morrocanization." The Istiqlal has had, of course, its own policies on these matters and its members in the government may very likely have gone more slowly than other Istiqlal members would have preferred. Most of these issues became increasingly important over the first three years of independence, so that by 1958 even the Istiqlal had made strong stands. The difference in the case of the Democratic party is that it was free to make such demands earlier and to take a much firmer position than those in positions of responsibility.[24] At the same time as the U.M.T. attack on keeping foreign troops in Morocco, the Democratic party printed a letter highly critical of the U.S. military "colonialism" in Morocco; this letter was followed by the motion of the National Council to evacuate all foreign troops.[25] From the time of independence the party maintained close contact with Egypt and often criticized Morocco's tardiness in establishing closer diplomatic relations with the Arab world. The Istiqlal declined participation in the Cairo Afro-Asian Conference of early 1958, where the Democratic party's delegation under Al-Ouazzani strongly supported the claim of Egypt to preeminence in the Arab world and defended the "unconditional" aid given Egypt by the Soviet Union.[26] Shortly after this, the Democratic party began organizing demonstrations in Casablanca and was forbidden to hold further public meetings.

Like Al-Fassi, the Democratic party has been extremely critical of the slow Arabization of the administration and schools and also of the failure to recover regions to the south of Morocco.[27] Perhaps the most emotional and persistent issue has been Algeria. In the summer of 1956, though still outside Morocco, Al-Ouazzani favored Moroccan armed intervention on behalf of Algeria. In the fall the party persisted in its appeal for a sympathy strike with Algeria on

[24] Again it should be cautioned that this is not a one-way maneuver. The Istiqlal criticized the Democratic party members in the first government in much the same way and raised issues that would be particularly embarrassing to them up until October 1956. The most outspoken factions within the party, such as Al-Fassi's Mauritania drive, are evidence of the same kind of phenomenon.

[25] *Démocracie*, May 27, 1957, p. 16.

[26] See the statement of Al-Ouazzani on his return. *Ibid.*, January 20, 1958, p. 4. There were also more statements about American bases in Morocco, though by this time the Istiqlal ministers were beginning to push the issue themselves.

[27] Al-Ouazzani called for integration of Ifni the month of the Franco-Moroccan Agreement. *C.M.*, March 24, 1956, p. 2.

the anniversary of her revolution, even after the strongly pro-Algerian U.M.T. had decided to bend to governmental wishes. The party renewed its pledge to Algeria in December 1956, while the government was struggling to reconstruct its rapport with France after the Meknes massacres. The Istiqlal continued to take a moderate, if not equivocal, position on Algeria during most of 1957, when the Democratic party called for "total solidarity for a single battle" and frequently welcomed F.L.N. delegates to its meetings in Casablanca.[28] There is no way to measure the effectiveness of this appeal, but it is perhaps significant that the most determined Democratic party move to exploit this issue at the Cairo Conference was not only followed by official restraint, but also by the Istiqlal's new interest in Algeria at the Tangier Conference.

The Istiqlal refrained from any direct attack on the Democratic party until 1958, though it wrote often of "colonialists' friends" and "political clubs." Sensitive problems were raised by the pro-Egyptian stand of the Democratic party. In the past an issue of the Democratic party newspaper had been seized for attacking the government's failure to relieve slum areas. But the Istiqlal had ignored the many charges of corruption and abuse of power by rural administrators; these charges claimed the summary arrest or other alleged discriminations against party militants throughout the countryside. The Istiqlal press, however, reacted to the Democratic party after the Afro-Asian Conference in Cairo and the subsequent rallies of the party in Casablanca. The Bachko meetings, named after the Casablanca *medina* where many of them were held, were denounced by the Istiqlal as seditious and a threat to the state.[29] Holding that the Istiqlal had no need to defend itself, the newspaper said that the state must take action against "sheep pastured by colonialists." The reaction of the U.M.T. was the most outspoken: "Ineptitudes of this kind would make one laugh if they did not carry very grave risk, since they proceed from the unveiled intention of misleading public opinion and have been made by types whose first concern is to sow doubt and despair among compatriots and to distract them

---

[28] *Rai Al-Amm*, January 8, 1957, Fr. Trans. See also *C.M.*, June 4, 1957, criticizing the government for signing the cultural convention with France during the Algerian struggle; also criticizing Moroccan moderation in the United Nations, *ibid.*, September 19, 1957, U.S. Trans.

[29] *Al-Alam*, January 21, 1958, U.S. Trans. For an account of how they were arranged, see *L'Action*, January 27, 1958, p. 10.

from constructive activities that the delicate circumstances now occupying the country impose on us. Truly we have pity on these individuals who, blinded by their ineffectiveness and impotence, choose, to make a profession from the opposition by selling their gelatinous conscience to the devil for destruction and putting their tainted pen in the service of foreign interests."[30] The invocation of national interest in the absence of any discussion as to how national interest is defined or how national goals may be changed was characteristic of the replies by the Istiqlal and the U.M.T. The renewed crisis in North Africa in the spring of 1958 was a partial vindication of many of the arguments that the Democratic party had put forward. The same arguments were used a year later by the progressive factions of the Istiqlal and the U.M.T. During 1959 the elder leaders of the Democratic party, including Mohammed Al-Ouazzani, gravitated toward the old Istiqlal, while the young leaders joined Ben Barka in the National Union.

The Sakiet-Sidi Youssef incident was the immediate provocation for the curtailment of party activity, which also applied to the Istiqlal. The orders were, however, much less disastrous for the largest nationalist party, which possessed an organization and governmental position to compensate for the restraints. Newspapers of the Democratic party were discontinued and public meetings were forbidden. This did not prevent Democratic party supporters from holding demonstrations in Fès, Casablanca, and Tangier, and offenders were imprisoned from three to four months. When one considers the many minor sanctions that could be brought to bear on Democratic party sympathizers, one must admit that the small meetings that took place are testimony to the party's strength. Although the activity of the Democratic party was severely restricted throughout 1958, the Political Bureau of the party was not hampered and on several occasions party leaders were consulted by the King. The party newspapers were authorized to reappear in February 1959, and organizational meetings of the party secretaries were planned.[31] Since middle ground between the positions of the two Istiqlal factions was hard to find in early 1959, now the Democratic party may well seek an even more extreme position than the new Democratic Istiqlal.

[30] *At-Talià*, editorial, in *Al-Istiqlal*, February 1, 1958, p. 5.
[31] *La Vigie*, February 15, 1959, p. 3.

Tribesmen Form a Party

Only in late 1957 did the Popular Movement emerge as a distinct political group. It remained illegal until the end of 1958. While the Democratic party relied on urban support, with a few tribal strongholds, the Popular Movement was a political expression of unquestionable rural strength and strong tribal support in many of the more retarded areas of the new country. It provides dramatic evidence of the pitfalls and opportunities of a new national political system which is developing in a society having an extremely broad range of social differentiation. With the social composition of Morocco and the stage of political organization, a party or political group tends to seek influence across the whole social spectrum of individual types. What are often distinguished as two subordinate societies in a new nation may work in harmony within a single political system and are by no means necessarily in conflict. The relationship established to increase influence on the national level may or may not be in harmony with the process of change which the more retarded members are experiencing—a secondary consideration for the moment. The relationship may also be very fragile and may quickly lose its harmonious relation to the social structures. Within the general requirements for the establishment of a nation there is, however, no necessary relation between the stage of social advancement of the members of a new nation and its national political system.

The history of the Popular Movement is also important for its demonstration of some of the problems of establishing a new party in a newly independent country, where there has been a strong nationalist movement. The Movement has been the most forceful concrete political expression of the tension that may occur between members of a new nation who are divided by vast social differences. These differences, it should again be cautioned, do not necessarily work to the detriment of either the national political system or the various societies that may be concerned. There are, nevertheless, serious difficulties in trying to establish a party on tribal loyalties and definite limitations in the kind of influence which the members of such a party can exercise or in the ways in which its leaders can organize the party itself. In the early months of the new government the Berber interests, which comprise the most intact tribes, were usually accepted as represented by Caid Lahcen Lyoussi.

Under Lyoussi's leadership the Berbers did not become a defined political group, though no doubt he laid the groundwork for the Popular Movement and personified many of the rural grievances that were later used. In the summer of 1956 the Istiqlal move to gain more control of the Council of Government had led to Lyoussi's first campaign among the Berber tribes. The Istiqlal claimed that the French were plotting to revive the old Berber policy in new form, although Lyoussi, Ahardane, and Dr. Khatib all had been above the slightest reproach in their loyalty to Mohammed V up to that time. Not until the trial of Addi ou Bihi was Lyoussi's role as interlocutor between the French and Addi ou Bihi revealed. Dr. Khatib and Ahardane were not implicated in the trial and were actually released in the midst of the proceedings. Though the plans for a rural party in 1956 cannot be documented, Lyoussi received a delegation of tribesmen from the Rif Mountains and claimed that this group of supporters would soon start a newspaper.

The Popular Movement developed slowly in 1957, when rumors of a new rural political movement were common.[32] In the meantime the leadership of the Movement had been taken on by Ahardane, then governor of Rabat province,[33] and Dr. Khatib, the former chief of the Liberation Army of the Rif. Moroccan speculation on the new political group did not appear publicly until an article in the Democratic party newspaper reported that the Popular Movement would include large rural Berber elements and be modeled after the Baath party of Syria.[34] Soon after this a curiously impatient note appeared in the same newspaper, asking for the publication of names of the leaders of the Popular Movement and reproaching it for its clandestine behavior.[35] In October 1957 the Popular Movement published its manifesto signed by a Koranic teacher, Haddou Riffi, of Rif province, but without names of its leaders. Like the doctrine of most opposition parties in Morocco, the Popular Movement included sweeping issues such as the slowness of the purge, vacillation regarding Algeria, and the presence of foreign troops.

The program was distinguished by its suggestion of a form of "Muslim socialism" and by a new union around Mohammed V as

---

[32] See *L'Action*, July 1, 1957, p. 7. In an interview with the Prince the paper's reporter asked his reaction to the rumors of a new rural party. He replied, "The formation of another movement risks being artificial."

[33] He came under fire from the U.M.T. early in 1957. See *L'Action*, February 25, 1957, p. 7. This may have been when the first moves were made to organize the new party.

[34] *Démocracie*, September 2, 1957, p. 12.   [35] *Ibid.*, October 7, 1957, p. 2.

the new *immam* or spiritual leader for all North Africa. A strong pro-Algerian proposal followed from Dr. Khatib's reluctance to discontinue the Moroccan Liberation Army's struggle to liberate all North Africa.[36] The growing resentment of the rural elements over the monopolization of the government by urban leaders was evident in the manifesto's aim "to realize equality among all social strata and to put an end to the grave differences in the standard of living."[37] Indirectly it objected to the monopoly of top governmental positions by urban Arab leaders and emphasized a desire "to put an end to all feudality under whatever appearance it may present itself." What justification these criticisms may have had is secondary to their revelation of how the new party sought to gain support and the differentiations on which it tried to build a political party. Its cautiousness was, in part, explained by the strict regulations still governing public associations and also by the risk of associating the new party with the colonialist Berber policy. The reality of tribal grievances was demonstrated a year later by the uprisings in the Rif.

The Movement was immediately banned for having organized without permission and Ahardane was removed from his post for making political statements while in high administrative office. This official action enabled the Istiqlal to portray the Popular Movement as subversive and colonialist. The Istiqlal angrily attacked those who "have not ceased to weaken national forces by divisions, disparagement or slander in order to reverse the current of history" and who "consciously or unconsciously erect ambushes and stab patriots in the back."[38] Ahardane was characterized as another Addi ou Bihi and the new party was accused of being part of a colonialist plot to recover Morocco. The Istiqlal press argued that the country should welcome administrative action to prevent "confusion in the people's minds" and reported that orders had been sent out from the Ministry of the Interior to arrest anyone found working for the Movement.[39] An article in the Istiqlal *Bulletin* alleged that the Movement was supported by members of the Protectorate regime, incapable persons from the first government, and advocates of the Berber *dahir*.[40] The fury of the attack on the new party was a good indica-

---

[36] Lacouture, *op.cit.*, pp. 160-161, notes that Ahardane was also a close friend of Ben Bella.

[37] Quoted from portion of manifesto in *L'Action*, October 14, 1957, p. 11.

[38] *Al-Istiqlal*, October 26, 1957, p. 3.

[39] *Al-Alam*, October 26, 1957, U.S. Trans.

[40] "Between Freedom and Anarchy," no. 11, November 1957(?), p. 1. It was

tion that it had potentially solid grounds for support and could become a real threat to the dominant nationalists.

The relation between the Popular Movement's program and its followers is hard to discover. This is by no means solely the case with the Popular Movement, but it is more marked here because of the idealistic Muslim socialist thread and also because the Movement spoke as much to persuade officials of its sincerity as to gain supporters. Ahardane confirmed that elements of the Movement had existed for two years and he forcefully denounced the Istiqlal device of outlawing the party under Protectorate legislation in order to brand its leaders as "traitors" and to claim for itself all patriotic honors. His cryptic observation that "we have not acquired independence in order to lose liberty" summarized the discontent of the Movement's leaders, but behind this concern was a vague but fervent doctrine derived from Islam and devotion to the King as *immam*. In modified form it might become persuasive among some rural elements, but it is difficult to see how it offers any precise solutions to Moroccan problems.

The leaders of the Popular Movement admit to being honestly frightened by the progress of Communism in countries where economic progress was made too slowly to neutralize mass discontent, and they therefore advocate the organization of a distinctly Muslim socialist system based on principles of Islam.[41] They are alarmed by the inroads that Communism is making in parts of the Moroccan government and among youth. As a solution they suggest that small countries defend their independence and religion by deriving their own doctrine and avoiding alignment with East or West. While there is a note of naïveté in this doctrine, it should also be recognized that it bears some similarity to the kind of mass enthusiasm and energy which more progressive members of the Istiqlal have tried to stimulate and direct into constructive effort. Although the Istiqlal activists do not have the same religious foundation for their doctrine or give such preeminence to the King, both the socialist

---

accompanied with a long explanation of the meaning of political freedom and argued that if personal aims or "destructive" goals were present in any party only anarchy could result. As is so often the case, the carefully simplified explanation of the party *Bulletin* contains some surprising examples. For example, here it was submitted that different parties must have their own programs and it cited "Democrats and Republicans of America and Labor and Conservative Parties in Britain." *Ibid.*, p. 2.

[41] Interview with Dr. Abdelkrim Khatib, Casablanca, July 3, 1958.

and neutralist doctrines have been advanced by young Istiqlal leaders. The leaders of the National Union defended their schism by the need for large sacrifices for the national welfare and disciplined mass action to overcome the human and physical limitations of Morocco.

Whatever was the exact discontent in the countryside that propelled the Popular Movement, it was sufficient to keep it alive during a clandestine existence throughout 1958. The King himself refused to discredit those who had fought for him in the resistance and, in his parting statement to Ahardane, noted that Ahardane had served his country well and rendered his Sovereign eminent service. The party's areas of strength in the countryside had been centers of Liberation Army activity like the Rif Mountains and the region of the Beni Snassen tribe near Oujda. Some following was also found in Casablanca, very likely among resistance members loyal to Dr. Khatib, and in the Middle Atlas, where Lyoussi had been involved with the Liberation Army. Activity was also reported north of Fès and in more isolated tribal regions of Rabat province, around Oulmes, where Ahardane had been a highly successful administrator before the exile of the King.[42] How a rural following could be organized around a national party and how it could express itself on the national level, even if legally recognized, was a delicate problem. Over the summer of 1958 there were repeated rumors that tribesmen, under the influence of the Popular Movement, were considering an armed revolt against the cities. In the fall the threat of serious bloodshed inspired a stiff government penalty of from five to twenty years in prison and fines up to two million francs for concealing arms. Before the party's future could be decided calmly, the tribal uprisings confirmed the need for more rural representation in national politics.

After a year of clandestine existence the leaders decided to hold a demonstration at Ajdir, a mountain stronghold north of Fès, where the Liberation Army had remained influential. To dramatize the meeting and to emphasize the Movement's opposition to Istiqlal tactics, it was decided to move the body of Si Abbés to a forest shrine. The rally of 5,000 Rifians was not brought under control until units of the Royal Army occupied the area. Dr. Khatib and Ahardane were arrested at their homes for illegal exhumation, unauthorized organization of a public meeting, and "outrages" against the agents

[42] See *Le Monde*, editorial, October 21, 1958, p. 1.

of authority. The Ajdir incident was the first in the series of tribal manifestations that led to the more serious uprisings of late 1958. There was no evidence to suggest that the Popular Movement purposefully inspired the tribal revolts, although its leaders were very likely respected in the regions of discontent. Had the political system been more sensitive to less violent forms of influence, the uprisings could probably have been avoided.

The best defense of the Popular Movement in this period was its own illegality, which had prevented it from forming a reliable organization and may have facilitated other efforts to subvert tribal loyalties. There were two other leaders with a background in the Moroccan Liberation Army and the Popular Movement who participated in the tribal revolts. Moha Ou Haddou, who began the uprising among the Beni Ouarain tribesmen, was one of the most difficult rebels to subdue. Abdallah Senhadji, one of the ex-commanders of the Rif Liberation Army, became the leader of the Alhucemas revolt, which also was one of the most serious. Though both these men were acknowledged to be associated with the Popular Movement, it is impossible to discover whether they acted with the consent or knowledge of the arrested leaders of the Movement. Had there been apprehension over Ahardane's and Dr. Khatib's taking active parts in the revolts or suspicion that they were behind them, it seems unlikely that the government would have released the leaders in the midst of the uprisings.[43] The available evidence on their behavior since release suggests that they did try to help the government during the tribal crisis. Although the Movement contained a strong pro-Algerian strain, which appealed to the ex-Liberation Army tribesmen, it should also be remembered that both top leaders were unquestionably loyal to the King and were devout Muslims. Both of these considerations also played an important part in the aims of the party.

There were reports that Dr. Khatib and Ahardane were in contact with friends of Ibrahim, although they left for Madrid the day before he was designated the new President of the Council.[44] The young Istiqlal faction might have been eager to undermine the old Istiqlal, both to bolster Ibrahim's government and to capture rural support for the new Istiqlal. Both the Movement and the progressive Istiqlal faction were generally agreed on the need for a program

---

[43] See *ibid.*, December 7-8, 1958, p. 1.
[44] *Ibid.*, December 18, 1958, p. 1.

of economic austerity, a degree of nationalization, and more help for the Algerian revolutionaries. The good faith of Ahardane and Dr. Khatib was confirmed when they returned from Madrid during the trial of Addi ou Bihi. They must have known that the proceedings would expose Lyoussi as a collaborator with the French plot of 1956-1957, but they were apparently confident that their own political records were clean. Both Ahardane and Dr. Khatib intervened on the side of order in the tribal uprisings and tried to persuade Moha Ou Haddou to leave his mountain stronghold.

The Popular Movement managed to survive all these intrigues and pitfalls. Before one assigns responsibility, one should note that the way in which traditional influence operates makes it difficult to predict the results of a given course of action. The general failure of the participants in a traditional political system to understand the national implications of their actions, or, therefore, to know when their goal has been accomplished, makes it even more unpredictable. The leaders of the Popular Movement may have been the unwitting actors in a chain of events that they could not control. Under the Ibrahim government, which certainly was not one to forgive persons of "colonialist" background, their trial was apparently completely forgotten. Early in February 1959 Ahardane announced the legal formation of the Popular Movement as a new political party.[45] Its headquarters were established in Rabat and plans were made to open offices throughout the nation. Ahardane and Dr. Khatib were received by the King, to whom they described their plans and announced their registration under the Charter of Liberties.

Although the Movement's influence is limited by the capability of its members, it should also be noted that either the Istiqlal or the administration is similarly limited in trying to control the tribesmen or to discredit the Movement. The influence of the leaders of the Movement in the rural areas is based on their positions in the social systems of the various tribes and on their prestige, established largely during the Army of Liberation campaigns, as devoted servants to the King, who is accorded similar prestige. The Istiqlal can neutralize or surpass such influence by discrediting the King, which they have been unwilling to do, or by breaking down the more primitive societies that enable men with tribal ties to organize. The latter course of action is limited by many factors, including the urban concentration of Istiqlal strength, the preoccupation of the government

[45] *Ibid.*, February 1, 1959, p. 3.

with external affairs and Rabat politics, and limitations of funds, resources, and skilled man power. The rural commune is the device most likely to integrate the tribes into the national political system in a way that could be more easily directed to the advantage of the Istiqlal and to reduce the importance of traditional influence in Moroccan politics. Paradoxically, the communes have been delayed by the postponement of the law on public liberties and the failure to agree on local electoral procedures. The paralysis of the advanced segment of the Moroccan political system has very likely contributed to the failure to integrate less active political participants in the new nation.

Intellectuals Without a Party

As the Popular Movement suggests the vulnerability of the Istiqlal in the countryside, so the Liberal Independent and Communist parties testify to the Istiqlal's invulnerability in the cities. These parties have some foothold both among intellectuals and a few civil servants. Being a more conventional political party, the Liberal Independents can be controlled more easily by official restraint than the Communists, though they both have been the victims of violence. Though the Liberal Independents have never approached the popular strength of the Istiqlal, they have an appeal to selected groups of intellectuals which the Istiqlal does not wish to lose. Even this highly limited influence of the Liberal Independents, whose continued existence has depended largely on their ministerial positions, was apparently sufficient to bring the wrath of the Istiqlal on them. The Istiqlal was probably more concerned over the ministerial positions than over the party's popular strength. The Istiqlal attack on the Independents began in late 1957 and, after a momentary suspension during the Ifni crisis, was renewed in early 1958. With the formation of the Balafrej government the Liberal Independent ministers were excluded from the government and little more was reported of their activities.

The history of the Liberal Independents begins with a small group of intellectuals, working for the King during the Protectorate, who found neither the Istiqlal or the Democratic party compatible.[46] As young instructors and students, they differed with the Istiqlal and formed a small intellectual clique after the war, when most of them

[46] Interview with Reda Guedira, Central Committee, Liberal Independent Party, Rabat, May 21, 1958.

were working in the palace. During the suppression of the nationalists Reda Guedira, a leading member and a minister in the first two governments, became a lawyer and helped defend terrorists in Rabat. Their close association with the Palace and their comparative freedom of activity in 1955 made the Liberal Independents useful during negotiations for independence. The party formally began with about 400 adherents, still led by the same men who had formed the small group fifteen years before. The King asked the party to select one member to participate in the first government and Guedira became Minister of State. In the second government he became Minister of Information and Tourism, and Rachid Mouline was also included as Minister of Civil Service. The leaders of the party are frank in admitting that their growth is due largely to the favorable publicity they received in government positions.

Unfortunately, the party does not release a credible membership figure.[47] The actual membership has no doubt varied considerably, depending on the fortunes of its leading members and the favorable publicity they could attract, which was supplemented by Guedira's position as Minister of Information. It is unlikely that the party ever had more than 50,000 members and it has probably lost many of these since it ceased being represented in the government in early 1958. Under the Executive Committee of fifteen members, offices are organized in the major cities, some of which have subordinate sections. The party claims—and may have had at one time—thirty sections, though only six sections were represented at a meeting in early 1958.[48] The Liberal Independents made a concentrated effort to organize support in the countryside in the latter half of 1957, which is when they were first directly attacked by the Istiqlal. Guedira made most of the arrangements for the King's official reentry into Marrakech in June 1957. This was the occasion for intensive recruiting by the party. The leaders claim that no headway was made in provinces where Istiqlal militants were the chief administrators, but surprising inroads were made in parts of Marrakech, Safi, Ouarzazate, and Tafilalet provinces. Aided by the poor agricultural year and possibly also by the initial rural disillusion-

[47] In this respect they are like the Democratic party and other opposition groups. Guedira claimed the impossible figure of 500,000 adherents. If all the stated membership figures were unquestionably accepted, nearly half of the Moroccan population would be members of a political party. This would be most remarkable, since about half the population is under twenty years of age.

[48] L'Echo, April 19, 1958, p. 3. They were Rabat, Casablanca, Marrakech, Beni Mellal, Kasba Tadla, and Khouribga.

ment at the difficulties entailed by independence, the party may have begun to establish footholds in the territory that was also being organized by the Istiqlal.

The attempts of the party to extend its organization have led to violence on several occasions. One party militant was wounded when a bureau was opened in Safi and the burning of the Rabat office led to a reprisal attack on an Istiqlal office. The Istiqlal's open criticism of the Liberal Independents shows the same kind of apparent premeditated timing and concentration that characterized their objections to the Democratic party and the Popular Movement. Party disputes are not a day-to-day affair with continuing criticism or drawn-out debates of party principles, but rather intensive efforts of a month or so duration to try to discredit the patriotism of the opposition's leaders. In October 1957 the Istiqlal Youth Congress specifically singled out the two Liberal Independent ministers for detailed criticism. Heavy criticism of both ministers continued throughout October during discussions of a new civil service law, municipal elections, and policy toward American troops. The Liberal Independents took positions opposed by the Istiqlal. The attack was renewed in January 1958, when the Minister of Information presented a draft press law and the party joined with the Democratic party in an intensive campaign against postponing legislation on public liberties. The Istiqlal-controlled Consultative Assembly recommended the abolition of both ministerial posts occupied by Liberal Independents; this was carried out by the Balafrej government. As had occurred in the government crisis of late 1956, international tensions in the spring of 1958 curtailed further party activity.

The program of the Liberal Independents is characterized by the generality found in all party platforms, most noticeable in the case of foreign policy. On the eve of the King's visit to the United States, the party favored retaining American bases in Morocco. Early in 1958 this stand was modified to favor seeking a mutually acceptable solution for the removal of the bases. During the 1958 ministerial crisis the party advocated immediate recognition of the principle of evacuation by the United States. The party also favored the return of Mauritania and the northern Spanish enclaves to Moroccan control—a popular issue that increased in importance throughout 1957. Algerian independence was naturally endorsed, but assistance was to be limited to diplomatic intervention and the formation of a North African consultative body. The only major international problem discussed at length in party documents was public liberties. Like the other parties at that moment, the primary concern was to avoid being in a "colonialist" position in international affairs and to guarantee the continued legal existence of the party.

The opposition party that is the most difficult to evaluate is the Moroccan Communist party. Declared illegal with the Istiqlal in December 1952, it has remained in a semiclandestine state since independence although its leaders have continued to circulate relatively freely. As with the activities of other opposition parties, everyone has an opinion or rumor concerning Communism in Morocco, but official sources and party documents have almost nothing to say. Though the Moroccan Communist party is sometimes defended as a purely national group, it is difficult to discuss it with any Moroccan without introducing the interests of Soviet Russia and the People's Republic of China in Morocco, North Africa, and the Middle East. The party's dual identity has thus been implicitly recognized, but conveniently overlooked as a form of foreign intervention.[49] As in many ex-colonies, Communism came to Morocco from Europe. During the reforms of the Popular Front the first French Communist cells were established in Casablanca. In the postwar period Communism in Morocco, like Communism in many other colonies, went through a short struggle to free itself from colonialist connections and domination. In 1944 the Moroccan Communist party condemned the Istiqlal independence manifesto, but reversed itself the next year when its French leader was replaced with the present Secretary General, Ali Yata.

The preindependence efforts of the Moroccan Communist party were probably directed mostly at the labor movement, but the domination of the Moroccan segment of the labor movement by the French Communists became increasingly difficult to justify. In 1951 and 1952 the Istiqlal began to realize that Communists manipulated colonialist problems to their own advantage, which could also work to the detriment of the Istiqlal. The Communist party's foothold in the labor movement remains and, like the original Communist influence in Morocco, is largely due to the Protectorate policy of ex-

[49] The national Communist parties act in coordination with international Communism and still bring the aura of true nationalist loyalty to Communist activity. Moroccans are, on the whole, aware of this, but tend to minimize its importance. This is only one of the more frustrating experiences for American diplomats in a new country, where the slightest sign of direct interference or personal influence of Americans may immediately be branded as subversive and "colonialist." See the short history of Moroccan Communism in Lacouture, *op.cit.*, pp. 162-166.

cluding other avenues of political expression. Although the U.M.T. has been outspoken on the advantages of Soviet assistance and the dangers of American aid, it has remained first and foremost a nationalist group. The U.M.T. also sent delegations to Russia and Communist China when the government was postponing any stand regarding Communist relations. Its international position is less equivocal, however, for it remained a full member of the free-world I.C.F.T.U., while having only an observer for the Communist-sponsored labor international.

Communist influence in Morocco is scattered and limited. Perhaps the greatest long-run threat is the attraction of Communism to advanced students in Morocco and France. The only Communist threat that Istiqlal officials admitted, except for some local activities, was the infiltration of their cells and youth section in Paris by Communist militants. Estimates of party sympathizers have run as high as ten to fifteen thousand, but the party probably does not have more than a thousand well-indoctrinated members.[50] It has been noted by Al-Fassi,[51] that the party is reported to have centers of strength in some ministries, especially the Ministry of National Economy. There are probably isolated Communist militants in most of the coastal rural towns, but the main strongholds are in the large cities of Rabat, Casablanca, Fedala, Meknes, Marrakech, and Safi. The party has managed to keep its press alive under semiclandestine conditions. A mimeographed French and Arabic news sheet has been distributed without official opposition since independence. In the summer of 1958, when other parties were suppressed, the Communist-oriented paper, *La Nation*, appeared and several bookstores for low-priced Communist literature were opened.

Like the other parties the Moroccan Communists have experienced some violence, but it was concentrated in the early months of independence when the urban resistance was being dissolved. Many of the early members of the urban terrorist cells came from the workers of Casablanca, who were also among the first to be unionized under C.G.T. auspices. The Communist secretary for Casablanca, Abdallah Al-Ayachi, was tortured by French police for resistance activities and another Communist, Abdelkrim Ben Abdallah, was supposed to have been among the founders of the Black Cross.

[50] *World Strength of the Communist Party Organizations*, Washington, Department of State, 1958, p. 29. See also Lacouture, *op.cit.*, p. 167.

[51] See article of Soviet relations, *Sahara Al-Maghrib*, translation in *La Vigie*, September 18, 1958, p. 2.

Three leading members of the party, including one of Ayachi's colleagues from the resistance and the alleged head of the party in Yata's absence, were attacked by gunmen and escaped while they were driving through the new *medina* of Casablanca. Nearly all of the incidents involving terrorists of Communist background took place in Casablanca except for the arrest of eleven members of the Black Cross near Marrakech. It is entirely possible that in this period the Communists were trying to align their supporters in the resistance like the Istiqlal. The political ramifications of these assassinations is even more confused regarding the struggle for liberation of Algeria, for some of the alleged Communists were of Algerian origin and very likely were first trained in terrorist techniques in Algeria. How many resistants of Communist sympathy were incorporated into the police force with independence is not known, but as one considers the efficiency of the Moroccan Sûreté, one realizes that they are probably not a serious threat.

The official status of the party was never clarified during the first three years of independence. Its Secretary General, Ali Yata, tried first to reenter the country shortly after the return of the King and a second time late in 1955. Two more unsuccessful attempts were made in 1957, when he received the same treatment.[52] On the eve of the arrival of the first Soviet ambassador to Morocco Yata made a third entry at Tangier, where he was permitted to stay after being questioned by the police. The Moroccan police appear to be very well informed on Communist activity in the country and on two occasions have taken serious countermeasures. In mid-1957 a Czechoslovakian business representative was expelled for his alleged role in organizing new Communist activity. During the labor discontent of the summer and fall of 1958 the police raided the Communist party office in Casablanca, seized its documents, and held thirteen officers. The Istiqlal paper reported that "despite the silence of the police" it had learned that papers were found linking the party to Israel and to certain espionage activities.[53] Whether the party wished only to publicize the treatment of Yata or if a more serious offense was involved was never clarified by the police.

[52] On the first attempt he got as far as the Rabat airport, where he spent the night, before being returned to France on the orders of the Resident General. The second attempt was through a telegram to the King. He requested permission again in January 1957 and was refused. He arrived by plane and was returned again in November 1957.

[53] *Al-Alam, La Vigie,* October 10, 1958, p. 2.

The tolerance the Moroccan Communists enjoy has probably been due to their extremely mild program and the consistent priority given to nationalist aims. The major point of their declaration at the time of independence was the necessity to abrogate the Treaty of Fès. The economic proposals of the party called for "liberation from capitalist grips" and some nationalization of land and mineral wealth, but were not aggressively socialist.[54] During the party maneuvers of the summer of 1956 suitable modifications were made by calling for the purge of "feudalists, traitors and collaborators," but these proposals were no more outspoken than the criticisms of the Istiqlal and the U.M.T. In fact, the party took pains to note that all three programs were similar, a fact which would enable the Istiqlal to serve "as a base for the formation of a new ministerial team." The most notable difference in the Communist program was its early demand for the evacuation of French troops and abolition of American bases. In general, the party's policy in Morocco has been characterized by its complete subservience to Istiqlal and U.M.T. aims. The Communists have neither the legal position nor the popular strength that would have enabled them to take a more aggressively doctrinaire line.

The position of the Moroccan Communist party is, almost unavoidably, affected by Morocco's relations with Soviet Russia and her policy in other parts of the world. Frequently sending felicitations and encouragement, Russia has carried out all diplomatic courtesies since independence. Early in 1957 a Soviet trade delegation arrived and a trade agreement was reached, which was renewed for 1958. During the Prince's visit to Cairo in the summer of 1957, he met with Shepilov and was invited to visit the U.S.S.R.[55] He later declined the invitation and cautioned Moroccan youth against the dangers of Communism. Delegations from the U.M.T., the Consultative Assembly, and several youth groups have visited the U.S.S.R. and China. Because of large imports of tea, which have resulted in a sizable trade deficit with the Chinese People's Republic, Morocco has had continued and important commercial relations with that country. In the fall of 1958 Balafrej and Khrushchev exchanged letters asking for diplomatic representation and the first Soviet am-

[54] Taken from party statement in *L'Echo*, August 26, 1956, p. 1, which quoted from party memoir of February 15, 1956.

[55] *C.M.*, June 21, 1956, p. 1. He was immediately called on by the French Ambassador in Cairo. Later Yata protested French pressure on the Prince that had caused him to decline the invitation.

bassador to Morocco arrived very shortly. The trend toward closer diplomatic relations with Soviet Russia will no doubt give prestige to the Moroccan Communist party, but it should also be recognized that it may carry hazards if Soviet policy conflicts with Arab interests.

The efforts of the Communists of Morocco to be unobtrusive and inoffensive places them in a somewhat different position than that of other opposition parties. The party wishes to preserve the small number of militants and followers now in the country. While imposed clandestineness would solidify its ranks, it now consists of little more than a few hundred indoctrinated Communists with their immediate following. To expect that the Communist presence in a new country can be prohibited is to deny the present structure of world politics. To assume that it is the same as Communist alignment of a new country is to misunderstand the most important issue in a new country—independence itself. Most leading Moroccans are well aware of the Communist activity in the country, though there may be a tendency to overestimate the ability of existing parties to restrain Communist activity if the present limited goals of the Communists were altered.[56]

At the time of the Hungarian revolts the Leader of the Istiqlal observed that even the Communists were not strong enough to suppress nationalist aspirations, though his view may have changed after the Soviet Army suppressed the revolution. The wrath of the nationalists where Communism conflicts with their interests is dramatically illustrated in Al-Fassi's condemnation of the Afro-Asian Cairo Conference, which the Democratic party exploited. Al-Fassi outspokenly condemned the conference for including a majority of Communists and for passing "Communist-oriented" motions. The nationalist flexibility was again demonstrated by the ability of the Istiqlal Leader to approve of Soviet relations a few months later and to defend the impartiality of the admittedly influential Communists in the Ministry of National Economy. So long as the Communist loyalties of Moroccan Communists are not in conflict with national goals and the party does not engage in widespread recruitment, it will no doubt be allowed to continue its semiclandestine life.

[56] In the early 1950's two bright young militants were sent to Algeria for contact and training with Algerian nationalists. There they came under the influence of Communist militants, disappeared, and next were heard of as leading Communist Algerians. Since they had been carefully selected by the Istiqlal for their loyalty, there was considerable consternation.

Formation of the National Union

The fifth opposition party in Morocco is the National Union of Popular Forces (U.N.F.P.) which was formed in early 1959 when the Istiqlal split. The dissent after the formation of the Balafrej government in May 1958 left little doubt that the Istiqlal leadership was severely divided. Over the summer of 1958 the conflict appeared to be confined to the party leadership and on several occasions there were signs of reconciliation. Bouabid often intervened to keep the discontent at a manageable level, and Ben Barka persuaded the union leaders to accept the compromise of submitting differences to a Congress of the Istiqlal. In the fall came the serious deterioration of the rural administration and the first signs of schism in the U.M.T. ranks. Both these events had repercussions in increased criticism of the Balafrej government and drove the dissident group closer together. When the Executive Committee lost Ben Barka in late November 1958,[57] there was no longer any official group to discuss compromise. By December the U.M.T. attacks on Balafrej made any reconciliation difficult, and the exposure of the deadlock on the Congress planning committee revealed that a solution within the party was most unlikely.

Beneath the party split were more profound political and social differences concerning the future of the Moroccan political system. The role of the nationalist party in facilitating the transition from a colonial to an independent political system is probably one of its most important contributions to the new nation. Depending on the range of social differentiation and level of industrialization, however, other factors may come into play that can feed back and destroy the solidarity of the nationalist party. Not all modern nationalist parties are predestined to split, but their futures depend heavily on the social structure of the new nation. New nations must undergo long-run social changes and withstand the shock of the immediate responsibilities of independence. The solidarity of the Istiqlal was preserved through the initial adjustment, but at the expense of preparing the party for the future. As the political system came to bear more on broad questions of social development and national political institutions, the differentiations in the party began to express them-

[57] He did not announce this until he had been expelled from the party. *La Vigie,* January 26, 1959, p. 2. The fact that it was not generally known is indicative of the rarefied political atmosphere among the party leaders and also of the possibility of a new reconciliation.

selves. The relative ease with which the Istiqlal's organizational framework enables identification of a more complex system of differentiation does not mean that this development was limited to the party. On the contrary, with independence the complexities of a country's social system are manifested more freely in politics. The solidarity of the party may have been increased with independence for a time, but the party eventually had to reconcile social differences that had been muted prior to independence.

Since the Istiqlal encompassed such a large share of the active political participants of Morocco, the formation of the U.N.F.P. provides an excellent opportunity to observe this transition among many of those who were more active. Early manifestations of the Istiqlal's difficulties are the *Bulletin's* articles concerning the future of the country and the meaning of the nation, which were supposed to be read to or by all members of the party. The Istiqlal needed to reorient its following to the concrete problems and sacrifices of the future, but in doing so it was contributing to the differences of opinion and reinforcing the divergence of interests among its members. The entire controversy in the party as well as for the nation as a whole is perhaps contained in the frequently repeated slogan, "Independence is not an end, but a means." There were undoubtedly many meanings attached to this slogan, but they were not expressed publicly or with clarity until the conflicts of 1958.

The reorientation of Istiqlal members was especially marked during the poor agricultural year, 1956-1957. Party commentary went beyond the material problems of the transition and tried to explain the difficulties and procedures of government. Sobering thoughts and real choices were described in the party's *Internal Bulletin*, which said: "The construction of a new thing in the country and the correction of errors requires time and financial ability. . . . The government's budget is so small that it is unable to change Morocco's position in all areas. We must understand . . . that independence is not a magic wand that will reverse everything in a short time. In the light of these two realities, we can say that we have not and that we shall not reach perfection in a short time."[58] The level of comprehension of a large proportion of the members was not high, and simplified explanations of basic political problems were constantly repeated. One article of the *Bulletin* went into great detail in out-

[58] "New Mind for a New Era," editorial in *Internal Bulletin* (New Series), no. 2, February 1957(?), pp. 1-2.

lining the basic characteristics of a nation, its land, its sovereignty, and the relations established among large numbers of citizens.[59] A similar rudimentary discourse on the significance of elections can be found, though with somewhat more outspoken favoritism toward the party than in other articles of basic political education.[60]

The comment of the *Bulletin* confirms the party's difficulties as participant in the government and as national spokesman. For the nation as a whole it is testimony to the problem of reorienting the high expectations of a newly freed populace and also of explaining new national goals to the people. In tracing the problems of the new era the *Bulletin* commented: "If any fault appears somewhere in a minister's actions, then such errors are undoubtedly not purposeful. The problems faced by the government are many and different and, therefore, no one should believe that his own question or local problem is the one that must be treated before all others."[61] The popular misunderstanding of the role of the new government appears to have reached proportions that handicapped the operation of government offices and also of party offices. The *Bulletin* became defensive in warning that "the people must not hasten to criticize the government's actions without reason. . . . It is also useless to submit complaints and send delegations to Rabat, since such actions mean anarchy."[62] A similar theme appeared in a later editorial, where the reasons for unrest among the people were listed and rationalized: "French civil servants remain in their posts because the country needs them; appointments of Moroccan civil servants cannot always agree with the wishes of everyone; unemployment and economic crises are not a result of independence; and lastly the people should not conclude the government is ignoring their interests when they are uninformed of its efforts on their behalf; . . . if we find a useless employee of the government that does not mean that all government employees are bad [and] if we do not receive advantage from a certain action, this should not be considered reason to criticize the government."[63]

The party activists were alarmed over these signs of failure and impatient to fulfill some of the high expectations. They also deplored the growing disinterest and apathy of party members, which

[59] "Our Nation" (New Series), no. 15, March 1958(?), p. 5.
[60] *Ibid.*, "Elections" (New Series), no. 5, June 1957(?), pp. 3-4.
[61] "New Mind for a New Era," *op.cit.*, p. 2.
[62] "Party's Activities" (New Series), no. 3, March 1957(?), p. 7.
[63] "Stability in Thoughts" (New Series), no. 5, May 1957(?), pp. 1-2.

was the subject of another revealing article in the *Bulletin*: "1) . . . The state of struggle still exists and the party's members must understand that they are still mobilized for the work needed by the party. 2) . . . The party has no honored positions to be given to lazy persons or to those who want to gain fame or prestige without working for their nation. 3) . . . The member who joins the party just to gain advantage will never find his place inside the party. . . . 4) . . . The party's members also have the right to draw the minister's attention to everything they may do poorly, through the instructors, officers and inspectors of the party."[64] The ideal role of an Istiqlal member was, however, subject to controversy among party leaders and probably a factor in the split of early 1959. The more activist, young group was much more prone to talk of the party in terms of mobilizing the country and stressed the need for constant discipline in the face of new threats to the nation. In general, the older leaders were more concerned with patronage and more likely to rely on the prestige acquired during the struggle to sustain the party. The Unity Road Project was a manifestation of the concrete, highly organized projects favored by the more ambitious organizers of the party, while the more complacent tended to view the party as simply a basis for justifying the Istiqlal's claim to mass support. The activists objected to government's becoming a "public service" which the party and population should passively enjoy. While the ideology behind this approach may be unclear, it should not be assumed that the more cautious thinking of the party elders was more appropriate. The para-military undertone of the activists may hold repercussions that they did not realize, but it also acknowledged the long social transition that was requisite to filling popular demands and establishing a political system of an advanced country.

Reports on the division of the Istiqlal as well as the statements of the leaders of the new party underscored the deeper significance of the schism. Lacouture wrote that for Ben Barka it was "the debut of the second phase of emancipation of the Moroccan people—a social stage succeeding a political stage."[65] For the country it was perhaps a question of whether the Istiqlal should become so inclusive and so militant as to begin to merge in significance, if not in actual structure, with the government. Ben Barka stressed the party's fail-

[64] "Responsibilities of Party Members" (New Series), no. 10, October 1957(?), p. 5.
[65] *Le Monde*, January 30, 1959, p. 6. The newspaper observed editorially that it was not sufficient "to see in this crisis the simple consequence of an error of organization or a rivalry of persons or of temperaments." *Ibid.*, January 29, 1959, p. 1.

ure to assimilate the "tidal wave" of new members from the U.M.T. and the resistance at the time of independence. Broader implications are found in the resolution of the Extraordinary Congress of the Regional Committees of National Union. The motion ended by specifying the challenge to the country of reconstructing its "colonialist" economy and giving all Moroccans a sense of participation in the new nation. "[The Congress] calls each citizen to realize the sense of this battle and to support voluntarily and conscientiously his part of the effort and the sacrifice for justice and equality. [It] demands that a real policy of austerity and work should be adopted in order to end certain habits of easy and luxurious life that are incompatible with the possibilities and tasks which are imposed."[66] When the Congress of the new party spoke of the "three years of weaknesses, negligence(s) and grave errors," there was little doubt but that it had in mind a different kind of political and social system than had yet been advocated by the King or the elders of the party.

Ben Barka's discussion of the role of party militants was extremely significant. He was, no doubt, eager to have many organizers join the new party, but his emphasis also disclosed different views on Morocco's future. "[The party] engages all militants to combat the campaign of confusion and demoralization undertaken by conscious or unconscious agents of colonialism . . . and to mobilize the popular masses in the enthusiastic drive . . . toward the accomplishment of the national objectives of liberation from the military and economic servitude as well as installation of a concrete democracy."[67] It was announced that steps would be taken to give militants an active role in the party; this had allegedly been discouraged by the inspectors of the old Istiqlal. Most of the militants had been trained since independence. The accuracy of Ben Barka's complaint was suggested by the promptness with which Al-Fassi replied, though his comment had a noticeably different emphasis. He also claimed that "profound modification of the party structure" would be made and that the way would be opened for "all militants, particularly the youth, to be fully assured of their responsibilities."[68] Al-Fassi thus tacitly admitted the weakness of the old Istiqlal, but his concern was still with their role as strictly party functionaries and his appeal to them was in terms of responsibility to the party.

[66] *La Vigie*, January 26, 1959, p. 2.
[67] *Ibid.*, p. 2.
[68] *Ibid.*, January 28, 1959, p. 1.

The U.N.F.P.'s federated organization ostensibly reversed the pattern of the old Istiqlal. Ben Barka emphatically denounced the system of inspectors, whom he characterized as the "civil servants of the Executive Committee." Their loyalty to Al-Fassi during the split suggested that Ben Barka may not have been uniformly successful in persuading the older party leaders to accept his reforms. He argued that the inspectors isolated the base of the party from its leadership and that some of the inspectors had not taken full advantage of opportunities to improve the party in their regions. In the new party there were to be only elected regional committees, which would be autonomous and coordinated for national purposes through an Administrative Commission. The Commission included eight men, of whom Al-Basri, the resistance chief, was chairman. Fifteen regional committees of Autonomous Provincial Federations were formed, which corresponded roughly to the same distribution as that of the old inspectors. Ben Barka became the Secretary General of the Casablanca Federation. Ben Seddik apparently had no office in the new party organization, although there were many union officers on committees. According to Ben Barka's plans, which must have been underway for some time before, each Provincial Federation would individually register under the Charter of Liberties and would provide an instrument of popular expression within the reach and control of the members in each province. Although this structure might be more suitable to conveying a sense of participation to the party's base, it is by no means certain that the base will have a more important voice in the direction of the Democratic Istiqlal than it had in the old Istiqlal.

The formation of the new party also raised new questions of the relationship between government and political parties. Over the preceding three years there were no major issues concerning administrative accountability or the neutrality of civil servants. Although Ibrahim was not openly associated with the new party, his position undoubtedly brought prestige to the new Democratic Istiqlal. Since Ibrahim had taken office under "personal title," he could not affiliate with the party. The influential Minister of National Economy, Bouabid, had openly condemned the Istiqlal Old Guard and had certainly encouraged the split, but he did not join the new party. Thami Ammar, Ibrahim's Minister of Agriculture, was well known for his agitation with the dissenting group and was among those expelled from the Istiqlal. Al-Fassi was of the opinion that the Min-

ister of Agriculture had broken the condition of nonparty alignment, on which the fourth government took office. Ibrahim and
Bouabid were not expelled in the first phase of the split because they
had not participated in the meeting to arrange the split, although
there was no doubt where their sympathy lay. The main target of
the Istiqlal's objections was, of course, Ben Barka, one of the first
to be expelled.

When the Inspector General of the Istiqlal was received by the
King in order to report on the party split, it was widely reported
that his mission was to have Ben Barka removed as President of
the National Consultative Assembly.[69] This was later denied, but
the subsequent attack on Ben Barka's alleged abuse of his office left
little doubt. The Istiqlal position is fully quoted, for it tells something about politics in general in the new country as well as the
bitterness the schism unleashed: "Mehdi Ben Barka, who has profited
for more than six months from his presence in the Executive Committee, who still profits from the secretariat of the National Assembly, which has become the local center of the separatist movement, who profits from his position as President of the National
Consultative Assembly, which confers on him a certain immunity
and a certain representative character to slander and organize his
dissidence in the shadow, giving himself the air of a man of the left,
a man who remains beside the people, has unveiled his game and his
true countenance."[70] There may have been a certain amount of
jealousy of the prestige and publicity that Ben Barka received from
his office, but hundreds of well-known Old Guard Istiqlal figures
had enjoyed similar recognition. To criticize his use of official facilities to manipulate the split was absurd, since nearly the entire
Executive Committee of the old Istiqlal had been carrying on party
business at work for years and no one had ever questioned its propriety. The King decided to remain above party squabbles and Ben
Barka kept his office, although a palace spokesman asserted that the
split would not affect the "mission or policy" of the Ibrahim government. The new party was clearly determined to avoid a clash with
central authorities and specifically warned its followers to avoid any
provocation of security forces.

Insofar as the more educated and more secure citizens of Morocco tended to remain with the Istiqlal, the new party was not

[69] See, for example, *Le Monde*, January 30, 1959, p. 6.
[70] *Al-Istiqlal*, January 31, 1959, p. 3.

likely to get much support from the civil servants and high government officials. There were some indications that the reformed Istiqlal was favored by some rural officials, mostly in areas where the resistance was thought to have placed many of its leaders in office. At Beni Mellal and Khouribga, Istiqlal officials were reportedly arrested illegally by *caids* loyal to the new party. In general, there seems to have been few local violations of governmental neutrality. By early 1959 Morocco appears to have reached a point where, at least among the most active political participants, institutional forms of influence were beginning to be used habitually. Though Morocco had not yet begun to approach the complex pattern of institutional influence found in advanced nations, different procedures and rules were beginning to apply to different problems in the political system as a whole.

The analysis of Moroccan opposition parties has demonstrated the difficulties of party politics where the institutional structure is rapidly changing or where mass appeal often on a charismatic base is frequently used. In the early stages of independence, the opposition has a serious handicap in trying to sustain its national authenticity while opposing the major national party. That the nationalists of the Istiqlal could feasibly split on a nation-wide basis is an indication of the rapid progress being made by Morocco. The problems of the opposition are partially disclosed by the similarities of their programs. To establish their identity they must challenge the meaning of the word "national" as commonly used by the preeminent party. Where the new political system emerges from a prolonged and ruthless struggle for independence, a challenge to the dominant nationalist group can easily lead to violence. The search for more persuasive goals, as well as the structure of internal politics, tends to focus opposition attention on international politics, which was particularly evident in the first three years of Moroccan independence. Once new institutions are developed, the parties are able to establish themselves in a new framework, though it is entirely possible that it may be quite meaningless in terms of the national political system. This does not seem to be the case in Morocco, where the influence of the King has provided an invaluable authority above party politics, while simultaneously providing a focus for Moroccans who are not sufficiently advanced to be active in parties. His position has probably been strengthened rather than weakened by the split of the Istiqlal, since the neutrality of the governmental structure has become more important. The tendency to concentrate on proving the supremacy of one's nationalist claim still persists in Moroccan politics, as all the parties demonstrate. Until the general level of political participation increases considerably it is likely to remain one of the major preoccupations of the parties.

Such a situation could and to some extent has resulted in simply an attempt to outbid the opponent's claim to nationalist fervor. The Istiqlal has been restrained to some extent by its responsibilities for the specific acts and policies put forward by its ministers in the government. The reiteration of its important role in achieving independence and the sacrifice of its followers are very likely encouraged by its reluctance to admit tacitly the controversial character of government. For similar reasons the Istiqlal refrains from specific attacks on an opposition group until they make inroads on its base or embarrass the government. To exert influence among the entire population requires activity that may spontaneously produce violence, as in the case of the Popular Movement, or that may be manipulated into being a threat to public order, as was the case with the Democratic party. So long as political interchange involves only the militant core of a party acting among its better-indoctrinated followers or submitting its grievances to the government in less dramatic forms, the Istiqlal has chosen not to call public attention to the matter. By avoiding debate or interexchanges on other terms the Istiqlal avoids admitting that national interest may itself be a thing of controversy and compromise and that by implication the party could have erred.

The Istiqlal by itself may have incorporated as much opposition activity as all the smaller parties combined. It is in closer contact with a much larger number of persons than all the opposition groups. By the use of national preeminence it has been able to represent and attract members from the wide cross section of social differentiation found in Morocco. The public split of Istiqlal factions in the summer of 1958 is itself testimony to the opposing strains within the party, which for several years withstood tensions that would otherwise have been expressed directly at the central level. In the absence of institutions and procedures for the airing and examination of policy alternatives the Istiqlal organization itself constituted a political subsystem within which will be found small groups closely aligned with the external groups identified in opposition parties. Though the Istiqlal has unquestionably benefited from the prestige of its many leaders in the Council of Government and members in the administration, its predominance has not been achieved by governmental advantages alone, nor has the opposition been reluctant to use these same advantages when it has been in positions of authority. The major party helped compensate for the unavoidable constraints on individual participation in national politics, which impose limitations that any political party would be compelled to recognize.

CHAPTER XI

DEVELOPMENT OF REPRESENTATIVE

GOVERNMENT

The Experimental Assembly

M OROCCO has shown continued interest in the development of representative government, though little progress was made toward this end in the first three years of independence. When one considers the other problems confronting the country as well as the requirements for meaningful representative government, one can well understand the results. The question is more justly examined from the viewpoint of what has been done to make some form of representative government possible. With the limitations and higher priority problems confronting the new nation, it is quite proper to inquire also if this form of rule was suitable during the early years of the transition. Each year the new country came close to being plunged into war: the arrest of Algerian leaders at the end of 1956, the Ifni affair at the end of 1957, and the inflamed hostilities over Algeria in 1958. Not until 1958 was there a single currency, civil service, or nationality law. The administrative areas of the country only began to change their colonial structure at the provincial level in mid-1958. The separation of administrative and judicial offices and the laws pertaining to these functions did not go into effect nationally until the end of 1957. The selection of a representative body by popular participation presupposes a variety of purely physical conditions for which the new nation lacked both time and resources.

For a country emerging from nearly forty years of colonial rule the past brings many handicaps to potential participants and leaders. The leaders of a nationalist movement, perhaps even more than their colonialist tutors, are accustomed to the unquestioned approval their earlier efforts received. The goal of independence has a simplicity and a self-justification that may affect the expectations of the new governors as well as the governed. For the mass of Moroccans the process of choice and compromise of an electoral process may seem strange, though at no time has such an ultimate purpose been opposed. Their capacity to participate is restricted by their educational level and by inadequate information. If they are strongly nationalist, they have submitted to the sacrifices and discomfort of the independence struggle almost solely on the basis of blind devotion to the nation. If they were opposed to or disinterested in this struggle, they are probably even more wary of placing their fortunes with the majority. So long as the operation of the government can be popularly associated with realizing the almost universally accepted goal of independence, the new political system may well be functioning in the most efficient and even most popular fashion possible.

Although the values placed on the nation in reference to its existence and in reference to lesser problems are not the same, they are more easily confused in the new nation. Where questions of diplomatic representation or a common currency are involved, for example, the nationalist appeal carries nearly full persuasiveness and the individual members of the nation may be led to sacrifice their lives for these interests. Below those questions that are more easily associated with survival comes a whole range of decreasingly important situations. Once the differentiation of responses and expectations begins, a new procedure must be found to create compromises or select alternatives. The new country may, of course, be governed more easily for the moment by coercion or may attempt to attach vital significance to every decision involving the nation. The apparent ease of such solutions places temptations in the path of political leaders, and also reinforces popular expectations that may jeopardize the formation of representative government. Perhaps the greatest threat to representative procedures is the facility with which apparently similar results can be produced in the new nation. Consensus can be manifested by many kinds of participation, of which many are not representative in the common meaning of the term, much less democratic. For this reason an induced response may not only discredit experiments in representative government, but may also contribute to a self-accumulative justification of the existing political system, which, in turn, makes any subsequent experiment more difficult.

With independence, groups and individuals begin to identify their particular interests and needs. So long as these interests do not conflict with the existence of the nation itself there are, of course, an endless variety of ways in which such groups or individuals might bring their influence to bear on national politics. It may be fair to describe representative government as a means of making decisions effecting highly differentiated national goals, where the participants possess a variety of ways of exercising their influence to achieve the desired goal. Representative government may thus be constrained by the few nationally understood goals; this is seen in the tendency of political parties to present almost identical programs. Due to the extreme range of social differentiation the precise meaning of goals advocated by a trade union may be incomprehensible to a tribal elder. The relatively low-level specialization of the retarded country means not only that it may be difficult to construct a single system of representative government that will be meaningful to all, but also that what can be done with any given system on the national level will be restricted. For a new nation to have a nationally representative form of government may mean having a form of government that cannot do very much, since it must be scaled to the situation of the most retarded member. The problem of representative government in a new nation is, then, not only the problem of the sheer physical limitations on the ability of some individuals to participate. In reference to the national political system as a whole the analytically parallel, and not derivative, problem is how nationally useful relationships can be established among all these members. If all the citizens were in a roughly equivalent state of social advancement a representative system similar to those in advanced countries might be constructed. The range of social differentiation as well as the particular qualifications of the members must be considered in the development of representative government.

Given some consideration of the complexity of the issue facing the new Moroccan government, the persistence displayed up to 1959 takes on a new meaning. Before returning to Morocco the King made it clear that Morocco would become a constitutional monarchy. He could, of course, with his present authority simply issue a constitution, but he has preferred to postpone the document until Moroccans are able to understand its significance and until some kind of popular assembly could participate in its composition. The most fully elaborated mission of the first Council of Government was: "The creation of democratic institutions resulting from free elections and based on the principle of separation of powers in the structure of a constitutional monarchy."[1] Early in 1956 the King noted that this could not be achieved until "conditions permit a free consulta-

[1] *Réalisations et Perspectives*, Ministry of Information, 1957, p. 8. The other two missions were simply to pursue negotiations with France and to manage public affairs.

tion of public desires,"[2] but he continued to take preparatory steps. The National Consultative Assembly was constituted in October 1956. In his inaugural speech the King excused the delay by saying, "It is necessary to proceed by steps in order to implant democracy . . . on foundations of political maturity, civic education and social advancement."[3] His determination to introduce a form of representative government was again repeated in the Throne Speech of 1956.

Three projects were intended to pave the way for popular participation: the National Consultative Assembly, an experimental electoral law, and the formation of rural communes. Plans were made for the Assembly before the first government crisis.[4] The Assembly was to be consulted on the budget and on "social, economic and political questions," which evolved into a fall debate on foreign policy and a spring debate on the budget. The debates were to be public, voting was to be done by a majority of those present, and ministers were obliged to be present when so requested by the King or when business related to their office was being discussed. Members could submit questions during the debates or in written form through the President of the Assembly, in which case the minister concerned was obliged to reply in one month. The King retained all authority over the Assembly. He could terminate any session at any time, remove any member, or dissolve the Assembly as he wished. In practice he has left the Assembly to its own devices and has made only an inaugural speech at the opening each fall and one special address during the troubled spring of 1957.

Although the debates have often been extremely critical of the government, there is absolutely no evidence that the King has tried to influence them. The members are given special protection against slander charges and immunity to arrest during the sessions. Except for the inaugural ceremony the King has never used his power of presiding and has left the management of the Assembly to its members and to the first President, Mehdi Ben Barka. There has been one extraordinary session—something which the King may convene as he desires. The Assembly has been consulted by the King on special problems and passed a motion on the crisis of early 1958 with which its meeting coincided. The King has consulted the President of the Assembly and the commissions frequently, especially on

[2] Interview of Mohammed V by Reuters, *C.M.*, January 14, 1956, Complement.
[3] *Réalisations et Perspectives, op.cit.*, p. 97.
[4] *O.B.*, no. 2286, August 17, 1956, "Dahir no. 1-56-179 du 25 hija 1375 (3 août 1956), portant institution d'un conseil consultatif auprés de Sa Majesté," pp. 900-901.

more controversial issues such as the evacuation of foreign troops and determination of boundaries. To add further to the prestige of the body, he has placed its representatives on several government agencies, including the Council of the Plan, the National Aid Committee, and the Court of Justice.

Though all the members were appointed by his approval, he chose to select personally only those who were not connected with formal organizations. The seventy-six members came from established categories of political parties, nonpolitical leaders, economic and social organizations, and diverse professional groups. Only the twelve delegates in the nonpolitical group, which represented the legal profession and the *oulemas* or religious scholars, were selected by the King. The other groups nominated their own delegates, including ten from the Istiqlal, six from the Democratic party, ten from the U.M.T., eighteen from agricultural associations, nine from commercial and industrial associations, and eleven from other professional associations. The nominations for these sixty-four members included most of the prominent leaders of the country who were not already in high government positions.[5] On the whole the members have shown an interest in their appointments, although several members who did not attend were removed early in 1958 and a minor adjustment was made late in 1957 to admit one delegate from the National Union of Moroccan Students (U.N.E.M.). Though the Assembly was not intended to be a representative body, the geographical regions of the greatest social and political advancement have well over half the seats. The same tendency to weight urban interests more heavily has been found in the breakdown of the members' professions. Roughly two thirds of the members were from unions, professions, commerce, or industry and the nineteen agriculture delegates were nearly all large landowners. The selection testifies to the advantage of organized interests in a new country and to the mechanical difficulty of giving means of expression to the socially retarded segment of the population. The King had no illusions on this shortcoming. He acknowledged that the delegates had been selected on the basis of "competence and experience" and frankly admitted that the method of designation was improvised.[6]

[5] The list of members appeared in the *O.B.*, no. 2304, December 21, 1956, "Dahir no. 1-56-258 du 15 rebia I 1376, portant nomination des membres de conseil national consultatif auprés de Sa Majesté le Sultan," pp. 1438-1441.

[6] *Réalisations et Perspectives, op.cit.,* p. 98.

The Assembly had four commissions to manage its affairs and to study the budget or other documents submitted by the King. They were the political, economic, social, and budget commissions, each having a president, two vice-presidents, and two secretaries. Only one Democratic party representative obtained office. The bureau of the Assembly, which has supervised the agenda and which directs debate, was solidly from the Istiqlal and the U.M.T. During the crisis of early 1958 the Istiqlal acknowledged the party's predominance in the Assembly and claimed to have a majority,[7] which was no doubt correct. In the 1957-1958 session the Democratic party lost its one post on the commissions, though its delegates continued to participate without apparent restraint after the party had been suppressed. To some extent the Assembly has become a forum for the Democratic party, since it was the party's sole direct contact with the government after the fall of 1956. The debates of the Assembly show that on the whole the Democratic party has received recognition in proportion to its strength in that body.[8] One of the important dilemmas of such an experimental representative body is that delegates tend to use their privilege on the presumption that the body has the authority of a properly elected popular assembly. Both the Democratic party and the Istiqlal early in 1959 not only aired justifiable complaints, but also used the Assembly as an authoritative source of party propaganda. To justify their immediate grievances each dissident group cast itself in the role of a fully qualified parliamentary opposition. The foundations of representative institutions are needed, but their construction may be easily abused by magnifying the body's significance to obtain short-term political gains.

The debates of the Assembly have included sharp criticisms of Istiqlal ministers by their own party colleagues. The question procedure has been used freely to provoke discussion of a variety of subjects. The Assembly's first motion concerned the general economic situation of the country; it frankly stated the reforms desired by the more progressive elements of the Istiqlal and the U.M.T. It called for a policy of austerity to combat the crisis which had been "aggravated by colonialist maneuvers for the purpose of maintaining the system inherited from the Protectorate and to sabotage all national effort for economic liberation."[9] The motion also advocated

[7] *Al-Alam*, April 27, 1958, U.S. Trans.
[8] See *Démocracie*, June 10, 1957, p. 4.
[9] *Assemblée National Consultative*, Session 1956-1957, "Motion sur la situation économique," December 3, 1956, p. 12.

more rapid Moroccanization of the civil service, the promulgation of a law on the civil service, and a law encouraging investment without endangering national sovereignty. Since the government was at this time engaged in reconstructing its relations with France after the Meknes incident and was still trying to settle many outstanding issues with her, this was a strong position and embarrassing to the Istiqlal ministers.

Early in 1957 the Assembly held its first major session in which Bouabid presented the operational budget for 1957. The meeting was subject to sharp criticism in advance by the U.M.T., who, like the Democratic party in later meetings, complained that they had not been given sufficient time to prepare. Though Morocco had been legally independent only ten months and the predominantly Istiqlal Council of Government had been in office only two months, the unions blamed the continuance of the "economic organization installed by the imperialist regime" for current economic troubles and demanded immediate revision of the structure put in place "by a minority of capitalists who made it an instrument to serve their interests."[10] The final motion[11] expressed regret over the short time for preparation, the failure to have consolidated the budget for the north and south, the refusal to submit the investment budget, and the tardiness in preparing civil service reform. Bouabid's report was approved, but attention was also drawn to the need for trained cadre and rural modernization. The license given the Assembly was evident in the final notations of the motion, which called for quick justice for those plotting against the state and an effort to expose those who "obstruct the march of the nation toward the achievement of its liberation." These elaborations on all national problems indicated that the Assembly meant to attribute to itself a role in current affairs as well as to conduct its specified discussions.

The Assembly continued to expand its role in the June 1957 debates on the investment budget for 1957. An Istiqlal militant directed sharp criticism at the Minister of the Economy regarding financial relations with France. The final motion was not so severe as that of the operational budget debate, but continued to assert the dangers of subversion and foreign intervention. The Assembly noted with approval its representation on the Council of the Plan. In the

[10] *At-Taliâ*, editorial translated in *Al-Istiqlal*, January 25, 1957, p. 5.

[11] *Assemblée . . . , op.cit.*, "Motion finale votée par l'Assemblée National Consultative à l'issue du débat sur le budget de fonctionnement," pp. 13-14.

tone of the Istiqlal activists the Assembly noted that the Plan could only be successful if based on a "mobilization of all national resources" and not on simple administrative changes. The 1957-1958 session of the Assembly opened with an address by Balafrej on Moroccan foreign policy. He was spared none of the awkward questions concerning delay in joining the Arab League, the status of foreign troops in Morocco, assistance for Algerian liberation, diplomatic relations with Communist countries, a rumored alliance with Iraq, Morocco's historic frontiers, and the American bases. His response[12] was introduced by an attack on the "destructive opposition" of some critics, though many of the most embarrassing questions had been posed by U.M.T. and more progressive Istiqlal delegates. The final motion voiced general approval of the government, but specifically endorsed independence for Algeria and noted that current efforts toward the evacuation of troops, unification of the territory, and economic liberation were insufficient. The session certainly anticipated the foreign issues that were to become crucial in 1958.

The 1958 debates reflected the previous year's experience. A calendar was organized for initial discussions in the Assembly bureau, for commission reports, and lastly for the debate of the entire Assembly. Over the preceding year the Ministry of the Economy had had time to initiate several changes in the budget, including the merger of the northern and southern budgets, allocation of income from phosphates to the equipment budget, and balancing of the operational budget; these changes were given the Assembly's approval and the Ministry was congratulated. The Assembly again commented on current political problems, to much the same effect as in earlier sessions. In presenting the budget Bouabid himself discussed the current governmental crisis. The Assembly approved his comment concerning "a lack of coherence and direction in the government and . . . absence of policy of true general expression of the national will."[13] The motions of the Assembly's Political Commission and Economic Commission contained a more detailed critique of the government's organization and activities, with an emphasis on the ministerial posts not controlled by the Istiqlal. The King continued his practice of enlarging the role of the Assembly throughout 1958 in the midst of increasing tension at home and abroad. To some extent consultations of Assembly officers compensated for the weak-

[12] *La Vigie*, November 14, 1957, p. 1.
[13] *Ibid.*, April 3, 1958, p. 1.

ness of the Balafrej Council of Government. A subcommission on frontiers was appointed, including Al-Fassi, who was not a member of the Assembly, to study a report of the Ministry of Foreign Affairs. In the summer of 1958 a special session was convened to discuss the Two Year Economic Plan for 1958-1959, which the Assembly criticized severely. Since the session happened to coincide with the American landings in Lebanon, the Assembly also condemned the intervention of foreign troops in the Middle East. When the question of foreign troops stationed in Morocco became an important issue during the summer of 1958, the King again sought and received Assembly support for troop evacuation.

In the fall of 1958 the political situation in Morocco was much too volatile to permit the selection of new delegates for the Assembly. Those who were then delegates had originally been appointed for two years. During the split of the Istiqlal the entire episode as it affected the Assembly is testimony to the unjustified significance that rudimentary institutions may acquire in a new country. Long before formal institutions are accompanied with appropriate changes in behavior they can become entangled in political controversies far beyond the purpose for which they were designed. It was generally agreed that the King decided not to attempt a new selection of delegates in order to avoid acrimonious debates that political tempers would surely have produced in late 1958.[14] Not only would it have raised the whole issue of the proportion of seats allotted to the various political parties, but it might have aggravated the growing division of the Istiqlal itself. The National Consultative Assembly was extended to May 1959, by which time it was hoped that elections could be held and a new assembly selected by some indirect voting system. For reasons that were never explained, but that probably rested on the bitter controversy mounting over the Balafrej government, the foreign policy debate was not held in the fall of 1958.

When the renewed Assembly was formally installed by the King, new elections for Assembly offices were held. Although the factions of the Istiqlal had ostensibly been reconciled when plans were made for a party Congress, the Istiqlal's impending split was startlingly revealed in the vote for officers. Of the seventy-six members of the Assembly, sixty-three were present. Ben Barka, who had been elected unanimously in the fall of 1956, received only a two-thirds vote. If the President of the National Consultative Assembly was embar-

[14] See *Le Monde*, October 21, 1958, p. 1.

rassed, the Vice-President, Ben Seddik of the U.M.T., must have been shocked. Without some questionable parliamentary maneuvering he might have been defeated and he was elected by far less than a majority of those present. Thirty-two members abstained on the second ballot and he was reelected by twenty-seven votes for and three against him. Ben Barka closed the session with a reiteration of the activists' demand for a "total mobilization of our human potential" and a thinly veiled dig at the more cautious members. The narrowly elected President called for a national sacrifice "in the spirit of equality and abnegation which leaves no place to monopolies or privileges bequeathed by the colonial regime."[15]

There were no doubts about the reflection of the party split in the debates of the National Consultative Assembly in January 1959. A special session was called to consider Moroccan policy when the French franc was devaluated for the second time. The debates began three days before the split of the Istiqlal. Bouabid made a presentation of the policy of adjusting the Moroccan franc but remaining in the franc zone. An equally long speech was made by Tahiri, a member of the moderate Istiqlal group, questioning the soundness of the policy of Bouabid and the Ibrahim government. The clash took place over the draft motions, since one had been submitted by the U.M.T. and another by more conservative Istiqlal members, mostly from the Union of Moroccan Merchants, Industrialists, and Artisans (U.M.C.I.A.). The latter group seems to have controlled the Economic Committee of the Assembly, which was supporting a policy more critical of the government. As a protest against the alleged favoritism of the President of the Assembly for the milder U.M.T. motion, the members of the committee left the chamber. The final motion is supposed to have been drafted jointly by the U.M.T. and the U.M.C.I.A., but the objections of the latter were revealed to the press after the party split. The final motion approved Bouabid's policy, but went on to state typical activist reservations on the slow progress of renovating the "colonialist economy," the failure to control exports and imports, and the delay in organizing Moroccan institutions to encourage investment.

The effect of the party split on the Assembly's future is difficult to predict. The vote for officers indicated that the moderates of the Istiqlal have a majority. The Istiqlal faction probably could not muster more than a third of the votes of the Assembly. They do,

[15] *Ibid.*, November 9-10, 1958, p. 2.

however, accrue prestige from their positions, like all the opposition parties, and control many of the top offices. When the Inspector General of the Istiqlal was received by the King to explain the party split, it was widely rumored that he hoped to have Ben Barka removed from his post as President of the Assembly. The Istiqlal later attacked him for using the Secretariat of the Assembly as the "local center for his separatist movement" and added that he "profit(ed) from his situation as President of the National Consultative Assembly, which confer[ed] a certain immunity and a certain representative character."[16] No doubt well aware that every Istiqlal minister had used his office to carry on party business, the King did not comment. Like the abuse of the U.M.T., this was one of the long-standing advantages that the Istiqlal had never questioned when it was united.

The National Consultative Assembly has come to have considerably more than an occasional advisory role. Though certainly not representative or explicitly making any claim to being such, it has gradually assumed some prerogatives of a fully organized and responsible assembly. Especially during 1958, when important elements were not represented in the Council of Government, they could be consulted through the Assembly. This practice tended, of course, to enhance the advantage of the critical groups who were not accountable—an advantage which the Old Guard Istiqlal did not hesitate to exploit early in 1959. The opportunities given to the dissident elements of the Istiqlal in 1958 certainly contributed to the party split, and the counterattack by Istiqlal moderates in the Assembly continued to inflame feelings in 1959. With the Istiqlal's efforts centered in Rabat's somewhat rarefied atmosphere, other projects for popular participation, like the rural commune, tended to be postponed. The danger of the political system's becoming an arena of intense intrigue and competition at the central level, while more distant members of the nation were forgotten, very likely encouraged the discontent in the countryside late in 1958. The continued squabbling in the Assembly in early 1959 probably contributed to the new surge of confidence in the King. While the more specialized political groups pursue their more particular goals, concentrating on immediate desires and expressing opinions only among the elite of the government may delay more far-reaching development of the political system. If the relation between the embryonic

---

[16] *Al-Istiqlal*, January 31, 1959, p. 3.

representative body and the mass of citizens appears to be only further repetition of political slogans, the new institution may be discredited. The experience gained by the Consultative Assembly has certainly been beneficial to the ultimate development of representative government, but alone it is not sufficient. If pursued in the absence of other projects for encouraging political participation, the experiment with representative government may become self-defeating and possibly detrimental to the nation itself.

Rural Communes and Popular Participation

The institutional reform for encouraging popular participation which will most probably be used as the basic electoral unit is the rural commune. The historical origin of the commune is of particular interest in the analysis of the present political system in Morocco, for it demonstrates that devices associated with the Protectorate or that have distinctly tribal origins are acceptable if Moroccan leaders can agree on their use. Although extremely sensitive on questions of colonial vestiges and also any continuance of Berber-Arab distinctions, the nationalists have been universal in their approval of the rural commune, or *jemaâ*, as the eventual basic political unit in the countryside. In its ancient form the *jemaâ* was a council of tribes or sections of tribes in the predominantly Berber areas, whose origins are nearly prehistoric. The French-sponsored Berber *dahir* of 1930 tried to institutionalize this ethnic division by reinforcing the more primitive communal structure. Under French rule they remained, however, largely a unit of administrative control as the pacification of the country advanced. Progress was carefully arrested at the level of development most useful to the Protectorate, though the communes were certainly not entirely detrimental to the tribes. Although the councils were carefully prevented from engaging in national politics, there were many beneficial results in cooperative enterprises to build roads, improve *souks* or markets, regulate and improve water supplies, and present tribal views as the councils were consulted.

Among the *dahirs* submitted to Mohammed V during the crisis of February 1951 was a new *dahir* on rural communes. Much to the surprise of the Resident General, the King did not oppose the plan to invigorate the communes.[17] Very possibly with justification, the

[17] See Julien, *L'Afrique du Nord en Marche, op.cit.*, p. 384.

King's reception of the plan aroused French suspicions that the King and the nationalists hoped to use the communes to extend their rural influence. By this time the King was a known nationalist figure throughout the country and the Istiqlal possessed footholds in many of the Berber regions. If the new communes were initiated with the explicit purpose of providing for the tribes a role in political and economic affairs, the French felt that they would very likely become another source of nationalist influence and that all delay in communal development would become the basis for nationalist complaints. There also was the risk of offending the pro-French *caids* and creating new opposition among the French *colons*. The French plan, which was designed to form much smaller units than the later Moroccan plan, called for 2,500 communes, of which only five hundred had been established by the end of 1953.[18] Under the *dahir* of 1951 communal elections were pigeonholed by the French, who continued to designate and carefully supervise local officials.

Administration of the communes was transferred to the Ministry of the Interior in the summer of 1956. The prerequisites of their utilization on the national level have delayed progress since that time. Plans were under way to have a new *dahir* prepared in the spring of 1958 defining the procedures and powers of the *caid*, local court, and communal council, but it did not appear. The most important missing items of legislation were the *dahirs* on electoral procedures and public liberties, without which the rural communes could not be organized in modernized form. Distracted by internal crises and international problems, the government was slow to enact basic legislation, although the preparations for the rural communes were nearly complete by 1958.[19] The law on public liberties, of course, also gave the small political parties legal protection that was extremely controversial. The government has been promising elections ever since early 1957, but government authorities felt that the electoral law should be coordinated with both the communal system and civic liberties legislation. Once an electoral law was published, it would have been most difficult to delay further the reforms which the Istiqlal very likely opposed while it remained united. The risk of this procrastination was seen in late 1958 when the Popular Movement, denied any legal avenue of expression and exploiting rural

[18] *Morocco, 1954, op.cit.*, p. 48. French figures are somewhat confusing on the progress of the commune plan, no doubt partly because there were second thoughts.
[19] Interview with Ahmed Bahnini, Director of Political Affairs, Ministry of the Interior, August 22, 1958.

discontent that was similarly without effective means of expression, broke into violent opposition.

The most important technical operation in reforming the communes was to divide the tribes into units that would be economically viable, politically manageable, and ethnically harmonious.[20] This monumental task was begun in the fall of 1957 for the southern zone. Those regions were completed by 1958 and work began on the northern zone, where both the terrain and the depressed economy made planning more difficult. The new plan was to include about 800 communes for the entire country, of which roughly 600 were to be in the southern zone and 200 in the northern zone. Nearly all of the communes had been designated by *caids* and there had been little effort to promote community development or cooperative enterprise with central support. The old system of communes was admittedly based on the tribal structure. The variety of the tribal structure in Morocco makes generalization difficult, but the French system envisaged about five communal councils for each tribe.[21] The small average membership of about 2,300 persons per commune and the division of many tribes into smaller units were in harmony with the French policy of careful control and isolation of the countryside. The new proposals envisage having about 10,000 members and allow for roughly one commune per tribe, but ethnic considerations are much less important. There are many instances of coincidence between tribes or sections of tribes and the new communes, but the overriding criteria have been to include an area where the people may convene without undue hardship, have some common economic and social problems to encourage cooperation, and have sufficient income to enable small local projects of their own choosing.

That the proposed local assemblies of the communes were to be disassociated from the tribal structure was made clear in the King's first speech to the Assembly, when he referred to their role in the "political education of the citizens and their participation in the management of their own affairs." His intention was repeated even more explicitly in the Royal Charter, which frankly stated, "The tribal structures . . . will not constitute a base for putting in place representative organisms."[22] That he needed to clarify this aim after

[20] Interview with Hassan Zemmouri, Assistant Director of Political Affairs, Ministry of the Interior, December 9, 1957.

[21] This is using the figures cited in *Morocco, 1954, op.cit.*, pp. 47-48, of 600 tribes and a total of about 3,000 communes.

[22] *Al-Istiqlal*, May 11, 1958, p. 3.

preparations had been under way in the predominantly Istiqlal government for over a year suggests that there may have been some
confusion in either administrative or Istiqlal circles concerning the
organization and purpose of the new communal system. Possibly
there was confusion in both areas. The administration might well
tend to rely on the more easily demarcated and well-known tribal
differentiations, on which the rural administration was already built.
On the other hand, the comment on the commune from Istiqlal
leaders has sometimes slighted the political role of the commune,
while stressing its function in the economic and social mobilization
of the rural population.

The structure of the communal system can best be judged from
the reports of the Itinerant Commission, which met with the high
officials of each province to prepare a statement on the division of
the communes.[23] The reports from the provinces of Fès and Tafilalet
were selected because they reveal the bewildering variety of problems
in planning communes. The northern province has a relatively rich
and modern agricultural economy in open plains. In the more primitive and arid southern province the people struggle along with
mountainside flocks or are scattered along the eroded valleys running through the pre-Sahara region. The commission noted that the
division in Fès province was facilitated by the local officials' familiarity with the old system and by the open plains. The task was more
difficult in Tafilalet where little had been done to modernize the
economy and where the tribal structure was stronger. The communes
envisaged by the Protectorate were too small to be helpful and not
well implanted. The small *souks* could not support a commune and
the dispersed occupations did not encourage central projects. Both
the livestock and rich olive groves of Fès supported active, large
souks where income could be derived for the commune. The problem was, nevertheless, complicated because much of the income was
controlled by large landowners living in Fès while many of the
local people had only the small wages of rural laborers.

Table 12 summarizes the major differences. In the poorer, more
rugged circles, like Goulmima, Ksar As-Souk, or Boulemane, the

[23] "Procès Verbale de la Réunion de la Commission Itinerante de Découpage à
Fès," October 4, 1957; and "Procès Verbale de la Réunion de la Commission Itine-
rante Découpage à Tafilalet," November 27, 1957. The representatives of the
Ministry of the Interior in both these meetings were Hassan Zemmouri and Scalabre.
All the examples given in this and the following paragraphs are from these two
reports. The ministry kindly agreed to permit the author to use two examples.

TABLE 12

Plan for Rural Communes of Fès and Tafilalet Provinces
(Average Membership, Caids, and Tribes per Commune)[a]

Province	No. of Com- munes	No. of Tribes	No. of Caids	Total Pop. (000's)	Aver. Memb. in Com- mune (000's)
Fès					
Circle of Fès-Banlieu	10	10	4	122	12
Circle of Karia Ba Mohammed	14	13	5	130	9
Circle of Sefrou	5	4	2	56	11
Circle of Boulemane	9	7	5	52	6
Circle of Taounate	13	10	5	119	9
Tafilalet					
Circle of Midelt	8	11	4	60	7
Circle of Erfoud[b]	8	12	5	91	11
Circle of Ksar As-Souk	5	7	3	30	6
Circle of Goulmima	9	8	4	54	6
Circle of Rich	10	25	7	73	7

[a] The number of communes has been taken from the "Procès Verbal . . . ," *op.cit.* The number of *caids*, tribes, and total population of the circles has been taken from the *Livre des Commandements, op.cit.* The population of the municipality of Fès and the pashalik of Sefrou has been excluded. The problem of quantitative estimates in a new country is suggested by the variance between the population figures given in these documents, although they are printed by two departments of the same ministry. The figures from the *Livre* have been used, although they tend to be slightly above the two Procès.

[b] In the commission report for the circle of Erfoud a commune is allotted to the Bureau of Taouz, an office created by the French and still used in areas of migratory tribes. For simplicity it has been counted here as a commune.

communes had a smaller membership. In the richer areas and in spots where travel was easier, membership reached the optimum of around 10,000, as in Fès-Banlieu, Karia Ba Mohammed, and the larger palmeries around Erfoud. The ratio between the number of tribes and communes varies unpredictably. The reports showed that no purposeless effort was made to break up tribal areas, which already, of course, displayed a certain social, economic, and political homogeneity that can be beneficial, but that where more important considerations of economic viability or communication were involved, ethnic lines were broken. The most consistent trend is to give each *caid* an average of two communes to supervise. As the rural-commune plan proceeds, however, the *caids* and *supercaids* will clearly play the key role. They are in a position to coordinate governmental aid to the communal projects while maintaining day-to-day contact with the communal councils.

The detailed appendices of the Itinerant Commission's reports show the many obstacles to rapidly integrating the rural population in national political life. To achieve economic viability, it was hoped that each commune would have resources valued at least a million francs and annual *souk* transactions of half this amount. Actually there were communes in the Fès area with resources valued at three million francs, most of which were owned by absentee landlords and represented by the productive olive orchards. In the same province existed a commune with resources of only about 100,000 francs, which condition was common in the south. In several instances the most easily demarcated area had no *souk*, and delicate negotiations were needed so that several communes could share income from the same market. In some areas of Fès improvements were jeopardized by the parceling of land into extremely small sections, while in other northern communes four fifths of the land was administered by *habous* or religious foundations. Around Midelt there were tribes of up to 5,000 without a *souk* and many small tribes were merged on the basis of common economic pursuits. One southern commune included 19,000 persons because they used the same *souk*, had a dispersed economy based on livestock grazing, and had the same ethnic ties. Along the Ziz river valley the scattered *ksars* or villages in the palm groves had to be grouped. Nearly all the communes of the Tafilalet province lacked sufficient resources, while the largest share of those in Fès are potentially workable.

The variety of local interests is not necessarily a handicap to developing communes that can be harmonious and constructive on the national level. Certainly considerable ingenuity will be required from the local administrative officials and, in turn, from their superiors in Rabat. The great differentiation of local problems can serve to encourage self-reliance and initiative in local affairs which, in turn, may help to clarify the difference between nation and locality. The existing social and economic diversity can help the tribesmen differentiate between what can be expected of central government and what must be done on a provincial or even circle level. These easily made distinctions in an advanced political system are implanted in a new, retarded nation only from experience. By their diversity the communes can set a pattern of directing influence at the level of political organization most suited to solve the problem and encourage defining the problems with which the political system is to deal in a limited way.

The risk on the national level, however, is that other circumstances in the political system will continue to postpone developing the more retarded members' capacity to participate in national politics, though the countryside may easily find other avenues of expressing its opinions and exerting its influence on the national level. The figures who exert influence in national politics may neglect increasing political participation for a variety of reasons. More active participants of all opinions may be unaware of the devices used to compel or persuade the less influential citizens to postpone their grievances or to overlook the shortcomings of the government. The full impact of the frequent appeals for continued nationalist solidarity because of past sacrifices to liberate the nation may have unintended and unanticipated consequences. By forestalling the development of an individual's capacity to participate in politics and by setting a pattern of imposing increasingly dire sanctions based on the survival of the nation, a self-justifying device for procrastination may be created. While there may be justifiable need for rationalization, it may also result in the accumulation of discontent among the nonparticipants and in their increased understanding of other forms of influence open to them. With sufficient tension of this kind the entire political system may collapse in civil war or some other form of violence.

The Istiqlal has generally supported the communal plan, but has revealed some equivalence and confusion regarding community development in the countryside. The more fervent Islamic leaders were first concerned with the commune as an instrument to facilitate the uniform application of Muslim law. Shortly after independence Al-Fassi sketched his idea of the model village, which would elect officers and have a consultative assembly at the level of the circle and province. He also expressed concern over the undemocratic customs of the tribes, by which he probably meant their use of customary law and the tendency to reject Muslim law. Later the progressive Istiqlal leaders, who did not take an interest in the commune until the approach of elections in 1957, discussed the communes in terms of a mobilization of popular energy for concrete, constructive purposes. Although the tribal *jemaâ* had been manipulated by the French to oppose nationalism and was also the seat of Berber customary law dreaded by devout Muslims, the party leaders began to refer to the democratic qualities of that ancient institution, which are generally presumed to be suitable for modern purposes.[24] Such a transformation might be possible, but it is doubtful if the presently existing tribal councils are capable of making such a transition without considerable help and direction from the government. This is a very different situation from the spontaneous and harmonious change predicted by party officials. To assume that qualities most needed in modern life will survive and will continue to function as desired is a self-deception that may ultimately work to the detriment of the communes. This assumption also appeared in the talk given at the *caid* school in which an official noted that Morocco's "appetite for democratic institutions"[25] was demonstrated by the harmony between the ancient councils and the pre-Protectorate kings. This statement is, at best, most disputable.

As the Itinerant Commission reports indicate, it is doubtful if the *jemaâ* in its present form is so easily transformed. Subsequent party discussion attached communal elections to demands for increased ministerial authority. To the extent that the Istiqlal had thereby committed itself to the *status quo* until popular bodies could be selected, it had also limited its ability to ask for more authority. During the crisis of early 1958 the problems were distinguished, but in early 1957, when the first speculations on elections began, the party showed deep interest in the commune. The main spokesman, Ben Barka, acknowledged the electoral role of the commune and also the historical roots from the *jemaâ*, but he was much more concerned with its economic and social contributions. He stressed his hope that the commune would become "the driving force in the total transformation of the country" and that from it would come "the fecund and dynamic spirit for the complete construction of the country."[26] Both international problems and the structure of the political system have worked to postpone this development.

[24] A typical example will be found in a statement of Balafrej, who is an experienced statesman and trained lawyer. *Al-Istiqlal*, March 30, 1956, p. 8. Late in 1958 Al-Fassi even suggested that the *moussem*, a tribal festival, once regarded as a heresy by orthodox Muslims, could have a constructive role in introducing tribes to national activities, *ibid.*, September 13, 1958, p. 15.

[25] *Ibid.*, January 11, 1957, p. 7.

[26] *Ibid.*, March 2, 1957, p. 3. It should also be noted that he displayed much more knowledge of other countries' experience with the commune and its organization in advanced nations. He very likely wrote the articles in *Al-Istiqlal* on the commune in Yugoslavia and France.

Elections in Search of a Role

The establishment of the communes, which had a joint social and political role, had to wait until a system for selecting communal officers could be agreed upon. These officers' functions also had to be related to those of other local administrative officials and to the larger popular assemblies that were to be indirectly elected. Although everyone may have been agreed on the commune plan, party relationships in Morocco made it difficult to arrive at an agreed electoral plan. Furthermore, officials were reluctant to hold elections during periods of international tension, which have recurred with discouraging regularity. Elections were placed among the most important purposes of the first and second Bekkai governments. On May Day, 1957, the King announced that elections were being planned for the coming fall. Shortly afterwards this was confirmed by the Minister of the Interior and received the Istiqlal's hearty endorsement. This decision introduced several weeks of bitter controversy among the parties—a revealing commentary on both the problems of planning and participating in elections in a new nation. To have suggested rural elections at this time seems most strange, since there were no indications that any plan existed, nor did the reorganization of the communes even begin until September 1957.

The Istiqlal was reportedly losing some support during the spring of 1957, partly from the poor agricultural year and partly from the initial disillusionment following independence. The Minister of the Interior, M'Hammedi, was reported to favor a system of *scrutin de liste* by majority,[27] which would certainly favor the Istiqlal. It would also simplify preparations for elections, for which there were only three months if the schedule of elections in October 1957 was to be kept. The improvisation that took place was criticized by both the King and the opposition parties. The Democratic party complained over the Istiqlal's interference with civil liberties and its predominance in the civil service. These claims may have been justifiable, but the Democratic party also used the occasion to open a campaign for "neutral" government of "National Union." How such a government would be formed or how it could contribute to fair elections was never explained, but it was certain that it would have given the Democratic party the national position it had lost in the fall of 1956. They later modified their views to ask only "to be consulted" and

[27] See *L'Action*, September 2, 1957, p. 10.

observed that, in the absence of any legislation on civil liberties and with the electoral census' being conducted by minor officials without provision for appeal or inspection, there were no guarantees that the elections would be able to reflect popular opinion.[28] When these grievances were sent to the King, the Istiqlal reacted strongly, charging the critics with trying to discredit an enterprise of the King and to delay the institution of a democratic government.

The King's intervention revealed that he would not be content with an improvised electoral system or with partial guarantees. Though M'Hammedi stressed "economy of text," the other ministers under Bekkai's leadership were officially reported to have dwelt on the importance of having each phase of the electoral process surrounded with guarantees.[29] After listening to various proposals the King submitted that the elections must be preceded with a careful study of their organization, even if it retarded them by some months. The next day a communiqué from the palace announced that the King had given instructions for a study of foreign electoral systems, with a view toward seeking the devices most suitable for Morocco. It stipulated that the citizens would have "the possibility of introducing all appeals concerning the establishment of electoral lists, lists of candidates and finally the holding of the consultation itself. . . . To this end His Majesty will designate the special commissions who will eventually make known the results." The charges that the elections were going to be arbitrarily directed by the Ministry of the Interior are to some extent supported by the firm intervention of the King at this time, especially in his explicit reservation that the commissions tabulating the returns would be personally responsible to him. By fall it was evident that preparations were insufficient for elections and the Ifni incident produced international complications. After consulting two French experts, M'Hammedi made a visit to study Tunisian elections. He announced that an electoral law was ready to be submitted to the King.[30] It was then reported that elections would take place in March 1958 and, later, not until August 1958. All these plans were postponed because of the crisis of the spring and summer of 1958.

[28] *Démocracie*, July 22, 1957, p. 3.

[29] Communiqué of Minister of Information, *C.M.*, July 25-28, 1957, p. 1, from which the quotations in this paragraph are also taken.

[30] *L'Action*, January 20, 1958, p. 11. The elections were subsequently announced for September 1959, and May 1960, when they were finally held. The circumstances and results of the election will be the subject of a subsequent study.

The only detailed electoral plan to appear by early 1959 was in the Istiqlal's *Internal Bulletin*.[31] The proposal favored voting rights for men and women at twenty years of age, though in the "transitional phase" a woman was to be either head of a family, carry a labor identity card, i.e., be a paid laborer, pay taxes on property or commerce, or have a certificate of elementary education. The electoral system suggested by the party relied heavily on the existing tribal or rural village structure. Each large village or group of villages was to select, "in accordance with the way that best suits their way of life," a president or sheikh. His function was unclear, except that he would "put into effect the group's decisions and represent the central authority." Much more explicit were his services for the central government: to carry out instructions from the *caid*; to keep order; to preserve public buildings; to issue official certificates; and to register births. Much less thought had gone into defining his local political role than into the question of how he could further the needs of his area. Important as this may be and, in a sense, as much of a prerequisite as it may be to a smoothly functioning electoral system, there was little attention as to how the local council would influence decisions concerning the village or how differences of opinion would be settled at the village level. While democratic government cannot blossom fully with a single reform, neither should the ultimate goal of new institutions be ignored. Indeed, there is no reason why some form of representative government is necessary, but it is unfortunate that other reforms should be presented under the guise of political reform—a practice that works to the disadvantage of both endeavors.

Evaluation of the Istiqlal's *Bulletin* must take into account that it is designed to be read to illiterate party members and especially to reach those members most distant from the centers of political activity. In July 1957 it carried an article on elections, which explained: "The meaning of elections is to choose one person from those who represent themselves as candidates or are presented by the party which you entrust to represent you in the defense of your interests or in the management of your affairs. . . . The holding of elections includes rights and duties for the elector and the candidate. Electors are completely free to vote for the person they like and no one can oblige them to use this right on behalf of any person they

[31] "Summary of the Istiqlal Party's Project for the Village Communes" (New Series), no. 4, April 1957(?), p. 4.

do not like. A delegate is to bear the responsibility of representing a part of the nation but when he feels incapable of carrying out this responsibility he must leave his position to someone who can carry out these duties. . . . To know your rights and duties it is necessary to get in touch with the party and to have complete information. Since elections are something new, the party members need explanations to carry out their duties."[32] The statement is interesting not only because its general impartiality, but also because impartiality is itself partially entailed by the electoral process in a new country. To be certain of widespread popular support the party could have used tribal loyalties and regional aims, but these are exactly the divisive forces which the Istiqlal had fought against and which the French had used to combat the Istiqlal. Having based their pre-eminence on the assumption of the party's popularity never yet tested by an actual head count, the Istiqlal could not belittle or abuse the procedure which it has continually claimed would vindicate its position. As an institution elections entail certain guarantees and procedures which the leaders of the party know very well and which they can deny only at the risk of jeopardizing their entire position in the political system.

The minority parties favored a system that would give their scattered membership more strength, single-member constituencies in the cities, and possibly a proportional representation system of counting in both cities and rural areas. The Istiqlal voiced the opinion that a system of *scrutin uninominal* might risk the "crumbling of the communal councils," while the *scrutin de liste* would permit the selection of "homogeneous teams conscious of the tasks to be accomplished."[33] That the Istiqlal did not feel free to delay, at least publicly, the progress of the electoral system does not mean that it was prevented from seeking popular support by appeal to preindependence fears. Possibly stimulated by the reported increases in the popularity of the Liberal Independents and also by the Popular Movement's success in the countryside, the *Bulletin* said: "Some indecisive persons and groups of traitors and feudalists have wanted to exploit these elections . . . to serve colonialist objectives. . . . Colonialism will not sit back these days, but will seek success through its supporters in the elections. . . . Some false organizations and parties of traitors may appear, particularly at the time of elections,

[32] "Elections" (New Series), no. 6, June 1957(?), pp. 3-4.
[33] *Al-Istiqlal*, October 12, 1957, p. 3.

to break popular solidarity. These organizations can always find the necessary support from colonialism, which offers them money to buy those of weak conscience and belief. . . . The Moroccan people must understand that the only way to preserve independence is to defeat the plots of these impostors, who do not rely on the national program of the Istiqlal party."[34] The question of colonialist influence was stressed in the meetings of the inspectors and the Political Commission. There also emerged two views on the role of elections, which had been implied to some extent in the differing interpretations of the commune. The difference was only one manifestation of the deeper cleavage of opinion among party leaders. In a speech to the Young Scholars of the Istiqlal Youth, Ibrahim maintained: "The citizen in a democracy of façade is a nonexistent citizen, since formal democracy is based on the 'law' not on daily realities. Under this regime the citizens are considered as equal in rights. It is a matter in reality of a false equality between the begging, starving citizen and the rich, powerful citizen. . . . No text of law can replace misery with prosperity, sickness with health or ignorance with knowledge. Formal democracy can be created in a month: it suffices only to rewrite the texts, publish them in the official journal, to foment the intrigues between such and such group. The goal we seek is not only to give liberty, but also the objective conditions permitting the citizen enjoyment of this liberty."[35] This position cannot be lightly dismissed, for it is the more broad economic and social problems of Morocco that have been the most troublesome internal obstacle to holding elections.

The Istiqlal, however, officially retained its position favoring elections, though with increasing reservations. In his interview with the King during the formation of the Balafrej government, Ben Barka reaffirmed his support for elections, but cautioned the King on the delay needed to prepare for them, on the other more pressing problems, and on the "imperialist intrigues and reactionary coalitions who camouflage themselves behind a so-called defense of democracy."[36] The difficulties were acknowledged in the Royal Charter, which repeated the King's desire to hold elections, but also noted the disastrous results that had occurred in other countries ending in "condemnation and degradation of parliamentary rule . . . political

[34] "At the Door of Elections" (New Series), no. 8, August 1957(?), pp. 5-6.
[35] Al-Istiqlal, March 1, 1958, p. 13.
[36] Ibid., April 20, 1958, p. 3.

disequilibrium . . . and lack of harmony." The Charter also noted that "democracy should be accompanied with the construction of a social and economic democracy." In his acceptance speech Balafrej expressed complete satisfaction with plans to hold elections and guarantee civil liberties for the free implementation of these elections. Without commenting on the work of the commission under M'Hammedi or the study of the problem up to that time, he also added that a new electoral commission would be appointed. Though throughout the year rumors continued concerning the promulgation of the basic legislation for elections, the Algerian question and the Popular Movement demonstrations led to further postponement.

By mid-1958 the intensified internal politics of Morocco made the delay in promulgating the Charter of Liberties and the holding of elections embarrassing for the Istiqlal and the King. At the base of the party, the party inspectors assured the militants that the "homogeneous" Balafrej government had not been formed to establish one-party rule. The Istiqlal reiterated that it had fought for liberty since independence and approved of a "constructive" opposition. It is quite possible that the ostensible priority that all Moroccan leaders had been giving to elections since 1955 had succeeded in establishing among the Moroccan populace expectations which were now beginning to feed back, to the discomfort of the leaders. Even the King publicly acknowledged the unanticipated obstacles which had arisen and confessed that the government had been "confronted with all sorts of difficulties, of which we anticipated neither the number or the complexity."[37] The admission of the mechanical problems was in itself important, but it was also significant that he made the admission before the National Assembly. The activist elements of the Istiqlal were well-represented in the Assembly and had often criticized the Balafrej government for postponing elections.

Morocco found herself troubled by the task of establishing some form of representative government when the advanced segments of the political system were already active in a quasi-representative body. The King anticipated the kind of sterile agitation that could take place in such an institution; this situation became apparent in some of the Assembly meetings. His decision to grant the Charter of Liberties in November, before the plan for elections was ready for promulgation, demonstrates the inverse sequence in which the

[37] *La Vigie*, November 18, 1958, p. 1.

institutions of the new country tend to be formed. In the Speech from the Throne the King repeated the obstacles to elections and went on to identify squarely the risk of institutions based on them: "The true danger is not in the absence of representative institutions, but resides in the establishment of a purely formal parliamentary regime, a factor of disorder and destruction, whereas an authentic democracy should be a factor of stability and construction."[38] With the promulgation of the Charter of Liberties it would become increasingly difficult to justify postponement of elections. The parties, particularly the newly formed National Union, were reluctant to accept the King's ruling as to their relative strength or his decision as to their appropriate role in governing. Elections will be an important test of the capability of the Moroccan population as a whole to participate in a national political system.

The question of establishing some form of representative government in a new nation introduces several difficult problems into the political system. Representative institutions require a set of rules. Ignoring for the moment how close these rules may come to the generally accepted concept of democratic or representative government, one sees that the new political system is itself poorly equipped to make rules. In Morocco the King reserved all sovereign powers and all legislation was subject to his approval. To the extent that the political struggle tends to cluster around personalities and the bureaucracy of the central government, the legislative process that is needed to select rules becomes a secondary consideration of most articulate participants. While the King's moderation and caution have been beneficial in some respects, they have also contributed to the confusion as to how particular groups or individuals were to focus their influence on a particular problem. In the absence of a long historical development of representative institutions such institutions are necessarily designed and promulgated in an arbitrary fashion. The use of defined procedures to exercise influence for specific purposes embodies a transition in the political system that should not be minimized. The King and the nationalists have all been subjected to a long struggle in which their political techniques were conditioned by a very different kind of setting. Decisions were made by a small caucus and in closely guarded clandestineness. Coercion was and—perhaps most important—tends to remain a form

[38] *Ibid.*

of influence, which representative procedures find difficult to control. Furthermore, the nation as a whole does not yet incorporate the specialized social and economic structure that tends to encourage groups to seek their aims outside the government.

Nearly every new need of the society as a whole or of a group of individuals tends to become a national problem. New institutions are not confined to supervising the administration and making laws on the relatively refined and predominantly political problems that are commonly submitted to the legislatures of an advanced nation. Decisions are not made on the basis of experience of actions and with the insights of dealing with similar problems for a generation. Only the most general kind of predictions can be made about the broad programs of social change upon which new countries embark. Concerning these, the most important decisions perhaps, there is very little disagreement, while concerning the interests of the specialized groups who might conceivably work out compromises within the framework of a representative government only a fraction of the population is directly involved. Thus it is not only that there is no way in which the retarded citizen can outline the best way to operate a rural commune or that he is not qualified to make decisions on monetary policy, but also that the merchant or doctor does not wish to have the tribesman telling him what to do. Emphasis alone on the limitations of the most retarded members may distort the problem of representative government, for it distracts attention from the inverse situation. In both instances the feasibility of the solution is limited by the least capable participant, but it is also the advanced member of the nation who wishes to preserve the kind of specialized and sophisticated influence used in his walk of life.

If for the moment the nationalists are accepted as a homogeneous unit, there are other complications both for the operation of some form of representative government and for its installation. As the National Consultative Assembly had demonstrated, the opposition groups had been given a forum that might have been exaggerated beyond its significance, but which was also almost invulnerable to criticism. Though these groups might be denounced as colonialist tools and political clubs, the fact remained that in a legislature their existence could not be destroyed. This, in turn, meant that the Istiqlal could never fully achieve the goal of preeminence. The maneuver used to combat the minor parties was to discredit their claim to influence by implying that they had not contributed to the liberation of the country or that since then they had worked against independence, often in collusion with a foreign power. The Istiqlal was understandably reluctant to establish any institution that would irrevocably defend the role of the opposition. To have an opposition means to the leading nationalists that the claims and goals that they wish to associate with the nation do not include all possible claims or all conceivable goals. In terms of the political system as a whole, this means that so long as political relationships from habit, intent, or accident tend constantly to be judged on the basis of the universal and exclusive claim of any one group, the progress of representative institutions is handicapped. Participation in such institutions means that there exists a defined area of common loyalties and mutual trust, which the contending groups in Morocco have not yet developed. For the explanation one must turn to the way in which the political system as a whole operates. It may be not only that leaders of the Istiqlal wish to preserve their preeminence, but also that if they were to sacrifice their superior claim both the political system and the specific institutions concerned would not be able to function.

Without accepting the slightly Marxist twist given to the views of the more outspoken activists of the Istiqlal, their contention deserves more careful consideration. The self-evident argument that the starving man cares little for the right to vote is likely to conceal a contribution to the analysis of politics in new nations. The great range of social differentiation does tend to alter the significance of the equal political privilege that representative institutions presume to exist in some form. Even with a modified electoral system, it is difficult to pose the goals of a legislative institution in such a way that the weight given to a particular rural unit, which may include many individuals, should be considered equivalent to that of an urban unit, which may represent fewer individuals. If such an institution is to act only on such matters as are of common concern within the political experience of all members of the new nation, it can obviously not make a very great contribution, nor can it probably handle alone the law-making needs of the new country. The citizens are not only limited by their capacity to exercise influence in different ways, but also by the different significance of the various problems that might arise. The capacity to act and the capacity to understand as psychological characteristics of the participants have their parallel significance in terms of the operation of the political system itself. Identification of the absence of understanding in the functioning of the political system is difficult, since it is, in a sense, a vacuum or a void where the political relationships simply do not exist. No institution can automatically fill the vacuum, and to expect it to do so is only to start a democratic system of government with a hopeless handicap.

CHAPTER XII

FORMATION OF INTEREST GROUPS

Industrialists and Merchants Unite

THE achievement of independence in Morocco has gradually destroyed the solidarity of the old nationalist movement, but to some extent the present struggle to survive has been almost as intense as the past struggle to exist. Occasionally less urgent problems have been phrased in terms of "existence" so that the country may enjoy the solidarity of the preindependence struggle. Some leaders advocated that the political system should continue to focus on survival and that all new relations should be based on this imperative. However, the discipline that the country manifested under colonial rule required effort and sacrifices that many are reluctant to make today. The possible temptation of an authoritarian political system was offset by the particular interests that were asserted after independence, though these too could conceivably have been enveloped in a highly directed and controlled political system. Special interests were formed on the basis of specialized endeavor of many kinds. Some of this activity has been predominantly political in its orientation, while other efforts have had predominantly social or economic purposes. In an advanced political system such groups generally are referred to as pressure or interest groups, but the conventional use of this phrase implies more institutional structure and regulated competition for influence than can be attributed to a new country. Indeed, one of the problems of the emerging political system is how to accommodate special interests while at the same time encouraging new forms of political participation and designing national institutions for all new citizens.

The problem is further complicated since the existing specialized groups are best prepared to use new national institutions. By their own advancement in the nation as a whole they tend to jeopardize the growth of other institutional relationships that might restrain, compromise, or detract from their purpose. This is by no means necessarily planned or intentional. The existing groups generally have a defined area of interest, their leaders know how to seek their ends within the governmental framework, and often the group is of sufficient importance to be able to bring certain kinds of threats to the existence of the nation itself. Their problem is, of course, that the influence they can exercise is limited to the kind of specialization upon which the group is based. In terms of national interest it may often be possible to justify the restraint or abolition of the group. The influential specialists of a new country wield a sword that may easily be turned against them. If merchants, for example, are inordinately successful in manipulating the administration through family connections or privileged knowledge of administrative procedures, they may demolish the importance of the differentiation on which their group was founded. Even more than pressure groups of advanced countries, nascent interest groups are denied the possibility of seeking influence by popular appeal. In the absence of the multiplicity of special interests or the institutional checks of an advanced society, their political activity may become simply intrigue and corruption at the central level, which, in turn, may result in discrediting such groups as the country as a whole progresses. The specialized group in a new country risks not only conflict with the national interest itself, which is a potential hazard for any group, but also it risks being surpassed by the rapid social and political change taking place in the country as a whole. As new institutions are designed and as new participants become active, the small group, in somewhat the same fashion as the political party, must adapt or risk extinction.

In less abstract form the same situation confronted the nationalists. Prior to independence the difference between small industrialist and worker, civil servant and student, or merchant and consumer meant little. Since independence the Istiqlal has tried to preserve the unity of purpose which it enjoyed during the previous struggle. But within its membership are found all the mentioned differentiations and more. Since the organization was based largely in the cities prior to independence and relied heavily on the more articulate sections of the population, the Istiqlal included many of the highly differentiated citizens. Although the party has encouraged the formation of special groups, possibly without fully realizing the implications of their activity, it has also tried to keep strong lines between these groups and the party. Formally and informally most of the large specialized groups in Morocco are represented in the party and most of them participate directly on the Political Committee. The largest and most important of these was certainly the U.M.T., whose conflicts with the party were sufficient to produce a break in 1959. The open conflict that has developed in this relationship is indicative of the kind of dissension that the party must try to avoid with other groups. The threat is not only the loss of members or revenue, but also the admission that the single party cannot encompass all the interests and resolve all the individual differences that are found in the new nation. Why the leaders of the Istiqlal should choose to attempt this is a psychological question beyond the intent of this study, but that they must find some way of doing it in order to fulfill their claim to preeminence is a political problem. Up to 1958 the party was surprisingly successful, though concessions, compromises, and sacrifices were made.

As the transition of the political system takes place, the relationship between the special group and the nationalist party changes. It should not be evaluated solely in terms of what the party does for the group in getting favors and recognition during the confusion of the transition. The party is, nevertheless, a useful and effective instrument for much action of the small groups in the early phase of the transition. As new civil servants are being placed with party approval, contacts are entrenched. Initially the specialized groups tend to be preoccupied with the reconstruction and adjustment of their internal organization and needs. As time passes there is very likely a tendency for groups to find their own direct channels of access to the government and even to try to have friends placed in key positions. As interests begin to be more clearly defined, there is a self-generating trend toward less and less dependence on the party. That most groups still prefer to keep at least a nominal position in the Istiqlal is, of course, an indicator that the usefulness of the nationalist movement does not instantaneously disappear.

Special interests want to be able to present opinions and claims in terms of national interest. After only three years of freedom Morocco was still too young and generally still too retarded to permit any interest to identify itself frankly and openly in opposition to other groups. The small number of such groups, which is a function of social, economic, and political development, helps explain the reluctance of groups to take firm, independent positions. They are not national in the way that most pressure groups of advanced nations represent a concern of many or even all persons, nor are they national in the sense that many other special groups contribute to an intricate and counterbalancing pattern of interests. To some extent their claim rests on the exact opposite presumption—that they are the sole representatives of major specialized interests and the members involved do not have alternative groups through which to express themselves. Such may actually be the case, but is also possible grounds for bringing them more closely under governmental supervision.

In addition to the U.M.T., three organizations clearly fall within the category of nationalist-sponsored interest groups: the Moroccan Union of Industrialists, Merchants, and Artisans (U.M.C.I.A.), the National Union of Moroccan Students (U.N.E.M.), and the Union of Moroccan Farmers (U.M.A.). The second of these is related to the whole issue of youth's role in the new country, which will be discussed as a separate problem. The early organization of the U.M.T. and the U.M.C.I.A. was testimony to the tendency to build on the most readily identifiable differences first and to give priority to economic problems. The delay in the growth of the landowners' group, the U.M.A., until 1958 is also of more general significance, as it suggests the tendency, in general, to postpone the rural problem. There are two areas where well-organized groups have failed to appear, though there has been a great deal of ostensible concern— feminist and literacy programs. They are interesting partly because qualified and interested leaders have not planned and worked for these interests. Both are indisputably national problems and both hold an appeal to a certain readily differentiated group of persons. The inability of the persons concerned to organize themselves has resulted in the unfortunate neglect of their needs—a fact which also sheds some light on how groups are formed in new countries. The Istiqlal claimed an interest, but the failure of the party to deal effectively with these problems reflected the tendency to attract first those whose influence was of immediate use. It may possibly also reflect the preference of the party and the government to postpone broad social changes whose implications for the political system are difficult to predict.

The U.M.C.I.A. was founded the month of independence, March 1956. The Secretary General since that time has been Mohammed Laraki, a wealthy Casablanca merchant and Istiqlal contributor. The group's first public bid for recognition was a motion presented to the King in mid-1956, which questioned the economic plan then in operation and asked that "competent economic organisms" be consulted on decisions involving the future of the economy. Subsequently U.M.C.I.A. delegates were selected for the National Consultative Assembly and also for the various economic boards of the Ministry of National Economy. By 1958 the U.M.C.I.A. was represented on the Council for the Plan and its various subcommissions, the National Aid Fund, and the credit-governing boards of the government, and it was consulted on most major economic questions.[1] Its function until its Congress in 1957 is not entirely clear, but it is generally agreed that it was formed originally from among the wealthier merchants and industrialists of Casablanca who wished to influence the formation of Moroccan economic policy.

Long before the terrorist struggle began in late 1952, many Moroccans had given large sums of money to the nationalists. During the terrorism the businesses of many Istiqlal contributors, including many prominent merchants and artisans of Fès, Meknes, and other cities than Casablanca, were closed for weeks at a time and the level of business was generally low. With independence these Istiqlal business leaders argued that if a truly Moroccan economic revival was to take place, they should have special recognition and even be given certain privileges. There is little doubt but that this was one of the major concerns of the early life of the U.M.C.I.A. During the early months of independence there admittedly was much favoritism in the issue of import and export licenses and other economic concessions controlled by the government. Resistance members were frequently compensated with licenses for lucrative enterprise, especially for shares of export and import transactions. Since these persons sometimes lacked the skills and experience to benefit from these privileges, they often optioned their licenses and quotas of goods to established merchants. The businessmen of Casablanca and other cities, who had information and experience, were probably preoccupied with the management of the affairs of the newly created merchants immediately after independence.

The available data on the organizational progress of the U.M.-C.I.A. suggests that progress was neither as rapid nor widespread as might have been reasonably anticipated. At the end of 1957 there were fourteen regional unions, which were based on centers of artisan and commercial activity rather than on territorial divisions. Almost 650 local unions had been formed, which had separate programs for industrialists, large merchants, small merchants, and artisans. The foundation of the U.M.C.I.A. has probably remained the

[1] Interview with Mohammed Laraki, Secretary General, U.M.C.I.A., Casablanca, September 26, 1958.

major industrial and more prosperous commercial families of Casablanca, where the organization started. The U.M.C.I.A. also formed special federations alongside the regional groupings for particularly important enterprises, such as commerce in tea and textiles and the transport industry. The U.M.C.I.A. was managed by a Directing Committee of the Secretary General, and an Undersecretary General, Secretary, Treasurer, and Assistant for each of the four categories of members. As a rule there are monthly meetings of the Administrative Commission of seventy members, which includes the Directing Committee, regional representatives selected in proportion to the number of members of each region, and also representatives of the special federations. Including the estimated membership among artisans, the U.M.C.I.A. claims approximately 170,000 members, but probably only a small fraction of this number are active members.

The group's concentration on the more prosperous and more easily organized businessmen is indicated by its weak organization of artisans. The Moroccan handicraft industry has been severely depressed ever since European goods were imported in large volume. The U.M.C.I.A. had carefully counted merchants and industrialists by 1959, but had not yet taken a census of artisans. There is no reason why the U.M.C.I.A. should have come to the aid of the artisans, but its failure to do so is evidence of its major concern with immediate economic interests. Of the 120,000 members from commerce and industry, nearly a third are in Casablanca. Like most interest groups, the U.M.C.I.A. conforms to the regions of advancement in the country as a whole. Of the 650 locals, about 400 are situated in the more highly developed provinces of Rabat, Fès, Meknes, and Chaouia.[2]

Like other organizations in the new country, the U.M.C.I.A. found that a congress, from which the group is supposed to emanate, could not be held until the initial substructure of the organization had been established. At the end of 1957 about 600 delegates met in Casablanca for the U.M.C.I.A.'s first Congress. When one is aware of the difficulties which the Moroccan economy had encountered since independence and the variety of interests represented by the businesses and regions represented at the Congress, one is not surprised that some very direct and embarrassing questions were posed.

[2] All organizational information comes either from the interview with Mohammed Laraki or with Omar Douiri, Undersecretary General for Artisans, U.M.C.I.A., Rabat, October 9, 1958.

One delegate asked for more precise information as to how profits from importing were divided and another asked what the group was doing to encourage the investment of Moroccan funds accumulated in private and foreign banks. Another delegate asked why the internal regulations of local unions were not standardized and why the Secretary General's report had not mentioned the trips taken at the group's expense.[3]

The main speaker of the Congress was the Minister of National Economy, Bouabid, who announced new legislation to create investment opportunities and to provide safeguards for private investment. He stressed the fact that future commercial and artisan interests lay with the development of Moroccan agriculture, which would increase the consumption and the total income of the small farmer and peasant. Though solicitous of the needs of the group, Bouabid also made it clear that the government would not tolerate the proliferation of intermediaries and excessive speculation in commerce which tended to increase prices. He was outspoken regarding the temptation that some members might have to reap quick benefits from the current difficulties of the nation and stated directly that "rapid and more or less speculative profits produce only an illusionary and passing prosperity."[4] The critical tone of his speech suggests that the U.M.C.I.A. may have been somewhat too ambitious in the pursuit of its special interests and perhaps somewhat short-sighted in its attitude toward the country's economic development.

With the sharpening of political differences in 1958 the U.M.-C.I.A. minimized its relation to the Istiqlal. There was increasing discussion of governmental commercial controls, particularly on tea imports. Though the group was probably in accord with most of the more conservative leaders of the Istiqlal, many of whom possessed large fortunes from commercial and industrial enterprise, the national activist wing's agitation for more governmental control of the economy and experimental nationalization projects very likely alarmed U.M.C.I.A. leaders. Although party leaders considered the group a parallel organization of the Istiqlal in late 1957, by the end of 1958 the U.M.C.I.A. had become very cautious. It claimed that it was not an official member of the party's Political Committee or

[3] *La Vigie*, December 29, 1957, p. 5, also noted that these interventions were "warmly applauded." The reference to the trips probably had reference to the frequent consultation of the U.M.C.I.A. officers with officials in Paris and also their several missions to Russia.

[4] *Ibid.*

in favor of any party, although it attended Political Committee meetings and a majority of its members were probably also Istiqlal members. The group's objections to the progressive opinions of some Istiqlal leaders and in particular to some motions of the National Consultative Assembly were publicly stated in the summer of 1958 as the party crisis developed. The U.M.C.I.A. rejected the move to "overthrow completely the structure of external commerce by recourse to measures of nationalization or statism, whose consequences will be disastrous,"[5] and made a special visit to the King.

Very possibly a response to the pressure brought by the U.M.-C.I.A. was the plan of Moroccan Chambers of Commerce for new elections soon afterward.[6] These institutions had been inactive since independence and had been used by the Protectorate as instruments of French economic interests. With an alacrity that is by no means generally expressed for such projects, the elections were begun in three weeks, with the hearty endorsement of the U.M.C.I.A. The U.M.C.I.A. apparently hoped that the elections would reinforce its position. U.M.C.I.A. objections had stressed the appointed character of the Consultative Assembly, and, therefore, its incapacity to speak with popular approval. The new Chambers of Commerce might well be able to claim more representative significance within their limited electorate, but they also serve further to differentiate the special interests of the commercial and industrial groups. The U.M.C.I.A. has also announced that Chambers of Craftsmen will be formed after similar elections for artisans. The elections will provide the U.M.C.I.A. with a new claim to national importance which will not depend on the Istiqlal.

In view of the requirements placed on large parties by the Moroccan social structure, it is surprising that the U.M.C.I.A. and the Istiqlal cooperated as long as they did. The split of the Istiqlal did not ease the tensions of party affiliation for the interest group and in some ways made affiliation more hazardous. The structure of the political system on the whole meant that both major parties looked to increasingly emotional issues to rally their following. Such tactics almost unavoidably conflict with the special economic interests of

---

[5] *Ibid.*, August 24, 1958, p. 3.

[6] *O.B.* no. 2398, October 10, 1958, "Dahir no. 1-58-322 du 23 rebia I 1378 (7 octobre 1958) modifiant le dahir no. 1-57-161 du 14 joumada II 1377 (6 janvier 1958) formant statut des chambres de commerce et d'industrie," p. 1664, and "Dahir no. 1-58-232 du 23 rebia I 1378 (7 octobre 1958) relatif à l'établissement, pour l'année 1958, des lists électorales des chambres de commerce et d'industrie," p. 1664.

the U.M.C.I.A. Ben Barka's policy, as expressed in the National Consultative Assembly and among the Istiqlal dissidents, had forced the U.M.C.I.A. to disassociate itself from party activity before the split. Al-Fassi advocated immediate and unconditional departure from the franc zone in early 1959—a stand which could hardly please the many Moroccan businessmen who enjoyed subsidies and privileges by affiliation with the franc zone. The structure of national politics was such that the U.M.C.I.A. could not risk backing a party while the structure of the Moroccan economy enabled the U.M.C.I.A. to exercise considerable influence without overt political associations.

The Moroccan Farm Bureau

Although progressing at a different rate, agricultural interests have begun to be differentiated in the Moroccan political system. It is interesting to note in particular that, as in the case of the U.M.-C.I.A., firm distinctions were not drawn until the crisis of the summer of 1958. At the time of independence the Istiqlal did not encourage the formation of an associated group for landowners, and agricultural laborers were included under the U.M.T. organization. The first Minister of Agriculture, who has since become the President of the Moroccan Union of Farmers, and some other high Istiqlal officials like Abdeljalil are large landowners. It is quite possible that the larger farmers found themselves sufficiently represented through personal contacts in the early months of independence. The organization of the farmers was undoubtedly delayed by the rural disorder in large areas until 1957. The farmers as a whole were not so well prepared as their urban colleagues to participate in an interest group. As a group the farmers do not possess the specialized knowledge and familiarity with government that specialized political activity requires.

The statistics on landownership suggest the complexity of the rural problem and the delicate political issues involved. There are about five million hectares of arable land owned by a million Moroccan families, or roughly five hectares per family.[7] Since many of the Moroccan landowners have large farms, there are thousands of

[7] See also Lacouture, *Le Maroc à l'Epreuve, op.cit.*, pp. 188-190; the estimates of Maurice Dupont, "Les interêts Françaises contre l'interêt de la France en Afrique du Nord," *Espirit*, 20e année, no. 192, July 1952, pp. 61-62; and Pierre Corval, *Le Maroc en Revolution*, Paris, Bibliotheque de L'Homme d'action, 1956, p. 38, who estimates that sixty-seven per cent of the French holdings are over 300 hectares. A hectare is just under two and a half acres.

small farmers living on two or three hectares of land. Another million hectares of land is cultivated by French landowners, though nearly three fourths of this land is owned by less than 5,000 Frenchmen. The French-owned land supports as laborers or under lease about 100,000 Moroccan families. If divided, it would provide each family with about ten hectares. The country would also lose large amounts of rural investment and considerable income from agricultural exports, which come from the large modern farms.

Though favoring the large landowners, the Protectorate was certainly aware of the possibility of creating a conservative, independent rural population from small Moroccan landowners. Shortly after the war a program of rural modernization was begun, but the costs of renting machines or paying for major improvements were too high for the small farmer. The new country has postponed resolving the ultimate disposition of the land under French ownership. The problem is extremely complicated since much of the land was seized under highly advantageous conditions, if not by force, although much of the subsequent improvement was the result of the investment and skill that French farmers brought to Morocco. Pending agreement on the Convention of Establishment, the government acquired the French rural modernization centers that had been built. A much more ambitious rural modernization program has been undertaken, but it was one which also gave rise to a new political awareness among the farmers and has also been involved in the foundation of the new U.M.A.

With strong support from the King the government began the cooperative cultivation program in the fall of 1957. Through the rural modernization centers the government purchased new tractors, cultivating implements, seed, and fertilizer that were dispersed or loaned to the farmers of each region. In its first season of activity the "Operation Plow" succeeded in cultivating and planting 160,000 hectares of land at a cost of about 2,500 francs per hectare.[8] The main obstacle to the program was persuading the small farmers living on plots of five or ten hectares to destroy boundaries and to create fields sufficiently large to enable economical use of machines.

[8] A lower average cost of 1,200 francs per hectare was reported in *Al-Istiqlal*, September 27, 1958, p. 8. The difference is accounted for by estimating whether or not the calculation is made on the basis of the total cost of the operation, the cost of new equipment, or only those funds that will not be returned to the government. The major expense was the purchase of 350 new tractors, which were used along with the approximately 150 in possession of the rural centers or lent by large farms.

To facilitate the mergers local farmers formed Committees of Management,[9] whose distribution gives some indication of the areas in which the first "Operation Plow" concentrated. Almost 600 committees were formed, of which three fourths were in Chaouia, Rabat, and Fès provinces. The others were also in the more advanced rural areas around Meknes, Beni Mellal, and Al-Jadiida.[10] The committees were selected by simple designation by the *caid*, by an election by the local tribal council, or by decision of the participants in the program themselves, by means of local opinion. Much of the success of these committees is due to the strong support given by the Istiqlal, although there were some places where committees could be formed only after Istiqlal members withdrew to allow local majorities of Democratic party members to direct the committee.

The immediate purpose of "Operation Plow" was, of course, to increase rural production and introduce the small farmers to modern farming methods. Less well-defined were its long-run implications for the organization and modernization of Moroccan agriculture. The director of the centers once claimed that "Operation Plow" would help create the spirit of cooperation needed in the rural communes, which might someday undertake similar projects.[11] Though officials working on the rural communes acknowledge the possible benefits to the commune, agricultural reform was not a major purpose of the commune plan in 1958. Bouabid also noted the contribution that "Operation Plow" might make to the political integration of the countryside in the new nation. However, the brief duration of "Operation Plow," which is concentrated in the short rainy season, and the increased taxes and debt for the small farmer have probably detracted from the spontaneous political regeneration that might have been hoped for. Under orders from the modernization centers the equipment arrives suddenly and works fast.

The slow development of rural communes has prevented them from becoming a vehicle to perpetuate the progress made in en-

[9] One humorous characteristic of their formation was that in the more retarded areas the farmers often selected the least capable of their group in order that no ambitious man would be able to dominate affairs and the committee would always be sure that its opinions would be heard.

[10] Some voluntary attempts were made to include more distant areas where the smaller area of cultivable land did not warrant making a major effort the first year. Thus, a drive was made in the Goulimime area to Agadir with the help of local large farms, and a later effort was made in the Larache area below Tangier.

[11] Lacouture, *op.cit.*, pp. 213. There are some reports that the ministers of the government themselves were somewhat divided over the operation and what its ultimate purpose should be. *Ibid.*, p. 211, outlines the crisscrossing of lines of authority in the rural program.

couraging local cooperation and consultation. Neither the resources nor the plans exist for auxiliary cooperative enterprises for marketing, purchasing, or storage. The program has been criticized by the Istiqlal for neglecting the social contribution it might make and for failing to establish a more permanent basis for cooperation. Although the Ministry of Agriculture issued a statement that the efforts being coordinated by the government did not preclude the formation of more permanent cooperative enterprises and committees, another Istiqlal official argued that the state did not possess sufficient funds to finance the total modernization of Moroccan agriculture and that, unless private and cooperative enterprise came to its aid, "Operation Plow" might become a kind of "giantism" the country could not support.[12]

Into this setting came the U.M.A., shortly after the government announced that "Operation Plow" for the year 1958-1959 would aim at cultivating nearly three times as much land as in 1957-1958— 450,000 hectares. A group of larger farmers in the Gharb plain had been organized by Nejjai, the first Minister of Agriculture, since the fall of 1957 and from time to time had made interventions on behalf of the farmers. Nejjai often spoke of the advantages that might accrue to the farmers by the cooperative processing and marketing of their produce, and over the summer of 1958 he organized the first regional unions of farmers in the Gharb and Chaouia plains. The U.M.A. was formally inaugurated by the King shortly after the expanded "Operation Plow" began. The monarch welcomed the new group and strongly recommended it to the small farmers; he assured them that it would be a "valuable interlocutor" with the government. The group was indirectly given prestige when the King announced at the same time that the government was going to study the complete revision of the rural taxation system and open new sources of rural credit. The King also had a word of advice for interest groups: "The unions and professional organizations incontestably represent among the population some groups which, although they differ by their social and economic activity, remain united by the sacred lines of citizenship. . . . They should not make the country an arena in which to oppose classes and ideologies but a field of emulation for the glory of the nation."[13] He suggested that the U.M.A. respect the

---

[12] The controversy was aired in *Al-Istiqlal*, September 27, 1958, pp. 7-9, and September 6, 1958, pp. 8-9.

[13] *La Vigie*, September 22, 1958, p. 1.

rural workers organized under the U.M.T. and that the large farmers help the small farmers to improve their methods and raise their income.

The organization of the U.M.A. is much like that of the U.M.C.I.A. The Superior Council consists of ten regional representatives, ten central officers, and eight representatives from specialized federations on livestock, rice, cotton, et cetera. The base of the organization consists of local unions, numbering nearly seventy in late 1958.[14] Though the U.M.A. undoubtedly benefited greatly from the hearty endorsement given by the King, it is unlikely that it has the claimed membership of 200,000. The distribution of its locals follows the agricultural advancement of the country. The U.M.A. leaders are well aware of the cautiousness of the small farmer and have also facilitated his membership by asking only 500 francs dues per year from the poorer farmers. For the rich farmer dues may go as high as 10,000 francs, with the just amount being determined by local committees. The U.M.A. has gone on record in favor of rural housing subsidies, tax exemption for farmers having less than four hectares, and more liberal credit terms. The organization has also consistently petitioned for an increase in the price of wheat, in opposition to the government's policy of lowering wheat prices as production has increased. The U.M.A. also hopes to organize more localized sharing of equipment by the large landowners and regional cooperatives for marketing, processing, and purchasing. There could be serious conflict between the U.M.A. and the government's rural modernization program, which hopes to draw its funds from the same activities and needs to minimize the importance of land boundaries for maximum success.

The government's program is limited by the human and material resources available to organize cooperative enterprises among small farmers. The way in which the small farmer is introduced to modern agricultural methods will certainly be important in determining his attitude as to the way in which his affairs should subsequently be organized and how his interests should be represented in the government. Very likely with this in mind Bouabid issued a statement shortly after the inauguration of the U.M.A. completely disassociating it from "Operation Plow." Government statements are seldom so specific or precise. He sharply drew the distinction between "the

[14] This figure and other organizational information, except as otherwise noted, come from an interview with Ahmed Ben Mansour Nejjai, Secretary General of the U.M.A., Rabat, October 25, 1958.

cooperative movement launched by official services, with all the necessary guarantees" and "private initiatives which are . . . neither patronized nor directed by the state."[15] Allowing that small farmers might have access to modern equipment through the efforts of the U.M.A. in advanced regions, he specified that such help was not included in the "official cooperative work of the 'Operation Plow'" and, therefore, is in no way guaranteed by the government or entitled to aid from the modernization centers. He forewarned that the responsibility for these efforts "falls totally on their organizers." The confusion and waste that would result from dual organization of the plowing in the parceled areas is self-evident.

Even more crucial in the long-run development of Moroccan agriculture is the way in which governmental participation may contribute to the social advancement of the small farmer. The "Operation Plow" has been most successful where land is already cultivated under one of the several forms of Muslim collective-ownership systems.[16] The government probably would like to see cooperative tendencies reinforced since they increase the effectiveness of the modernization program. On the other hand, the U.M.A. envisaged including those farmers working exploited land collectively, plus those working under the *khamis*, or Muslim sharecropping system. While the U.M.A. program has advocated cooperatives for processing and marketing farm products, it has avoided any suggestion that land should be cooperatively owned. It is precisely in those areas where the limited cooperative effort of the government has so far had most success, and where a basis exists for converting the land into a system of cooperative ownership more easily, that the U.M.A. and the government may conflict.

The Istiqlal has carefully avoided making any policy statement on this problem. One party militant, however, has squarely posed the inconsistency of the party's advocacy of private ownership with the needs of agricultural modernization; he has suggested that the party "proceed toward the general collectivization in the exploitation of land, but preserve property rights in the sense that each individual will receive a share of production which belongs to him as a func-

[15] *La Vigie*, September 25, 1958, p. 2. See also comment on his statement in *Le Monde*, September 24, 1958, p. 4.

[16] *Al-Istiqlal*, September 27, 1958, p. 8, noted that the Management Committees "were much more successful in collective lands than in private land." Government officials also noted that the Management Committees in areas of melk land were more easily perpetuated as reform groups after the major operation by the government was completed.

tion of his land and work."[17] The political implications of the private landowners' interest group have not escaped notice. The Moroccan Communist party attacked the "colonialist-inspired" attempt of the "rural *bourgeoisie*" to draw strength from the small farmers, whose interest lay in cooperative ventures.[18] Like the U.M.C.I.A., the U.M.A. may find that the pursuit of its interests will contribute to further clarification and definition of the government's position on this crucial area of reform. It is almost certain that the U.M.A. and the U.M.C.I.A. will give their support to the moderate faction in the party split. Their positions as the most specialized interest groups were underlined by their refusal to associate publicly with either Istiqlal group after the party split. In the Assembly debates on devaluation of the franc the representatives of the U.M.A. and U.M.C.I.A. joined in opposition to the U.M.T. motion. Although their political tendencies might be characterized as generally conservative, it should be noted that the Left-Right spectrum hardly holds in Morocco and that these groups may find some of Al-Fassi's policies equally repugnant.

The Silent Half and the Students

Moroccan youth do not form an interest group with the solidarity or precise purpose of landowners and businessmen. The past generation is sharply differentiated, especially among the politically active segment of the population. The difficult adjustment that young Moroccans have been compelled to make over the past thirty years may, to some extent, help explain both their generally higher level of political activity and also their difficulty in finding a new role. Nearly eight tenths of the rural exodus have been estimated to be under thirty years of age and two thirds in the ten- to thirty-year group.[19] They undoubtedly played a leading part in the resistance and continue to lead the trade unions. Though the Istiqlal has no figures in the age composition of its members, it is generally conceded that those under thirty are more active. Over the past ten years in par-

[17] *Al-Istiqlal*, September 27, 1958, p. 9.
[18] *La Nation*, November 3, 1958, p. 1. The main reform suggested by the Communists was the same as that of Nejjai—reduction and abolishment for some cases of the land tax. Curiously, noting that it might increase the subemployment already existing in the countryside, the party was hesitant on further mechanization of agriculture.
[19] P. Suisse, "L'exode rural," *Bulletin Economique et Social du Maroc*, v. XIX, no. 68, 4e trimestre, 1955, March 1956, p. 463.

ticular the Istiqlal has undoubtedly had a strong appeal to uprooted and confused young people.[20]

The youth of Morocco is by no means homogeneous, socially or politically. It is difficult to measure the differences between those who only recently participated in modern life and those who have been privileged to enjoy contacts with the West all their lives, those from tribal communities or the countryside and those of longer urban experience, or those who have completed their educations and received secure positions as opposed to the newer arrivals. The use of the word "youth" itself in the new nation denotes something of the group's significance because it refers not only to those in puberty and adolescence, but also to young adults and often adults between thirty and forty years of age. Perhaps the sharpest distinction exists between those who are the product of French culture and those from traditional Moroccan schools. The distinction has taken on excessive significance, possibly because the former group also contains most of the more wealthy young Moroccans, who were able to prepare themselves for important positions in the new government. It would be a mistake to assume, however, that political views conform to these differentiations, for the whole spectrum of political opinion can be found among youth of similar age, income, and educational background.[21]

The political orientation of Moroccan youth defies generalization. There is undoubtedly a large proportion that remains aloof from politics or confines its political activities to discussions with small groups of friends. Among the young leaders of the Istiqlal, who are closely watched by youth, exists the activist, more progressive wing generally dominated by Ben Barka and Ibrahim, while there is also the relatively more conservative young group of Douiri, Boucetta, Kadiri, and Tahiri. An unfortunate tendency is to judge youth by the opinions of organized groups, especially those of the advanced students in the U.N.E.M. In a country where a third of the population is under ten years of age and half under twenty, it would obviously be misleading to use the term "youth" so loosely. Even the

[20] See the comment of Paul Buttin, *Le Drame du Maroc*, Paris, Editions du Cerf, 1955, chapter v, pp. 99-110, and regarding the Istiqlal see particularly pp. 107-108.

[21] See the comment on French educational influence in Pierre Corval, *op.cit.*, pp. 2-23. His implication that youth has unfortunately been dominated by French culture is more or less a lament for the inevitable. Since independence Moroccans continued to prefer French schools and have used the French model in their university.

entire Istiqlal Youth program has reached, at most, only about 100,000 young people, of whom many participate in sport and scout activities quite apart from the political life of the party. Young people as a whole in Morocco are probably most strongly influenced by their schools, though of the 620,000 Moroccan students, only about 50,000 were at the secondary or advanced level of education in 1958.[22]

On the whole, most young Moroccans are uncertain as to what their political role should be, though they are almost universally intensely patriotic and scornful of any vestige of the Protectorate if they are old enough to recall the regime. They have high expectations of the changes that independence can produce in their country and they feel strong ties to the rest of the Arab world.[23] Advanced students have not hesitated to express themselves. Thus, the Paris students, who are probably the most active politically, have frequently sent to the government petitions expressing their views. The students in the traditional universities of Fès and Marrakech have also unified to present petitions and even to hold hunger strikes for reforms in their living conditions, for modern education, and for equal opportunity for positions in government.[24] Perhaps the main contrast between the youth of Morocco and their elders is that their political views, once developed, are much more intense and their attitude toward the government as an instrument of reform much less passive. The young Moroccan is probably less tolerant of inefficiency, procrastination, and rationalization than are his elders. This is more than the usual impatience associated with youth, for those few en-

[22] See "Recensement des Elèves des Etablissements d'Enseignement du Maroc," Rabat, Ministry of National Education, February 11, 1958.

[23] Unhappily the shortage of Arabic instructors and the lack of Arabic educational materials has forced the government drastically to curtail its original Arabization program in the schools. In the fall of 1958 the new Minister of Education announced that all instruction in science and math would henceforth be given in French and that language instruction in the first two primary grades would be limited to French except for religious instruction. Partly as a result of the rapid expansion of the number of students, the primary-grade cycle had to be increased one year to maintain the quality of education. For 1958 it was also decided to admit only 60,000 new students to compensate for the 120,000 admitted in 1956, and 200,000 in 1957. These were all undoubtedly very hard decisions to make and constitute a major revision of plans that was very embarrassing for the government. There are now two million youth of school age in Morocco and their numbers increase by about 120,000 per year.

[24] The first strike was for equal access to high civil service positions and for equivalent status with the diplomas issued by modern Muslim and French schools. A second strike was for new equipment, new courses qualifying them for positions in government, clarification and standardization of the examination procedures, and improved living conditions. They apparently had the support of the *oulemas*, for the instructors addressed the letter. Many of these changes have been made, including access to the civil service and many new scholarships.

joying educational opportunities are generally much more interested in national and international affairs than students at comparable levels of education in advanced countries. All young Moroccans realize that their new opportunities were made as a result of independence and that their futures rest with the nation's progress.

In their struggle for independence the nationalists have long been aware of the importance of youth and have accorded it special recognition. In 1933 the Hassan Scouts were begun, with young Prince Moulay Hassan as honorary president. The group soon took on a paramilitary structure and participated in the riots of the 1930's. Several sports clubs were founded after the war with Istiqlal support, though the Moroccan scout movement was forbidden by the French, who had apparently learned of its usefulness to the nationalists.[25] There were some indications that the older scouts acted as internal police for the Istiqlal and also that they participated in the resistance in groups. Abdeselam Bennani, now assistant Secretary General of Istiqlal Youth and a scout leader, was one of the organizers of the Casablanca resistance. Although a Democratic party member was the first Director of Youth and Sports in the Ministry of National Education, the Istiqlal faction became the largest scout group. There are now about 30,000 scouts organized under a Hassan group, which is affiliated with the Istiqlal Youth, 8,000 affiliated with the Muslim scout group, a few hundred still active under the Abdallah group of Democratic party affiliation, and approximately 3,000 organized by the Israeli scouts.[26] Late in 1958 the Director of Youth and Sports succeeded in forming a federation of Moroccan scouts. Though the Moroccan Scout Federation will certainly be dominated by the Istiqlal Hassan Scouts, scouting has lost much of its former political orientation.

The government does not take an active part in the organization of youth, but provides facilities and subsidies for existing groups. This means, of course, that the Istiqlal, who has been by far the most aggressive in the organization of youth, has no doubt received most help. There are indications that even the Istiqlal Youth organization has not been entirely successful by the party's standards. The party claimed that nearly 100,000 young Moroccans participated in its activities over the first two years of independence.

[25] See Rezette, *Les Partis Politiques Marocains, op.cit.,* pp. 78-79, 311-312.
[26] Interview with Omar Mezzour, Director of Youth and Sports, Ministry of National Education, Rabat, February 14, 1958.

TABLE 13

Estimated Participation in Istiqlal Youth Activities in 1956 and 1957[a]

Activities	1956	1957
Hassan Scouts	10,000	30,000
Association for the Education of Youth	4,000	6,500
Popular Child Care Group	1,000	5,000
Young Scholars	4,000	7,000
Sport	15,000	25,000
Renaissance Association (girls)	—	2,000
Youth Hostel Group	500	1,000
Culture and Arts Group	5,000	8,000
Builders of Independence	—	12,000
Total	39,500	96,500

[a] Interview with Abdelkrim Fellous, Secretary General, Istiqlal Youth, Rabat, February 26, 1958. These totals are generally confirmed by the Directorate of Youth and Sports. The two groups without figures in the 1956 column were not started until 1957.

To the youth groups under Istiqlal sponsorship should be added the Young Workers of the U.M.T., claiming 10,000 members, a national ski club of about 5,000, several small Israelite youth groups and scouts, and the Muslim scouts numbering about 8,000. Much youth activity continued to enjoy royal patronage and the Prince's birthday has become the occasion of a large youth demonstration.[27] The party is very firm regarding the identity of membership in the youth groups and in the party itself. An Istiqlal youth has all the obligations of a regular party member and except for the Hassan Scouts, who are constrained by the rules of the World Scout Federation, each youth takes the same party oath. The Istiqlal Youth are represented in the central organization of the party by their own Secretariat at party headquarters and in the Political Commission of the party. There is no way of evaluating to what extent the opinions of Istiqlal youth have actually influenced party decisions, though there are reports that party leaders are sensitive to discontent among the young members.

The Istiqlal Youth organization demonstrates many of the same characteristics as other political activity in the new country. Efforts

[27] The 1958 youth fete, during the Istiqlal tension in the government, did not appear to have been so enthusiastically received as former ones. There was also a rather humorous incident over objections to borrowing 2,000 camp beds and 160 field tents from the United States Air Force, whose presence had not yet been officially recognized by the Moroccan government.

are highly centralized in the Secretariat at Rabat, whose officers supervise all important meetings at the national or regional level. A cadre training program devoted only to youth was comparable to that undertaken by the entire party. During 1956 youth cadre were trained in Rabat, probably under the same program as that used by the party. In 1957 special Istiqlal youth schools were organized at Casablanca, Fès, Marrakech, Oujda, and Azrou, which gave courses for from one to three weeks to about 1,000 young members. Most of these sessions were held during the summer or school vacations. The candidates were selected by the administrative body of each Istiqlal Youth group with the final approval of the Rabat office. As in the party cadre school, the caliber of the officials who are willing to instruct in these courses suggests the importance which ministers and party officials attach to the indoctrination and training of youth. In contrast with the subjects given in the general party cadre school, the young people study specialized subjects that require a considerably higher general level of education.[28]

As the membership figures of the Istiqlal Youth suggest, it has developed by campaigns concentrated on specific groups. Immediately after independence the greatest effort was made in sports and scouting—areas where the party had some experience and areas which were familiar to the youth then associated with the party. The first Congress of Istiqlal Youth was held at the end of March 1956 and, like most congresses that have been held in the new country, was primarily a demonstration of solidarity. The results of the 1956 Congress and also the 1957 Congress were remarkably accurate predictions of future problems. The General Motion of the first Congress[29] anticipated the economic crisis of the new country and asked for new public works and austerity measures. The most indicative of the future problems was the outspoken demand for a "homogeneous government representing a solid political party," which the Istiqlal did not officially adopt until three months later. Perhaps most characteristic of the views of young Moroccans was their observation that "it is indispensable to undertake a second internal liberation in order to get rid of the pernicious traditions and the defects of the colonialist regime."

The second Istiqlal Youth Congress was preceded with a frank report on the progress that the youth groups had made over the pre-

---

[28] See the outline of courses and speakers in *Al-Istiqlal*, January 11, 1958, pp. 8-9.
[29] *Ibid.*, April 6, 1956, p. 3.

ceding year and a half;[30] this report provides considerable insight into the problems of more active Moroccan youth. The Hassan Scouts were credited with their effort at training new cadre and were provided with a Technical Committee, whose purpose was mainly to help the older scouts move on to more "constructive and productive areas." The sports sections were criticized for their internal disputes and hopefully unified around a newly chosen national Superior Committee. Likewise the Young Scholars were criticized for their failure to develop leadership or to accomplish the minimum goals set the year before. The most severe criticism was directed at the regional officers of the Istiqlal Youth, whose coordination of youth activity and publications was reported to be extremely poor. They were said to have lacked initiative and perseverance in overcoming the problems of organization and to have allowed relations with the central office to deteriorate. New directions emphasized that the essential goal of all youth activity was party membership and that under no conditions should the youth groups cut the "primordial line" between themselves and the party.

The second Congress met at an interesting time in the transition of the new country, September 1957, or almost a year after the Istiqlal had had virtually a "homogeneous government," favored in early 1956. The organization had taken on a more purely Istiqlal identification and there was no participation by palace or high government officials. The motions of the second Congress were much more specific and denoted much more closer association with the activist wing of the party than those of 1956.[31] The absence of palace representation was probably just as well, for the Royal Army was urged to free itself from dependence on the French Army and to conduct a purge. There were also demands for a second list of collaborators; for a purge of the administration; a protest against "phantom parties," probably meaning the Popular Movement; and an unusually outspoken denunciation of the two Liberal Independent ministers of the Council of Government. Although these opinions may have been proposed by the mentors of the organization, they were enthusiastically received and form an important part of the indoctrination of this segment of Moroccan youth. By cultivating excessively high expectations the party may be jeopardizing its own control of the organiza-

---

[30] "Rapport général sur le 2ème Congrés des Jeunesses Istiqlaliennes tenu à Tangier," Rabat, General Secretariat, Istiqlal Youth, n.d., from which all information in this paragraph was taken.

[31] *Al-Istiqlal*, October 5, 1957, p. 14.

tion, but it may also reflect the informed judgment of the move-ment's leaders that without these goals the party's prestige among the youth would be lost in any case.

The differences of interest among the various youth groups have to some extent defeated any Istiqlal intentions of constructing a high-ly disciplined, militant youth movement. Of the 100,000 Istiqlal Youth, only those in scouting and the Builders of Independence groups have a military organization. Of course, all Istiqlal Youth are exposed to party indoctrination, but not under circumstances where their behavior is as closely controlled as in potentially para-military groups. The proliferation of orientation committees and rep-rimands for poor organization testify to the difficulties of sustaining a strong organization in the nonmilitary groups and, more impor-tant, of keeping close liaison with Rabat. The announcement in late 1958 that the Istiqlal Youth were again undergoing a reorganization suggests that trouble still existed. The party leaders again expressed hope that the party youth would become "a driving element, the propagator of the ideals and doctrine of the party." The new or-ganization was supposed to create "greater cohesion among the di-verse organizations and multiply contacts between the members of the central commission and the local sections."[32] The party expects youth to become militants and to make concrete contributions. The Builders of Independence are very likely the model of the ideal youth group. As the core of the militant youth under Istiqlal super-vision they are of special interest because they were organized as a result of a postindependence project, Unity Road.

The entire concept of Unity Road is possibly of more political sig-nificance than the road or the youth group.[33] It was a demonstration of the kind of youth activity favored by the activist wing of the party and an example of the kind of interministerial, coordinated effort the faction suggested. The highly planned effort by the government was able to multiply its results by a mobilization of approximately 10,000 young people who lived for the summer under paramilitary conditions. More conservative leaders of the government have not

[32] *Ibid.*, October 11, 1958, p. 5.
[33] Also of interest is the existence of only a handful of Moroccan leaders who possess the skills and imagination to conceive and execute such a project. Equally significant in evaluating the Moroccan political system is that the inspirer, Ben Barka, was compelled and chose to manage the most petty details of the operation himself. For larger-scale achievements the country would need not only more persons with organizational skills, but also more capacity to delegate authority in the planning and execution phases.

expressed themselves on extending this kind of activity, but the failure to repeat the effort in the summer of 1958 suggests that it was quietly discouraged.

The project was envisaged as a school for militant youth, who would return to their homes and villages "to guide, direct and undertake projects of local improvement."[34] The volunteers were assembled in camps along a fifty-kilometer trail north of Fès, which connected Taounate and Ketama in the Rif Mountains. The road became a symbol of national unity by assembling volunteers from all parts of the country for the first time and by improving a link between the two Protectorate zones. The prodigious task of organization is evident in the detailed plans for transporting volunteers to and from the sites and the carefully scheduled camp activities. As plans progressed the King became the patron of the project and a special committee of ministers was established to coordinate the logistics, transport, and indoctrination of the young people. Volunteers receiving some assistance from Royal Army units and local tribes worked from 5:30 A.M. to 12:00 noon on the road itself. The afternoons and evenings were left free for military drill, physical training, and conferences. Leisure activity was supervised by 300 specially trained monitors. The cadre training program is of special interest since the monitors were given fuller explanations of the purpose of the project. Their training was planned by the Istiqlal and the candidates came almost entirely from the Istiqlal Youth. Ben Barka described them as *"avant-garde* animators who have the constant desire to rebuild the masses with their full adhesion and to give the people the means for reflection."[35] The instruction on civic education and community development that the cadre of the Unity Road received indicates that the party hoped the group would continue to mobilize the countryside. Though this kind of popular mobilization did not result, it is perhaps not entirely due to the discouragement the program appears to have encountered in some official circles.

The response to the cadre school and the Unity Road as a whole did not include many volunteers at advanced educational levels, as might have been anticipated. The U.N.E.M., although it made a special appeal through its organization, did not provide many college students. In 1958 the U.N.E.M. confessed that college students had failed to support the project and chided advanced students for

[34] *Al-Istiqlal*, June 1, 1957, p. 1. [35] *Ibid.*, June 29, 1957, p. 12.

considering themselves above manual labor with their fellow citizens.[36] Only ten monitors had advanced bilingual education and twenty-two had advanced education in Arab institutions.[37] Two thirds of the cadre were from the coastal provinces and very few came from more isolated regions. The modernized student's scorn for menial chores and also a limitation on the future usefulness of the monitors are indicated by the large majority of students from Arabic schools—roughly two thirds.[38] While the tendency for the more traditional and less privileged youth to predominate raises doubts as to the sincerity of the more advanced students, it also means that the project did more for less privileged young people. Organizers of the cadre school were of the opinion that the cadre school's experience confirmed the view that students of French and traditional urban schools held their uneducated comrades from the countryside in low repute.

Without efforts to follow up the project, the indoctrination and organization of the Builders of Independence has probably been of limited value to the party. A survey of the volunteers[39] showed that two thirds were illiterate and that nearly half spoke a Berber dialect. The traditional orientation of the group is indicated by about half favoring polygamy, a third depending on family choice of spouse, and two thirds participating in *moussems* or tribal festivals. Only about a third of the volunteers were employed, of whom the vast majority worked in agricultural and forestry occupations. Almost nine tenths of the volunteers listened to the radio and nearly half of

[36] *Ibid.*, June 1, 1958, p. 14. This is interesting evidence that the French influence is more subtle and profound among the educated young Moroccans—even of progressive opinions like the U.N.E.M.—than they realize. They may also have acquired this attitude from their elders, who generally frown on manual labor and have servants in large numbers.

[37] "Note statistique sur le recrutement des stagaires de l'école des cadres," École des Cadres, Rabat, September 5, 1957, p. 2.

[38] About thirty per cent were from bilingual schools and the remaining four per cent were the advanced students, of whom three fourths were from Arabic schools. Slightly over one half of the Unity Road cadre were under 22 and almost eight tenths were under 26, so that they had many years of Istiqlal Youth participation open to them.

[39] Unfortunately the results of the survey can be used only with considerable reservations. Though it is claimed that a copy was returned by each participant, *Al-Istiqlal*, March 16, 1958, p. 7, only 320 were used for the preliminary analysis. Many of the volunteers were illiterate and filled in the questionnaires with the help of the monitors. On the opinion questions it should also be remembered that they were being subjected to a fairly intense political indoctrination during their afternoons and in their contact with the monitors from the Istiqlal Youth. All the results appeared in *ibid.*, pp. 8-9, and *ibid.*, March 23, 1958, pp. 8-10.

them selected newscasts and commentary as their favorite program. A fourth of them had joined the party between 1952 and 1955 and another fourth before 1952; this fact confirms opinions that veterans of the rural resistance strongly supported the project. Clues as to their political attitudes were that two thirds viewed the future with optimism and selected the King's return as the happiest moment of their lives. The Builders of Independence may have contributed to the party's organization in the countryside, but they also place difficult obligations on the party as a result of the enthusiasm and hopes raised during the Unity Road project. When the Builders of Independence from Tafilalet and Ouarzazate provinces were mobilized as unarmed guards in the late spring of 1958, there were unsubstantiated reports of unrest among militant youth in the southern provinces. A less calculable implication of the Builders of Independence is the influence it may eventually give the Istiqlal in the Royal Army, until now generally regarded as politically uncommitted.

Among the college youth there was only one clearly defined interest group, the U.N.E.M. It possessed many characteristics of the other interest groups, having readily identifiable membership criteria and easily identified immediate interests. The U.N.E.M. asked for and received representation in the National Consultative Assembly, although the opinions of college youth vary greatly and it is doubtful if a majority belong to the U.N.E.M. The first organization for Moroccan college students, organized by the Protectorate in 1951, was the Association of Moroccan Students, which appears to have undergone all the strains and divisions of Moroccan politics. The U.N.E.M. was founded late in 1958 and was courted by representatives of both the Western and Communist-sponsored student internationals, rather as was the case with U.M.T.[40] The reorganization in Rabat involved serious internal schisms and resulted in the arbitrary removal of the local officers, who apparently belonged to the Democratic party. By the U.N.E.M.'s second Congress in the fall of 1957, its political character was much more in evidence and unmistakably of Istiqlal quality. The internal divisions of the U.N.E.M. persisted in new form. The students from the Moroccan traditional universities and from Egyptian, Syrian, and Spanish universities

[40] Even before the formation of the U.N.E.M., Moroccan college students were attending congresses on behalf of both internationals and debating the question of their ultimate affiliation. See *Al-Istiqlal*, November 30, 1956, p. 9.

formed a disconnected opposition to the dominant element from French-language institutions in Morocco and France. The Democratic party continued to protest that the association was dominated by the Istiqlal, which was very likely correct.

The questions on which the U.N.E.M. could agree were North African unity and Algerian independence, but the internal split of the U.N.E.M. persisted. Early in 1958 three members of the Executive Committee resigned and organization was temporarily under the Administrative Commission. The third Congress of the U.N.E.M. confirmed that, whatever had been the internal disputes of the last three years, the group was now solidly aligned with the Istiqlal and most sympathetic to the critical party faction. The motions were sufficiently extreme to delay their publication in Morocco, though excerpts appeared in the foreign press.[41] The Royal Army was called an "army for parade." Most outspoken were the proposals to limit the powers of the Chief of Staff of the Army, the Prince Moulay Hassan; to purge the army of "antinational and antipopular elements"; to reduce army expenses and to end its dependence on foreign officers; and, lastly, to install a system of conscription "to permit the formation of an army of the people." The foreign-policy proposals, much firmer than anything yet advanced by Balafrej, called for diplomatic isolation of France and diplomatic relations with Soviet Russia and the Republic of China. The final motions also favored nationalization of mineral exploitation, public utilities, and transport; collectivization of land belonging to *colons* and "feudalists"; and a nationally directed cooperative for artisans.

In the subsequent confusion a U.N.E.M. delegation called on the King to reaffirm its loyalty, while numerous corrections and denials appeared. By early 1959 the U.N.E.M. was apparently still divided over political affiliation. Although one of its officers participated in the meeting to form the progressive Istiqlal, the group decided to remain "apolitical" vis-à-vis the split. The intellectual youth of Morocco seems to be as varied in their sentiments as those of any other country.

Interests Without an Organization

Two less well-defined groups deserve mention—the illiterates and women; their situations are to some extent similar to that of youth.

---

[41] *Le Monde*, August 3-4, 1958, p. 9. They later appeared in *Al-Istiqlal*, August 16, 1958, p. 16, and August 23, 1958, pp. 12-13.

Their common need is the rudimentary qualifications to participate in an advanced society, which is not easily made the basis for an organization without outside help. They are not of special interest because of their present importance in the political system, but because of their potential importance. Adequate treatment of illiteracy and feminist problems requires a vast social change which the political system has not yet encouraged, though some steps have been taken to increase literacy. Certainly there is no a priori reason why the political transition of Morocco should be compelled to deal with the question of literacy and feminist reform, but it can reasonably be asked within the framework of this inquiry how one explains that very little has been done. Both issues ranked high in the nationalist preindependence goals and constitute severe limitations on political participation that the nationalists have professed to favor. There have, of course, been limitations of resources, cadre, and leadership that confront every major social change in the new nation.

An explanation may be suggested by reversing the question and asking why these men and women have not yet been able to make their influence felt in Moroccan politics. Unlike the organized interest groups who have direct means of influencing the government and like the youth who have a varied social background and limited capacity to participate in politics, illiterates and women have few ways of exercising influence. While more influential groups and individuals may be well aware of the problem, they are free to postpone seeking a solution because of the structure of the political system. Whether a choice of convenience or of necessity, it is a course of action that avoids adjusting the political system to the influence of individuals whose interests and expectations may be difficult to predict. Less easy to prove, but certainly possible, is that perpetuating these political and social handicaps may jeopardize the political system. Those excluded from active participation may seek more extreme methods of political expression. When a political system confesses its inability to solve the problems that are also used to rationalize neglecting the needs of citizens, it has reached a serious impasse.

The limited effort that has been made to combat illiteracy demonstrates considerable ingenuity and has met with an enthusiastic response. This effort has also been handicapped by poor coordination and party interests, like most other national programs. One project existing under the Ministry of National Education gave instruction from about forty rural centers. Though the instruction is probably superior to that of the Istiqlal-sponsored drives, it has not extended far from the major cities. The government project was begun by the first Minister of Youth and Sports, who was from the Democratic party. He succeeded in forming five centers in Casablanca, which rejected the new Istiqlal minister in late 1956 and then were won over by direct appeals. The Istiqlal effort, the League for the Education of the Base and to Combat Illiteracy, was formed from several nationalist organizations but received most of its financial support and organizational framework from the party. Initially sponsored by the King and other national figures, it survived largely from party support and from the demands of party members for basic education. In its early stages the League received personal attention from Ben Barka. The newspaper *Al-Manaar Al-Maghrib* was especially designed for illiterates and was established with a large subsidy for special type fonts from the Istiqlal.

The League, like the feminist effort, benefited from the enthusiasm of independence. On the whole women have been more interested in it than men, as is verified by the figures of the first two years:

TABLE 14

Estimated Participation of Men, Women, and Teachers
in the Literacy Campaigns of 1956 and 1957[a]

	1956	1957
Male participants	325,000	137,000
Female participants	25,000	25,000
Teachers	10,000	5,000
Completed course	110,000	40,000

[a] Interview with Ahmed Cherkaoui, Editor, *Al-Manaar Al-Maghrib*, League for . . . , August 27, 1958. See also the article on the 1956 campaign by Henryauc de Chaponay, "Lendemain de fête du Maroc," *Esprit*, vol. 24, no. 240-241, July-August 1956, p. 149.

Though the number of participants roughly halved over the first two years, the number of women remained the same—a fact which testifies to their interest in self-improvement. The main campaign has been coordinated with Ramadan each spring, though the party continues to instruct throughout the year, with lessons that are repeated in *Al-Manaar*. In the first year no diplomas were distributed, but 40,000 were given in 1957 to those completing two years' study.

The first campaign was not directed at any particular region, but a special effort was made in Marrakech and Ouarzazate provinces in 1957 and was planned for the Rif area in 1958.[42] The League's organizers are well aware of the inconsistency of the quality of the instruction, but also are gratified by the spontaneous reaction that has enabled them to reach thousands of illiterates with sparse resources. With due allowance made for the shortcomings of the League's activity, its success tends to confirm the claims of more activist leaders of the Istiqlal that much could be done by directing popular enthusiasm into self-improvement projects.[43]

The feminist movement has progressed less than any other national effort since independence. There are even some indications that since 1955 Morocco has suffered relative losses in integration of women as equal members of the society. The Princess Lalla Aicha, who before independence sometimes upset elder Istiqlal officials with her speeches and demonstrations for feminine equality, took an evasive and cautious position when asked about the future of feminist reforms after independence.[44] Moroccan women have, nevertheless, demonstrated their ambition in the literacy drives and have not been reluctant to assert their rights under the new divorce laws.[45] The Istiqlal has a feminist organization, but since 1956 its activity has steadily decreased. There were few indications of specialized activity and mass meetings were organized mostly for political purposes on national holidays. The progress of women is handicapped by the lack of trained personnel, as the slow progress of feminist organizations in the Ministry of National Education suggests. At independence all the women directing the Ministry's fifty-two women's centers were French and two years later only half of these centers had been able to find Moroccan women capable of taking over their supervision.[46] There is, nevertheless, little evidence to sug-

[42] Interview with Ahmed Cherkaoui, Editor, *Al-Manaar Al-Maghrib*, League for . . . , August 27, 1958.

[43] The problem of linguistic training is not limited to the programs discussed here, nor is it as simple as this short treatment might suggest. Many Moroccans also need instruction in French in order to assume responsible positions in commerce and industry, where the vocabulary is still almost completely French. The Ministry of Public Works has been giving French courses to workers in Casablanca, though this has aroused some misgivings among more Arabist-minded officials.

[44] See Lacouture, *op.cit.*, p. 329.

[45] Interview with Ali Benjelloun, Cabinet Director, Ministry of Justice, October 29, 1958. He claimed that the rise in the recorded number of divorces included many women who went to court in self-defense now that the new divorce code gave them legal protection.

[46] Lacouture, *op.cit.*, p. 392.

gest that much has been done to direct or encourage popular interest and ambitions.

The feminist leadership of Morocco is on the whole monopolized by women with French cultural interests and secure positions in urban society. There are some indications that young working women in hospitals, infirmaries, and schools resent the domination of women's activities by this largely urban group.[47] There are reports that in the cities, where one might expect most rapid progress, middle-class Moroccan husbands have discouraged social equality for women in their homes. Since the men are frequently oriented to traditional symbols of status, they prefer their wives to wear veils and robes rather than adopt modern dress and behavior.[48] The Istiqlal party inspectors were not very concerned with feminist activity and discussed it during interviews only when directly asked. A typical example is probably to be found at Oujda, where the inspector claimed four or five thousand female members, all in the city of Oujda, out of a membership of 100,000. A party inspector in the south reported that, where he could find leaders, women's activities progressed more rapidly among the tribes, where women tend to have more equality, than in the predominantly Arab communities. The country will not be able to pay the price of keeping its women under retarded conditions indefinitely, but it is apparent that little progress has been made during the early years of transition. Like the problem of illiteracy, the reform of women involves a major social change both of the tribal structure and of traditional Muslim family life in the cities. The influence of women in the emerging political system has not yet been felt, and women certainly do not constitute a distinct group. But they have many common problems which the new government has not yet considered.

Although the organization and development of Moroccan interest groups is similar to those in more advanced countries, the significance of these groups in the political system as a whole is much different. An interest group presumes that a limited number of persons possessing certain qualifications can be organized around a fairly

[47] See Lacouture's conclusion, op.cit., pp. 334-335, on the feminist movement. One working girl compared them to the old French controleurs civiles of the rural administration and argued that a true female renaissance would come only from working-class leadership.

[48] See the comment of ibid., pp. 325-326. He suggests that this is especially the case in the more traditional cities, Fès, Tetouan, Salé, Meknes, or Marrakech, rather than in Rabat or Casablanca. See also his comment on the return of the veil. Ibid., p. 319.

specific need. The stage of social development of a newly independent country is such that, in fact, very few specialized needs can be found. There are very few interest groups in Morocco as compared with their intricate multiplication and overlapping in advanced countries. This is only explained in part by the educational, financial, and other limitations. The tendency to confine the activity of small groups to a few organizations is also derived from the difficulty during the transition of harmonizing with national problems the immediate demands of such groups. The low level of education in the trade unions, for example, may have helped them preserve their solidarity, but so also has a critical economy, where both the U.M.T. and the U.M.C.I.A. have on many instances had little choice but to favor the same policy. Thus, there is not only relatively more effort than in an advanced nation to make group demands compatible with national interest, but there is also more difficulty in the prerequisite act of particularizing national goals. As the transition progresses these goals become increasingly specialized, but the effect has not been to multiply interest groups since nationalist solidarity is still needed and satisfaction can be found by direct representation in government.

The smaller number of interest groups simplified the problem of the way in which to exercise influence. These groups are less likely to seek influence through political parties than would be the case in advanced nations because party activity is restricted and the institutions by which party policy could be implemented, if it did exist, are not yet formed. An interest group, therefore, tends to demand and to get direct representation on the commissions and rudimentary representative institutions that have been formed. Unfortunately this may very likely jeopardize the development of a freer, open political system, for, as the groups find that their members can be satisfied and that the organization can establish national prestige without an association with a political party, the party may tend to become an anachronism. The result is not nearly so regrettable for citizens who enjoy status in the urban or modern pursuits as for the vast majority of the nation, which is socially retarded and unorganized. Even the nationalist movement, as has been the case with the Istiqlal, may concentrate on preserving harmony among specialized interests. It is caught in a dilemma between its claim to nationalist solidarity, so important to its prestige in the retarded areas of the new nation, and the needs of its modernized members. As has occurred in Morocco, specialized groups do define their interests and learn how to wield influence much more rapidly than the socially retarded mass. The national crises, both internal and international; the concentration of cadre, by virtue of the structure of social change; and the direct access enjoyed by interest groups all tend to exaggerate the differences between the few who are organized and the many who are not.

CHAPTER XIII

CONCLUSION

MOROCCAN politicians frequently assert that ¦
their country have political significance. ¦
eral expositions of the importance of ¦
observer is likely to pass such statements off as ¦
countries of Morocco's diversity, however, the ma ¦
a handy rule of thumb. The intuitive understand ¦
may be difficult to formalize and, thereby, base¦
found knowledge of the political system than tha¦
scientist can acquire. Most of the dramatic even¦
years of Moroccan independence were foretold ¦
though they could not always speak their min¦
some allowance for personal differences, their lor¦
were remarkably similar. The difficulties of in¦
creased political participation on the national ¦
anticipated by nearly all experienced Moroccan ¦

While the political scientist does not wish to ir¦
systematic academic endeavor does require ¦
and comparative value of inquiry be specified. ¦
in systematic study cannot become so fixed on ¦
istics of the situation at hand that he renders ¦
drawing more general conclusions. The cultur¦
political quirk may seem obviously suited to ¦
larly difficult problem in the analysis of politi¦
is itself nullified by the impossibility of comp¦
is claimed. A thousand explanations could b¦
of a thousand unique events without advanc¦
in political studies. The description might or ¦
some later studies, but the full explanatory v¦
not be approached. In practice it is almost ir¦
shearing away of related facts if only becau¦
human powers of concentration, description ¦
tion. However, the fascination of the uniqu¦
dents are reluctant even to identify their ¦
analysis, not to mention the more distant an¦
they hope to contribute. It is very possibly ¦

405

unknowingly the victim of an author's intellectual sorting process than to endure the impositions of an analysis that can be separated from the data as other uses may be found.

This study of political change in Morocco has proceeded from the more specific and descriptive early chapters to more general and analytical chapters. The first four chapters dealt with politics in conventional terms, while CHAPTERS V to VIII began to use some of the concepts briefly sketched in the Introduction. CHAPTERS IX to XII emphasize the analytical framework of the book, although still dealing with major problem areas in Moroccan politics. In this way it is hoped that the study will be useful to those bringing other schemes to bear on the Moroccan scene, as well as that it will alert the student of comparative politics to what seem to be promising avenues for theory formation. Although there is still much data collection to be done in the study of underdeveloped countries, it is in the realm of theory and concept formation that progress has been slowest. To some extent our ignorance of underdeveloped countries has encouraged more careful and thoughtful generalization, since we have had to maximize the value of the available data and proceed fully aware of our lack of intuitive insight, rather like the case of Soviet studies. Over the past decade more and more studies have appeared that apply more refined methodological techniques in the study of new nations, and more recently there have been several inquiries aimed at forming very general theory.[1]

Before outlining more carefully the framework used here, some preliminary observations on theory formation may be helpful. No systematic or hopefully scientific theory can be indiscriminately applied to any situation. One of the most difficult problems in designing theory is to arrive at and then to use consistently a single unit of analysis. This study, like most political studies, has jumped from discussion of groups to parties, from parties to formal institutions, and from government to populace. There has been relatively little concern with whether or not all these units could be discussed in the same terms, although it was pointed out from time to time that functional relationships vary considerably under different circumstances. However, one unit, the nation, has been discussed throughout in the same terms, namely, the four categories of influence briefly introduced in CHAPTER I. Agreeing on the usefulness of this unit is

---

[1] See, for example, Daniel Lerner, *The Passing of Traditional Society*, *op.cit.*; and David Apter, *The Gold Coast in Transition*, Princeton, Princeton University Press,

only a first and elementary step in improving our explanatory tools, and, indeed, has been suggested before.[2] The political scientist is certainly no more intent on explaining everything about the nation than, say, the economist is intent on explaining everything about the firm. Both may produce poor theories and both may define peculiar characteristics or relationships concerning the unit that they are especially eager to explain. Though still in the process of development, the particular concern of the political scientist is usually identified as the political system, whose concrete referent is most often the nation. These propositions, of course, do not constitute a theory until the word "political" can be translated into some operational concepts, which is the reason for the fourfold classification of influence.

"Political system" is simply a phrase used for convenient reference to a particular way of observing and relating kinds of influence in relation to the nation. Assuming that the above ideas can successfully be put into operational terms leads to certain additional complications, although present research indicates that influence relationships are amenable to empirical study. It is, at present, physically most ambitious, if not impossible, to apply a particular research design to all members of any one nation at any one time, especially in the case of an underdeveloped nation. To enable closure of the theory in manageable form it is suggested that attention be directed to particular national problems. In other words, the forms of influence or the political system could be studied, much as has been done in this inquiry, in reference to actual situations or specific needs of the new country. This modification is done on a strictly *ad hoc* basis and must be used with extreme care. Interpretation solely in relation to arbitrarily selected national problems would sacrifice the comparative value of the scheme, since it would have to assume that, in order to apply, the same concrete problem had the same significance in each political system. It would also forfeit the framework's claim to logical validity, since it would be increasingly difficult, rather than easier, to refine the meaning of the concepts in their most general form as empirical study progressed.

Much remains to be done before this or any other scheme can begin to form a basis for a general theory of politics. There is no fully qualified theory of political behavior as yet, but each attempt makes subsequent efforts easier and also provides certain heuristic advan-

[2] Leonard Binder, "Prolegomena to the Comparative Study of Middle East Governments," *op.cit.*, pp. 651-668.

tages for current investigations. As was briefly outlined in the Introduction and as much of the content of the book suggests, a roughly drawn distinction between the active and less active participants in national politics seems useful in discussing the politics of a new nation. In much the same manner, but with the ease of greater familiarity with the distinction involved, the Moroccan experience with a variety of national problems can be analyzed in reference to the way in which actions were influenced by the roughly described active and inactive portions of the population. For the student less interested in theory and concept formation itself, this distinction will probably enable him to perform the analysis contained in this study and to explore the conclusions that it reaches. In other words, for practical purposes a more complex theory is not needed. The disadvantage is, of course, that the failure to extract maximum theoretical significance from empirical findings does not aid in the formation of more general theory or contribute to the testing of existing theory by comparative analysis.

The contrast in political participation can also be explored in terms of the fourfold classification of forms of influence. For example, the active participants seem to be those persons who are most skilled in the use of institutional influence and, to a lesser extent, coercive influence. For some purposes it may be sufficient to use the word "active" in its conventional meaning, but, as inquiry proceeds and evidence accumulates, terms of this kind are reexamined and refined. The translation of the single distinction into a fourfold distinction has both analytical and practical significance. One of the indications of useful theory is its amenability to translation into other kinds of theory or its contribution to more general theory, which is being done in an elementary way in this case. The practical implication is also important, for the fourfold distinction enables more precise discussion of a wide range of behavior that has usually been excluded in the study of comparative politics. "The politically active" or "the institutionally skilled" is a rough characterization of the participant in the political systems of advanced countries. Indeed, the study of comparative government has traditionally dwelt on those countries displaying highly developed institutional behavior. One of the major problems in the study of newly forming countries is how to study political behavior where national institutions are in process of being formed and where much influence is being exercised outside the conveniently formalized structure of institutions. The assertion that institutions are less reliable foci of analysis in new nations has become almost commonplace, but the problem of how one may study politics on the national level in the absence of such self-defining and self-regulating areas of behavior remains one of the most difficult issues in theory formation.

With these statements on the relationship of this inquiry to the theory of comparative politics, the more general observations that this study leads to may take on additional meaning. For example, the confusion and vagueness of the goals of most political groups in Morocco has been repeatedly stressed throughout the study but bears some reexamination in the light of various suggestions offered here. There could be no more misleading tendency than the frequent reference to policy, plans, and prospects of new nations in the same manner as to those of more advanced nations. Most informed persons make appropriate reservations, but more than this is needed in designing a more general framework for comparison and analysis. The wide range of social differentiation and its corollary for political analysis—a relatively small number of politically active persons—is fundamental to an explanation of the nebulous policy of many new countries. As many of the documents cited in this investigation indicate, there is still much Moroccan political propaganda devoted to the most rudimentary indoctrination. The attempt of some Moroccan writers to magnify the national consciousness of their countrymen and to claim an historic national identity of use in modern circumstances is further evidence. Without disparging the intent of such writers and without asserting that their effort is entirely dysfunctional in relation to present national requirements, it is perhaps possible to add that this search for national identity also tells something about the way in which the political system operates. The most difficult feat is transposing this phenomenon into a form suitable for analysis and capable of some measurement.

In the early phase of a new nation's existence the politically active segment appears to possess certain advantages, which are derived from its accompanying generally higher level of social and economic development. The less active segment may be neglected or even related through coercive forms of influence while the initial adjustment and organization of the new political system takes place. For many reasons the tendency is to concentrate development efforts on the politically active segment or perhaps those that might be placed in border-line positions. This group has invariably led the struggle for independence and its immediate cooperation is usually essential to the initial order and stability of the new country. In Morocco, for example, the large-scale agricultural-aid program of "Operation Plow" has been concentrated in the more advanced and profitable rural regions. The concessions to the workers are manifold and economic reforms of all kinds, favorable or disfavorable, directly concern a relatively small group. This is not to imply anything good or bad about the way in which decisions have been made in Morocco, but simply to point out that politics in a new country are restrained by the existing level of development and by the most pressing problems.

The Moroccan experience demonstrates that there is a process of reorientation of participants whose political behavior is highly institutionalized. The problem is certainly not the same for all parties or groups. The U.M.T., for example, found that representing the workers in a new nation required increasing participation at the national level. The U.M.C.I.A., on the other hand, has tended to minimize its association with national politics and, like the newly formed U.M.A., become more specialized. Explanations for these developments can be offered in less sweeping terms than generalizations about the system as a whole, but either the twofold or fourfold classification can lead to better explanations. Both the U.M.C.I.A. and the U.M.A. were limited in their exercise of influence by their own dependence on highly institutionalized behavior. The U.M.C.I.A. had special interests which it knew how to serve, although the solution of the U.M.A.'s political role was less clear. The retarded state of much of the Moroccan agricultural community raised subsidiary issues of the way in which the traditional peasant would be modernized, and, indeed, on at least one occasion this group profited from the charismatic influence of the King to build their organization.

The U.M.T. was led more directly into politics due to the pressing poverty of many of its members and the convictions of some union leaders regarding the best solution to Moroccan problems. Its widely dispersed and desperately impoverished following constituted a national problem that surpassed the capability of any single organization, including the U.M.T. As inexperienced participants, many of the new union members found the appeal of nationalism more understandable than the technical controversies and plans that preoccupy unions in more advanced countries. In order to respond to growing capabilities for participation, the U.M.T. became more active in national politics and began to use forms of influence less characteristic of the prototype of union institutions. By so doing the U.M.T. was very likely relieving considerable tension in the working force and, thereby, performing a national service, but it also offended the more experienced union members. The span of social differentiation was sufficient to include union members having highly specialized needs and considerable familiarity with institutionalized political behavior. These were the men who left the U.M.T. to form the old Istiqlal's Committee of Autonomous Unions. It seems likely that the industrialized working force of every new country will experience tensions of this kind, although the different capacities for participation may be accommodated within one organization front or the various forms of influence many used more discreetly.

The same procedure of analysis could be followed in explaining the development of the Istiqlal, and very likely the development of the nationalist movements in other countries. The nationalists may also encounter an additional complication. They may admit so many members that they include most of the politically active as well as a large proportion of the less active citizens. In practice it is not unusual to assert that the political system of certain new nations converges with the nationalist party or is consumed by nationalist fervor, but these assertions have been most difficult to translate into a form amenable to testing and comparison. The error is not nearly so much the original insight, but the reluctance to adopt analytical tools capable of handling generalizations about national political systems.

To some extent it is simply a reluctance to admit that political parties, like political behavior in general, are different in new countries. The Istiqlal, like other nationalist parties, tried to use all forms of influence or appeal to both active and inactive citizens. Where a party succeeds in doing this the actual situation begins to approximate the analytical structure in a way that seems much easier to understand due to our erroneous but understandable tendency to attribute the same significance to parties in new and old nations. Where a party does not succeed in doing this, more parties begin to appear, some of which may rely heavily on certain kinds of influence that the old party finds difficult to use, as is the case with the Popular Movement's use of traditional influence or organization of the politically less active countryside. There is also the intriguing possibility that the party system will atrophy as it confines itself, voluntarily or involuntarily, to the more active segment of the population. There are some indications that this happened to the Egyptian Wafd and also to several nations in the Levant between the wars.

An ostensible paradox of the Moroccan experience is that the Istiqlal party, which at the moment of independence may have been the most important, concrete structure in the political system, split three years later when it had the opportunity to take full responsibility for the government. The split is more readily understood if the analysis provides a means for studying the way in which influence was exercised in the intervening period. From the time of independence the Istiqlal and other parties used forms of influence that are generally barred to parties in more advanced nations. Three years from independence, however, the initial rules were being formed for the use of influence in the national political system. The smaller Moroccan parties were given legal protection in late 1958, but could not hope to enjoy the prestige of the predominant nationalist party. The relations among the Moroccan parties tell more about the Istiqlal than they do about the party system. The political system as a whole, however, did not change so fast as the ways in which parties could exercise influence. This is not to imply that the procedures embodied in the Charter of Liberties or labor legislation are not desirable or advisable, but only to point out that the party was operating with essentially the same national patterns of influence over the entire period. What appeared in the party system as a split of the Istiqlal was an adjustment to new patterns of influence on the national level in more generalized terms. The fact that two parties could exist with members in all social strata and distributed throughout the country was an indication of the remarkable advancement of the Moroccan political system since independence.

In summarizing the Moroccan experience, it is helpful to identify, first, the conflicts that have arisen in a political system where all the defined forms of influence are evident or where there was sufficiently widespread participation to indicate that both politically active and less active were exercising influence. The importance of the charismatic relationship between the King and the people is undoubtedly the most striking characteristic of Moroccan politics. With the diversity and complexity of Moroccan social structure, it is probably the only force that could have brought Morocco successfully through the major crises since independence. Even more important for the future of Morocco, it is important to note that it is one of the most effective means of bringing such a diverse group of citizens into contact with national politics. Such a figure has difficulty in dealing with detailed empirical problems, which are imposed by the nation, and sustaining his position. The areas of tension concerning the monarchy have not arisen so much in relation to the use of traditional and coercive influence as in relation to the place of institutional reforms, which tend to relate more directly to the politically active. The conflicts concern not only reforms affecting the advanced segment of the population, where the King has made large concessions, but also reforms concerning the extension of institutional devices to those less closely associated with government. For the activist groups in the country, generally represented by the U.N.F.P., institutions are also a means of achieving rapid social and economic change.

In the case of Morocco, the Istiqlal was confronted with a monarch whose popularity challenged the party's and whose influence was of a form that the Istiqlal could exercise in only a much more limited way. The King could and did change the rules of national politics. That he is a strong leader is fairly obvious, but how his actions relate to the entire political system is more difficult to analyze. To state simply that the monarchy accounts for the division of the Istiqlal is not very helpful and also implies that Mohammed V was motivated in a way for which there is no evidence. For those who seek explanations of political behavior in terms of conflict there were differences of opinion, but the common ground of the King and the Istiqlal was much greater. Although the King enjoyed a form of influence that the Istiqlal did not have, both would no doubt sincerely admit that each was essential to the country. Even the few known critics of the monarchy have made only indirect and qualified statements of disapproval and never utter such words before a large Moroccan audience. They do not make even mild criticisms without multiple assurances of loyalty. Motivationally this may be simply self-interest but their actions also reveal certain characteristics of the new political system that no one can ignore.

The King is able to appeal to the politically less active for a combination of reasons, which include, among other things, his religious position, his martyrdom over the two years of exile, and his reputation as a leader of the independence struggle. In relation to the entire country Mohammed V has a kind of mystical influence, perhaps shared to a small extent with Al-Fassi. In moments of national crisis, such as the merger of the Liberation Army, his commands are more compelling to a larger share of the population than those of any other single person. As the crises of Algerian politics continued and as internal conditions become more oppressive, the country tended to rely more and more both on the King's charismatic influence and on the use of coercive influence. Both these tendencies were resented by the more active citizens, as the statements of both elder and younger nationalists indicate. Their dissatisfaction, unreasonable as it might have been, was well founded for several reasons. It meant, first, that the institutional forms of behavior on which the party relied heavily were proportionately less important. It also meant that the development of new institutions, social and economic as well as political, was postponed. Even so, it should also be remembered that the Istiqlal itself, when threatened with destruction in early 1959, did not rely on its institutional structure nearly so much as on the charismatic influence that Al-Fassi wielded.

Neither the King nor the old Istiqlal progressed as rapidly as the progressive Istiqlal seems to have wished. Even the most progressive leaders of the new opposition party would probably admit that the monarch had an important function in the new country and that as a party they could not extend their influence so widely as could Mohammed V. What the Democratic party seems to have been proposing indicates their ambitiousness and their advanced thinking. For the charismatic influence of the King, as an abstract goal they advocated influencing national action by appeal to the nation. This is, of course, achieved in both democratic and authoritarian political systems of advanced nations, where imperatives are attached to the existence of the nation. These commands are understood by all and are generally above controversy. As authoritarian political systems have demonstrated, however, reliance on such imperatives for a wide range of political action tends to require an almost constant threat to the existence of the nation. The new party may well find that it is difficult to convey an abstract notion of the state to the less active citizens without sustaining a state of agitation that itself may delay or even prevent the economic and social progress they desire.

As the King's own restraint has demonstrated, charismatic influence has limited usefulness in achieving the rapid social and economic progress that Morocco wishes. Coercion is even more doubtful, especially over long periods of time. Where new countries have relied heavily on these forms of influence, their politics have been characterized by a turbulence and extraordinary unpredictability. While wider participation in national affairs may well be a prerequisite to other forms of progress, it is doubtful if participation under the imperatives of passionate nationalism is any more helpful than participation in the form of devotion to a monarch. For parties and others desiring the extension of institutional behavior, it seems quite possible that impersonally controlled imperative behavior is less suitable than personally exercised imperative or charismatic influence. In a certain sense the U.N.F.P. demonstrates a lack of confidence in itself. The only future course that Morocco or any other new country has will entail more specific and more intricate institutional structures, all of which contribute to more active political participation or greater reliance on the use of institutional influence. Furthermore, the politics of Europe suggests that dynasties that wished to survive were much more adaptable to modern life than were dictators.

Allal Al-Fassi also deserves closer examination. As an individual, the Leader of the Istiqlal displayed difficulty in adapting to national political life. In reference to the political system his actions were sometimes almost meaningless in the setting of independence. His persistent condemnation of French intentions and his quixotic campaign for liberation of the Sahara seemed unreasonable in the first phase of independence. The entire orientation of the Leader made him difficult to work with, particularly for the young party leaders who thought in more specific and concrete terms. Furthermore, they were excluded from sharing Al-Fassi's influence by the way in which he exercised it, since the charismatic appeal is incompatible with group rule. The isolation and invulnerability of a charismatic figure were poorly suited for dealing with the day-to-day details of government. The system began to grow without Al-Fassi. In late 1958 he consented to enter the political arena within the institutional framework by trying to form a cabinet and he was defeated. His appeal meant little to the modern group of leaders in Rabat. Nationally he was overshadowed by the King, although Al-Fassi might have converted his appeal into votes if the political system had been sufficiently institutionalized. He returned to the actual leadership of the Istiqlal after the crisis of late 1958, when his unquestioned authority and crusading behavior were once again harmonious with party needs.

Widespread political participation on the national level via institutional channels presupposes a level of understanding that may not be reached for a generation. The general progress of the traditional segments of the population as well as their increased political participation also means the gradual disappearance of the tribes. Only one clear-cut attempt was made to rally national political strength on the basis of tribal loyalties—that of Lahcen Lyoussi in the fall of 1956. Though the Popular Movement may well exploit tribal customs in its mobilization of the countryside, it carefully avoids any hint that the traditional order per se has a permanent role in the nation or should be privileged with any specially designed form of representation. The fury with which nationalists, both conservative and progressive, attack the rurally based party indicates their inability to use the same forms of influence and, to some extent, their awareness of their failure to provide for all Moroccans' political needs. It will be greatly to the advantage of the older nationalist parties as well as to Morocco that the countryside learn the ways of more sophisticated political behavior as rapidly as possible. Although the nationalists strenuously insist that they do not wish any privileged position in the new nation for the service in liberating the country, it also is interesting to note that their insistence on preeminence in the political system is, in fact, such a claim. The split of the Istiqlal will, of course, make such behavior more difficult in the future.

In explicitly rejecting tribal structure as the basis for implementing the new Moroccan rural communes the King acknowledged a requirement agreed upon since independence. Moroccan leaders seem to be aware that superficial implementation of political reforms is easy to accomplish without basic economic and social reforms. Charismatic and coercive relationships are not necessarily harmonious with the introduction of new institutional relationships, either on the national level or among smaller groups within the nation. Morocco has, on the whole, been extremely fortunate that her leader, Mohammed V, has generally been in agreement with more institutional reforms. Conversely, most Moroccans who are active in the network of institutional relationships existing in the new country have also displayed understanding by acknowledging that simply multiplying the institutional relationships among the advanced segment of the population will not in itself solve Morocco's major problems. One risk of any new country is that those best prepared to participate in politics in ways similar to those employed in advanced countries will only contribute to the existing disparities. This has been seen particularly in the case of economic reforms, where the easiest and often the immediately most profitable course is to increase the specialization of developed areas and established industries. The same can occur in the realm of political affairs and can have similar disastrous results by broadening the gap between those prepared to participate in national politics and those still heavily restrained by traditional ties.

There are many shades of opinion among those most intricately involved in the existing institutional framework of Morocco. The vagueness and general agreement of their goals, even between the factions of the Istiqlal, can be partially explained by consensus regarding those outside their network of institutional relationships. There has been surprisingly little discussion of the future value of the existing institutional structure as participation increases and social change takes place. The system is not suited to dealing with political problems on a national scale with a high degree of participation, and day-to-day problems are, in fact, often decided upon with participation limited to those having known requisite skills. The advanced segment of the nation must not only face the more easily discernible problems of the future of the country as a whole, but must fashion the existing national institutional structure into an effective and harmonious pattern of relationships. This is probably a much more difficult task than that facing the leaders of advanced nations. The graft, waste, and purely personal interests that may delay this effort are by no means unique among new nations, but are probably a much greater threat to the new nation.

In the early period of independence there appears to have been a lamentable trend toward multiplying the relationships among the politically active while neglecting or ignoring the less active new citizens. The leaders of a new nation do not necessarily have a choice in this emphasis, especially where stormy international conditions distract attention and drain resources. What may not be realized is that maintaining the *status quo* of the less active segment is both a relative and an absolute loss in extending political participation. The advanced portion of the populace tends to reap the benefits of even reduced social and economic progress as well as the satisfaction of increased political participation through groups, parties, and formal institutions. In this way the political problems of a new country may become more severe with independence, but it is seldom that affairs

417

deteriorate to the utterly senseless bloodletting that so often takes place during the struggle for self-government. Recently Western observers have begun to realize that social and economic change does not necessarily contribute to free or even effective political development, although our analysis has often displayed the same absurd deterministic assumptions of our largest ideological competitor. There are encouraging signs that the leaders of new nations are also beginning to realize that political progress is every bit as difficult as industrial progress, and probably a good deal more difficult.

BIBLIOGRAPHICAL NOTES

S INCE IN THE UNITED STATES there are few good collections of literature on contemporary North Africa and very little material in English, this bibliography is mainly of interest to specialists. The most important recent addition is by Nevill Barbour (ed.), *A Survey of North West Africa (The Maghrib)*, London, Royal Institute of International Affairs, 1959. For a summary of twentieth-century events see Rom Landau's *Moroccan Drama: 1900-1955*, San Francisco, American Academy of Asian Studies, 1956. A better work and probably a more authoritative one is Charles-André Julien's *L'Afrique du Nord en Marche*, Paris, Julliard, 1952. Both authors are definitely sympathetic with the nationalists. For recent events there are two works, both by Frenchmen. Robert Rezette's *Les Partis Politiques Marocains*, Paris, Armand Colin, 1955, is a fascinating attempt to apply Duverger's suggestions for the study of political parties and allegedly received help from Protectorate authorities. More recent is Jean and Simonne Lacouture's book, *Le Maroc à l'Epreuve*, Paris, Editions du Seuil, 1958, which is written in the intriguing style of French reporters. An account of the Istiqlal's struggle up to the late 1940's is Allal Al-Fassi's *The Independence Movements of North Africa* (translated from Arabic by H. Z. Nuseibeh), Washington, American Council of Learned Societies, 1954. Lorna Hahn's *North Africa: Nationalism to Nationhood*, Washington, D.C., Public Affairs Press, 1960, is a sympathetic and useful account which includes material on the other North African nationalist movements and their interrelationships. Some evidence on the Moroccan resistance and the Algerian conflict will be found in Michael K. Clark's *Algeria in Turmoil*, New York, Praeger, 1959, although the volume is extremely pro-French.

The English reader might also enjoy two first-hand accounts by correspondents in Morocco during the fighting: Marvine Howe, *The Prince and I*, New York, Doubleday, 1955, and Edmund Stevens, *North African Powder Keg*, New York, Coward-McCann, 1955. A tormented account of a young Moroccan caught between two cultures is Driss Chraibi's *Le Passè Simple*, Paris, 1955, which received literary recognition in France. Two novels set in Morocco are Paul Bowles' *The Spider's House*, New York, Random House, 1955, which deals with a young Moroccan's introduction to terrorism, and Peter Mayne's *The Alleys of Marrakech*, Boston, Little, Brown, 1953.

Most scholarly work on Morocco has, of course, been done by Frenchmen. The two histories are Charles-André Julien's *Histoire de l'Afrique du Nord: Tunisie, Algerie, Maroc*, Paris, 2nd ed., 1952-1953, and H. Terasse, *L'Histoire du Maroc*, Casablanca, 1949. The former is generally regarded as superior and is also found in a first edition of 1931. The prevailing controversy prevented French political scientists from writing much about the Protectorate before 1955, but there are a variety of anthropological studies. Robert Montagne's is one of the most famous and his *Les Berbères et le Maghzen dans le Sud du Maroc*, Paris, Alcan, 1930, was one of the first studies. He later edited a study of tribal movements toward cities, *Naissance du Prolétariat Marocain*, Paris, Peyronnet, 1950, and also wrote a short, pro-French account of the nationalists, *Révolution au Maroc*, Paris, France-Empire, 1953. The other major anthropological study is Jacque Berque's *Structures Sociales du Haut-Atlas*, Paris, 1955. Roger Le Tourneau has written a study of pre-Protectorate society in *Fès avant le Protectorate*, Paris, 1952.

The most plentiful source on contemporary affairs concerns the Protectorate and is made up from memoirs of French officials, all of whom bring some bias to the subject: Gen. Georges Catroux, *Lyautey le Marocain*, Paris, 1952; Gilbert Grandval, *Ma Mission au Maroc*, Paris, 1956; Maréchal Alphonse Juin, *Le Maghreb en Feu*, Paris, 1956; Boyer de Latour, *Veritiés sur L'Afrique du Nord*, Paris, 1956; and Daniel Guerin, *Aux Service des Colonies: 1930-1953*, Paris, 1954. Other accounts of Protectorate politics, which also reflect something of the difficult times in which they were written are: Paul Buttin, *Le Drame du Maroc*, Paris, 1955; Pierre Corval, *Le Maroc en Révolution*, Paris, 1956; Jean d'Esme (pseud.), *Le Maroc que Nous Avons Fait*, Paris, 1955; Robert de Montvalon, *Ces Pays qu'on n'appelera plus Colonies*, Paris, 1956; and Fulbert Taillard, *La Nationalisme Marocain*, Paris, 1947.

There are several works on the Moroccan economy. Although Albert Ayache is reportedly a Communist, his *Le Maroc: Bilan d'une Colonisation*, Paris, Editions Sociales, 1956, is a well-documented account of economic and social conditions up to independence. Two studies by Frenchmen are Paul Ripoche, *Problèmes Economiques au Maroc*, Rabat, n.d.(1954?), and Jacques Milleron, *Regards sur l'Economie Marocaine*, Rabat, 1954. French statistical services were quite good and provided the basis for two studies done since independence by the Planning Service, Ministry of National Economy, Rabat: *L'Evolution Economique du Maroc,* 1958, and a recent study of the interim plan for 1958-1960. The English reader will get a very good account of the major problems from the United Nations' study, *Structure and Growth of Selected African Economies,* New York, 1958. Many specialized studies as well as quarterly statistical accounts of the Moroccan economy appear in the *Bulletin Economique et Social du Maroc,* Rabat, Institute for Advanced Studies, which has appeared for many years.

The student of contemporary politics is soon forced to use periodicals and rely on interviews, as this author has done. Of the French newspapers, probably *Le Monde, France-Observateur,* and *L'Express* are the most objective, though North Africa is seldom discussed rationally by Frenchmen. The French quarterlies, *L'Afrique et L'Asie* and *L'Espirit,* have also contained some excellent articles and reports on Morocco. French-run newspapers in Morocco are *La Vigie Marocaine, L'Echo du Maroc, Courier du Maroc,* and *Petit Marocain.* Due to their vulnerability, they are more careful than newspapers printed in France and are particularly useful for reproductions of official communiqués and statements that are otherwise almost impossible to find. *Al-Ahd Al-Jadiid* is the official government newspaper, but it is strongly pro-Istiqlal. The Istiqlal party has an Arabic daily, *Al-Alam,* and a French weekly, *Al-Istiqlal.* The Democratic party published an Arabic daily, *Rai Al-Amm,* and a weekly, *Démocracie,* also. The U.M.T. has its own Arabic paper, *At-Taliâ,* and it also began a French newspaper, *L'Avantegarde,* representing National Union opinions. The Communist party publishes papers in French and Arabic, and the Popular Movement announced plans for a newspaper early in 1959.

Although various offices of the Moroccan government publish press releases, reports, and communiqués, they are of limited value because of poor distribution and filing. The Royal Palace, the Ministry of Foreign Affairs, and the Secretariat (sometimes Ministry) for Information and Touring under the President of the Council of Government all disseminate information. From time to time individual ministries have also published their own propaganda. Under the Ministry of Information two useful chronicles appeared: *Réalisations et Perspectives,* 1957, and *Le Maroc à l'Heure de l'Independence,* 1958. The government now publishes the *Bulletin Offi-*

ciel, which is available in French, Spanish, and Arabic. It contains a wealth of information, but reflects French distaste for useful indexing. The last census was in 1952, the *Annuaire Statistique de la Zone Française du Maroc*, Statistical Services, Cherifian Government, 1953, but another is planned.

For the English reader, by far the best accounts of current events are the informed reports of Charles F. Gallagher, Jr., who writes for the American Universities Field Staff, New York. Balafrej had an article in *Foreign Affairs*, 1956, pp. 483-489, called "Morocco Plans for Independence." Julien has had three articles in *Foreign Affairs*, 1940, pp. 680-699; 1951, pp. 445-455; and 1956, pp. 199-211. On foreign policy John Marcum's article in the *Western Political Quarterly*, 1957, pp. 301-317, and Lorna Hahn's article in *Foreign Affairs*, 1958, pp. 302-314, are both good. Analyses by the author dealing with more recent development have also appeared in the *Western Political Quarterly* and the *Middle East Journal*. The problem of cultural change is considered by Benjamin Rivlin and R. Vaurs in the *Annals of the American Academy of Political and Social Science*, 1956, pp. 4-9 and pp. 17-25. Probably the best summary is Senator Mansfield's report to the Senate Foreign Relations Committee, Washington, Government Printing Office, 1958. There are at present several English and American scholars working on Moroccan problems, so that the amount of reliable and scholarly material should increase over the next few years.

INDEX

Abdeljalil, Omar, 42, 129, 263
Abdelkrim, Al-Khatabi, Mohammed, 27, 46, 53, 67, 171
Abdelrazak, Mohammed, 228; interview, 274n.
Abdu, Mohammed, 30, 31
Addi Ou Bihi, 11, 127, 136, 139, 143, 203, 213, 216ff., 313, 320
administration, since independence, 101, 103, 110-24, 144, 160, 215, 303; see also civil servants, Interministerial Commission, Commission for Professional Training; Abuse, 303; Planning, 117; Training, 192-3ff., 114, 116, 123; Transition, 90, 92, 102, 121-33
administrative reform, 118, 125
Afro-Asian Cairo Conference (1958), 333
Agadir, 26, 27, 175-6, 178, 182, 203-6, 253
Ahardane, Mahjoub, 103, 168, 180, 212, 215, 216, 320, 323
airports, 12
Ait Ba Amrane Tribe, 179, 205
Ait Youssi Tribe, 199
Aix-Les-Bains, 83
Aix-Les-Bains Conference, 222
Ajdir incident (1958), 212, 323
Akchouch, Si, 217
Al-Afghani, Jamal Din, 30
Alaouite dynasty, 26
Al-Ayachi, Abdallah, 330
Al-Basri, Fqih Mohammed, 107, 169, 177, 182, 228, 229, 262, 339
Al-Fassi, Allal, 7, 25, 31, 34, 36, 40, 42, 44, 48, 52, 60, 64, 66, 71, 76, 84, 86, 88, 90, 97, 107, 108, 122, 135, 147, 159, 167, 169, 171, 174, 175, 179, 196, 197, 198, 201, 222, 225, 229, 235, 239, 242, 260, 295, 298, 306, 338, 352, 361, 381, 387, 413, 415; quarrel with Mohammed Ouazzani, 41
Al-Filali, Abdellatif, 140
Algeria, 61, 101, 103, 115, 133, 153, 168-73, 178, 212, 222, 290, 316, 328, 331, 344, 351, 398, 414; Popular Movement, 324
Algerian independence, 170
Algerian National Liberation Front, 169, 171, 290
Algerian refugees, 208
Algerian war, 82, 87, 91, 101, 200, 204-5, 207, 216, 290, 321
Algerians, in Oujda, 206

Al-Glaoui, Thami, 11, 28, 60, 68, 73, 136, 162, 179, 241
Al-Hassan, Ahmed, 163
Al-Hizb, 220
Alhucemas, 209, 213, 214, 217, 324
alim, see ulema
Allaliynes, 44
Al-Maghreb, 31n., 34
Al-Manaar Al-Maghrib, 400
Al-Mandjara, Mahdi Saadi, 30n.
Al-Mokri, Mohammed, 86
Al-Ouazzani, Brahim, 50
Al-Ouazzani, Mohammed, see Ouazzani
Al-Ouazzani, Thami, 49
alumni associations, 36, 57
American bases, see United States-Moroccan relations
Ammar, Thami, 110, 262, 339
Aneggai, Abderrahmin, 214
Anti-Atlas Mountains, 27
Aouad, Mohammed, 104, 110
Arab League, 32, 51, 52, 53, 65, 67, 69, 70, 290, 351
Arab-Moroccan relations, 389
Arab ties, 65
Army of Liberation, see Liberation Army
arrest, 234
Arslan, Chekib, 31, 35, 37, 41, 47
artisans, 16, 20, 59, 380
Asensio, Gen., 50
Association of North African Muslim students, 36, 39
Atlantic Charter, 58
At-Taliâ, 231
Ayache, Albert, 10n.

Baath Party (Syria), 320
Bachko meetings, 317
Bahnini, Ahmed, interview, 356n.
Bahnini, M'Hammed, 110, 140, 151
Balafrej, Ahmed, 25, 32, 36, 41, 51, 59, 64, 76, 97, 103, 104, 105, 107, 129, 147, 150, 166, 221, 222, 224, 242, 260, 270, 295, 351, 368, 398; see also Third Council of Government
Beigbeder, Col., 49
Bel Larbi, Naceur, interview, 122
Ben Abbès, Al-Bachir, 140, interview, 76n.
Ben Abbès, Dr. Youssef, 110
Ben Abdallah, Abdelkrim, 168, 330
Ben Abdellai, Abderrahim, 110
Ben Al-Arabi Al-Alaoui, Si Mohammed, 30, 60, 95

Ben Amar Hamidou, Si Mohammed, 207
Ben Arafa, Moulay, 54, 73-4, 79, 82-5, 88, 158
Ben Bachir El-Riffi, Driss, 139
Ben Badis, Si Abd Al-Hamid, 30n.
Ben Barka, Mehdi, 59, 61n., 102, 104, 106, interview 106, 108, 128, 137, 148, 150, 165, 170, 182, 222, 225n., 227, 230, 238, 260, 268, 295, 298, 334, 337-8, 340, 347, 352, 361, 367, 388, 395
Ben Bekkai, M'Barek, 83, 86, 89, 91, 96, 100, 103, 149, 197, 207, 284, 363; *see also* First and Second Councils of Government, Popular Movement
Ben Bilou, Ahmed, 262
Benchekroun, Mohammed, interview, 236n.
Ben Driss, Abdelaziz, 122, 136, 263; interview, 29n., 178
Ben Hamou, 179
Benier, Charles, 19n.
Beni Mellal, 200, 264, 341
Beni Ouraighel tribe, 217
Beni Ouarain tribe, 212, 214, 217, 324
Beni Snassen tribe, 168, 174, 207, 253, 323
Benjelloun, Abdelkader, 309, 312, 315
Benjelloun, Abdellatif, 140, 170
Benjelloun, Ali, interview, 115n.
Ben Miloudi, 212
Bennani, Abdelselam, 158, 390
Bennani, Hachimi, interview, 285n.
Bennani, Mohammed, 228
Bennouna, Abdelselam, 46, 48
Bennouna, Abdeselam, Si, 47
Bennouna, M'Hammed, 25, 29
Bennouna, Mehdi, 51, 54
Bennouna, Taib, 51-2, 54
Ben Seddik, Maghjoub, 72, 224, 228, 262, 274, 279, 287, 291-2, 339, 352
Ben Slimane, Si Fatimi, 86, 89
Ben Youssef, Mohammed, *see* King Mohammed V
Berbers, 22, 60, 64, 68, 69, 73, 83, 200, 215, 257, 319, 356, 396; *see also* Beni Ourain, Beni Ouraighel, Beni Snassen, tribes, Traditional Influence
Berber-Arab Differentiation, 198, 258 (Table 10)
Berber College of Azrou, 64
Berber Dahir (1930), 30, 34, 35, 37, 47, 199, 355
Berber resistance, 27
"Berber Tract Plot," 200
Berger, Morroe, 6n.
Berguent, 208
Berkane, 169, 209
Bertrand, Pierre, 14n.

Bidonville, *see* Slums
Binder, Leonard, 6n.
Black Crescent, 163
Black Cross, 160, 331
Black Hand, 158, 163
Bled, *see* rural administration, tribes, early Istiqlal Organization
Bled Al-Makhzen, 25, 27
Bled As-Siba, 25, 27
Bouabid, Abderrahmin, 59, 60, 96, 104, 105, 107, 127, 129, 142-3, 147, 150, 221, 227-8, 230, 261, 278, 292, 334, 339, 350, 351, 352, 379, 383, 385
Bouabid, Maoti, 110
Bou Arfa, 107, 182, 212, 228, 297
Bouazza, Taib, 72, 191, 274
Boucetta, M'Hammed, 77, 106, 227, 261, 388
Boulemane, 201
Boutaleb, Abdelhadi, 286, interview, 314n.
Boycott, 65
Boyer De Latour, Gen., 85
Brazzaville, conference, 58
Bromberger, Serge, 169n.
brotherhoods, *see* religious brotherhoods
budget, 66-8, 347, 350, 351 (1950)
Builders of Independence, 394

Cabinet, *see* Councils of Government, Crown Council, Royal Cabinet, Secretary General of the Government
Caid, 186, 359, 384; school, 192, 195, 361; *see also* administration, civil servants
Cairo, 169, 170, 171, 332; Afro-Asian Conference (1958), 102, 316
Casablanca, 60, 64, 76, 78, 106, 149, 150, 158, 162, 163, 169, 230, 238, 254, 263, 264, 272, 278, 292, 296, 323, 400; Strike (1952), 13, 54, 72, 157, 273
Catroux, Gen., 84
cement, 21
census, 14
Ceuta, 162
Chami, Abdelhai, 241
Chambers of Commerce, 380; Craftsmen, 380
Chaouia, 22, 26, 255, 283, 384
charismatic influence, 7, 110, 116, 125, 130, 214, 218, 268, 412-15, 416
Charter of Liberties, 134, 151, 196, 339, 368, 412
Charter of Public Liberties, 150; *see also* public liberties
Cherifian Phosphate Office, 19, 297
Cherkaoui, Ahmed, interview, 400n.
China, *see* Peoples Republic of China
Chiguer, Messaoud, 104, 144

Churchill, Sir Winston, 57

"Circle," 189, 193; *see also* rural administration

citizenship, 133-4

civil liberty, *see* public liberties

civil servants, 339, 341, 375; nationalists, 57; "nontitled," 118; "Mixed cadre," 118; "reserve cadre," 118; "Titled," 118; transition, 91

civil service unions, 284

clandestine activity, 34, 62, 77, 323, 333; *see also* resistance, Army of Liberation

Clark, Michael K., 169n.

coercive influence, 8, 11, 27, 110, 116, 145, 157ff., 165, 183, 217-8, 268, 311, 345, 370, 408, 413-16

Cogny, Gen., 175, 178-9, 207

collective bargaining, 165, 286; *see also* trade unions

Colombe-Bechar, 175

"colons," 81

Commission of Inquiry (1958), 140; for professional training, 114, 117; on Revision of Legislative texts, 151; *see also* Interministerial Commission

commissions and trade unions, 270

Committee of Aid for the North, 112

Committee for the Defense of Morocco (1932), 48

Committee of the Franc Area, 91

Committee of National Action, 39, 42, 47; 35 (1929)

Committees of Management, Operation Plow, 383

communications, 123, 233, 257

communism, 149, 163, 164, 168, 272, 299n., 322, 351; (1949), 67; (1952), 72; and Istiqlal, 332

Communist China, *see* People's Republic of China

Communist party, 302, 326, 329-34, 387

comparative politics, 405-17

consensus, 345, 417

Confederation of the North African Trade Unions, 290

conscription, 398

constitutional monarchy, 71, 126, 128ff., 146, 221, 346

Consultative Assembly, *see* National Consultative Assembly

consumer goods, 20

Convention of Establishment, 92, 382

corruption, 374

Council of Government, pre-1955, 66-8, first, 96-101, second, 101-2, third, 103-4, fourth, 105-11; *see* Table 3, pp. 98-99

Council of the Plan, 348, 350, 377

Council of the Resistance, 168, 176, 180; *see also* Resistance, Liberation Army

Court of Justice, 139, 348

Crown Council, 95, 126, 143, 224

Czechoslovakian arrest, 331

dams, 12

Daoud, Mohammed, 47, 49

decision-making, 112, 122, 124, 129, 155, 232, 267, 271, 307, 315, 363, 369-70

Democratic party (P.D.I.), 102, 149, 161, 173, 197, 235, 286, 302, 304, 308-18ff., 349, 363, 397, 414; independence negotiations, 86, 97; Istiqlal, 101, 317; resistance, 309; U.M.T., 276; arrests, 311; Congress, 314; goals, 314; Political Bureau, 312; school, 314; split (1959), 318; tactics, 313

demography, *see* population

De Rivera, General Primo, 28

Despois, Jean, 21fn.

D'Esme, Jean, 26fn.

Destour party, Tunisia, 30

Deutsch, Karl, 5

devaluation, 109

diplomatic conventions, 91; *see also* convention of establishment

divorce, 116

Djerada, 297

Douar, 202; village, 360; *see also* rural administration

Douiri, Mohammed, 77, 106, 227, 261, 388

Douiri, Omar, interview, 378n.

Doukkala, 22, 287

Doukkali, Sheikh Bouchaib, 30

Draa valley, 205

drought (1957), 102

drug traffic, 211

Dubois, André, 89

economic development, 19, 105, 112, 127, 209, 211, 271, 288, 290, 349, 377, 398; plan for (1958-59), 352; planning, 113; policy, 377; reform, 97, 107; *see also* Council of the Plan

economy, 12-21, 65, 222, 271, 289, 352

education, 12, 106, 209, 210, 249, 267, 388, 398

Egypt, 28, 47, 50, 54, 56, 67, 84, 86, 88, 102, 222, 309, 312, 316, 411

election (1950), 66 (1951), 70

elections, 104-5, 109-10, 126, 137, 147-8, 262, 306, 336, 352, 356, 363-8

electoral planning, 344, 347

Emerson, Rupert, 5

espionage, 331

executive, *see* King's Role, council of government, administration, crown council, Royal cabinet

fascism, 46-50, 52, 59
Faraj, Dr. Abdelmalek, 104
Fardel, J, 21n.
farming, 381; income, 17-18
farm workers, 283
Faure, Edga, 83, 81fn. 85-6; Faure, Edgar, 81fn.
Fellous, Abdelkrim, interview, 391n.
feminist, 220, 224, 376, 401-2
Fès, 26, 27, 41, 162, 176, 197, 217, 255, 264, 358; riots (1934), 36
fishing, 20
forces of order, 109, 119, 165, 181; unions, 285; *see also* police
foreign policy, 102, 315, 351, 290; trade, 17; troops, 288, 316, 348, 351, 352; *see also* United States, French Army
Forichon, R, 10n.
Foum Al-Hassan, 179
Franc zone, 381
France, Vichy, 57
Franco, Gen., 32, 45, 48
Franco-Moroccan Agreement (1956), 55, 81, 91, 94, 124, 161, 172, 222
Franco-Moroccan relations, 78, 80-1, 90, 101, 102, 115, 119, 121, 130, 139, 143, 159, 165, 172, 205, 262; *see also* Judicial Convention, Military Convention, Technical Aid Convention
free schools, *see* Istiqlal Party, free schools
French aid, 121, 122
French Army, 91, 159, 167, 172, 174, 175-7, 178, 184, 203, 332
French colonial administration, 16, 25-7, 31, 32, 61, 67, 70-3, 78-9, 81, 94, 137, 186, 193, 217
French colonial policy, 59, 81, 146, 357, 382; conservatives, 81, 84, 85, 158; currency, 352; National Assembly, 79, 85; National Committee for Liberation, 58; National School of Administration, 123; Popular Front, 32; prosperity; Socialists, 48; trade unions, 40, 72, 272; technical assistance, 91, 177; union, 66; West Africa, 205; *see also* Convention of Establishment

gendarmerie, 285; *see also* forces of order, police
Geneva, 170
Gennoun, Abdallah, 47
geography, 21-4, 46
Germany, 51

Gharb, 22, 26, 255, 283, 384
Ghazi, Mohammed, 30, 34
Governors, 191, 194, 197, 205; *see also* rural administration
Grandval, Gilbert, 81-3
Great Britain, 51
groups, 12, 112, 348, 373, 384, 403; Chp. XII, 373-404
Guedira, Réda, 97, 101-2, 327
Guillaume, Gen., 54, 70
Gzennaia tribe, 217

habous (religious foundation), 95, 360
Hached, Farhat, 72, 273
Hague court, 71
Hajbi, Houcine, 262
Hajjaj (Pseud.), 175
handicraft industry, 378; *see also* artisans.
High Atlas Mountains, 22, 186, 253
High Council for National Defense, 127, 181
Hopkins, Harry, 57
Hungarian revolt (1956), 333

Ibrahim, Abdallah, 104, 106, 108, 109, 166, 215, 224, 227, 262, 278, 285, 289, 297, 324, 339, 352, 367, 388; arrest, 1958, 285; *see also* fourth Council of Government
Ifni, 138, 171, 177, 205, 210, 290, 326, 344, 363
illiteracy, 220, 396-8
income disparities, 18
independence, 82, 310, 328, 336, 344, 373, 405, 417; Manifesto (1944), 58ff., 228, 242, 329; negotiations, 55, 74-92
Indo-China, 13, 69
industry, 13, 20
influence, 107, 145, 154, 252, 267, 342, 345, 361, 369, 399, 403; Chp. XIII, 405-18; *see also* political system, political participation
inheritance, 116
institutional influence, 8, 110, 123, 128, 130, 134, 155, 181, 184, 202-3, 217-18, 267, 272, 279, 286, 291, 298, 299, 325, 337, 341, 354, 366, 369, 373, 403, 408-16; reforms, 105-6, 111, 128; *see also* legislative reform
interest groups, *see* groups
Interministerial Commission, 111, 114, 149; Social Affairs, 113; *see also* administration, Commission for Professional Training
International Confederation of Free Trade Unions (I.C.F.T.U.), 274-5, 330

International Labor Code, 297
investment, 13, 105, 259
Iraq, 290, 351
irredentism, 102, 134, 167, 175, 204, 221, 348, 352
Islah, 311; and the Istiqlal, 226-7; leadership, 56; membership, 56; National Committee, 47; organization, 49-50; party, 45-56, 169, 222; resistance, 55; and southern nationalism, 52; and Spanish, 55; and tribes, 52; and Unity party, 53
Islam, 30ff., 33, 35, 90, 265, 322; see also Pan-Islam
Israel, 331
Istiqlal, 5, 96, 209, 213, 219-69, 293, 296, 352, 384, 390, 398, 400, 412; administrative commission, 261; arrests (1952), 72; cadre, 63, 219, 232-43, 256, Table 8, 237; cells (1945), 61-2, 240, 249; civil servants, 154; Committees of Action and Vigilance (1960), 263; Committee of Autonomous Unions (1959), 296; communications, 61, 77, 254, press, 238; Communist party, 332; congress, 90, 147, 195, 221 (1955), 106, 227ff., 228-32, 263-5 (1959); Democratic party, 317; elections, 365ff.; Executive Committee, 44, 60, 61, 63, 144, 220, 223, 226, 251, 261, Table 7, 223; finance, 38, 259; and first government, 96; goals, 58, 86, 105, 135, 147, 154, 219, 223, 239, 265; governmental policy, 108, 121, 125, 129, 141, 144, 150, 165, 263; inspectors, 62, 233, 250-1, 254, 263, 338, 402; Inspector General, 233; instructors, 62-3, 249; Islah, 49, 53-4; and King, 58, 69, 265; leadership, 41, 57, 59, 86, 222-4, Table 7, 223, 226, 232, 241-2, 252, 334, 339; linguistic characteristics, Table 10, 258; Liberation Army, 165-6ff., 178; membership, 38, 43, 60, 66, 71, 335, Table 11, 280; National Council, 97, 135, 147, 195, 219, 224; negotiations, 80, 83, 86, 96; opposition, 304; organization, 42 (1937), 59-62 (1945), 70 (1950), 60 (1951), 75 (1952), 221 (1956), 225-6, 233-60, Table 9, 247; party free schools, 34, 45, 54, 60, 64; Popular Movement, 321; Political Committee, 107, 221, 224, 226, 251, 263, 268, 270, 374; postwar history, 57-74; press, 61, 64, 227; Provisional Executive Committee, 158; regional committees, 62 (1945); regulations, 41, 245, 250; Royal Army, 181; rural administration, 195, 198, 201; resistance, 157-9, 167-70, 172, 226, 252; U.M.C.I.A., 379; U.N.F.P., 322-3; split, 59, 107, 109,

117, 126-7, 130, 151, 165, 182, 229-32, 241-3ff., 302, 352, 354, 380, 394, 401, 416; Superior Council, 44 (1937), 61 (1945), 63 (1945); trade unionists, 226, 249, 254, 259, 273, 287, 293, 295; tribes, 40, 249, 257; youth, 64, 102, 138, 222, 224, 261, 328, 367, 389-92, 392; see also Islah, nationalism, U.N.F.P., Ben Barka
Italy, 315
itinerant commissions, see rural communes, planning

Jerma, see rural communes, tribes, Berber
Jewish minority, 97
Joly, F., 21n.
Jorio, Mohammed, 275
Judicial Convention, 115
judicial reform, 106, 111, 114, 123-4, 139, 194; see also Muslim law
Juin, Gen. Alphonse, 33, 54, 65, 66, 73, 84-5, 309
Julien, Charles André, 57fn.

Kadiri, Abdel Kader, 388
Kachkate (Louis-Gentil), 297
Kasba Tadla, 200
Kemal, Mustapha, 30
Kenitra (Port Lyautey), 162, 264
Keukjian, Emanuel, 16fn.
khalifa (village official), 188
Khalifa of Tetouan, 49, 52, 55, 80, 94, 186, 190
khamis (Muslim sharecropping system), 386
Khatib, Dr. Abdelkrim, 158, 168, 170, 173, 174, 180, 212, 215, 216, 313, 320; interview, 322n.
Khemisset, 172, 214
Khenifra, 172
Khouribga, 264, 296, 341
King Mohammed V, 7, 36-7, 57, 63-9, 88, 93, 105, 127-8, 162, 180, 199-203, 207, 293, 298, 304, 310, 320, 322-5, 340, 346-57, 363, 368-9, 376, 384, 395, 397, 412; and Algeria, 208; exile, 54, 67, 77, 78, 80, 140, 158; and Liberation Army, 174; and Liberal Independent party, 326; Paris visit (1950), 67; political role, 108, 110, 116, 124-9, 137, 140, 143, 148, 151, 154, 173, 184, 194, 213, 304, 341, 364; return, 83, 88-9; symbol, 74, 244; Tangier speech (1947), 52, 68; U.M.T., 276, 287ff., 296
Koenig, General, 84-5
Korea, 13, 69
ksar (village), 360

Labonne, Eric, 63-4
Labor, code, 286; exchanges, 279; force, 276; *see also* U.M.T., workers
Lacoste, Robert, 79
Lacouture, Jean and Simonne, 16n., 106, 128, 337
L'Action du Peuple, 35
Laghzaoui, Mohammed, 63-4, 68, 164; *see also* police
La Nation, 330
land, 18, 195, 332; distribution, 207; ownership, 17, 42, 195, 360, 376, 381, 398; utilization, 17
Landau, Rom, 28n.
language differentiation, Table 10, 258
Larache, 162
Laraki, Abdelouad, 311
Laraki, Abdelwahab, 172
Laraki, Mohammed, 376; interview, 377n.
Laval, Premier Pierre, 37
League for the Education of the Base and to Combat Illiteracy, 400; *see also*, literacy
Lebanon, 57, 290, 352
legal reform, 106, 111
legislative power, 128
legislative reform, 114
legislature, *see* national assembly
Lejeune, General, 90
Lemaigre-Dubreuil, Jacques, 79-81
Lerner, Daniel, 9n.
"Letter of the Seventy Five," 77
Liberal Independent party, 97, 102, 138, 149, 302, 326-9, 366, 393; and first government, 101, 104, 304
Liberation Army, 11, 55-6, 75, 82, 85, 89, 103, 107, 125, 135, 139, 143, 159, 161, 167-76, 179-80, 204-5, 209, 214, 245, 311, 413
literacy, 9, 117, 249, 376
Lyautey, Marshall, 27
Lyazidi, Ahmed, 63
Lyazidi, Mohammed, 30, 35, 40, 42, 44, 59, 86, 108, 171, 214, 224
Lyoussi, Caid Lahcen, 95, 143, 173, 196, 198ff., 198-201, 216, 262, 313, 319, 323, 416

Madagascar, 84
Madrid, 170
Maghrib Unity party, 49
makhzen, 3, 93-4ff.
Mansour, Mohammed, 228
manufacturing, 20
March, James A. Jr., 7n.
Marmoucha, 169, 171
Marrakech, 26, 102, 176, 197, 200, 238, 263

marriage, 116
Massizli, René, 58
mass politics, 10n.; *see also* political participation
Mauritania, 24, 32, 175, 179, 328
Medboh, Captain Mohammed, 110
Medkouri, Driss, 262
Meknes uprising (1956), 13, 42, 101, 148, 178, 204, 317
Mendes-France, Pierre, 79, 80
merchants, 59; *see also* U.M.C.I.A.
Messaoud, Si Abbès, 169-70, 175, 212
Mezziane, Ahmed, 217
Mezzour, Omar, interview, 390n.
M'Hammedi, Driss, 59, 64, 97, 108, 138, 195, 196, 262, 363
Middle Atlas Mountains, 22, 27, 107, 168, 170-1, 174, 200, 217, 238, 323
migration, 16
Military Convention, 178
mining, 19, 21, 42
Ministry of the Interior, 162, 164, 185, 198, 194, 278, 286, 293, 363; *see also* police
Ministry of Justice, 206
Ministry of Labor, 283
Ministry of National Defence, 101, 207-8, 213
Ministry of National Economy, 101, 113, 330, 333, 377; *see also* Royal Army
Ministry of National Education, 399
Ministry of Public Works, 101, 117, 211
Ministry of Youth and Sports, 400
moqaddem (village official), 188
Moha ou Hammou, 212, 217, 324
Mohammedia (Fedala), 162
Mollet, Guy, 90
monarchy, 129, 134, 153-5ff., 157; *see also* constitutional monarchy, King Mohammed V
Montagne, Robert, 10n., 26n.
Montel, Pierre, 85
Moroccan Federation of Labor, *see* U.M.T.
"Moroccanization," 118, 121, 122, 164, 288, 350
Moroccan Union of Industrialists, Merchants, and Artisans, *see* U.M.C.I.A.
Moulay Hassan, *see* Prince Moulay Hassan
Mouline, Rachid, 101, 327
moussem (festival), 396
M.P. (*Movement Populaire*), *see* Popular Movement
municipal government, 188
Muslim Brotherhood, 310n.
Muslim law, 114, 116, 361; *see also* divorce, inheritance, marriage
Muslim World Conference (1932), 48

Naciri, Mohammed Mekki, 49-52

Nador, 165, 176, 206, 209, 213, 214

National Aid Committee, 348; Aid Fund, 377

National Consultative Assembly, 12, 113, 147, 154, 164, 181, 279, 305, 347-55, 368, 397; *see also* institutional influence

National Front, 53, 70

nationalist goals, 25, 32, 37, 49, 75, 145, 154, 244, 273, 310, 318, 336, 366, 399, 403, 409; income, 16, 185; leadership, 25, 321, 344; symbols, 29, 59, 196, 395; *see also* King Mohammed V, symbol

National Party for the Realization of the Plan of Reforms, 42

National School of Administration, 123

National Union of Merchants, Industrialists, and Artisans, *see* U.M.C.I.A.

National Union of Moroccan Students, *see* U.N.E.M.

National Union, *see* U.N.F.P.

nationalism, 25, 130, 296, 334, 341-2, 355, 370, 373; and Islam, 31

nationalists intellectual development, 25-34, 38, 106, 326, 398-9

nationality, *see* citizenship

negotiations for independence, 71, 74-92, 101, 161; *see also* Franco-Moroccan relations

Nejjai, Ahmed Ben Mansour, 384; *see also* U.M.A.

Noguès, Gen., 34, 39

"Nondependence," 290

North African Liberation Committee, 169

Nuseibeh, Hazem Zaki, 30n.

"Operation Plow," 18, 382, 384, 410

opposition politics, 142, 155, 305, 315, 318, 368, 370; Istiqlal attitude toward, 304-8, 340-3; *see also* Popular Movement, Democratic Party, National Unions, Liberal Independents, Communists, political participation

opposition parties, 139, 151, 220, 341, 342; *see also* political parties

Oran, 168, 206

Ouassou, Si Tahar, 86

Ouazzan, 27

Ouazzani, Mohammed Hassan, 32, 37, 40, 43, 54, 64, 308, 310; Fassi quarrel, 41

Oued Zem uprisings, 83, 160

Oujda, 26, 206-9, 214

Oulmés, 212

pacification, 25-7

Palestine, 47, 67

Pan-Arabism, 31, 46

Pan-Islam, 31, 32

Paris, 168, 389

party politics, *see* opposition parties, political participation, political parties

P.D.I. (*Parti Démocratique de l'Indépendence*), *see* Democratic Party

Paux, Gabriel, 57

Peoples Republic of China, 106, 329, 330, 332

per capita income, 18, 21

peseta, 210

Pétain, Gen., 28

Peyrouton, Gen., 39

Pinay, Anton, 83, 84

Pineau, Christian, 90, 91

Plan of Reforms (1934), 37, 48

police, 106-7, 119, 122, 126, 129, 149, 152, 159, 163-4, 176, 200, 212, 284-5, 292, 331; Director of the Sûreté, 208; organization, 164-6

political differentiation, 31; *see also* political participation; institutional influence

political participation, 5, 9, 11-12, 14, 117, 125, 128, 131-2, 147, 150, 155, 165, 199, 202, 219, 245, 261, 266, 267, 298, 303, 341, 343, 346, 355, 361, 370, 373, 386, 399, 405, 408, 415, 417; *see also* influence, political system, political parties

political parties, 109, 128, 129, 147-6, 150, 152, 162, 200-1, 252, 260, 263, 266, 267, 300, 303, 310, 319, 341-2, 352, 363, 366, 375, 403, 411; and civil service, 201; party police, 159, 160, legal definition, 152

political system, 75, 106-7, 110, 115, 118, 123, 125, 129, 134, 148, 154, 165, 166, 168, 184, 185, 198, 201, 202, 218, 220, 243-4, 266, 272, 276, 286, 300-1, 303, 305, 308, 310, 312, 319, 324, 334-5, 341, 342-6, 354, 361, 369-72, 373, 380, 381, 399, 402, 405-17; *see also* influence, political participation, political parties

popular control, *see* rural commune, elections, representative government

Popular Front (1936), 39, 49, 329

Popular Movement, 103, 138, 148, 167, 180, 198, 205, 209, 212, 215, 230, 235, 302, 307, 319-26, 366, 393, 411, 416; and Istiqlal, 321

population, 14-16, 21, 185, 276

ports, 12

Présence Française, 79, 81, 86, 90

President of the Council of Government, 95

President of the French Republic, 83

press, 40, 43, 47, 103, 106, 109, 146, 149, 153, 328; *see also* public liberties, Charter of Liberties

pressure groups, *see* groups

Prince Moulay Hassan, 127, 174, 180, 207, 217, 332, 390, 398

Princess Lalla Aicha, 401

Protectorate, 4, 11-12; *see also* French colonial administration, Spanish colonial administration

provincial administration, 188-9; *see also* rural administration, governors, Oujda, Taza, Agadir

public associations, 149, 321; *see also* public liberties

public liberties, 63, 78, 103-4, 105, 132, 145, 145-6, 221, 308, 329, 356, 363; *see also* Charter of Liberties, press, public associations, Royal Charter, arrests, police

purge, 114, 118, 132, 134-5, 154-5, 215, 350, 398; and U.M.T., 288

Pye, Lucian, 6n.

Qadiri, Boubker, 224

Qarawiyn, 34, 36, 42, 60, 311

Rabat, 22, 149, 238, 278, 325

rainfall, 22

Raisouni, Moulay Khaled, 50, 162

regional administration, *see* provincial administration, rural administration

religious brotherhoods, 33, 35, 44, 71, 73, 137, 160

representative government, 105, 130, 148, 186, 230, 305, 345, 365, 368; *see also* National Consultative Assembly

resistance, 54, 69, 74-5, 78, 103, 140, 158, 225, 229, 252, 285, 377; Committee of Revolution, 169; "Coordination Commission," 169; and independence negotiations, 80; leadership, 77, 157; urban, 163-4; *see also* violence

Rezzette, Robert, 44, 59n.

Rich, 213

Rif, 24, 55, 107, 168-70, 200, 206, 213; Mountains, 221, 253, 323, 395; Republic, 28; tribes, 52-5; uprising, 27-9 (1920), 85, 172 (1955-56), 210-11 (1958), 212-17 (1958)

Riffi affair, 140

Riffi, Haddou, 320

Rio de Oro, 175

roads, 12

Roosevelt, Franklin D., 57

Royal Army, 101, 109-14, 119, 126-7, 129, 138, 152, 159, 166-7, 173-84, 203, 208, 212, 285, 323, 393, 397-8; and Liberation Army, 173; organization, 180; *see also* coercive influence, Ministry of National Defense

Royal Cabinet, 94-5; *see also* Crown Council, King, political role

Royal Charter (1958), 103, 105, 128, 151, 357, 367

rural administration, 107-9, 124, 134, 147, 157, 163, 185-218; abuse, 197-8ff.; northern region, 210-11; organization, 189, 194; transition, 193; *see also* tribes, popular movement

rural commune, 105, 186, 192, 325, 347, 355-62, 383, 416; workers, 385; *see also* traditional influence, rural administration

Russia, *see* communism, Soviet Union

Rustow, Dankwart, 6n.

Safi, 26, 328

Sahara Desert, 27, 171, 174-6, 203, 205, 235, 262, 415

Sakiet-Sidi-Youssef, 102, 149, 290, 318

Salafiya doctrines, 29-30

Sbihi, Omar, 86

Schuman, Frederick, 71

scouts, 36, 64, 390

scrutin de liste, 366; *see also* elections

scrutin uninominal, 366; *see also* elections

Secretary General of the Government, 94, 126, 151

Senhaji, Abdallah, 158, 169, 170, 210, 217, 324

"separation of powers," 114-15, 124-31; *see also* King's role, National Consultative Assembly, Council of Government, constitutional monarchy

sheikh, *see* rural administration, provincial administration

Simon, Herbert A., 7

slums, 10, 13, 102, 317

social change, 252, 399, 417

social differentiation, 6, 215, 300, 319, 342, 346, 371, 374, 388, 409, 411

souk (market), 186, 190, 202, 360

Souk El-Arbaa du Gharb, 161, 311

Soussi, Si Mokhtar, 95, 140

Sous valley, 27, 170, 204

Soviet Union, 316, 329, 330, 331-2, 398

smuggling, 211

Spanish colonial administration, 24, 27, 32, 51-5, 67, 94, 113, 143, 159, 171, 186, 209, 275, 309, 311; Civil War, 48

Spanish colonial policy, 45ff., 49, 217; French relations, 51, 80; foreign policy, 51

Spanish Moroccan relations, 91, 143, 162, 205, 209-10, 213, 216; Republic, 47; zone integration, 210-11

Speech from the Throne, 67 (1947), 146 (1955), 148 (1956), 135 (1957), 138 (1958), 142, 183, 369

split of the Istiqlal, *see* Istiqlal, split

St. Cloud Declaration (1955), 88-9, 96, 146
stockpiling, 13
strikes, 106, 292
students, *see* youth, college, Oarauign
Suez crisis (1956), 200
sugar, 21
supercaid, 189, 193, 360; *see also* rural administration, provincial administration
Superior Council of the Plan, 113
Supporters of Truth, 34
Sûreté Nationale, *see* police
Syria, 57, 320

Taalbi, Sheikh Abdel Aziz, 30n., 41
Tafilalet, 203, 213, 358
Tahiri, Mohammed, 117, 262, 352, 388
Tangier, 26, 46-7, 60, 91, 94, 101, 170, 188
Tangier conference (1957), 149, 317
Tangier speech (1947), 52
Tanana, Mohammed, interview, 56
Tarfaya, 183, 188, 194
tariffs, 105
Taza, 26-7, 174-6, 197, 213-7, 238
Tazi, Si Abdelkader, 29
teachers, 297-8; *see also* education
technical aid, 118-9; Convention, 121; training, *see* civil service, administration training
Tetouan, 46, 47, 94, 170, 209, 275
Terrasse, Henri, 26
terrorism, 77-82, 162-3; *see also* violence, urban resistance, Présence Française
Throne Council, 80, 83, 86
Tindouf, 175
Torrès, Abdel Khalek, 48-9, 51, 53-6, 66, 170, 222, 224, 227
trade unions, *see* U.M.T.
traditional influence, 8, 107, 110, 185, 196-8ff., 203, 218, 268, 319, 325ff., 411, 413
transportation, 12
Treaty of Fès (1912), 14, 25, 26, 87, 89, 90, 91, 94, 96, 332
Treaty of Madrid (1880), 133
tribes, 11, 22, 33, 40, 42, 44, 107, 115, 159, 165, 173, 179-80, 185, 190, 201, 253, 313, 357-8ff., 384, 402, 416; northern, 46; pre-independence, 26, 52, 64, 69, 70, 73, 83; and Popular Movement 196, 198, 214, 319; uprisings, 11, 143, 183, 323; *see* Meknes uprising, Taza, resistance, Liberation Army; *see also* Gzennaia, Taza, Abdelkrim, rural administration, popular movement, rural commune, Beni Ouraighel, Beni Ourain, Beni Snassen
Tunisia, 30, 72, 82, 87, 103, 127-8, 149, 273, 290

ulema (religious scholar), 35, 204
U.M.A. (*L'Union Marocaine des Agriculteurs*), 376, 381-7, 410; organization, 385
U.M.C.I.A. (*L'Union Marocaine des Commerçants, Industrialistes et Artisans*), 352, 376-81, 410; organization, 377-8; and Istiqlal, 379
U.M.T. (*L'Union Marocaine du Travail*), 40, 72, 75, 106, 113, 138, 153, 165, 215, 216, 225, 229, 291, 317, 330, 350, 352, 374, 410; Administrative Commission, 282; cadre school, 279; congress (1955), 282; finance, 275, 283; foreign policy, 271; history, 270-9; and Istiqlal, 293; and King, 278; National Bureau, 282; National Council, 282; organization, 275-6, 279-91; rural administration, 195; split, 276 (1956), 291-301 (1959); youth, 289; *see also* workers, I.C.F.T.U.
U.N.E.M. (*L'Union Nationale des Etudiants Marocaines*), 166, 183, 348, 376, 395, 397-8
unemployment, 109, 211, 276
unions, 249, 348
United Nations, 53, 54, 56, 58, 60, 67, 70, 72, 91; New York Information Office, 71
United States, 57, 69, 138, 315; air bases, 69, 290, 328, 332, 351; landings (1942), 51; and Spain, 53; troops, 316
Unity party, 53, 54, 149; of Naciri, 50, 53; *see* Naciri
Unity road, 211, 337, 394-5ff.
U.N.F.P. (*L'Union Nationale des Forces Populaires*), 107, 264-5, 298, 318, 334-41, 353, 369; Administration Commission, 339; Autonomous Provincial Federation, 339; and Istiqlal, 322-3, 339; goals, 109, 371, 337; and King, 265, 302; organization, 339
urbanization, 9, 22, 254

Valino, Garcia, Gen., 54, 55
Viénot, Paul, 39, 41
villages, 188, 250; *see also* rural communes, rural administration
violence, 36, 40, 44, 59, 63, 69, 72, 74, 77, 79, 82-3, 101, 107, 149ff., 153, 166, 198-9, 207-8, 212, 230, 245, 295, 302, 306, 310, 324, 328, 330, 342, 344; at independence, 157-62; mass, 166, 318; pre-independence, 157-63; tribes, 211-18; *see also* uprisings, Casablanca strike (1952), Meknes incident, Bachko incident, coercive influence, terrorism
Von Grunebaum, G. E., 31n.
voting qualifications, 365; *see also* elections

women, *see* feminists
workers, 16, 20, 54, 72; Table 11, 280; farm, 297; fishing, 292; mining, 272, 297; phosphate, 292; port, 292; *see also,* U.M.T.
World War I, 27
World War II, 45, 50, 59; landings, 51, 57

Yata, Ali, 329, 331
Youssfi, Abderrahmane, 170, 177
youth, 36, 64, 102, 138, 198, 322, 332, 348, 376; college students, 36, 330, 389, 397; communism, 330; and Istiqlal, Table 13, 391; resistance, 159; U.M.T., 391; *see also* scouts, education, U.N.E.M.
Yrisson, Henri, 84
Yugoslavia, 106

Zaghloul, Saad, 29
Zeghari, Mohammed, 101, 180
Zemmouri, Hassan, 110; interview, 357n.
Zerktouni, 168, 158
Zhiri, Kacem, 228

ST. MARY'S COLLEGE OF MARYLAND
ST. MARY'S CITY, MARYLAND